Liberalizing Foreign Trade

Volume 7

Liberalizing Foreign Trade

Edited by
*Demetris Papageorgiou, Michael Michaely, and
Armeane M. Choksi*

Volume 7

Lessons of Experience in the Developing World

BY   *Michael Michaely, Demetris Papageorgiou, and Armeane M. Choksi*

Basil Blackwell

First published 1991

Basil Blackwell, Inc.
3 Cambridge Center
Cambridge, Massachusetts 02142, USA

Basil Blackwell Ltd
108 Cowley Road, Oxford, OX4 1JF, UK

Library of Congress Cataloging in Publication Data
Liberalizing foreign trade/edited Demetris Papageorgiou, Michael Michaely, and Armeane M. Choksi.
p. cm.
Includes index.
Contents: v. 1. Liberalizing Foreign Trade. The Experience of Argentina, Chile, and Uruguay – v. 2. Liberalizing Foreign Trade. The Experience of Korea, the Philippines, and Singapore – v. 3. Liberalizing Foreign Trade. The Experience of Israel and Yugoslavia – v. 4. Liberalizing Foreign Trade. The Experience of Brazil, Colombia, and Perú – v. 5. Liberalizing Foreign Trade. The Experience of Indonesia, Pakistan, and Sri Lanka – v. 6. Liberalizing Foreign Trade. The Experience of New Zealand, Spain, and Turkey – v. 7. Liberalizing Foreign Trade. Lessons of Experience in the Developing World
ISBN 0–631–16666–1 (v. 1). ISBN 0–631–16673–4 (v. 7). ISBN 0–631–17595–4 (7-vol. set).
1. Commercial policy. 2. Free trade. 3. International trade.
I. Papageorgiou, Demetris, 1938–. II Michaely, Michael, 1928–. III. Choksi, Armeane M., 1944–.
HF 1411.L497 1989
382'.3–dc19   6003762703
                                                              88–37455
                                                                   CIP

British Library Cataloguing in Publication Data
A CIP catalogue record for this book is available from the British Library.

Typeset in 10 on 12pt Times
by TecSet Ltd
Printed in Great Britain by T. J. Press Ltd., Padstow

Contents

List of Figures

List of Tables

About the Editors

Demetris Papageorgiou is the Chief of the Country Operations Division in the Brazil Department of the World Bank. He has served as a senior economist in the Country Policy Department and as an economist at the Industry Division of the Development Economics Department.

Michael Michaely is Lead Economist in the Brazil Department of the World Bank. Previously he was the Aron and Michael Chilewich Professor of International Trade and Dean of the Faculty of Social Sciences at the Hebrew University of Jerusalem. He has published numerous books and articles on international economics.

Armeane M. Choksi is Director of the Brazil Department in the Latin America and the Caribbean region of the World Bank. He is co-editor with Demetris Papageorgiou of *Economic Liberalization in Developing Countries*, and has written on industrial and trade policy.

Acknowledgments

This volume is the synthesis of an extensive research project, in the course of which many debts have been incurred. First and foremost, we wish to acknowledge the contributions to this synthesis of the 32 authors of the 19 country studies. Their participation goes beyond the fundamental research from which the comparative inferences of the volume are drawn. In many collective and individual meetings over the life of this project – from the stage of designing and formulating the studies to the discussion of structure, hypotheses, and findings of the synthesis – their ideas, suggestions, and comments were invaluable.

Similarly helpful in providing insights, forming a sounding board, and critically evaluating the research were the members of the project's external advisory board: Robert Baldwin, Mario Blejer, Jacob Frenkel, Arnold Harberger, Ian Little, Michael Mussa, Richard Snape, and Martin Wolf. Richard Snape's continuous collaboration was particularly significant.

This project could not have been started and sustained without the involvement of many colleagues at the World Bank. Our prime debt is to S. Shahid Husain, Vice President of Operations Policy and subsequently of the Latin America and the Caribbean Region, for his strong support and encouragement; and to Anne O. Krueger, Vice President, Research, when the study was implemented who, drawing on her vast experience in earlier studies, greatly helped us in the design and formulation of this research and provided a continuous stimulus. We also wish to mention Vinod Dubey, Basil Kavalsky, and Bevan Waide, whose support and advice were instrumental in launching the project; and Deepak Lal, Sarath Rajapatirana, and Marcelo Selowsky who, as members of the Bank's internal advisory board, contributed continuously to the project's progress.

Ioannis Kessides is the author of the statistical analysis reported in Appendix A2 of this volume. Noga Lewin and Christos Kostopoulos set up and managed the extensive statistical data base on the countries. For research assistance and data processing, we are also indebted to David

Barol, Janet Entwistle, Barbara Lyman, Jill Minneman, Jacqueline Saettone, and Panos Varangis.

A necessary condition for undertaking such a large-scale research is efficient administrative machinery. This was designed and implemented by Sappho Haralambous, the project's first administrator, and subsequently maintained by Maria Lozos. They were greatly helped by Isabelle Kim, the project's secretary. Diane Cashman monitored the proceedings of the project's conferences and prepared their summaries.

Philippa Shepherd assumed the daunting task of editing the study – contributing immeasurably to its readability, consistency, and order – and of preparing the study for publication. Several country studies were edited by Phillip Sawicki, and several chapters in the present volume by Bruce Ross-Larson and Ann Beasley. Rebecca Kary managed the final production of the volumes. Masha Adamantiades, Kristin Pfeister, and Linda Snyder worked long hours to help prepare the manuscripts for press, and María-Teresa Sánchez patiently and proficiently typed many versions of this volume. And finally, Shirley Kessel took on the demanding task of indexing each volume and compiling a comprehensive index for the whole series.

The research presented here was managed at the World Bank and was financed by a generous grant from its Research Committee. Inferences of the research, however, are solely the responsibility of the authors, and are not necessarily the position of the Bank or any of its officials.

Demetris Papageorgiou
Michael Michaely
Armeane M. Choksi

Editors' Preface

The General Objective

"Protection," said the British statesman Benjamin Disraeli in 1845, "is not a principle, but an expedient," and this pronouncement can serve very well as the text for our study of *trade liberalization*. The benefits of open trading have by now been sufficiently demonstrated and described by economic historians and analysts. In this study, we take them for granted and turn our minds from the "whether" to the "how."

The Delectable Mountains of open trading confront the pilgrim with formidable obstacles and there are many paths to the top. The direct route seldom turns out to be the best in practice. It may bring on rapid exhaustion and early collapse, while a more devious approach, skirting areas of excessive transition costs, may offer the best prospects of long-term survival.

Given the sharp diversity of economic background and experience between different countries, and indeed, between different periods in the same country, we should not expect the most favorable route to turn out the same for each country, except perhaps by accident. There are fundamental principles, however, underlying the diversities and it is our thesis that a survey and analysis of a sufficiently broad spectrum of countries over sufficiently long development periods may serve to uncover them.

With this object in view, we set out to study as many liberalization experiences as possible and aimed at including all liberalizations in developing countries in the post-world war period. However, the actual scope of this study had three limitations. First, we restricted the study to market-based economies. Second, experiences with highly inadequate data had to be excluded. Third, to be an appropriate object of study, an experience had to be of some minimum duration. Applying these criteria, we were left with the study of liberalization experiences in the 19 countries listed at the end of this preface. This final, concluding volume presents the synthesis of the country analyses, whereas six earlier volumes contain the country studies.

Definitions

"Trade liberalization" implies any change which leads a country's trade system toward neutrality in the sense of bringing its economy closer to the situation which would prevail if there were no governmental interference in the trade system. Put in words, the new trade system confers no discernible incentives to either the importable or the exportable activities of the economy.

By "episode" we mean a period long enough to accommodate a significant run of liberalization acts terminating either in a swing away from liberalization or in a period where policy changes one way or another cease to be apparent.

The "episode of liberalization" thus defined is the unit of observation and analysis employed in each of our country studies.

Identification of Liberalization Episodes

There are three main indicators of a move in the direction of neutrality: (a) a change in the price system; (b) a change in the form of intervention; (c) changes in the foreign exchange rate.

Price System

The prices in question are nominal protection rates determining consumption patterns and, more importantly, effective protection rates affecting production activities. Any change which lowered the average level and distribution of rates of protection would count as a move toward neutrality. Typically, such a change would arise from a general reduction in tariffs, but it might also be indicated by the introduction, rather than the removal, of instruments of government intervention, or even, indeed, by the raising rather than the lowering of the incidence of government intervention. An instance of this might be the introduction of export subsidies in a protective regime previously biased against exports and favoring import substitution. Another instance might be the introduction or increase of tariffs on imported raw materials and capital goods in a regime where tariffs have previously escalated over the whole field, with the zero and lower rates applying on these imports.

Form of Intervention

The form of intervention may be affected by a change in the quantitative restriction (QR) system itself or by replacing QRs with tariffs. Although the actual changes might be assigned price *equivalents*, it is not feasible to assign price equivalents to their comprehensive effects. Moreover, the reactions they induce are so different from responses to price signals that they are better treated as a separate category.

The Exchange Rate

A change in the level of a *uniform* rate of exchange, since it does not discriminate between one tradeable activity and another, is not of itself an instrument of intervention. A move from a *multiple* to a uniform rate would, however, be equivalent to a change in intervention through commercial policy instruments; changes in the rate would modify the effect of commercial policy instruments already in being, for example, where QR systems are operated through the exchange control mechanism itself or where tariffs effective at an existing rate become redundant at a higher rate. Failing detailed studies of the impact of exchange rate changes on QRs or tariffs we take as a general rule that a formal and real *devaluation* constitutes a step towards liberalization.

Policies and Results

We do not take the actual degree of openness of the economy as an indicator in itself of a liberalization episode. Liberalization policies may commonly be expected to lead to an increase in the share of external trade but this is not an inevitable result. For instance, if, starting from a state of disequilibrium, liberalization is associated with a formal devaluation imports may actually fall. Therefore attempts to detect liberalization by reference to trade ratios rather than to policy *intentions* would be misleading. Exceptionally, however, the authors of the country studies have used trade performance as an indication of liberalization, particularly where actual changes in imports can be used to measure the degree of relaxation, or otherwise, of QRs.

Measurement of Degrees of Liberalization

In each country study we have attempted to indicate the degree of liberalization progressively attained by assigning to each year a mark for performance on a scale ranging from 1 to 20. A mark of 20 would indicate virtually free trade, or perfect neutrality, a mark of 1 would indicate the highest possible degree of intervention. These indices are subjective and peculiar to each country studied and in no way comparable between countries. They are a rough and ready measure of the progress, or otherwise, of liberalization as perceived by the authors of the country study in question. They reflect, for instance, assessments of nominal and effective rates of protection, the restrictiveness of QRs, and the gap between the formal exchange rate and its equilibrium level.

Analysis of Successful Liberalization Exercises

To arrive at criteria of what makes for success in applying liberalization policies, the following questions might be asked in our studies.

1   What is the appropriate speed and intensity of liberalization?
2   Is it desirable to have a separate policy stage of replacement of nonprice forms of trade restrictions by price measures?
3   Is it desirable to treat productive activities during the process of trade liberalization uniformly or differentially?
4   If uniform treatment is indicated, how should it be formulated?
5   On what pattern of performance of the economy is the fate of liberalization likely to hinge?
6   Is it desirable to have a stage of export promotion? If so, what should its timing be in relationship to import liberalization?
7   What are the appropriate circumstances for the introduction of a liberalization policy?
8   How important are exogenous developments in deciding the sustainability of liberalization?
9   Finally, what *other* policy measures are important, either in their existence or absence, for a successful policy of trade liberalization?

Lurking behind many of these issues are the (potential) probable costs of adjustment of a liberalization policy and, in particular, its possible impact on the employment of labor.

Scope and Intention of our Study

The general purpose of our analysis is to throw up some practical guidance for policymakers and, in particular, for policymakers in developing countries where the economic (and political) climate tends to present the greatest obstacles to successful reform. It is for this reason that (as already explained) we have based our studies on the experience of a wide spread of countries throughout the developing world. All country studies have followed a common pattern of inquiry, with the particular analytical techniques left to the discretion of the individual authors. This approach should yield inferences on the questions raised above in two different ways; via the conclusions reached in the country studies themselves, and via the synthesis of the comparative experience of trade liberalization in these countries.

The presence of a common pattern of inquiry in no way implies that all country studies cover the same questions in a uniform manner. Not all questions are of equal importance in each country and the same quantity and quality of data were not available in all countries. Naturally, the country studies differ on the issues they cover, in the form of the analysis, and in the structure of their presentation.

The country studies are self-contained. Beyond addressing the questions of the project, each study contains sufficient background material on the country's attributes and history of trade policy to be of interest to the general reader.

The 19 countries studied classified within three major regions are as follows.

Latin America

Argentina	by Domingo Cavallo and Joaquín Cottani
Brazil	by Donald V. Coes
Chile	by Sergio de la Cuadra and Dominique Hachette
Colombia	by Jorge García García
Perú	by Julio J. Nogués
Uruguay	by Edgardo Favaro and Pablo T. Spiller

Asia and the Pacific

Indonesia	by Mark M. Pitt
Korea	by Kwang Suk Kim
New Zealand	by Anthony C. Rayner and Ralph Lattimore
Pakistan	by Stephen Guisinger and Gerald Scully
Philippines	by Geoffrey Shepherd and Florian Alburo
Singapore	by Bee-Yan Aw
Sri Lanka	by Andrew G. Cuthbertson and Premachandra Athukorala

The Mediterranean

Greece	by George C. Kottis
Israel	by Nadav Halevi and Joseph Baruh
Portugal	by Jorge B. de Macedo, Cristina Corado, and Manuel L. Porto
Spain	by Guillermo de la Dehesa, José Juan Ruiz, and Angel Torres
Turkey	by Tercan Baysan and Charles Blitzer
Yugoslavia	by Oli Havrylyshyn

Coordination of the Project

Armeane M. Choksi, Michael Michaely, and Demetris Papageorgiou, of the World Bank's Latin American and Caribbean Region, are the directors of this research project. Participants in the project met frequently to exchange views. Before the country studies were launched, the common framework of the study was discussed extensively at a plenary conference. Another plenary conference was held to discuss early versions of the completed country studies, as well as some emerging general inferences. In between, three regional meetings were held to review phases of the work under way. An external Review Board consisting of Robert Baldwin (University of Wisconsin), Mario Blejer (International Monetary Fund), Jacob Frenkel (University of Chicago and Director of Research, International Monetary Fund), Arnold Harberger (University of Chicago and University of California – Los Angeles), Richard Snape (Monash University), and Martin Wolf (Chief Economic Leader Writer, Financial Times) contributed to the reviewing process of the country studies and of the synthesis volume.

Volume 1: Liberalizing Foreign Trade. The Experience of Argentina, Chile, and Uruguay;

Volume 2: Liberalizing Foreign Trade. The Experience of Korea, the Philippines, and Singapore;

Volume 3: Liberalizing Foreign Trade. The Experience of Israel and Yugoslavia;

Volume 4: Liberalizing Foreign Trade. The Experience of Brazil, Colombia, and Perú;

Volume 5: Liberalizing Foreign Trade. The Experience of Indonesia, Pakistan, and Sri Lanka;

Volume 6: Liberalizing Foreign Trade. The Experience of New Zealand, Spain, and Turkey;

Volume 7: Liberalizing Foreign Trade. Lessons of Experience in the Developing World

Demetris Papageorgiou, Michael Michaely, Armeane M. Choksi

1

Introduction

Scope of the Study

That a liberal is preferable to a restrictive trade regime is by now generally accepted, and a substantial body of empirical research carried out over the last 20 years supports this conclusion. The mere statement gives no clue, however, as to how liberalization is best achieved. Little is known about the essential attributes of a *change* from one regime to another: of a move away from a distorted trade policy regime toward a more neutral one. It is this issue of the timing, phasing, and sequencing involved in the design and implementation of a trade liberalization policy that forms the subject matter of the present study.[1]

There are many ways of proceeding from a protective to a liberal regime. With some programs, the long-term gain may be offset by an initial net loss to the economy; and some programs will be more sustainable than others. The fact that a particular type of program pursued in two different economies or at different times in the same economy has proved successful may be purely fortuitous. Nevertheless, it is to be expected that successful programs will exhibit certain general principles that are common over a sufficiently large number of countries and over a wide range of stages of development. This study attempts to identify these principles by way of empirical investigation carried out over a wide range of countries.

---

1 Several comparative studies of liberalization experiences are already available in the literature. Principally, in a major OECD study (1970), six country experiences were investigated, with conclusions drawn in Little, Scitovsky, and Scott (OECD, 1970, vol. VI). A later project, at the National Bureau of Economic Research (1974–8), studied ten countries and was synthesized in the volumes of Jagdish Bhagwati (1978) and Anne Krueger (1978). The comparative experience has also been analyzed in Bela Balassa and Associates (1982). While these earlier studies have highlighted the potential benefits of liberalization, and (primarily in Krueger) have drawn attention to some necessary conditions for its survival, they have mostly not addressed the issues of timing and sequencing that are the focus of the present project.

The Issues

The following are the principal issues:

1 the speed of implementation;
2 the attributes of each stage;
3 the circumstances in which the program is launched;
4 the relationship between trade liberalization and other economic policies.

In all these issues, income distribution aspects as well as political considerations are involved alongside the concern for economic efficiency. A brief discussion of the nature of the issues follows.

Speed of Implementation
It is obviously desirable to realize the benefits of liberalization as quickly as possible. In addition, radical policies may be expected to be more credible, hence leading to stronger responses. In a context free of all rigidities, and where capital of all sorts is malleable, the full and immediate implementation of liberalization in one stage would seem to be the right course. But in reality there are a number of inhibiting factors.

When protection is removed from an activity, whether partially or totally, production is likely to decline. The activity will contract and fewer resources – physical capital (including natural resources) and labor (both "raw labor" and human capital in general) – will be employed in it.

There would be no waste if these displaced resources could be immediately directed to another, potentially expanding, sector. But capital goods are often specific to the sector in which they are employed, and the contraction of that sector would leave them at least partially unemployed. The same applies to human capital, which is largely sector or occupation specific. If "raw labor" were transferred fully to the expanding sector, the reallocation of factors would be beneficial even in the short run: unemployment of capital indicates that it could not yield any rent, since its marginal product (given the new set of prices) is zero or negative, in which case its unemployment is superior to its employment in the existing (contracting) activity. But two factors may hinder the transfer of labor. First, the reservation wage of labor – higher than the value assigned at the margin to leisure – may be higher than the expected wage rate in the expanding sector (which is the marginal product in that sector of raw labor and of the nonspecific element in human capital). Second, the capacity of the potentially expanding sector to employ extra labor depends on the provision of extra capital or managerial resources which may not be readily available.

The wider the differences in attributes of different sectors, the less mobile the factors (as, for instance, between urban and rural sectors), and the shorter the time available for adjustment, the more will employment be disrupted. Aside from the effect of unemployment on the economy's welfare, it may be expected to diminish the chance of the program's survival. Avoiding high unemployment should therefore be a consideration in any scheme of liberalization. This, presumably, would be an argument against a very rapid process.

The change in relative prices resulting from a liberalization program will tend to reduce the rewards of both physical and human capital in a contracting sector, while there will be a corresponding increase in sectors that may benefit from the program. Therefore, where price changes are large or suddenly applied, a considerable redistribution of income is likely to ensue. To the extent that this is the outcome, another argument for gradual change, announced well in advance, would be introduced. The status quo may enjoy a special esteem in the eyes of both the public and the policymakers, and a policy that upsets the status quo would generally be reckoned to be "unfair." A wholesale redistribution of income may thus make the relevant program harder to sustain – a consideration arguing for a gradual approach.

However, even though public resistance is greater the larger the relative change in prices and the greater the redistribution of income, there is the risk that a slow multistage program will entail a sustained political struggle which may distort it or prejudice its success altogether.

Attributes of Stages
1 The first point for consideration is the shift between *forms* of protection. Government interference in imports (and, though to a lesser extent, in exports) often takes the form of quantitative restrictions (QRs) rather than, or in addition to, tariffs (or export taxes). Indeed, the term "liberalization" is very often understood as a shift from a QR system to protection through tariffs, rather than as the lowering of protection involved in a tariff system. In an economy in which QRs are indeed prevalent, the first question should be: should the liberalization process start by shifting from QRs to protection through tariffs, while leaving the level of protection much as it was, or would it be better to lower protection gradually through a gradual relaxation of the QRs?

Shifting protection to the price mechanism must have a few major benefits. It may, first, help to eliminate any unintended – sometimes unrecognized – lack of uniformity in the protection system brought about by a system of QRs that necessarily entails a multitude of *ad hoc* discretionary decisions. Thus an apparent change in form becomes, in effect, also a change in the level of protection, lowering the variance involved in it. A shift to the price mechanism renders the system transparent and predictable, and should encourage greater efficiency in the production processes and the elimination of rent seeking. It also makes it possible to announce future levels of protection in advance, thus facilitating rational decision making by economic agents. While it is notionally possible for economic agents to translate QRs into price equivalents, this is difficult and complicated. A program of price changes would be simpler and easier to understand. This argues for a shift from QRs to tariffs at the outset.

As against this, the time needed to convert from one system to another would tend to hold up the liberalization process. Moreover, the substantial impact on income distribution involved in a wholesale shift from QRs to tariffs (that is, the elimination of large scale rents in favor of the taxpayer) may make it harder to sustain the liberalization program.

2 How should the export sector figure in a liberalization program? Highly protected economies generally exhibit a strong bias against exports. As will be explained later, export promotion measures in such regimes would constitute an act of trade liberalization, and may form part of a liberalization process.

To lower protection of an import-substituting industry would lower its price by comparison with exporting and nontradeable activities. Resources would then tend to move to the latter sectors, as well as to import-substituting activities not previously favored by protection. Exportable activities would thus automatically become relatively more profitable; but if they were boosted by export promotion incentives, they would more easily absorb the resources displaced by the lowering of protection. In addition, even if these resources were rapidly absorbed, they would be drawn to some extent into the nontradeable sector. This would tend to lead to a current account deficit, with the possibility of a balance-of-payments problem that might jeopardize the liberalization program. This may indicate the desirability of promoting exports – by subsidies, reduction of taxes on exports, or a formal devaluation (which would tend to boost the import substitution sector as well as the export sector and, together with import liberalization, to bring about a change in the structure of the former).

There are several potential sequencing orders. One would be to bring about a relatively large price increase in the export sector, via a formal devaluation or export subsidies, to coincide with the initial stage of import liberalization. This should increase the response of the export sector and reinforce export expansion. If, however, there were a considerable time lag, balance-of-payments problems and unemployment would still not be avoided at the initial stage. An alternative way might be to initiate export promotion in advance of import liberalization. But a rise in exports unaccompanied by a decline in highly protected import substitutes might result in inflationary pressure rather than the reallocation of resources. Moreover, any delay in the actual initiation of import liberalization may put the whole process at risk.

3 Should tariff reductions be uniform? One of the advantages of introducing tariff reduction uniformly is simplicity and "fairness." The selective treatment of different sectors involves arbitrary decisions, uncertainty and political friction. But the responses of different industries will not be uniform. Therefore, where the contraction of a certain activity is likely to generate particularly high unemployment, this would constitute a potential case for special treatment.

If a uniform set of rules for tariff changes is adopted, whether in a pure form or in some combination with a differential treatment, various alternative formulations of this set may be selected – again, in a "pure" way or in some combination of these alternatives. One is an *equiproportional* ("across-the-board") reduction of protection of various activities. This path has the advantage of leading to an increased convergence of protection rates and a gradual reduction of the variance in the protection system. Another possible method is to reduce protection rates by equally large *absolute* amounts. In the initial stages, however, this method might increase the dispersion in the system of protection rates. A third alternative, which is superior on *a priori* grounds, is the "concertina method": in the initial stage of the policy, all tariff rates above a specified ceiling are lowered to that ceiling, with no change in other tariffs; in the next stage, this is repeated with a lower ceiling; and so on.

Circumstances Favorable to the Introduction of Liberalization
Situations of either inflation or high unemployment are presumably not conducive to a successful liberalization. Failing a remedial change in the exchange rate, inflation leads to a deterioration in the balance of payments, a situation which should make the maintenance of a liberal import regime especially difficult.[2] Where unemployment is high, the transitional cost in terms of extra unemployment may make liberalization unacceptable. A severe balance-of-payments crisis, due not to inflation but to exogenous factors such as crop failure or a serious deterioration in the terms of trade, would likewise not seem to be propitious for introducing a trade liberalization program.

These considerations suggest that a liberalization program is most likely to succeed if introduced in conditions of internal and external equilibrium. But other considerations may indicate the opposite: severe economic difficulties may actually stimulate a resolve to undertake remedial measures and see them through.

---

2 An exception would be an inflation *caused* by a balance-of-payments surplus (say, due to increased capital inflows or to improved terms of trade). In this instance, trade liberalization may be considered an anti-inflationary device.

Trade Liberalization in the Context of Other Economic Policies
In the case of an economy suffering from inflation and balance-of-payments difficulties, a program of liberalization would presumably be likely to survive only if undertaken in conjunction with stabilization measures. Even where the difficulties are not so acute, the nature of accompanying macroeconomic policies – the foreign exchange rate policy and fiscal and monetary policies which determine aggregate demand – would be likely to influence the fate of the program.

Restrictions operating in markets other than that of external transactions in goods and services, for example price controls, wage controls, and subsidies, must also be taken into account. A trade liberalization program may be accompanied by relaxation of these intervention measures. Sometimes changes of this nature may result directly from trade liberalization, in which case the relationship and the sequencing are obvious. Thus, for instance, the elimination of QRs would normally be followed by the abolition of domestic rationing and price conrols of imported goods, rather than the other way around. In other instances, these obvious sequential relationships would not exist. In any case, all these elements might have a bearing on the effectiveness and success of liberalization programs.

Finally, the relationship between the sequencing of trade liberalization and the liberalization of external capital movements warrants particular consideration. Granting that the eventual liberalization of both the goods and the capital markets is beneficial, general theory as yet affords no guidance as to whether a first stage, or *partial* removal of restrictions in the goods market, should be accompanied by *no* liberalization of the capital market, *complete* liberalization, or something in between; nor whether liberalization in the capital market should precede, follow, or be concurrent with the liberalization of goods.

Our focus here is *trade* liberalization. Other policies may have been more important to policymakers at the time: liberalizing trade may have been quite subsidiary. But in the present context all other policies are regarded as "accompanying," examined only to discover their role in determining the fate of trade liberalization.

The Method of Research

The present investigation is empirical. It seeks to clarify the issues set out above by studying the history of actual liberalization programs and searching for the general principles at work. This is most effectively done by reviewing a large number and variety of cases: the larger the number of observations, the greater the validity of the inferences. We have therefore, subject to the following qualifications, attempted to cover all liberalization experiences in the post World War II period.

1 The object of this study is to reveal rules which may be applied in the design of trade liberalization in *developing* countries. Since it may be presumed that the nature of the economies in developing countries, the way they respond, and the feasibility of using various policy instruments tend to differ from those of *developed* economies, we have excluded from the study the investigation of liberalization policies in developed economies – of which post-war Europe would have provided the bulk – except where they undertook liberalization programs at an earlier, less developed stage.

2 Similarly, the subject matter of the study is the implementation of liberalization policies in *market economies*: the nature of centrally planned economies and the context in which a trade liberalization is undertaken in them are so different that lessons drawn from experiences in one category of economies would be of limited validity for the other. We have therefore excluded centrally planned economies with the exception of Yugoslavia, as a borderline case.

3 A substantial body of data, of reasonable quality, is essential for the investigation of the issues involved: where such data are mostly missing, the liberalization experience cannot be studied. In fact, no country's whole history has been abandoned on this score. But several earlier liberalization experiences in countries covered in the study could not be explored.

4 Similarly, since this is an analysis of experience, very recent liberalization policies could not be studied: a history of at least three or four years from the introduction of liberalization to the start of this study (in 1984) was thus a necessary requirement. This has not ruled out several liberalization experiments that were ongoing and, judged by policy announcements, still at an early stage when the study was launched; but other present-day experiences, primarily in several African countries, could not be analyzed.

5 Finally, in line with the former observation, only *actual* liberalization attempts form the body of this study. Liberalization policies that were announced but either were never implemented or were abandoned very quickly could not be the subject of a study that investigates effects of a policy in order to relate them to the policy's fate. For the same reason, the present study does not raise the question of why liberalization policies have not even started in various economies.

This leaves us with 19 countries, each of which has been studied by a single author or team as follows: *Argentina* (D. Cavallo and J. Cottani); *Brazil* (D. V. Coes); *Chile* (S. de la Cuadra and D. Hachette); *Colombia* (J.

García García); *Greece* (G. C. Kottis); *Indonesia* (M. M. Pitt); *Israel* (N. Halevi and J. Baruh); *Korea* (K. S. Kim); *New Zealand*[3] (A. C. Rayner and R. Lattimore); *Pakistan* (S. Guisinger and G. Scully); *Peru* (J. J. Nogués); *Philippines* (G. Shepherd and F. Alburo); *Portugal* (J. B. de Macedo, C. Corado and M. L. Porto); *Singapore* (B.-Y. Aw); *Spain* (G. de la Dehesa, J. J. Ruiz and A. Torres); *Sri Lanka* (A. G. Cuthbertson and P. Athukorala); *Turkey* (T. Baysan and C. Blitzer); *Uruguay* (E. Favaro and P. T. Spiller); *Yugoslavia* (O. Havrylyshyn).

Analysis of the country studies has followed a uniform framework in which the issues involved in designing and implementing a liberalization policy have been defined by ten primary questions.

1   What is the appropriate speed and intensity of liberalization?
2   What circumstances are favorable for introducing trade liberalization?
3   Should productive activities be uniformly or differentially treated during the process of trade liberalization?
4   If uniform treatment is indicated, how should it be formulated?
5   Should there be a separate stage for replacing nonprice forms of trade restrictions with price measures?
6   Is an export promotion stage desirable? If so, how should it be timed in relation to import liberalization?
7   How important are exogenous developments to the survival of liberalization?
8   On what pattern of performance of the economy is the fate of a liberalization policy likely to hinge?
9   What independent policy measures contribute, either by their presence or absence, to the success of trade liberalization?
10 How best should a trade liberalization policy and the liberalization of external capital transactions be sequenced?

A minimum core of analysis constructed around these issues has been followed in the country studies. But individual studies are much richer in substance and less uniform than the list of core issues would suggest: they have pursued additional more specific issues, have focused on different aspects, according to the country's circumstances, have provided substantial historical descriptions and data, and have followed a variety of analytical techniques.

Clearly, only very partial inferences about some of the issues could be drawn from the analysis of a single country's experience. Considerably more may be expected when the wealth of experiences studied in the

3 New Zealand is the only instance of a liberalization experience in a *developed* economy which is included in this study. It was added when it was found that an ongoing study of their experience investigates the issues central to the present project, and that New Zealand's liberalization history might help in shedding light on them.

separate country analyses is synthesized. This synthesis is provided in the present volume.

Inferences have been drawn in a variety of ways. To start with, hypotheses of relationships have often been suggested by the country studies. These hypotheses have then been investigated through comparing experiences, using the collective evidence of the liberalization episodes as a set of observations. In the main text this is done in a rough rather than a precise and rigorous manner; but most of the propositions derived are also supported by a more formal econometric analysis, presented in a separate appendix.

While the primary issues that have been elaborated here serve to focus the analysis, neither the country studies nor the synthesis uses them as a framework for *presenting* the findings. Some are more important and some more researchable than others; and inferences about some are derived indirectly through answers to differently formulated questions. Thus, while the reader would usually be easily able to appreciate each chapter's relevance to one or more of the primary issues, the presentation of this study follows its own logic. And, like the country studies, the synthesis ranges beyond the core defined by the list of primary issues.

Besides the econometric appendix, two further appendices are attached. One suggests some propositions on the basis of theoretical analysis, primarily where the experiences studied were not sufficient to yield empirical inferences. The other summarizes the liberalization histories of the individual countries from which the inferences in this synthesis were derived. But the accounts are extremely concise, merely outlining the experiences in general: to understand and appreciate these experiences in any depth, the manuscripts of the country studies are indispensable.

Part I

The Introduction and Fate of Liberalization

2

Episodes of Trade Liberalization

"Trade liberalization" is defined as any act that would make the trade regime more "neutral" – nearer to a trade system free of government intervention. Such acts may take two forms: changes of price instruments – primarily tariffs – and relaxation of QRs.

An "index of liberalization" provides a shorthand synthetic description of the experience of individual countries. The index shows both a potential trend movement of the nature of the trade regime and periodical fluctuations of the severity of trade interventions.

Partly through the index, "episodes of liberalization" are delineated for each country. The "episode" is defined as starting with a substantial act of liberalization and terminating at a time when no further significant liberalization is undertaken (often a point at which the process of liberalization is reversed). These episodes are the basic units of observation and analysis for the study.

Trade Liberalization: a Move toward Neutrality

Literally, trade liberalization means freeing the flows of trade between the country concerned and its (actual or potential) trade partners. It thus implies the lessening of government intervention in these flows. But suppose that a government removes QRs from 100 trade items and imposes new restrictions on 50 others. Would that be a "liberalization"? Not necessarily, not even if the volume of imports of the newly freed trade flows exceeds that of flows that have just been eliminated by new restrictions. "Lessening" must be evaluated in terms of the impact of any intervention on the operation of the economic system. In fact, a movement that appears to be more government intervention could actually lessen interference and thus qualify as a liberalization.

We shall call a "liberalization" any change that makes the country's trade system more "neutral." A trade system is completely neutral if it operates precisely as it would with no government interference of any sort. A trade system with no government interference whatsoever would thus be, by definition, neutral; but conceivably a system with many interventions could also be neutral if it perfectly simulated free-market operation. Be that as it may, the less the operation of a trade regime deviates from the way it would work under complete neutrality, the more neutral it is. A movement that leads in this direction is a "liberalization"; a change that increases the deviation is its opposite.

The intervention at issue is solely and specifically that which is directed at the trading system. A consumption tax on an importable, for instance (or its equivalent, a system of a tariff and an equal tax on domestic production), may be expected to affect imports. But it is neutral in its impact on the cost of an import versus an import-competing activity. Hence, although it alters trade flows, it is not, in our definition, a deviation from neutrality, and its removal or imposition (or its reduction or increase) is not a liberalization or a de-liberalization. The same is true for similar measures, such as general production subsidies, as long as they are not directed specifically and differentially at trade versus domestic activity. In other words, the study's concern is with trade liberalization rather than with liberalization of the economy as a whole.[1]

A Change in Form

Trade liberalization, thus defined, could be manifested in two ways. One is a change in the form of intervention: a move from direct government regulation through rationing – QRs – to intervention through the use of

---

1 A presumption still exists, however, that trade liberalization reduces government distortion of the economic system: a neutral economy is likely to be a less distorted economy. This is not, of course, logically inevitable; trade interventions may conceivably be so constructed as to offset the effect of the nontrade government intervention. For instance, an export subsidy may happen to be relevant primarily in those sectors in which minimum wage legislation applies. Thus, a system with trade interventions might be globally more neutral, in the sense of deviating less from a situation devoid of government intervention, than a system without trade intervention but with other government interventions. But, though possible, this seems unlikely. The experiences of the countries covered in this study as well as others would suggest, first, that in countries in which trade intervention is minimal, domestic intervention is constrained by the necessity to compete with the outside world, and is therefore also likely to be minimal. Such countries are indeed facing a policy of approximate "global neutrality." Second, no evidence suggests that as a rule, or even often, trade intervention offsets other government interventions; it is thus plausible that trade liberalization does tend to lower man-made distortions.

the price mechanism – most often, tariffs. This abstracts from any potential change in the level of protection that may be involved in the change of form: a shift from the use of a QR to the direct application of its price equivalence – the replacement of the QR by an equivalent tariff – would still be expected to have an impact on the economy (probably even a far-reaching one (see chapter 10)) and will bring the economy closer to neutrality: it would thus constitute a liberalization. In practice, the change would not be expected to replace a QR with its *precise* price equivalent. Thus, while a change of QRs to a price equivalent, as a change in form, constitutes liberalization, the difference between the price actually set and the price equivalence of the former quota may be a move toward or away from liberalization, depending on the direction of the change. In one instance this would be unequivocal: when the quota is prohibitive its price equivalence is infinite. Any price (tariff) actually set cannot exceed it, so that the price-change element involved in the move away from the QR would be toward liberalization or at worst immaterial, but never *de-liberalization*.

Changes in the Price System

The other manifestation of liberalization is a change in the price system: that is, a use of price instruments in a way that changes relative prices in the economy. The prices that matter here are the effective protection rates, as the signaling prices for production activities, and the nominal protection rates as signals for consumption. A move toward neutrality would be a change that reduces the average level and dispersion of the system of these rates of protection. In fact, if protection rates are defined so that they incorporate an exchange rate adjustment, the issue of *average* levels of protection disappears: this average, properly defined, must be zero, with some positive protection rates in the system and inevitably some negative rates as well (see Corden, 1971, chapter 5; Michaely, 1977, chapter 4). Thus defined, a move to neutrality would be simply a reduction of the dispersion of the protection rate system.

Changes in the relative prices system would be introduced via changes (a) in tariffs and other trade taxes or their equivalents (special levies, appreciated price estimates of imports for custom duties, "price-equalization" funds, and so on); (b) in subsidies or, similarly, their equivalents; (c) in the severity of QRs (as represented by their price equivalence or quota profits, which have just been discussed); and (d) in the formal system of the foreign exchange rate.

Trade Taxes and Subsidies
The intervention system concerned of course includes export taxes and subsidies as much as import taxes (tariffs) and subsidies. Introduction or

intensified use of these instruments would sometimes, as remarked earlier, be a move toward liberalization. An important case in point is export subsidies. A restricted trade system frequently involves an anti-export bias, encouraging import substitution and discouraging exports.[2] Any action to encourage exports in this situation would be a move toward neutrality (and hence an act of liberalization)[3] whether it were accomplished through reducing export taxes – involving a reduction of government intervention – or, as is very common, through subsidizing export activities – entailing *increased* government intervention.[4] Another instance where new or intensified government intervention would be liberalizing in its effect concerns tariffs on imported inputs (intermediate and capital goods). A system of trade restrictions will frequently have a strong element of "escalation": no tariffs, or very low tariffs, on imported primary inputs, and particularly high tariffs on finished consumer goods. The absence (or low level) of tariffs on inputs, given the output tariffs, leads to (a) a discrimination against the local activities that compete with the imported inputs (the exchange-rate-adjusted protective rates of these activities would be negative) and (b) an increase in both the level and the dispersion of the effective protection rates of the activities that produce the final goods. By contracting these effects, the imposition or increase of tariffs on inputs would most probably be a move toward neutrality.

Changes in the Formal Exchange Rate
If a system of *multiple* formal exchange rates[5] exists, this is conceptually equivalent, on the trade side, to the existence of a single rate combined with a system of tariffs and subsidies; that is, the multiple exchange rate system introduces a dispersion into the system of nominal and effective protection rates. Hence, any change in the formal exchange rate system would constitute a step toward or away from liberalization. Specifically,

2 When exchange rate adjustments are made, import substitutes as a whole would be found to have positive rates of protection, whereas exports would face negative protection rates.
3 Brazil's liberalization experience consisted mostly of such export-promoting acts.
4 This statement refers to exports and import substitutes as a whole, as if each consisted of one good. In fact, export promotion could be carried out in a nonuniform way, increasing the dispersion of protection rates within the export sector. And this might, all changes considered, be a move away from neutrality.
5 "Formal" exchange rates are distinguished from "effective" exchange rates. The latter include the "formal" exchange rates as well as tariffs, trade subsidies, and so on; as such, they are obviously involved in the process of liberalization. The former (which may also be referred to as "posted" exchange rates) are rates announced as such by the government and used for foreign exchange transactions through the banking system. The "formal" rate may or *may not* be the official exchange rate: the "effective" rate may be one of several formal exchange rates which exist simultaneously, or even none of them.

the shift from an existing system of multiple exchange rates to a single rate would normally be an act of liberalization.[6]

Does a change of uniform exchange rate constitute an act of liberalization (or its reversal)? Strictly speaking, the answer is negative. Had "neutrality" of the trade regime been defined as the outcome in a market free of *any* government intervention, the answer would have been different: setting an exchange rate would alter the price ratio of tradeables to nontradeables, leading away from neutrality; and changing the exchange rate toward or away from its equilibrium level would then be an act of liberalization or its reversal. But in our definition, which is restricted to government intervention through trade or commercial policy instruments, a change in the exchange rate would not be conceptually a representation of liberalization or its reverse.

Nevertheless, exchange rate changes are bound to affect the degree of restrictiveness of commercial policy instruments. Perhaps the most telling example is the degree of trade restriction through QRs, which, whether they are administered through the exchange control mechanism or otherwise, must be affected by a change in the exchange rate. Similarly, tariffs that are effective with one exchange rate may become redundant with a higher rate, thus lowering the effective level of the tariff. Conceptually, such changes should be captured by observing directly the trade policy instruments involved: estimated quota profits would change and hence the tariff levels implied by the QRs; or the estimated effective (nonredundant) levels of tariffs would change. These changes, in turn, would constitute a liberalization or its reverse. In practice, however, such estimates are rarely made and, in their absence, the changes in the exchange rate, assuming their expected impact, would come to represent acts of liberalization (or de-liberalization). Thus, given the proper context, a formal devaluation may be – and for several liberalization episodes is – a step of liberalization in its own right.[7]

A Change in Policies

Finally, "liberalization" is defined here by policies rather than by outcomes. Specifically, it is not defined by the "openness" of the economy, as measured through some trade ratios. Certainly a policy of liberalization may be expected to lead to an increased share of external trade in the country's economy. Normally, imports will increase (the local production

---

6 "Normally," rather than inevitably, because an existing system of multiple exchange rates may conceivably be designed so as to offset the impact of tariffs and subsidies.

7 Such a statement implies that the devaluation concerned is *real*, genuinely moving the rate of exchange closer to its equilibrium level.

of import substitutes will decrease); and exports, too, will increase either because they have been directly encouraged via subsidies or lowered taxes or because resources have shifted from import-substituting activities. But this result is not inevitable. First, if liberalization is associated with a formal devaluation, as it often is, and starts out in a situation of disequilibrium, imports may fall while exports increase; and the attempts to identify liberalization through the import ratio, or even through the aggregate trade ratio, may be misleading. Second, when liberalization is manifested as a mere change in the form of protection, this would by definition mean no change in imports. Nevertheless, in the absence of direct price observations, authors have occasionally used actual trade performance as an indication of liberalization, especially in instances where QRs were supposed to be relaxed in some way and actual changes in imports (particularly of final consumer goods) were used as indicators of the existence or absence of such relaxation.

The Index of Liberalization

In each country study, the degree of liberalization, in the sense just discussed, is represented by an index number – one for each year. The movement of the index thus depicts, synthetically, the history of each country's trade regime (figures 2.1–2.19).

The index is designated on a scale from 1 to 20, 1 standing for a regime with the highest degree of intervention possible and 20 for the most liberalized regime – a system of completely free trade (or, conceptually, one which perfectly simulates free trade).[8] Between 1 and 20, the index is designated in integers, with no pretensions to representing fine distinctions.

---

8 A system with a single uniform rate of tariff on all imports of goods and services and of subsidy to all exports would be such an equivalent (it should be recalled that only intervention in *trade* flows is considered here: such a uniform tariff/subsidy would still amount to a differential tax on capital flows). In fact, no such perfect simulation, or even its rough approximation, has ever been observed.

A completely free-trade situation has not been found in the 19 countries studied here, nor, probably, will it be found in any other country (save, perhaps, Hong Kong), either in the post World War II period or in any other. The situation for which the number of 20 is assigned in the index should be interpreted as something like "as free a trade system as may feasibly be expected to be found." Of the 19 countries, only Chile achieved that position at the height of its liberalization.

Similarly, a system with the "highest possible degree of intervention" probably does not exist: in any system, some further intervention, taking the economy further away from neutrality, must technically be possible. Thus the index of 1 is assigned to as high a degree of intervention as may be realized in a *nonsocialist* economy.

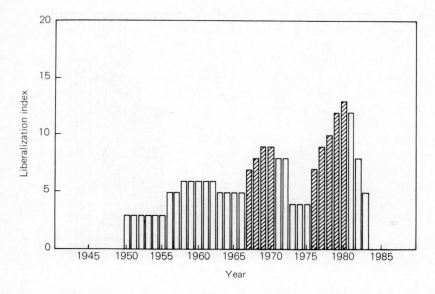

Figure 2.1 Trade liberalization index, Argentina, 1950–1983. The shaded areas delineate episodes.

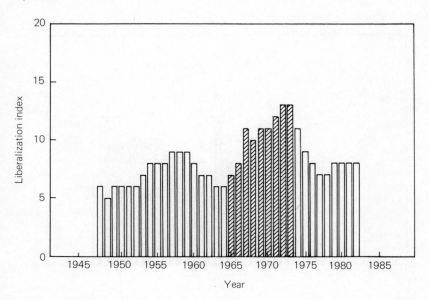

Figure 2.2 Trade liberalization index, Brazil, 1947–1982. The shaded areas delineate episodes.

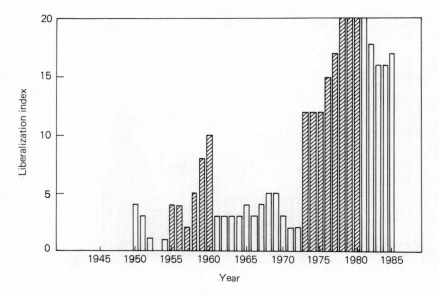

Figure 2.3 Trade liberalization index, Chile, 1950–1985. The shaded areas delineate episodes.

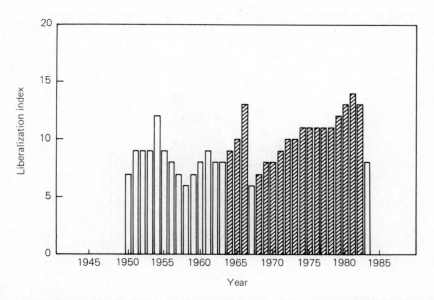

Figure 2.4 Trade liberalization index, Colombia, 1950–1983. The shaded areas delineate episodes.

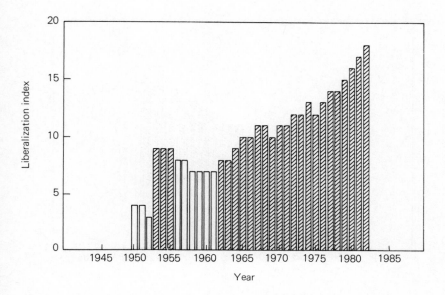

Figure 2.5 Trade liberalization index, Greece, 1950–1982. The shaded areas delineate episodes.

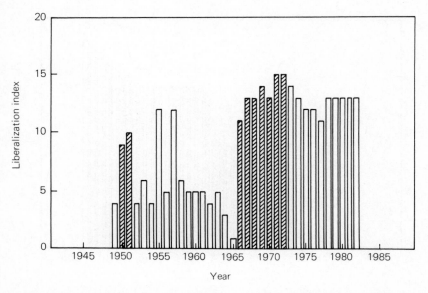

Figure 2.6 Trade liberalization index, Indonesia, 1949–1982. The shaded areas delineate episodes.

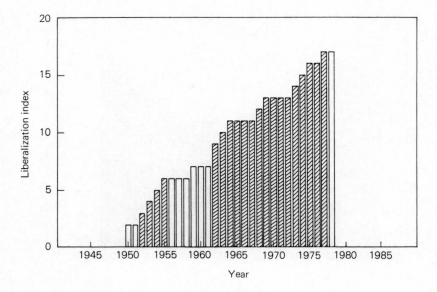

Figure 2.7 Trade liberalization index, Israel, 1950–1978. The shaded areas delineate episodes.

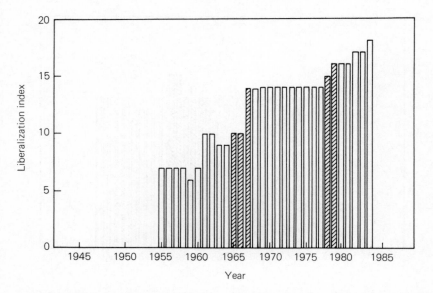

Figure 2.8 Trade liberalization index, Korea, 1955–1984. The shaded areas delineate episodes.

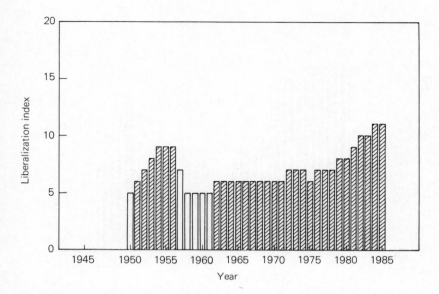

Figure 2.9 Trade liberalization index, New Zealand, 1950–1985. The shaded areas delineate episodes.

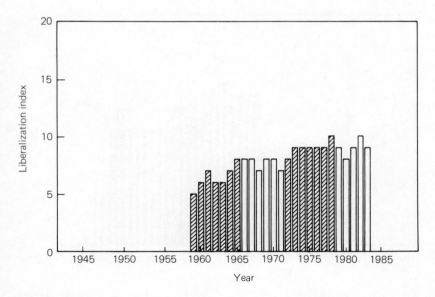

Figure 2.10 Trade liberalization index, Pakistan, 1959–1983. The shaded areas delineate episodes.

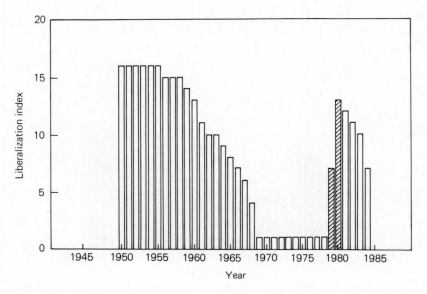

Figure 2.11 Trade liberalization index, Peru, 1950–1984. The shaded areas delineate episodes.

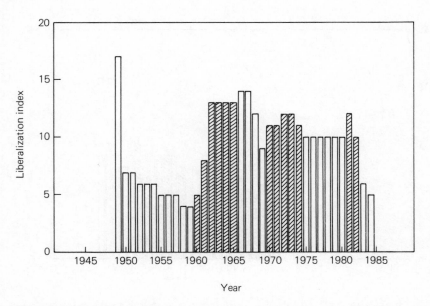

Figure 2.12 Trade liberalization index, Philippines, 1949–1984. The shaded areas delineate episodes.

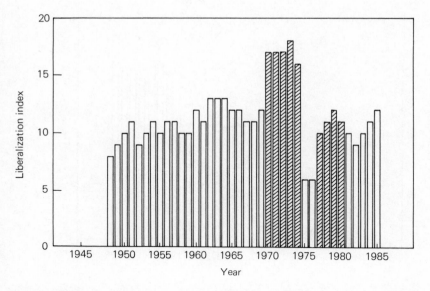

Figure 2.13 Trade liberalization index, Portugal, 1948–1985. The shaded areas delineate episodes.

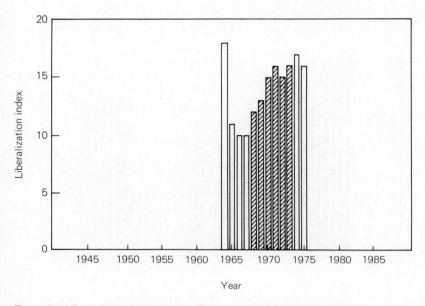

Figure 2.14 Trade liberalization index, Singapore, 1964–1975. The shaded areas delineate episodes.

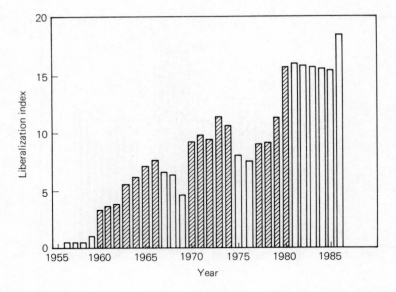

Figure 2.15 Trade liberalization index, Spain, 1955–1986. The shaded areas delineate episodes.

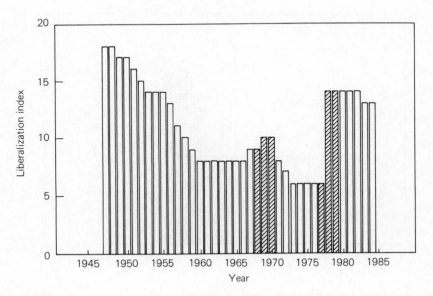

Figure 2.16 Trade liberalization index, Sri Lanka, 1947–1984. The shaded areas delineate episodes.

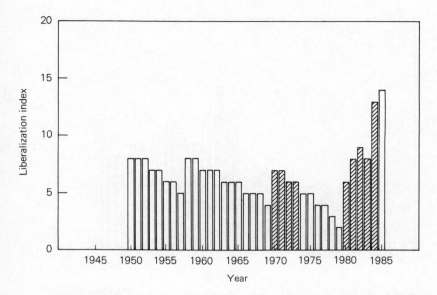

Figure 2.17 Trade liberalization index, Turkey, 1950–1985. The shaded areas delineate episodes.

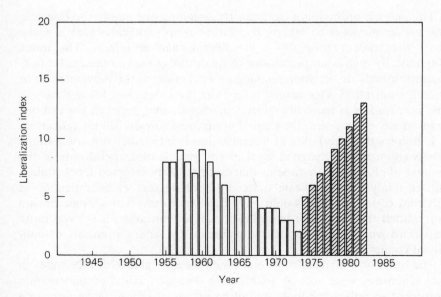

Figure 2.18 Trade liberalization index, Uruguay, 1955–1982. The shaded areas delineate episodes.

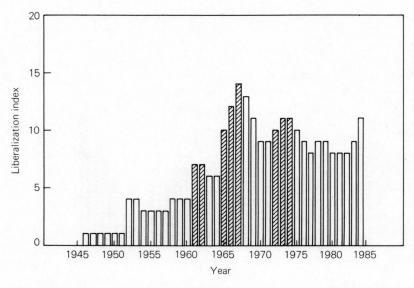

Figure 2.19 Trade liberalization index, Yugoslavia, 1946–1984. The shaded areas delineate episodes.

The index is ordinal, not cardinal. By assigning one number to one year and higher numbers to others, the author simply indicates that in some years the trade regime was more liberal than in others. The index emphatically makes no pretension to quantitative measurement. Its fluctuations merely depict strengthening or weakening of the movement to or from liberalization. One cannot infer from the index that, for instance, in one year trade was more liberal than in another by x percent; nor can one read, at any given point, the degree of progress toward full liberalization.

It follows that the index of liberalization is inherently not comparable *across countries*: its assigned level in any year is meaningful only in the context of changes over time in that country. Any assigned level could – and certainly does – indicate quite different degrees of liberalization in different countries. This would have been true even had a single person determined the indices of liberalization in all countries; it is even more important when the indices are constructed by separate authors of individual country studies.

The bases on which authors determined the annual levels of the index in their countries were sets of quantitative data or qualitative information presumed to reflect the basic definition of liberalization (as an approach toward neutrality). These were often data on nominal and effective rates of protection, on the prevalence and degree of restrictiveness of QRs (other than as their representation in quota profits, hence in protection rates), on the degree of anti-export bias, on the distance of the formal exchange rate from its equilibrium level, on the structure of imports – in particular, the share of final consumer goods in the total – and similar measures. Often, impressionistic information about phenomena such as the degree of friction in the administrative machinery was involved. Sometimes a declarative act such as the signing of an agreement with another country or a group of countries, or merely the announcement of a scheme (without as yet any action), may be involved in the estimate. No general formula was applied, nor was there any mechanical weighting of sets of indicators in the estimation of any individual index. In the end, each index reflects the best judgment of its authors, based on the data available and reached by whichever method suited the authors best.

The synthetic overview provided by the indices of the nature of the trade regimes in the 19 separate countries shows, for each country, a trend of development over time (if any) toward or away from liberalization. But no inference should be made on the basis of anything like a slope of a trend line – a procedure which would be legitimate only if the index were a cardinal measure. More important than the trend are *oscillations* of the index over time, which form the bases for delineating the liberalization episodes.

Liberalization Episodes

An episode of liberalization starts at a point at which a significant policy change toward liberalization was implemented. It ends with a reversal or when no further policy trend in either direction is apparent. A significant step toward liberalization is judged by two criteria. First, the policy chnage must be of some substance. A one-point increase in the index (provided no further change follows) would not qualify.[9] Second, the liberalization policy must be in force for some reasonable time. Thus even when an act in the direction of liberalization is quite substantial but lasts no more than a year, no "episode" will be indicated: analysis of the consequences of so short an episode would be impossible and even irrelevant. The minimum length of an episode is thus set at two years, because the present study analyzes the implementation of a liberalization policy mostly by examining

9 In general, a one-point change in the index is too small to carry much weight, since the index involves a strong judgmental element. And the placing of a one-point step is also often arbitrary: a moderate process of liberalization (or, less often, of its reversal) often advances over a long period, with no radical change in any given year, and the author would assign along this process a step (or steps) of one-point change with no strong justification for the selection of the particular year.

its consequences. No such examination will be feasible, or even relevant, if the policy has been very short lived. More generally, this is an extension of the principle of studying implemented policies rather than mere intentions, or of why liberalization policies have *not* been undertaken when and where they have not.

The duration and intensity of an event are also important in determining when an episode has ended. A slight reversal, or pause, for just one year, followed by a resumption of progress toward liberalization would be judged an interruption rather than the end of an episode: the period of "no change" would have to be long enough to justify a designation of an end of one liberalization episode and the beginning of another. An exception is made for Israel, where an "episode" is described as over when no pause or reversal is evident. In Israel, liberalization was proceeding in one way or another for decades, but a crucial change in its nature led the authors to designate this change the end of one episode and the beginning of another. For New Zealand, where similar changes in the nature of the policy were less crucial, the authors have preferred to designate such sections as "phases" of a single episode. Several liberalization episodes (in Uruguay, New Zealand, and Turkey) were on going at the time they were analyzed. For these, the present (that is, the time of the study) has arbitrarily been designated as the "end" of the episode. The fate and full impact of these episodes cannot yet be determined, but they have all by now been in force long enough to justify their inclusion in the individual country analyses and in this synthesis.

The episodes of liberalization are designated by shaded areas in the individual indices of liberalization (figures 2.1–2.19). Not all have been analyzed in detail in the country studies, sometimes because the available data, though sufficient for at least some parts of the intercountry analysis of the present synthesis, were inadequate for the in-depth investigation of the country study. Some of these neglected episodes will be included in the further analysis undertaken here. On occasion – Turkey's liberalization of 1958 may be the most obvious example – data limitations have led country authors to exclude a period of liberalization altogether from their list of episodes. Conversely, in one country study – the Philippines – the authors have carefully analyzed a period, in the early 1980s, from which interesting country-specific inferences could be drawn but which was too short to qualify as an episode, as defined here: trade liberalization measures began to be reversed (in 1982) just one year after they were introduced. In the intercountry comparison this period will be neglected. Thus, the episodes observed in the synthesis (table 2.1) are approximately, but not precisely, those analyzed in detail in the country studies. Whenever more than one episode appeared in the country's experience, the episodes are identified by chronological numbers ("Argentina 1," "Argentina 2," and so on). The

Table 2.1 Episodes of liberalization

Latin America		Asia and Pacific		Mediterranean	
Argentina 1	(1967–70)	Indonesia 1	(1950–1)	Greece 1	(1953–5)
Argentina 2	(1976–80)	Indonesia 2	(1966–72)	Greece 2	(1962–82)
Brazil	(1965–73)	Korea 1	(1965–7	Israel 1	(1952–5)
		Korea 2	(1978–9)	Israel 2	(1962–8)
				Israel 3	(1969–77)
Chile 1	(1956–61)	New Zealand 1	(1951–6)	Portugal 1	(1970–4)
Chile 2	(1974–81)	New Zealand 2	(1962–81)	Portugal 2	(1977–80)
		New Zealand 3	(1982–4)		
Colombia 1	(1964–6)	Pakistan 1	(1959–65)	Spain 1	(1960–6)
Colombia 2	(1968–82)	Pakistan 2	(1972–8)	Spain 2	(1970–4)
				Spain 3	(1977–80)
Peru	(1979–80)	Philippines 1	(1960–5)	Turkey 1	(1970–3)
		Philippines 2	(1970–4)	Turkey 2	(1980–4)
Uruguay	(1974–82)	Singapore	(1968–73)	Yugoslavia	(1965–7)
		Sri Lanka 1	(1968–70)		
		Sri Lanka 2	(1977–9)		

comparative observation and analysis of these episodes will form the core
of this synthesis.

3

Intensity and Sustainability of Liberalization Episodes

Episodes of liberalization are classified according to their *intensity* – the *strength* of the undertaking and the *speed* of implementation – and their *fate* – completely sustained, partially sustained, and totally collapsed.

Strong liberalization policies tend to be sustained over the long run. Strong episodes generally start with a substantial step of liberalization. Liberalizations that start hesitantly are more likely to end in reversal and failure.

A restrictive trade regime tends, with time, to be self-reinforcing: the longer it has been in force, the stronger should be the attempt to change it and, in general, the less likely is such an attempt to succeed. Weak liberalizations that follow another unsuccessful attempt to liberalize have even less hope of survival, but when they follow a successful liberalization, even weak policies are quite likely to succeed. In general, if a first liberalization is successful, a long-run persistent course of liberalization is most likely to follow. The other extreme – a series of failing liberalization attempts – is not common: it is fully represented only by the history of Argentina.

A period of roughly six years seems to be suggested as a dividing line: once a liberalization experiment lasts five years without reversal, it is most likely to be sustained over the long run. This may be because a policy that lasts that long must either have survived a political change or been associated with a stable government, and because a period of six years is adequate to establish a pervasive interest in the survival of liberalization.

Intensity

To reveal and analyze connections between the success or failure of a liberalization policy and the speed and intensity of its implementation is clearly a core subject for the present investigation. We cannot measure these elements any more precisely than we could quantify liberalization levels; but we can nevertheless give some general idea of the degree of gradualism involved in an episode.

Assessing the degree of gradualism calls for judgment about intensity as well as duration: the liberalization episodes studied in the project will thus be classified as "strong" versus "weak" as well as "fast" versus "slow" (table 3.1). Obviously, a "strong" and "fast" episode will be "abrupt," whereas a "weak" and "slow" episode is "gradual."

The classification is based on the index of liberalization, supported by the detailed descriptions of the episodes. Although an ordinal rather than a cardinal measure, the index still expresses the degree of intensity of a trade liberalization policy within the context of a given country. An element of arbitrariness is bound to be present in our scheme of classification

Table 3.1 Intensity of liberalization episodes

	Strong episodes		Weak episodes	
Fast episodes	Argentina 2	(1976–80)	Argentina 1	(1967–70)
	Chile 1	(1956–61)	Colombia 1	(1964–6)
	Chile 2	(1974–81)	Indonesia 1	(1950–1)
	Greece 1	(1953–5)	Philippines 2	(1970–4)
	Indonesia 2	(1966–72)	Portugal 1	(1970–4)
	Israel 1	(1952–5)	Portugal 2	(1977–80)
	Peru	(1979–80)	Sri Lanka 1	(1968–70)
	Philippines 1	(1960–5)	Turkey 1	(1970–3)
	Singapore	(1968–73)		
	Spain 3	(1977–80)		
	Sri Lanka 2	(1977–9)		
	Turkey 2	(1980–4)		
	Yugoslavia	(1965–7)		
Slow episodes	Brazil	(1965–73)	Greece 2	(1962–82)
	Colombia 2	(1968–82)	Korea 1	(1965–7)
	Israel 2	(1962–8)	Korea 2	(1978–9)
	Israel 3	(1969–77)	New Zealand 1	(1951–6)
	Spain 1	(1960–6)	New Zealand 2	(1962–81)
	Uruguay	(1974–82)	New Zealand 3	(1982–4)
			Pakistan 1	(1959–65)
			Pakistan 2	(1972–8)
			Spain 2	(1970–4)

(diminished, we hope, by the reading of the detailed accounts of the episodes but compounded further by being largely based on the judgment of the authors of this synthesis). The more extreme cases would be less vulnerable in this way – there would be little dispute that the Chilean experience in the 1970s and the Greek in the 1950s were strong, or that the attempts in Pakistan and Turkey's 1970–3 episode were "weak." But classification of intermediate situations might be more open to doubt.

Sustainability

In analyzing what makes for durability in a liberalization attempt three categories of policy record are distinguished: "sustained" episodes, "partially sustained" episodes, and "collapsed" episodes.[1] A liberalization episode that, for its duration, has either kept progressing or, at least, not been reversed is classified as sustained; others, more tentatively included in the category, are episodes that are still in progress (Uruguay, New Zealand 3, and Turkey 2). In several cases policy has been reversed, but even so the trade regime has remained significantly more liberalized than before the attempt to liberalize. These episodes are classified as "partially sustained." Where policy reversals have led liberalization back to, or below, its pre-episode level, the episode is described as "collapsed."

The question arises as to how long a liberalization attempt must be maintained in order to qualify as "sustained." We took the extreme position of not regarding as "sustained" any episode that has been reversed at any time. But a strong argument could be made that a policy that survives over a considerable length of time and is then reversed should be viewed as a "sustained" policy which *independently* of its course and outcome has been followed by a different policy, owing to some exogenous circumstances. The most obvious instance is Brazil's eight-year episode of liberalization, from 1965 to 1973. No unequivocal resolution of this problem is obvious, so qualifications are mentioned when the individual episodes concerned are being analyzed.

The classifications (table 3.2) involve, as usual, a speculative element. The decisions represented in the table are the product of the combined judgments of the country authors and of the authors of this synthesis. In the event, the virtually complete concurrence of all observers indicates that the arbitrariness is probably not crucial.

---

1 Throughout the text the term "sustained" describing a liberalization is freely interchanged with the terms "survived" and "successful." The symmetrical opposite term "failed" is interchanged in this text with the terms "collapsed" and "reversed."

Table 3.2 Sustainability of liberalization episodes

Sustained		Partially sustained		Collapsed	
Chile 2	(1974–81)	Colombia 2	(1968–82)	Argentina 1	(1967–70)
Greece 1	(1953–5)	Pakistan 1	(1959–65)	Argentina 2	(1976–80)
Greece 2	(1962–82)	Pakistan 2	(1972–8)	Brazil	(1965–73)
Indonesia 2	(1966–72)	Philippines 1	(1960–5)	Chile 1	(1956–61)
Israel 1	(1952–5)	Philippines 2	(1970–4)	Colombia 1	(1964–6)
Israel 2	(1962–8)	Portugal 2	(1977–80)	Indonesia 1	(1950–1)
Israel 3	(1969–77)	Spain 1	(1960–6)	New Zealand 1	(1951–6)
Korea 1	(1965–7)	Spain 2	(1970–4)	Peru	(1979–80)
Korea 2	(1978–9)	Spain 3	(1977–80)	Portugal 1	(1970–4)
New Zealand 2	(1962–81)			Sri Lanka 1	(1968–70)
New Zealand 3	(1982–4)			Turkey 1	(1970–3)
Singapore	(1968–73)			Yugoslavia	(1965–7)
Sri Lanka 2	(1977–9)				
Turkey 2	(1980–4)				
Uruguay	(1974–82)				

Intensity and the Fate of Liberalization Episodes

We now look at the fate of separate liberalization episodes in relation to their intensity, that is, whether they were strong or weak.

1 In Argentina, the first liberalization episode (1967–70) was weak; it failed (in the sense of collapsing within several years). It was followed by a second liberalization episode (1976–80), which was strong, and has also failed.

2 In Brazil, the only liberalization episode (1965–73) was strong (although it started weakly). It has failed; however, the classification of the Brazilian liberalization as "failure," we recall, is open to doubt, in view of its rather long period of survival.

3 In Chile, a strong first liberalization attempt (1956–61) with a weak first stage, ended in failure. The second liberalization (1974–81) was strong and has been sustained.

4 In Colombia, the first, weak, liberalization episode (1964–6) failed; the subsequent (1968–82) episode was strong and was partially sustained.

5 In Greece, a strong first liberalization episode (1953–5) was sustained. It was followed by a weak episode (1962–82), which has also been sustained.

6 In Indonesia, the first liberalization episode (1950–1) was weak and failed. The subsequent episode (1966–72) was strong and has been sustained.

7   In Israel, a strong liberalization episode (1952–5) was sustained. It was followed by another liberalization, performed in two stages (1962–8 and 1969–77), both of which were strong and sustained.

8   In Korea, the two liberalization episodes (1965–7 and 1978–9) were both weak and both sustained.

9   In New Zealand, a weak first liberalization attempt (1951–6) failed. It was followed by another weak episode (1962–81), which this time has been sustained, and still another ongoing weak episode (1982–4).[2]

10   In Pakistan, both liberalization episodes (1959–65 and 1972–8) were weak and partially sustained.

11   In Peru, a single liberalization attempt (1979–80) was strong and failed.

12   In the Philippines, the first liberalization episode (1960–5) was strong and was partially sustained. A second episode (1970–4) was weak and was also partially sustained.

13   In Portugal, a weak liberalization episode (1970–4) ended in failure. The subsequent attempt (1977–80), again weak, has been partially sustained.

14   In Singapore, a single strong liberalization episode (1968–73) has been fully sustained.

15   Of Spain's three liberalization episodes, the first (1960–6) was strong (although its initial steps were not) and partially sustained. The second (1970–4) was a weak episode and was again partially sustained. The final strong attempt (1977–80) has been partially sustained.

16   Sri Lanka's first weak liberalization episode (1968–70) ended in failure. The second attempt (1977–9) was strong and has been sustained.

17   In Turkey, similarly, a first liberalization attempt (1970–3) was weak and failed; the second episode (1980–4), in which liberalization was strong, has been sustained.

18   In Uruguay, the single liberalization episode (1974–82) was strong and has been sustained.

19   Yugoslavia's strong liberalization episode (1965–7) was partially sustained. The subsequent weak attempt (1972–4) failed.[3]

This summary description is represented graphically in figure 3.1. An inference which seems to emerge rather clearly from this record is that *strong* liberalization attempts tend to be sustained. A reading of the histories of liberalization, as well as the observation of the indices of liberalization, indicates that these are mostly episodes which *start* with significant, rather than minor and marginal, steps of liberalization. Weak, hesitant liberalization attempts, on the other hand, tend to end up in failure rather than to gather momentum and develop eventually into a

2 Starting in 1986 – beyond the period covered in this study – the pace of liberalization in New Zealand has accelerated, making it definitely a strong policy.
3 The latter attempt at liberalization in Yugoslavia is not analyzed in detail in this study.

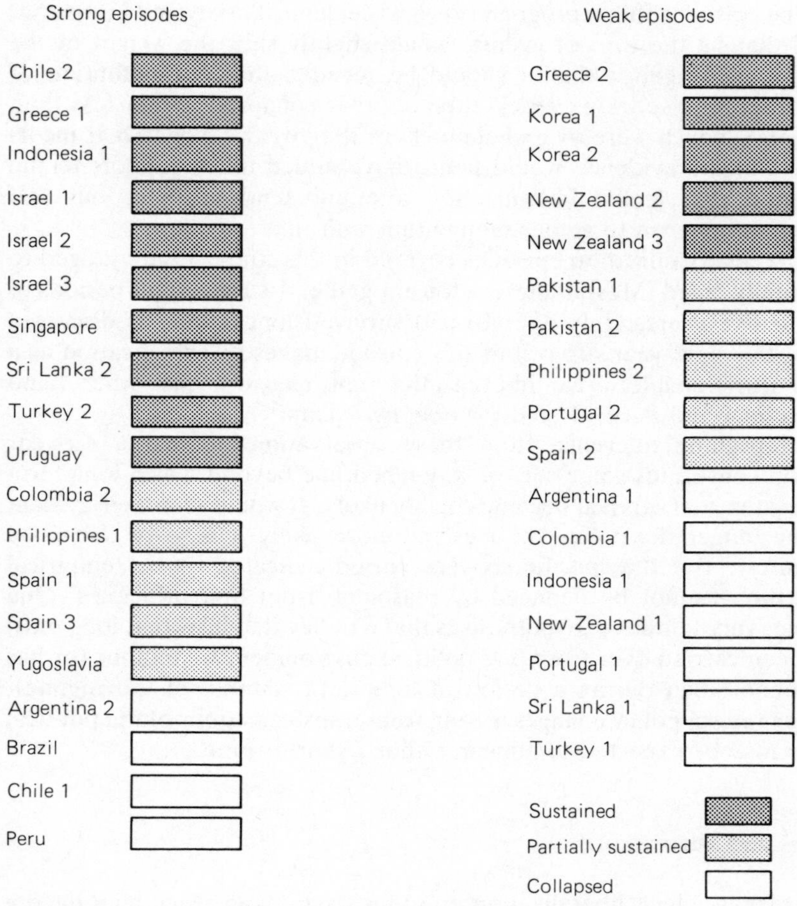

Strong episodes   Weak episodes

Chile 2	▓▓▓		Greece 2	▓▓▓
Greece 1	▓▓▓		Korea 1	▓▓▓
Indonesia 1	▓▓▓		Korea 2	▓▓▓
Israel 1	▓▓▓		New Zealand 2	▓▓▓
Israel 2	▓▓▓		New Zealand 3	▓▓▓
Israel 3	▓▓▓		Pakistan 1	☐
Singapore	▓▓▓		Pakistan 2	☐
Sri Lanka 2	▓▓▓		Philippines 2	☐
Turkey 2	▓▓▓		Portugal 2	☐
Uruguay	▓▓▓		Spain 2	☐
Colombia 2	☐		Argentina 1	☐
Philippines 1	☐		Colombia 1	☐
Spain 1	☐		Indonesia 1	☐
Spain 3	☐		New Zealand 1	☐
Yugoslavia	☐		Portugal 1	☐
Argentina 2	☐		Sri Lanka 1	☐
Brazil	☐		Turkey 1	☐
Chile 1	☐			
Peru	☐			

Sustained	▓▓▓
Partially sustained	▒▒▒
Collapsed	☐

Figure 3.1 Strength and sustainability of liberalizations. Brazil's classification as "collapsed" is ambiguous; see text.

durable liberalization. This inference is fully supported by the experiences of Greece, Indonesia, Israel, Singapore, Sri Lanka, Turkey, and Uruguay, and to some extent also by the record of Chile (in which the strong first liberalization attempt started weakly) and of Yugoslavia. The evidence is mixed for Argentina, Brazil (in which, in view of the length of the episode, "success" or "failure" is not clear), Colombia, New Zealand, Pakistan, the Philippines, Portugal, and Spain, but runs counter to the inference only in Peru (where the single strong liberalization attempt resulted in failure) and New Zealand (where a persistent liberalization has developed from several minor liberalization episodes).

Two qualifications should be mentioned. First, an eventual collapse of the three episodes still in progress (in New Zealand, Turkey and Uruguay), should that be the turn of events, would slightly shift the weight of the evidence. But against that it should be recalled that our definition of liberalization episodes excludes attempts that collapsed within less than two years – which were overwhelmingly of the "weak" type. Their incorporation in the evidence would hence have added much support to the contention that feeble liberalization attempts tend to peter out and collapse rather than to gather momentum with time.

Of the 36 liberalization episodes covered in this study, 13 are judged to have totally failed. Most of these – ten altogether – survived for periods of three to five years. Only one (Brazil) survived longer but, as discussed earlier, the eight-year survival of this episode makes its classification as a failure questionable. Two liberalization episodes, on the other hand (Indonesia 1 and Peru), lasted for only two years.[4]

An intriguing inference from these observations is that a six-year duration constitutes some sort of watershed line beyond which long-term or at least partial survival becomes highly likely. It would seem self-evident that the longer the policy survives the more likely it is to be sustained indefinitely. But the specific six-year period indicated by the empirical observation cannot be deduced by reasoning from first principles. One possible, very tentative, hypothesis is that a policy that lasts that long must have been carried over from one political environment to another (or has been undertaken during a period of long-term stability of the regime), whereas radical policy changes arising from transformations of the political regime may be expected to appear within a shorter time.

Success and Succession

The order in which liberalization episodes have taken place may have a bearing on their eventual fate.

Of the 19 "first" liberalization episodes ("first" refers also to *single* liberalization attempts in countries' histories) only five were fully sustained: in Greece, Israel, Korea, Singapore, and Uruguay. All but Korea's episode were "strong" liberalization attempts. Three others – Pakistan, the Philippines, and Spain – were partially sustained: of these, the episode in Pakistan was "weak," while the other two were "strong." In the remaining 11 countries – the majority – the first liberalization attempt did not survive. Most of these attempts (seven out of the 11) were "weak." Put

4 But here, again, the definitional procedure should be recalled: a survival of at least two years was required to designate a liberalization attempt as an "episode." Without it the number of very short-lived liberalization "episodes" would have appeared to be much larger.

differently: six of the ten "strong" first-time attempts survived, fully or partly, but only two of the nine weak attempts survived. The inference that the strength of a liberalization effort is important for its survival seems, then, particularly pertinent for first attempts.

In all five countries in which the first liberalization attempt survived, a long-term course of liberalization, with at most minor temporary reversals, has been set. The clear inference from this observation is that, judging from past experience, a sustained (probably strong) episode of liberalization is likely to lead a country toward a persistent long-term policy of trade liberalization. This empirical inference would be only slightly weakened were the Brazilian experience to be regarded as a case of sustained liberalization which has eventually been reversed.

In almost all of the 14 countries in which the first liberalization attempt either collapsed or was only partially sustained, further attempts have been made. Leaving aside Peru, in which the failed liberalization attempt is too recent for further policy courses to be expected, Brazil is the only country that has not tried again once the first attempt failed. Of those 12 countries in which repeated attempts have been made, in half of them – Chile, Colombia, Indonesia, New Zealand, Sri Lanka, and Turkey – fully sustained liberalizations have resulted. In five more – Pakistan, the Philippines, Portugal, Spain, and Yugoslavia – liberalization has been partially sustained, whereas in only one, Argentina, has the further attempt resulted again in an unqualified collapse. The notorious "Latin-American pattern" of repeated liberalization attempts that keep ending in failure is thus, strictly speaking, peculiar to a single country – Argentina. Counting separately all subsequent attempts (that is, second and third liberalization episodes) the majority – 13 out of 19 – appear to have been fully sustained and five have been partially sustained. Only one, Argentina's second episode, has definitely failed.

The strength of the liberalization attempt thus seems, in the empirical probabilistic sense, to be less crucial for the fate of subsequent episodes than for first experiences. Much, however, depends on the fate of the first episode. Of the 12 attempts to liberalize that followed a failed first attempt, not one *weak* subsequent liberalization has fully survived when a *strong* first attempt had failed; and in only one instance (New Zealand) has a repeated weak effort fully survived following the prior collapse of another weak episode. An earlier failure, particularly of a serious liberalization attempt, would seem to require that a subsequent attempt must be strong if it is to succeed, whereas, when it follows a prior success, even a weak further liberalization is likely to survive. The impact of previous success or failure on subsequent attempts is presumably a function of the extent of credibility attached to government policies derived from these prior experiences. It is, of course, also possible that repeated successes are not so much the result of a learning experience as a reflection of fundamental forces that operate in a country throughout its history of attempted liberalization, and which establish the fate of its liberalization attempts.

The inferences about the potential effect of past experiences of liberalizations tie in with a similar issue, namely the relationship of the fate of liberalization attempts to a country's history of restriction of trade. It would seem reasonable to expect that, the longer lived and more stringent the trade restrictions are, the more radical is the transformation that must be effected by liberalization; hence, presumably, the less likely is a liberalization policy to survive (although, of course, the larger are the gains to be expected should it be sustained).

Table 3.3 classifies all liberalization episodes by the length of time and intensity and preceding trade restrictions. Once more an element of arbitrariness is inevitable. Episodes are described as having had a "long" or "short" history of "severe" or "moderate" preceding trade restrictions. Some association of these two dimensions naturally exists. Specifically, very few "severe" restrictive regimes are found to have been "short" (only three). Nevertheless, the two dimensions should be kept separate. For each dimension, episodes are recorded separately by the categories of "sustained," "partially sustained," and "collapsed."

Both length and intensity of restrictiveness, particularly in combination, appear (in the probabilistic sense) to influence the fate of a trade liberalization attempt. Notably, of all the 12 *first* liberalization episodes that followed a long period of severe restrictions, only two (Greece 1 and Uruguay) have survived fully; two others have survived partially. When preceding restrictions had been either long but moderate or short but severe, the outcome seems to have been mixed. None of the three attempts at first liberalization undertaken after a period of both short and relatively moderate restrictions (Colombia 2, Philippines 2, and Singapore) has fully collapsed. These observations appear thus to conform, roughly, with our *a priori* hypothesis (table 3.3).

Histories of persistent and intensive trade restrictions are notably frequent in Latin America. This may be one explanation of the particularly high incidence in this region of failures of liberalization attempts.

An important implication of these observations is that a regime of trade restrictions is, in time, self-reinforcing. The longer it lasts, the harder it will be to reverse, and the more protracted thus does its life become. In view of our earlier observations, this would in turn imply that a liberalization attempt needs to be strong to survive, particularly in countries with a pervasive history of restricted trade.

Table 3.3 Sustainability of liberalizations and history of the trade regime

Severity of restrictions	Duration of restrictions	
	Long	Short
Severe	*Sustained*	
	Chile 2	Israel 1
	Greece 1	
	Indonesia 2	
	New Zealand 2	
	New Zealand 3	
	Sri Lanka 2	
	Turkey 2	
	Uruguay	
	Partially sustained	
	Philippines 1	Portugal 2
	Spain 1	
	Collapsed	
	Argentina 1	Indonesia 1
	Argentina 2	
	Brazil 1	
	Chile 1	
	New Zealand 1	
	Peru	
	Sri Lanka 1	
	Turkey 1	
	Yugoslavia 1	
Moderate	*Sustained*	
	Greece 2	Singapore
	Israel 2	
	Israel 3	
	Korea 1	
	Korea 2	
	Partially sustained	
	Pakistan 1	Colombia 2
	Pakistan 2	Philippines 2
	Spain 2	
	Spain 3	
	Collapsed	
	Colombia 1	
	Portugal 1	

4

The Introduction of Liberalization: Circumstances and Motives

Often liberalizations have been introduced "under distress" when the country was suffering severe economic difficulties: an acute balance-of-payments crisis, rapid inflation, or a drastic decline in income and employment. On occasion, such failures have led to a perception of a total economic collapse, sometimes accompanied by a drastic change of the political regime. But almost as many liberalization policies have started under "placid" conditions, with no obvious malfunctioning of the economic mechanism. These liberalizations have often been undertaken following the success of an earlier liberalization experiment. In between are liberalizations introduced when the economy was experiencing some difficulties but these were not severe enough to lead to a perception of crisis.

Liberalizations introduced "under distress" have tended to be intense (strong and rapid) and have consequently also tended to survive better than other liberalization experiments. Those implemented under "placid" circumstances have survived nearly as well, particularly when they followed earlier successful liberalizations. The "in-between" category – lacking either the intensity born of crisis or the encouragement of earlier success – has had the weakest record of sustainability.

The topic of this chapter is the relationship between the circumstances in which liberalization attempts are launched, the typical motives for adopting the policy, and the nature and fate of the attempt. The discussion is based purely on the facts and interpretations established by the authors of the country studies, rather than on an independent search.

Initial Circumstances

Needless to say, some circumstances more commonly attend the launching of a liberalization than others (table 4.1). And, of course, some circumstances will be mutually exclusive. Various elements tend to go together but will still be mentioned separately if one does not totally include the other.

Change of Political Regime

A trade liberalization, as a major economic policy decision, has often been undertaken upon a radical change in the political regime – defined here as a political discontinuity – in the sense that the new regime is not expected to abide by the basic commitments of its predecessor (see chapter 9).[1]

Fourteen liberalization episodes, in ten countries, have been associated by the authors of the country studies concerned with such change of regime. Two episodes followed an obviously violent and radical change: Chile 2 and Indonesia 2. Indonesia's first liberalization also followed a radical change – from colonial rule to independence. Pakistan and Sri Lanka, while differing in the ways they introduced the changes, have a similar pattern of alternating regimes, with incoming governments introducing liberalizations following retrogressions by their predecessors. This is true for both of Pakistan's liberalization attempts and for Sri Lanka's two liberalization episodes. In Argentina, no similar "cycle" of events seems to have taken place; nevertheless, both its episodes followed a change of political regime, as did Brazil's single (but rather long) liberalization episode. The third liberalization attempt of Spain also came in the wake of a transformation of the political regime, although in this case the degree of discontinuity is probably modest enough to make it a borderline candidate for qualification as a "change in regime." Finally, liberalization in Singapore followed shortly after the collapse of the Federation with Malaysia – an event which both led to a perception of crisis and freed the country to pursue its own policy.

---

1 We may, however, define a liberalization episode in a given country as having followed a change of political regime while later we shall classify this country as one with a "stable" regime. This would be true when no further change appears within a reasonably long time after the implementation of the liberalization policy. Obvious examples are the second liberalization episodes of Chile and Indonesia, which will be mentioned shortly.

Table 4.1 Initial circumstances

Episode		Date of launching of episode	Change of political regime	Perception of complete economic collapse	BOP crisis (or a deterioration)	High inflation	Exogenous shocks	Favorable BOP	Favorable combination of economic circumstances
Argentina	1	1967	x		x	x			
	2	1976	x	x	x	x	x		
Brazil		1965	x			x	x	x	
Chile	1	1956		x	x	x	x		
	2	1974	x	x	x	x	x		
Colombia	1	1964							x
	2	1968							x
Greece	1	1953			x			x	
	2	1962							x
Indonesia	1	1950	x						x
	2	1966	x	x	x	x	x		
Israel	1	1952		x	x	x			
	2	1962					x	x	x
	3	1969							x
Korea	1	1965							x
	2	1978							x
New Zealand	1	1951						x	x
	2	1962							x
	3	1982							x
Pakistan	1	1959	x					x	x
	2	1972	x					x	x
Peru		1979				x			
Philippines	1	1960	x						x
	2	1970			x				
Portugal	1	1970							
	2	1977	x						
Singapore		1968	x				x	x	x
Spain	1	1960			x	x			
	2	1970						x	x
	3	1977	x		ø	x			
Sri Lanka	1	1968	x		ø		x		
	2	1977	x					x	
Turkey	1	1970			x				
	2	1980		x	x	x			
Uruguay		1974			x	x	x		
Yugoslavia		1965			ø	x			
Number of episodes 36			14	6	15	13	10	8	16

BOP, balance of payments; ø, deterioration.

Perception of Complete Economic Collapse

When things get bad enough, radical departure from existing policies becomes more attractive. It follows, however, that a liberalization policy undertaken in such a climate would make sense only if introduced in conjunction with changes in other major policy instruments.

People often become unhappy with various manifestations of economic performance; but a consensus that the economy has collapsed completely and can no longer function without radical transformation is less common: six liberalizations in five countries studied in this project have been introduced under such circumstances. In one country, Chile, this was true for both its liberalization episodes, more so for the second episode than the first. Other instances are Argentina 2, Indonesia 2, Israel 1, and Turkey 2.

Besides this group, Spain is again a borderline case: the general view when its first liberalization episode was launched in 1960 was that, while not quite in a state of total collapse, with its present policies the country was facing an economic dead end.

Balance-of-payments Crisis

A major element of "total collapse" must be a balance-of-payments crisis[2] – in all seven instances of "collapse" just mentioned a balance-of-payments crisis was present. In other instances, a balance-of-payments crisis was evident without a general perception of total collapse: Argentina 1, Philippines 2, Turkey 1, and Uruguay. And several started under a condition – short of a crisis – of acute balance-of-payments deterioration: Greece 1, Spain 3, Sri Lanka 1, and Yugoslavia. Altogether, nearly half the episodes started under circumstances of severe deterioration of the balance of payments. Once more, this would indicate that the liberalization policies must have been connected with a more comprehensive policy package.

High Inflation

Unsurprisingly, our observations found a nearly one-to-one correspondence between the behavior of the balance of payments and the behavior of inflation on the eve of adoption of a liberalization policy. Inflation was high in all the instances in which liberalization followed a severe balance-of-payments deterioration except Philippines 2, Sri Lanka 1, and Turkey 1. And only a single liberalization – Brazil's – was launched in a situation of rapid inflation *without* a severe balance-of-payments deterioration.

Exogenous Shocks

In a few instances, liberalization followed an exogenous shock. The most common such shock was a deterioration of the terms of trade – whether attributable to a fall in export prices in economies with highly concentrated exports or to an increase in the price of imports, predominantly of oil in 1974. Terms-of-trade deteriorations were evident before Chile 1, Argentina 2, Brazil, Indonesia 2, Sri Lanka 1, and Uruguay. In three other instances, exogenous shocks of a different nature have been identified as

2 As usual, such "crisis" is not easy to define with any precision. In our usage of the term, we follow again the descriptions provided by authors of the country studies. Most often, the "crisis" would be a perception that either at present or very shortly the country would not be able to maintain the size of imports necessary (at least in the short and medium run) to maintain economic activity at any reasonable level.

germane: the imminent exhaustion of the German reparation payments in Israel's second liberalization episode; the announcement that Greece's foreign aid from the Marshall Plan would shortly come to an end with the expected outcome of a balance-of-payments deterioration; and the prospective departure of the British military forces from Singapore with its potential economic consequences.

An exogenous deterioration of the terms of trade may naturally be expected to contribute to a balance-of-payments crisis. Indeed, in almost all instances where a liberalization episode was launched following a terms-of-trade deterioration, a situation of balance-of-payments deterioration also prevailed – the only exception being Brazil's liberalization episode.

A Favorable Balance-of-payments Position

Paradoxically, the position of the balance of payments at the inception of several of the episodes, far from approaching crisis, was particularly healthy. Clearly, urgent demand for policy change would not be the prime impetus in such circumstances; the important ingredient here would be that relaxation of import barriers would not be impeded by foreign exchange constraints, even in the absence of any accompanying policy measures. The balance of payments was in surplus at the launching of Singapore's experience, and evidently healthy at the inception of Korea 2, Spain 2, Sri Lanka 2, New Zealand 1 (following a terms-of-trade improvement), and both of Pakistan's attempts (the authors of the Pakistan study consider the availability of foreign exchange the crucial factor in determining the policy cycle in the country). The balance of payments was also favorable when Brazil's episode was launched (although the rationale given for the role of this circumstance would not be relevant here, since the policy primarily involved action on the exports side) and at the introduction of Israel's second liberalization episode (accompanied here, however, by an expected imminent and significant deterioration).

Combinations of Circumstances

In concluding this section, we look at the most common combinations of the various opening circumstances.

Three instances stand out as occasions in which all the circumstances of crisis are found: a perception of total economic collapse, highlighted by an acute balance-of-payments crisis and a rapid inflation, accompanied (probably not by accident) by a drastic change of the political regime (in all cases, incidentally, a military takeover). These were the circumstances when the second liberalization episodes of Argentina, Chile, and Indonesia were introduced. Three other episodes – Chile 1, Israel 1, and Turkey 2 – share a similar set of attributes, but *without* a political upheaval (and not necessarily involving a terms-of-trade deterioration). Together, the six may be classified as liberalization policies introduced in crisis conditions.

In five other episodes – Argentina 1, Spain 1 and 3, Uruguay, and Yugoslavia – the two important ingredients of severe deterioration are found (balance-of-payments crisis and rapid inflation); but these phenomena were apparently not sufficient to give rise to a general perception of economic collapse. With the former group, these 11 episodes may be classified as liberalization policies launched in circumstances of *distress*.

In contrast 16 episodes – almost half of all the attempts – may be said to have been undertaken in a "normal," or even a rather favorable, economic situation. This characterizes all attempts made in Colombia, Korea, Pakistan, Peru, and Singapore; New Zealand 1 and 2 and Indonesia 1 (though here the policy was *planned* when circumstances were less propitious); Philippines 1, Israel 2 and 3, and finally, Greece 2 and Spain 2 (see table 4.1).

Between these two sharply distinct sets of circumstances lie various combinations in which economic performance is not particularly favorable nor even altogether placid, but would not quite qualify as distressed. These may be, for instance, situations of balance-of-payments deterioration but without any unusual inflation; or the other way around. These hybrid combinations of circumstances apply to all the remaining liberalization episodes (Brazil, Greece 1, New Zealand 3, Philippines 2, Portugal 1 and 2, Sri Lanka 1 and 2, and Turkey 1).

Initial Circumstances, Intensity, and Survival

If we look at the role of the initial circumstances in the context of the intensity (strength and speed) of implementation (see chapter 3, table 3.1) several patterns emerge.

First, both the strength and speed of the policy seem to be related to the degree of economic duress under which this policy was introduced. Thus, the six episodes launched when the economy was generally perceived to be in a state of total economic collapse (three of them also occasions of radical political change) were all classified as both strong and fast – that is, the pace of policy implementation was highly intense. Of the five episodes undertaken under severe economic circumstances, four were also strong – either both strong and fast (Spain 3 and Yugoslavia) or strong and slow (Spain 1, Uruguay). The "weak" exception – Argentina 1 – was nevertheless fast.

By contrast, roughly half the liberalization episodes launched under placid comfortable circumstances belong to the "weak and slow" category – which, moreover, consists exclusively of the nine "comfortable circumstances" countries. This strong association suggests that no "hesitant" implementation of a liberalization policy would be undertaken under any but economically favorable circumstances – the absence of severe balance-of-payments deterioration, of rapid inflation, or of some negative exogenous shocks. As we shall see later, the employment situation did not play much of a role in this context, and in no single country study has it been mentioned as a relevant circumstance when liberalization policy was adopted.

The converse – that *every* liberalization undertaken under favorable circumstances would be weak and slow – is not true. Nevertheless, only four out of a total of 20 liberalization experiences that started under favorable circumstances were of the "strong–fast" category, as opposed to eight of the 11 attempts introduced under distress.

Of the eight "in-between" episodes (in which initial economic circumstances were neither fully comfortable nor seriously wrong), five appear to be weak and fast: it appears that when economic performance on the eve of the policy introduction is flawed, but not terribly so, the policy tends to be enacted quickly, but also to constitute only a minor departure from the past.

The connections observed earlier between the strength of a liberalization episode and its survival suggest a corresponding relationship between "initial circumstances" and sustainability. Indeed, a pattern does emerge. The liberalizations (all of them strong and fast) that followed a perceived economic collapse have also, not surprisingly, tended to survive more than other episodes – altogether the numbers involved are too small to generalize with confidence. Of the six episodes concerned, four (Chile 2, Indonesia 2, Israel 1, and Turkey 2) have fully survived; two (Chile 1 and Argentina 2) failed, even though for the latter a radical change in regime accompanied the economic collapse (the only instance in which this occurred).

The episodes least likely to endure, on the other hand, seem to be those in which some failure of the economy (including a balance-of-payments deterioration) is apparent but not a perception of a total collapse (categories of "severe distress" and "partial deterioration" in chapter 5, table 5.1). Of the 14 such episodes, only four (Greece 1, New Zealand 3, Sri Lanka 2, and Uruguay) have fully survived (all four having the "strong" character). Four more (Philippines 2, Portugal 2, and Spain 1 and 3) were partially sustained, whereas the other six attempts (Argentina 1, Brazil, Portugal 1, Sri Lanka 1, Turkey 1, and Yugoslavia) all concluded with complete reversals.

The performance of the liberalizations undertaken under "placid" circumstances (last category in table 5.1) is mixed: their proportional representation in the three categories of sustainability is rather similar to the aggregate of all liberalization episodes. The group is not uniform. Some of the liberalization episodes followed from ideological convictions; the motives for others were more indeterminate. Several were policies that followed up earlier successful stages of the liberalization process in the countries concerned – as such, even the "weak" ones should be likely to survive. In only four countries has a liberalization policy survived fully while starting from a position of calm rather than of economic distress: the second liberalization episode of Greece; the opening liberalization episodes of Singapore (which required only a single episode) and Korea; and the later liberalization policy of New Zealand.

In sum, liberalizations implemented under extreme distress seem the most likely to succeed, followed by those starting from "normal" economic performance. Least likely to survive, apparently, are those initiated in circumstances in which some economic failure is perceived but short of a complete economic collapse.

Motives for Liberalizing

The motives for implementing trade liberalization are summarized in table 4.2. The circumstances and motivations for introducing a liberalization policy sometimes overlap, most obviously in the case of *a change of political regime* which, in and of itself, may stimulate a change of policy. Sometimes the impetus is a *profound*[3] ideological difference: a new regime would introduce the policy change to signal its orientation and as a measure of credibility of its professed beliefs. On other occasions, a new regime may use a change in trade policy as an instrument for shifting power from one group to another.[4]

In two of the instances where the political regime changed just before the introduction of liberalization (table 4.1) specific motives for liberalizing trade, related to the political change, were discerned. In the episodes of Portugal 2 and Spain 3, trade liberalization was at least partly related to the wish to join the European Common Market, which in turn was perceived, beyond its potential economic benefits, as an instrument for ensuring the survival of the newly formed democratic regimes. In addition, the first

3 "Profound" is emphasized: any undertaking of a liberalization policy, following a policy of trade intervention and discrimination, must involve some change in modes of thinking of policymakers. We look here, however, for a more fundamental change which would make trade liberalization a natural outcome.

4 The authors of Pakistan's study note that in its second liberalization episode (1972–8) a change in the *power structure* was involved, with the liberalization policy serving as an instrument for accommodating the new structure. This is obviously a "political" motivation for liberalization, but it falls short of a change in ideology or political philosophy.

Table 4.2 Motivations for liberalization

Episode		Date of launching of episode	Change of political regime	Ideological change	Resource allocation and growth	Increased exports	Combat inflation	Multilateral commitments
Argentina	1	1967						x
	2	1976	x	x	x	x		
Brazil		1965	x			x		
Chile	1	1956				x	x	
	2	1974	x	x	x	x		
Colombia	1	1964				x		
	2	1968					x	
Greece	1	1953		x	x			
	2	1962						x
Indonesia	1	1950						
	2	1966	x	x			x	x
Israel	1	1952			x	x		
	2	1962			x			
	3	1969			x			x
Korea	1	1965				x		x
	2	1978					x	x
New Zealand	1	1951						
	2	1962						
	3	1982			x			
Pakistan	1	1959		x		x		x
	2	1972						
Peru		1979			x			x
Philippines	1	1960	x		x			x
	2	1970			x	x		x
Portugal	1	1970						
	2	1977	x					x
Singapore		1968		x		x		
Spain	1	1960		x				x
	2	1970						x
	3	1977	x					x
Sri Lanka	1	1968			x	x		
	2	1977		x	x			
Turkey	1	1970				x		x
	2	1980			x			x
Uruguay		1974	x	x	x	x		
Yugoslavia		1965		x	x	x		
Number of episodes	36		8	10	14	15	4	16

liberalization policy attempt in the Philippines followed a political change which, though falling short of a "change of regime," nevertheless provided a motivation for liberalization. "Political factors" – specifically the wish to reduce corruption – are cited by the authors of this country study as the major motive for launching the policy.

Profound ideological change and a change of political regime could be expected to be intimately related. But they are not identical: roughly half the episodes of liberalization that started with a change in regime – Argentina 1, Brazil,[5] Indonesia 1, Pakistan 2, Portugal 2, and Sri Lanka

5 In Brazil's liberalization, policymakers did view their policy as a radical departure, but they nevertheless shared with their predecessors the fundamental tenet that trade flows should be controlled by the government.

1 – were unaccompanied by profound ideological change. On the other hand, in three instances political–economic ideology shifted *without* a change in the political regime. All were perhaps instances of moderate rather than revolutionary conversion but were nevertheless quite wide in their scope. One was the first trade liberalization in Greece, in which a conservative parliamentary government came to power. Another was the trade liberalization of Yugoslavia, which was one manifestation of a more universal shift in the perception of how the economic mechanism should work. The third was Spain's first episode (1960–6) which was fueled by a conviction that a sharp economic and political turn from closeness and seclusion to openness and integration was needed.

Better resource allocation and faster growth appears (as it should) to be the prime economic motivation in many of the liberalization episodes. But this is not universal, at least not explicitly; it is missing in about half the episodes.[6] Important instances in which this motivation seems to be absent are the liberalization policy of Brazil, Colombia 1 and 2, Greece 2, Indonesia 1 and 2, New Zealand 1 and 2, the Portuguese attempts, and Turkey 1. In both Singapore and Spain, "opening the economy" was the fundamental motive for the liberalization policies; but, once more, resource allocation was not explicitly mentioned – although, at least for Singapore, such awareness should probably be assumed. For both Korean episodes a motive cited was the "protection of domestic consumers" – implying more awareness of consumption gains than of impacts on resource allocation. In the case of Pakistan, the authors note explicitly that better resource allocation was *not* a motivation for either of its liberalizations.

An increase in exports, as an expected outcome of liberalization, is often mentioned as an important motivation for the policy.[7] The motive has, in fact, been present in at least one of the liberalization episodes in most of the countries studied. The impact on exports as a motive is mentioned in Argentina's second liberalization episode; it appears to have been a primary impetus for Brazil's liberalization and Colombia's second episode, and an element in both liberalization experiences of Chile, and in Israel 1, Korea 1, New Zealand 2, Pakistan 1, Singapore, Turkey 2, Uruguay's

6 The "explicitness" should be emphasized here. In several of the instances which we shall enumerate as *not* having been motivated by this element, an important motivation mentioned explicitly was the need to "open the economy" or some similar term. This may reflect an implicit understanding of the impact of integration into world trade on resource allocation, but such understanding is not self-evident.

7 Since an anti-export bias is an almost universal condition before liberalization, by lowering this bias liberalization may normally be expected to increase exports. The impact on exports has usually been mentioned, however, not so much in such a general abstract context as in the framework of liberalization measures which were applied *directly* to exports (such as, for instance, the removal of export taxes, the granting of export subsidies, or a devaluation of the formal exchange rate as part of the liberalization package).

ongoing liberalization experience, and Yugoslavia's experiment (1965–7). For two episodes – Philippines 2 and Sri Lanka 1 – the motive appears to have been not export expansion in general but the encouragement of nontraditional exports specifically. Finally, in Turkey's first liberalization attempt (1970–3) exports are not singled out: it is the improvement of the balance of payments as a whole – encouragement of exports as well as capital inflows, and discouragement of imports – that impelled the adoption of a liberalization policy.

In a relatively small number of instances the use of a liberalization policy – via its effect on the size of imports and on prices of importables – to *combat inflation* is mentioned as a significant motivation. This was so in Chile's first liberalization episode and in Colombia 2, Indonesia 2, and Korea 2. Surprisingly, only for the Indonesian and Chilean episodes was inflation particularly high on the eve of the adoption of the policy.

Quite often *accommodation of other countries or multinational organizations* appears to have been a motive for liberalization. The need to respond to wishes of external political entities or to undertake certain trade reform measures to qualify for some association with a multinational economic (primarily trade) organization has often been a significant (though rarely the sole, or even prime) impetus for liberalization. Association with the European Economic Community (EEC) has been particularly important: a prime motive in Greece 2, and important in Israel 3, Portugal 2, and Spain 2 and 3. (The potential association with the EEC was also important, used by the government as an argument for the inevitability of liberalization, in Israel's second episode.) Still within the European context, the Organization for European Cooperation and Development (OECD) has played some role in the liberalizations adopted in Spain's first episode, as well as in both Turkey's episodes – in both countries in conjunction with an International Monetary Fund (IMF) involvement in policies. Compliance with the wishes of the World Bank, the IMF, or a foreign (mostly the US) government, separately or jointly, is thought to have promoted the first liberalization attempts in Argentina and Pakistan, both of the Korean and Philippine episodes, Peru's attempt, and the second attempt at trade reform in Indonesia and Turkey.

Motivation and Sustainability

Past experience gives surprisingly little indication that a liberalization attempt's survival depends significantly on any particular motive, or combination of motives, for its adoption.

To start with, the explicit motivation of enhancing the economy's growth and improving its resource allocation is common enough to appear frequently in all the "sustainability" categories. This is also true for the other common motive of using liberalization as an instrument of export expansion. The *combination* of the two motives – which comes close to providing an explicit economic rationale for liberalization under a trade intervention regime with an anti-export bias – does appear to predominate in the liberalization episodes that survived, and to appear less often in those attempts that eventually collapsed or were only partially sustained. But the difference is not obvious enough to allow a strong inference about the relevance of this set of motivations to the durability of liberalizations.

The same is true of the motivations related to the political regime and economic ideology. Five liberalization attempts carried out following a radical change in the political regime also involved a profound change of economic philosophy. All of them were highly intensive – both strong and fast. Three have survived fully: Chile 2, Indonesia 2, and Sri Lanka 2. Of the other two, Argentina 2 has been fully reversed and Spain 3 has been only partially sustained.[8] The size of this group is clearly too small to allow any credible inference about sustainability.

Does the desire (or necessity) to accommodate *other* political entities or economic organizations play a role in determining the final fate of liberalizations? A liberalization undertaken in response to this motivation, without any strong commitment of policymakers or obvious perceived benefits, might last only as long as pressure to accommodate persists. But the opposite outcome is also possible: the existence of a commitment, formal or otherwise, to outside entities may make a policy reversal harder because it is more costly.

Particularly favorable to the persistence of liberalization should, it seems, be a policy undertaken within the context of association with a multinational trade agreement. In this framework, the international commitment of the country would be more specific and more binding, the benefits of membership, or association, better perceived, and the costs of absence of adherence to the agreement more pronounced than when liberalization is undertaken unilaterally. In the experiences studied here, the only relevant multinational trade agreement – the EEC – has been important, even vital, in the policy undertakings of four Mediterranean countries. In the second liberalization episode of Greece (1962–82) and in Israel's third episode (1969–77), it should be noted, the episodes followed earlier attempts that had fully survived and persisted for a considerable length of time. The experience of Portugal and Spain has been quite different. The former's second liberalization attempt (1977–80) and the latter's second (1970–4) and third (1977–80) undertakings, also conceived within the framework of association with the EEC, have been only partially sustained. If any inference is permitted from this very limited scope of observations, it is that the framework of a multinational commit-

8 The difference in sustainability of liberalizations within this group of countries cannot be explained by the survival of the political regime. In Spain, as well as in Chile, Indonesia, and Sri Lanka, the political regime has been stable since the change preceding the introduction of liberalization. In Argentina it has not been, but the collapse of liberalization preceded by far the collapse of the political regime.

ment and the desire to share in a multinational agreement may contribute to the survival of liberalizations once some fundamental other elements are in operation: the external commitment may prevent minor and temporary aberrations. But when such fundamental components are absent, the multinational framework would *not* ensure survival.

The same inference may be derived from the fate of other liberalizations that were influenced by the urging of outside entities – most often the US Government, the World Bank, or the IMF. These were as likely to survive or to fail as liberalizations adopted purely on the country's own volition. Apparently, again, the timing was influenced by the need to accommodate, but the longer-term course and fate of the liberalization was probably determined by influences that owed only little to the relationships with outside organizations.

5

The Attributes of Liberalization

Often, trade liberalization has been undertaken in the context of an overall stabilization policy, which usually included a nominal currency devaluation, a restrictive fiscal policy and – less frequently – a tight monetary policy. Even without this context, a nominal devaluation has most often accompanied trade liberalization, so that it became the most common attribute of a liberalization policy.

In about a third of all liberalization episodes, a "full menu" of the major components has been adopted: a relaxation of QRs, a lowering of tariffs, and a formal devaluation. This pattern characterizes almost all the liberalization introduced "under distress" and most of the *intense* liberalizations. The pattern of components thus also correlates strongly with the chance of survival of a liberalization experience.

Almost as frequent has been a pattern of QR relaxation combined with devaluation, but without the lowering of tariffs. This combination too is much more frequent in liberalizations implemented "under distress" than among those initiated under "placid" conditions.

Another substantial segment of liberalization policies consisted essentially of a relaxation of QRs. Thus, relaxation of QRs was present – often as the sole or principal element – in most of the episodes.

Pre-announcement of the course of the liberalization process figures in less than a third of the episodes, and implementation has rarely followed the pre-announcement faithfully. Nevertheless, a clear association exists between the fact of the pre-announcement and the long-term sustainability of the policy.

In this chapter, we first enumerate the elements, or components, that have tended to appear with some frequency in the design of liberalization policies. We then proceed to distinguish common patterns of the uses of these components, to survey some other attributes of liberalization episodes that are not related to a specific component, and to distinguish common relationships between attributes of liberalization and circumstances of introduction of the liberalization policy, the motivations for it, and the likelihood of its survival.

Direct Elements of a Trade Reform

Relaxing Quantitative Restrictions

The relaxing of QRs is important enough to merit a separate chapter (chapter 10). Here, we mention only some salient features.

In most of the liberalization episodes some reduction in the severity of QRs was an ingredient of the policy package. It was missing in only seven instances: Brazil, Greece 2, Israel 3, New Zealand 3, Philippines 2, Portugal 1, and Turkey 1. For several of these (Greece, Israel, and New Zealand) QRs either had not been significant to start with or had been mostly removed in earlier episodes. In other instances – Brazil is the main example – liberalization primarily took the form of direct use of policy instruments to promote exports. Thus, in almost all cases in which QRs were prevalent and trade reform consisted primarily of import liberalization, the contraction of QRs was an important component of the liberalization policy. In a smaller number of episodes, the contraction of QRs was at once of major proportions and the primary element of liberalization. Chapter 10 gives detailed attention to this group of 11 liberalization episodes.

Tariff Reduction

Reducing tariffs, something that may be regarded as an essential element of a typical trade liberalization, has in fact been far from universal. It appears in fewer than half the episodes (16 of 36). Tariff reduction was notably rare in the first (or single) liberalization episodes of the countries studied: in only six (of 19) was it part of the liberalization policy. Tariff reduction was central, on the other hand, in two of the three liberalization episodes that were the *third* liberalization phases in the countries concerned.[1]

---

1 The three episodes (Israel 3, New Zealand 3, and Spain 3) are too few to suggest any conclusion. Moreover, for Israel, the episode was *defined* as such owing to the shift of the liberalization policy from the relaxation of QRs to the contraction of tariffs. New Zealand, recorded here as *not* having resorted to tariff reductions, has entered such a phase after the conclusion of its "third episode" in 1984.

The frequent absence of tariff reductions is associated, first, with the observation that the liberalization often starts with the removal of QRs as the sole element, delaying tariff reductions to later stages (which may or may not be implemented). The relaxation of QRs could even be – and on five occasions was – accompanied by an increase in tariffs to compensate for the removal of protection that QRs formerly provided.[2]

Second, in principle a process of trade liberalization may entail increasing rather than contracting tariffs and subsidies for other reasons than compensating for the removal of QRs; according to our definition, this would be a liberalization if it led toward neutrality. Two obvious examples are involved, one frequent, the other rare. In an economy which discriminates against exports, the granting (or increasing) of export subsidies (or the reduction of export taxes) would be a liberalization. This has happened quite often – with or without a reduction of import duties. On the *import* side, too, a move toward neutrality might be achieved through the *imposition* (or increase) of tariffs where they are absent (or low). Specifically, these would be tariffs on production inputs and, in most cases, capital goods. Often advocated, such an increase has not been practiced much. The move toward neutrality through tariff increases (except as a substitute for removing QRs – the case just discussed) explains not one absence of tariff reductions.

Tariff Unification

On many occasions, liberalization policy has included an explicit unification of tariffs. Although this could be done through an increase of some tariffs when others are unchanged or lowered, this has rarely happened. Most tariff unifications were performed through tariff reductions.

One way of unifying tariffs would be to have no overall rules of tariff determination but to change each sectoral tariff to increase the uniformity of the system. If, however, a more universal rule, or set of rules, is applied, several main methods may be followed. Of these, the simplest is the proportional across-the-board cut of all tariffs, which would reduce the overall level of the tariffs but with no change in dispersion.[3] Another is the "concertina method." The highest tariffs are reduced first, then the next highest tariffs, and so on. This method will increase uniformity – reduce dispersion – even for importable activities subject to positive tariffs, a uniformity that will keep increasing as the process continues. Obviously, all sorts of combinations are possible.

---

2 These were the episodes of Israel 2, Philippines 1, Singapore, Spain 1, and Sri Lanka 2. In Turkey 2, some such tariff increases were introduced along with some reductions of tariffs on other imports.

3 For the sectors concerned, the proportional across-the-board tariff reduction would be equivalent to an *appreciation* of the currency with no change of tariffs.

In practice, no method has been used purely. Chile 2 is the only case that comes close to the application of the concertina method, whereas Greece 2 comes close to the use of the proportional across-the-board rule. Combinations of the two rules, or some variants, were used in Israel 3, Spain 2, and Spain 3. Uruguay added the element of time: in the first stage only the highest tariffs were lowered; in later stages all tariffs were gradually reduced. Tariff unification systems without a rule (or with elaborate combinations of various rules) were used in Argentina 1 and 2, Brazil, Colombia 2, Peru, and Portugal 2.

Direct Export Promotion

Direct export promotion is found in many liberalization episodes. Export subsidies were introduced or (mostly) increased in 16 episodes. In two, export subsidies to some activities were combined with the reduction or abolition of export taxes on other activities (Argentina 2 and Brazil). In two others, the introduction (or increase) of export subsidies to nontraditional exports was accompanied by the imposition (or increase) of export taxes on traditional exports (Argentina 1 and Philippines 2). In Sri Lanka 1 and 2 incentives were provided to the nontraditional activities, with no change for the traditional sector.

The introduction of incentives for some exports when others do not enjoy them has two contradictory effects: it leads the trade regime toward neutrality in one way – narrowing the gap in protection between these activities and importables – but it moves away from neutrality in creating (or increasing) gaps in protection rates among exportables. Thus it is impossible to state with certainty that this combination of measures indeed constituted a "liberalization."[4] In other instances, export incentives alone were involved, applied broadly but not uniformly: Colombia 1, Indonesia 2, New Zealand 2, Pakistan 1, Singapore, Spain 1, 2, and 3, and Turkey 1 and 2.

Reduction of Export Incentives

Just as many liberalization packages had direct export incentives, others applied direct disincentives. Such a reduction may be implemented through the removal or lowering of export subsidies or through the imposition of export taxes. Doing this makes sense only if a formal devaluation (not normally coming under the heading of export incentives)

---

4 A very significant devaluation was undertaken in the Philippines when the second episode was launched. This apparently led to a substantial reduction in the severity of QRs. When this consideration is added, the question mark raised by viewing direct trade instruments alone disappears.

is undertaken at the same time. The direct export disincentives would partly offset the impact of the formal devaluation, leading to a smaller increase – yet an increase – of the effective rate of foreign exchange for exports. Indeed, all applications of disincentives to exports are associated with a formal devaluation. Export taxes were imposed in Pakistan 2 and (through a differential exchange rate) Philippines 1. In Philippines 2, such taxes were imposed only on traditional exports, whereas nontraditional activities enjoyed increased export subsidies. This pattern also characterizes the experience of Argentina 1. Export *subsidies* were removed or substantially lowered in Greece 1, Israel 2, Korea 1, Peru, and Yugoslavia.

Accompanying Policies in Trade Liberalizations

Liberalization as Part of a Stabilization Policy

Often a trade liberalization was part of a more comprehensive stabilization package. The usual nontrade components of such a package are an exchange rate devaluation, a restrictive monetary policy, a contractionary fiscal policy, and some form of an incomes (wage–price) policy. In a large proportion of the countries in this study, one or two of the trade liberalizations were part of more comprehensive stabilization schemes: Argentina 1 and 2, Brazil, Chile 1 and 2, Indonesia 2, Israel 1, Spain 2, and Turkey 1 and 2.

Devaluation

Stabilization policies have universally included the element of devaluation. Devaluation has been a common – sometimes crucial – instrument of trade liberalizations even when these were not associated with a stabilization package. In several episodes it was the central element: Greece 1, Israel 1, Philippines 1 and 2, and Turkey 1 and 2.[5] In most other countries, a significant devaluation was an element of at least one trade reform episode: Argentina 1 and 2, Chile 1 and 2, Israel 2, Pakistan 2, Portugal 2, Spain 1, 2, and 3, Sri Lanka 1 and 2, and Yugoslavia. In Peru, a devaluation preceded the liberalization by close to a year, and the two may have been related.

---

5 For Greece 1 the removal of QRs was another policy foundation. As stated earlier, devaluation has very often led to a relaxation of the intensity of QRs, thus serving as an instrument of liberalization. In Greece, however, these two were implemented simultaneously. A classic case of changing QRs after the devaluation is Israel 1.

Contractionary Fiscal Policy

An apparently indispensable element in stabilization packages has been a contractionary fiscal policy.[6] Only in Turkey 1 was fiscal policy expansionary. And only in Philippines 1 and Sri Lanka 2 was a contractionary fiscal policy practiced without its being an element of an overall stabilization. A contractionary fiscal policy accompanied most liberalizations. Fiscal policy was expansionary only for Israel 2, New Zealand 3, Peru, Spain 3, Sri Lanka 2, and Turkey 1. As the discussion later in this chapter shows, the association of expansionary policy with the failure of liberalizations is strong.

Tight Monetary Policy

Restrictive monetary policy, another pillar of stabilization policy, accompanied liberalization policies somewhat less frequently than tighter fiscal policy. Even when the liberalization was part of a stabilization package, monetary policy was sometimes expansionary rather than contractionary: Argentina 1 and 2, Portugal 2, and Turkey 1. Monetary policy was restrictive in Brazil, Chile 1 and 2, Colombia 1, Indonesia 2, Israel 1, Spain 1, and in a mild way Turkey 2. In addition, tight monetary policy accompanied several liberalizations that were not part of an overall stabilization policy: Korea 1, Spain 3, Sri Lanka 1 and 2, and Yugoslavia.

Wage–Price Policy

On some occasions, a wage–price policy was practiced when liberalization was introduced, mostly with a comprehensive stabilization policy: Argentina 1 and 2, Brazil, Chile 1, and Turkey 2. A wage–price policy was also applied in Greece 1 and New Zealand 3. These two groups had radically different liberalization outcomes.

The Real Exchange Rate

Strictly speaking, the real rate of exchange is not a policy instrument. It is the outcome of the nominal rate of exchange and of fiscal and monetary policy. But its change, as one attribute of liberalization policy, is important. This is discussed in some detail in chapter 13. To summarize here: in most countries the real exchange rate *increased* with the introduction of trade liberalization; in some instances, the rate remained substantially

6 Contractionary is used here to indicate the nature of the *change* in policy, that is, tightening of fiscal policy. Even after tightening it may – and very often will – have an expansionary effect on the economy.

unchanged; a falling exchanging rate accompanied the liberalization policy in less than a quarter of the episodes.

Patterns of Liberalization Policies

Frequent Combinations of Policy Measures

QR relaxations and tariff reductions, the two pillars of a liberalization policy, might be expected to appear together. But this combination appears in only 11 episodes (of 33 with the relevant information). Much more frequent is the relaxation of QRs alone – without changing the tariff structure (or accompanied by some increase in tariffs to offset the removal of QRs). This was the pattern in more than half (18) of the liberalization episodes. Much more rare is the adoption of tariff reductions alone – without changing the QRs. It occurred in only three episodes: Greece 2, Israel 3, and Brazil. In the first two of these, QR reductions were absent simply because earlier phases of the liberalization had abolished (or drastically reduced) QRs. Only Brazil, with initially high tariffs and intensive QRs, opted for a liberalization that touched only on tariffs.[7]

We turn now to trade reform measures concerning both imports and exports. Once more, in only about a third (12) of all liberalization episodes were measures related to both exports and imports.[8] Most liberalizations involved changes in the import regime alone (only in Brazil, New Zealand 2, and Turkey 1 did liberalization consist mostly of measures related to the export trade).[9]

---

7 Indeed, had it not been for the introduction of *export* subsidies – lowering the anti-export bias and partly approaching neutrality – Brazil's experience probably would not have qualified as a "liberalization." It is likely that QRs were and mostly remained the binding constraint, so that the changes in tariffs were not very relevant to the protection system.

8 This statement refers, obviously, to measures of export *promotion* – encouraging export activities and transactions. As has been noted before, changes in import policies were accompanied on numerous occasions by a *reduction* of export subsidies (or by the imposition, or increase, of export taxes) to offset (partially or completely) the effect of a formal devaluation. As before, it should be noted that the classification of an episode as one in which export *promotion* was involved is, on occasions, arbitrary. This is particularly true in those instances in which not only were promotion measures confined to only a segment of exports (usually nontraditional activities) but, moreover, export *taxes* (or reduction of subsidies) were applied to other activities (commonly the traditional sector).

9 Also, while both trade flows were involved in the first liberalization experience of Pakistan (1959), the major emphasis of this policy was on measures of export promotion.

A word of caution should be added to prevent misinterpretations. Many instances are found, in the countries covered in the present project as well as in others, where export promotion measures were adopted *without* at the same time reforming the import regime. But aside from the cases surveyed here, these were not substantial enough to amount to the introduction of a "liberalization episode."

Devaluations almost universally were in conjunction with the relaxation of QRs (with or without a tariff reduction). In none of the three episodes where only a tariff reduction occurred – Brazil, Greece 2, and Israel 3 – was a devaluation introduced. In just two instances – Philippines 2 and Turkey 1 – a formal devaluation was undertaken without the direct relaxation of QRs (or the lowering of tariffs).

In sum, six main patterns can be distinguished.

1 *The full menu* (a reduction of QRs and of tariffs, accompanied by a formal devaluation): Argentina 1 and 2, Chile 2, Greece 1, Pakistan 2, Portugal 2, Spain 1 and 3, and Yugoslavia. In only three of these episodes did formal devaluation result also in a real exchange rate devaluation: Chile 2, Greece 1, and Portugal 2. In just two instances – Argentina 2 and Spain 3 – the liberalization package also contained export promotion measures (in all the rest, export incentives were either lowered or remained unchanged).[10]

2 *Relaxation of QRs accompanied by a devaluation* (but with no general tariff reductions): Chile 1, Colombia 2, Indonesia 2, Israel 1 and 2, Pakistan 2, Philippines 1, Sri Lanka 1 and 2, and Turkey 2 (in which tariff reductions followed several years later).

3 *Relaxation of QRs and of tariffs* (but without an accompanying devaluation): Korea 2, Peru, Spain 2, and Uruguay. In none of these instances was there a real devaluation. Nor were export promotion measures applied.

4 *Relaxation of QRs alone* (with no changes in tariffs or in the formal rate of exchange). For half of the eight episodes in this category the relaxation of QRs was the *sole* instrument: Indonesia 1, Korea 1, and New Zealand 1 and 3. In the other half, export promotion measures were an added element: Indonesia 2, New Zealand 2, Pakistan 1, and Singapore.

5 *Reduction of tariffs alone*: Brazil, Greece 2, and Israel 3. Only in Brazil was this combined with the application of export promotion, the major element of liberalization. In Greece, her agreement with the EEC required also the reduction in QRs but not until the early 1970s.

6 *Devaluation alone*: Philippines 2 and Turkey 1. In both cases, the devaluation was accompanied by export promotion measures.

Liberalization as a Process

For most countries the liberalization episode comprised a sequence of steps (beyond the possibility of carrying out liberalizations, over the long haul,

---

10 Another instance of the full menu, not included generally in this synthesis, is the latest stage of implementation of liberalization in New Zealand (starting in 1984).

in a sequence of episodes). These steps may or may not have been designed or defined beforehand. In only about half the episodes characterized by a continuous liberalization was some intended future scheme announced when the liberalization was first implemented (or even later): Argentina 2, Chile 2, Greece 2, Israel 2 and 3, Korea 2, Peru, Philippines 1, Portugal 1 and 2, Spain 2, and Uruguay. In a broad ill-defined manner, pre-announcements of the future course of liberalization were also made in Singapore, Spain 1, Turkey 2, and Yugoslavia.

In most other episodes, the liberalization was a continuous process without a pre-charted or pre-announced course. And in six instances the liberalization package was launched in a single step: Argentina 1, Greece 1, Pakistan 2, Sri Lanka 1 and 2, and Turkey 1.

Relationship of Policy Patterns to Initial Circumstances and Motivations

Is there, as would be expected, a relationship between the application of different elements of a liberalization policy and the initial circumstances and motives behind the introduction of the policy? To find the answer, table 5.1 cross-classifies all liberalization episodes by the initial circumstances and the policy components. No strong and fast relationship exists between these two variables, but several weaker tendencies emerge. These are the following.

1 In liberalizations undertaken under distress (the first three groups in table 5.1), the liberalization consisted almost universally of the full menu – or at least of the relaxation of QRs combined with a devaluation. That is, the policies were rather comprehensive and, primarily, included the element of devaluation: in this group a devaluation was missing only in Uruguay. In about half the episodes the exchange rate depreciation also appears to have been real. The granting, or increasing, of export subsidies is also frequent in this group.
2 In liberalizations undertaken under favorable circumstances, the full menu of policies is virtually absent. Devaluations appear only in a few instances, and real depreciations are even less frequent. This contrast is no surprise. Situations of crisis or severe balance-of-payments deterioration make a more comprehensive policy feasible. In particular, they call for a devaluation. If circumstances are favorable, on the other hand, the pressure to devaluate is weak or absent. In these episodes, the more frequent emphasis is to relax QRs.
3 For episodes that fall between the two extremes, the full menu again is virtually absent. Devaluations are more frequent than in episodes that start from favorable circumstances but less frequent than in liberalizations introduced under distress. Most common in this category is the granting or the extension of export subsidies. These presumably are

Table 5.1 Attributes of liberalization and circumstances of its introduction

Circumstances	Attributes							
	a	b	c	d	e	f	g	h
Full crisis								
Argentina 2	x							x
Chile 2	x						x	
Indonesia 2		x					x	x
Perception of collapse								
Chile 1		x					x	
Israel 1		x						
Turkey 2		x					x	x
Severe distress								
Argentina 1	x						x	x
Greece 1	x						x	x
Spain 1		x						
Spain 3	x							x
Uruguay			x					
Yugoslavia	x							
Partial deterioration								
Brazil					x			x
New Zealand 3				x				
Philippines 2						x		x
Portugal 1								
Portugal 2	x						x	
Sri Lanka 1		x					x	x
Sri Lanka 2		x					x	x
Turkey 1						x		x
Favorable circumstances								
Colombia 1								
Colombia 2		x						
Greece 2					x			
Indonesia 1				x				
Israel 2		x					x	
Israel 3					x			
Korea 1				x				
Korea 2		x						
New Zealand 1				x			x	
New Zealand 2				x				x
Pakistan 1				x				x
Pakistan 2		x						
Peru				x				
Philippines 1		x						
Singapore				x				x
Spain 2				x				x

a, the "full menu": relaxation of QRs; reduction of tariffs; devaluation.
b, relaxation of QRs; devaluation.
c, relaxation of QRs; reduction of tariffs.
d, relaxation of QRs alone.
e, reduction of tariffs alone.
f, devaluation; no change in the import regime.
g, depreciation of the real exchange rate.
h, measures of export promotion.

instances in which the relaxation of QRs relies on other measures. But unlike the liberalizations introduced under distress, the pressure for a more comprehensive policy package is not strong enough. The main exceptions are Sri Lanka 1 and 2.

Not much can be said about how the attributes of liberalization are related to motives. The reason for this is that no clear-cut differentiation by motivation was possible. There does not seem to be any relationship between an explicit motive of liberalization – such as the wish to improve resource allocation and enhance growth – and a formal devaluation. Devaluations are as likely where any specific motive is formulated as where it is not. Nor does there appear to be a relationship between the formulation of export expansion as a motive and the practice of granting (or extending) export subsidies as part of a liberalization policy. Once more, export subsidies are as likely to appear when the motive of export expansion is articulated as when it is not. One expected relationship that does appear, albeit weakly, is between the adoption of the full menu of liberalization elements and the combination of a change in the political regime with a profound ideological conversion. Most instances of such a combination are characterized by a full liberalization menu – and vice versa. But the number of episodes is too small to put much faith in such a relationship.

Attributes, Intensity, and Survivability

Attributes and Intensity

Some attributes of the liberalization policy should be associated with its intensity: that is, a strong (or a fast) policy package should consist of certain elements, while a weak (or a slow) policy measure will consist of others. Some such associations are indeed observed.

A strong relationship seems to exist between the intensity of a liberalization policy and the number of major policy elements. Specifically, the highly intensive – both strong and fast – liberalization efforts overwhelmingly comprise either the full menu or the two major policy elements of a QR relaxation and a devaluation. The obverse is also true: most of the full menus belong to episodes that are both strong and fast (the exceptions – Argentina 1 and Portugal 2 – are weak and fast). All the strong and fast episodes, without exception, contain the element of a QR relaxation and all but Indonesia 2 and Singapore involve devaluation as well. In addition, the liberalization attempts characterized as strong and slow mostly use devaluation. But in the weak liberalization attempts, whether fast or slow, devaluation appears to have been practiced only in roughly half the episodes.

Not surprisingly, the liberalizations that are part of a comprehensive stabilization policy are substantially stronger and faster episodes than others. Nearly half these highly intensive liberalization efforts are part of stabilization schemes, while the frequency of this association is much lower elsewhere. And looking at the reverse relationship, more than half the liberalization–stabilization packages are strong and fast. At the other extreme, of the eight episodes designated as both weak and slow, none was undertaken with a stabilization package.

In view of the strong relationship between a stabilization policy and a contractionary fiscal policy, the latter should be associated with the intensity of a liberalization policy. If anything, this association is even stronger than that between the intensity of liberalization and the presence of a stabilization policy. Of 13 strong and fast liberalization episodes, a contractionary fiscal policy appears in eight. Only four other instances of such fiscal policy are found in all the other (more than 20) episodes. Naturally, a contractionary fiscal policy is absent from a liberalization attempt that is both weak and slow.

There is some association between the strength of a liberalization episode and the likelihood that export promotion will be one of its components. The latter is found in half the strong liberalizations (whether fast or slow) but in only a quarter (four of 16) of the weak.

In sum, a strong liberalization policy, especially if fast, is likely to contain a larger mix of major policy elements than other liberalizations. It would in all instances involve a relaxation of QRs, and it would be likely to involve a formal devaluation accompanied by a tight fiscal policy.

Attributes and Sustainability

In examining the relationship between the attributes of a liberalization policy and its likelihood to survive (on which much more is said later), it must be noted that the number of observations is much too small to arrive at any rigorous conclusions.

In general, the components of liberalization grouped earlier as "direct elements" of policy reveal no general association with the likelihood of survival. This is true for individual components, for their various combinations, and for the size (number of major elements) of the policy package. (The exception appears to be a policy consisting solely of relaxing QRs, without even a devaluation. In most of these instances – there are only eight – the liberalization policy survived.)

Nor does it matter whether the liberalization is part of an overall stabilization policy. Such liberalizations are as likely to survive, or collapse, as other liberalizations implemented on their own. But a distinction must be made. Liberalizations in which a stabilization policy is absent fall into two groups. In one, a stabilization policy is required but not undertaken, and the liberalization is likely to collapse. In the other, stabilization is not required, and the liberalization policy is more likely to survive.

Nor is there a relationship between a formal devaluation, the frequent companion of liberalization, and the durability of liberalization. Liberalizations appear to be as likely to survive, or collapse, with or without a devaluation. But a tight fiscal policy does increase the likelihood of survival. With only a small number of observations, however, this relationship is weak and uncertain.[11]

The association between the change of the *real* exchange rate and the sustainability of liberalizations is strong. With only two exceptions (Sri Lanka 1 and Portugal 1) among 12 observations, the liberalization either fully or partially survived when the real exchange rate increased,[12] whereas all seven liberalizations immediately followed by a decline of the real exchange rate were doomed to collapse.

The evidence – admittedly rather weak – suggests a negative relationship between a wage–price policy and the sustainability of liberalizations. Once more, the number of such episodes is small – seven altogether. But the pattern is interesting nevertheless. Of these seven, five were presumably undertaken in the context of an overall stabilization: Argentina 1 and 2, Brazil, Chile 1, and Turkey 2. With the exception of Turkey 2 these episodes eventually collapsed. In the other two episodes that were not part of a stabilization scheme (Greece 1 and New Zealand 3), the liberalization policy did survive. If any inference is permissible, it is that a wage–price policy – perhaps because it indicates certain circumstances or the absence of other necessary policy measures – is not an accompaniment to a durable liberalization.

Finally, a distinct association seems to exist between pre-announcement and sustainability. Again, the relationship is not foolproof: in Argentina 2, Peru, Portugal 1, and Yugoslavia the pre-announcement element was present but the attempts nevertheless collapsed completely. Even so, in the clear majority of such policies, the liberalization attempt did survive, either fully (in Chile 2, Greece 2, Israel 2 and 3, Korea 2, Singapore, Turkey 2, and Uruguay) or at least partly (Portugal 2 and Spain 2 and 3). Once more, the survival of these episodes does not necessarily mean *adherence* to a pre-announced course – a rare exception rather than the rule.

11 To prevent misunderstanding, the policy measures under consideration are those adopted on, or shortly after, the liberalizations. They are not those undertaken several years later.
12 Looking at the reverse relationship, about half the liberalizations that fully survived involved an accompanying increase of the real exchange rate. This may not look very impressive. But it should be noted that the other half consisted overwhelmingly of follow-up episodes in countries like Greece, Israel, or New Zealand, in which liberalization was continuous.

Part II

Transitional Impacts on Income and Employment

6

Liberalization and Unemployment

The relationship of trade liberalization and unemployment is
a crucial policy issue. Liberalization, requiring structural
changes, may lead to transitional unemployment: labor
displaced in a contracting sector would not be immediately
absorbed in an expanding sector. The causality may also run
in reverse: the emergence and existence of unemployment,
whether due to trade liberalization or not, may lead to
abortion of the liberalization policy.

The study finds surprisingly strong evidence that neither of
these two potential relationships has been strong in
liberalization experiences. Rarely could any substantial
unemployment be assigned to the introduction of trade
liberalization, and even more rarely has a liberalization
policy been reversed because of unemployment, whatever its
origin. These inferences are as true for highly intense,
strong, and rapid liberalizations, as for others that were
weak or slow. These findings are clearly a crucial
consideration for deciding how gradually a trade
liberalization policy should be implemented.

Liberalization may be expected to incur a short-term[1] transition cost in the
form of unemployment. Most obviously, there is a potential (gross)
"disemployment"[2] effect: the reduction of employment in sectors that
contract following introduction of the policy. But it is the size of the "net"
effect of the policy – taking into account, that is, the impact on the

---

1 In chapter 1 we specified the reasons why, *a priori*, short-term – but not long-term – costs
may be expected to follow the introduction of liberalization in the form of loss of product and
unemployment.

2 This term has been coined by Oli Havrylyshyn, in his country study of Yugoslavia.

expanding activities – that determines the economic loss due to unemployment. This is our first issue for inquiry.

In turn, unemployment has a role to play in determining the fate of a liberalization. At issue here are the *context* of unemployment, independent of the liberalization, in which the policy takes place, and the public's (including, of course, policymakers') *perception* of the *relationship* between the policy and the creation of unemployment. The second question we seek to answer, then, is: what is the role played by unemployment – whether truly resulting from liberalization, only perceived to be so, or even entirely unrelated – in the implementing and the eventual fate of the trade liberalization policy?

Disemployment

To estimate the disemployment effects of liberalization one must separate the impact of the policy in various sectors from that of a plethora of other economic variables, whether macroeconomic instruments and performances or sector-specific developments. Precision is thus clearly impossible; nevertheless, in several country studies the available data made a rough analysis possible, yielding approximate results that may suggest, at least, ranges of the "true" impact.

The most direct way to estimate the disemployment effect of liberalization would be to relate changes in employment directly to the measures used to implement the policy. This has been carried out in two country studies: Israel and Singapore. In the Israel study, the effect of liberalization on employment was estimated through a simulation exercise. First, changes in import ratios and export volumes arising from the changes in relative prices of exports and imports brought about by the tariff reductions of 1968–77 were estimated. Input–output ratios were then used to assess the fall in employment attributable to increased imports and the rise attributable to increased exports. From this the direct impact of liberalization could be identified. The Singapore study estimates a model in which several magnitudes of economic performance, including employment, are explained in each sector by a group of variables that includes the degree of restrictiveness of quotas (represented by a dummy variable) and the level of tariff protection.

Another method of estimation is to relate the employment effect not to the instruments of liberalization but to its presumed manifestation. Specifically, this is an estimate of the effect of the increase in imports, presumed to follow from liberalization, on employment and disemployment. Two variants of this method are found in the country studies. One – followed in the studies of Colombia, Spain, and Yugoslavia – is a quantitative estimate of the disemployment resulting from the presumed displacement of factors from local production in specific sectors by the realized imports. (The distinction between this method and the Israeli procedure is that the latter starts from the anticipated effects of *price* changes on the trade volumes.) The other, more common, approach is simply to find out whether this effect exists or not: the *sign* rather than the *size* is established. Most often, the variable representing the change in imports is not actual size (through rate of change) but share – whether in production or (less often) in consumption. Causality, in this method, is sought through the intersectoral observation of the two variables involved (changes in imports and in employment). A problem of this approach is that it inevitably involves some element of what we have referred to as the *net* impact of liberalization on employment.[3] This approach has been followed in the studies of Korea, Peru, Singapore, Spain, Turkey, and Uruguay[4] and, in a less rigorous form, in the studies of Brazil and the Philippines.

An altogether different method of estimation, through the comparison of observed employment with a simulated value, was used in the study of Chile's major liberalization episode (1974–81). There, differences of actual production and employment from an expected *trend* were estimated, where the trend was adjusted by the expected impact of changes in relevant variables. These differences were assigned to the liberalization policy. This procedure of estimation was applied to the manufacturing sector as a whole, and to subbranches within it.[5]

---

3 Suppose, for instance, that liberalization leads to equal increases of imports and exports of a sector. The net effect on the sector's employment should be zero (disregarding possible differences of employment-to-output ratios within sectors). In the method discussed, no causal relationship would be found despite the (presumed) fact that an increase of imports displaced some local resources within the sector.

4 In the studies of Singapore and Spain this method was used in addition to those described above.

5 The country study of Chile should be consulted for a full description of this method. In summary, it consists of the following steps: (a) estimate an expansion path for manufacturing (or individual branches within it), based on the ratio of manufacturing output to gross domestic product during 1960–70; (b) estimate the expected response of the sector to changes in the terms of trade; (c) from (a) and (b), estimate (provisionally) the expected sectoral output during the years 1976–81; (d) estimate a path of recovery from the recession of 1975 (unrelated to liberalization) to full employment in 1979; (e) adjust, accordingly, the expected output estimated in (c). This yields the expected sectoral output; (f) use an employment–output elasticity to find (provisionally) from (e) the expected sectoral employment; (g) adjust (f), however, by deducting a gradual elimination of existing "overemployment" in 1973, estimated from past trends. This yields the sector's "expected" employment. Finally, (h) deduct from this expected value the actual sector employment. This yields the unemployment assigned to liberalization.

The liberalization effect on production is estimated, similarly, by deducting the expected value in (e) from actual sectoral production. This, in turn, is divided into a "price effect" and a "supply effect" (movements *on* and *of* the supply curve). The former is estimated by applying supply elasticities to price changes yielded by tariff reductions. The latter is then a residual.

Moving from methods to inference, and starting with the two studies that estimate directly the impact of *instruments* on employment, we find that the Israel simulation exercise reveals a significant negative impact of liberalization on employment. The disemployment (gross) effect of liberalization, through an increase of competing imports, is estimated to be about 11 percent of industrial employment. This would be only partly offset, to the extent of 2 percent, by an expansion of exports, yielding a net decline of 9 percent of industrial employment. The authors emphasize that this is an overestimate, since it overlooks completely any effect of liberalization other than through the direct response to price changes. In the case in question, this price-generated effect would be expected to take place over almost a whole decade, so that adjustment should have been easy. In the event, other economic factors easily swamped the presumed effect of liberalization and so no unemployment – in the industrial sector or elsewhere – was evident throughout the decade of this liberalization experience. The opposite was true for Israel's two earlier liberalizations, in both of which (1952–5 and 1962–8) unemployment was quite severe for a while – in 1953 and in 1965–7. Both spasms, however, must be assigned to macroeconomic processes arising from restrictive fiscal and monetary policies; in the first period, as part of a major stabilization package, and in the second, probably as a result of accident as well as some design. Liberalization could not have contributed – in the second episode it had not yet even manifested itself through increased imports.

The results from the Singapore study are different, and instructive. A significant relationship is found between employment and the restrictiveness of quotas: the looser the quota constraints are, the higher is the level of employment. As long as quotas are highly restrictive, changes in tariffs are not significantly related to changes in employment – not surprising, of course, if quotas are the binding constraint. Once quotas become loose, however, tariff reductions too appear to affect positively the level of sectoral employment (see chapter 10). (But actual levels of tariffs, and hence changes in them, were quite low in Singapore throughout.)

In Chile, the impact of liberalization on employment varied considerably between sectors. The effect, predictably, was found to have been positive in the subsectors of exportables and negative in the import-competing branches. The largest negative impact was in the sectors of electrical and nonelectrical machinery, where employment was reduced by nearly half. For the manufacturing sector as a whole, the reduction of employment appears to be within the range of 9–10 percent. But in the first two years of the period investigated for this purpose (1976–7) the impact on the manufacturing sector as a whole appears to have been positive – probably because concrete tariff reductions were still small (owing to general tariff redundancy) whereas the favorable effect of the change of regime (the "supply effect") was substantial. As a result, only three out of 16

manufacturing subsectors show a consistent negative impact of liberalization on employment throughout the period. Furthermore, the outlook
changes entirely when the "net" magnitude is analyzed (next section).

The three country studies that identify the disemployment effect by
estimating the employment content of increased imports turn up an
employment impact of some consequence. It is lowest for Colombia
(1968–82), for which the estimates show unemployment in the manufacturing sector ascribable to liberalization as exceeding 1 percent in only three
years: 1970 (2.2 percent), 1981 (2.2 percent), and 1982 (1.4 percent). Over
the period as a whole, estimated in terms of value added, about half the
aggregate loss of employment in the industrial sector is assigned to the
textiles industry. In Spain 1, the disemployment is estimated at close to 5
percent of industrial employment, or somewhat above 1 percent of the
economy's aggregate employment; in Spain 2, it is estimated at 2.4 percent
of industrial employment; in Spain 3, this declines to less than 1 percent of
industrial employment (or 0.6 percent of total employment). In Yugoslavia's liberalization episode (1965–7), the estimated disemployment at
the peak year (1967) is about 7 percent of industrial employment.

Estimated in this way, liberalization is bound to lead to disemployment.
Indeed, if liberalization leads to any structural changes, it must, by
definition, create disemployment somewhere in the economy. But where
large sectors and the actual employment patterns of the sectors are
involved, disemployment is not a foregone conclusion. Indeed, the findings
yielded by relating actual sector employment changes to changes in
sectoral imports (usually imports ratios) commonly suggest quite a weak
relationship. In Brazil's liberalization, the evidence seemed to indicate no
association between imports and employment except in the textiles sector,
in which a sharp increase of imports was accompanied by the absence of
increase (but not by a decrease!) in employment. In Korea, a rank
correlation analysis of sectoral changes in imports and in employment
shows no significant relationship for the first liberalization episode
(1965–7), whereas it is negative and significant for the period 1975–80
which contains the second liberalization episode (1978–9). In Peru,
unemployment as a whole (in Lima) did not increase during the two-year
episode; in the following year, 1981, it did increase, but as much in the
sector of consumption goods, in which import competition increased
substantially during the liberalization, as in the sectors of intermediate and
capital goods. An intersectoral correlation analysis of the changes in
employment and in import shares from 1980 to 1981 has revealed no
significant relationship. In the Philippines study, sparse data precluded
rigorous analysis, but the available evidence suggested strongly that in only
one (small) sector of those in which decontrol during the first liberalization
episode (1960–5) led to increased import ratios could a fall in employment
be attributed to the liberalization. In Singapore, in addition to the test

mentioned above, sectoral retained-import ratios and employment were correlated for eight annual changes, yielding relationships with contradicting signs in various years and generally quite weak. In Spain (again in addition to the method of analysis mentioned earlier), a rank correlation analysis of the import-to-consumption ratio and employment does not show any significant relationship during the first (1960–6) and the second (1970–4) liberalization episodes. (The authors caution, however, against inferring too much from a poor data base.) In Turkey's first liberalization episode (1970–3), the authors note that large increases of employment (and production) occurred in many import-competing sectors. A rank correlation analysis of changes in employment and in import ratios yielded a positive coefficient, although of low significance. Finally, a similar analysis in Uruguay, carried out for various sections of the period of the liberalization episode (1974–82), yielded mostly insignificant coefficients.

The overwhelming impression gained from these findings of the country studies is that import ratios and employment were correlated either very weakly or not at all. This inference could have two, probably complementary, explanations. One is that, when liberalization is undertaken during a general economic expansion in the country, sectors in which production expands relatively more will have a particularly large rise in demand for imported inputs and (owing to short-term constraints on the supply of domestic intermediate inputs) might realize increases in import ratios. If final and intermediate goods of the sectors are not distinguished – and often this distinction could not be made, or not sufficiently clearly – employment will appear to be positively related to import ratios.[6] The other explanation is that this form of analysis introduces some element of the net impact of liberalization on employment. If all adjustment is made rapidly within a sector – factors move from one segment of it to another – increased import competition will not yield unemployment. The findings thus may suggest – though they do not provide definite evidence – that much adjustment of employment following liberalization takes place within individual sectors.

This argument brings us to the really important issue: the possible net short-term effect of liberalization on employment.

The Net Impact of Liberalization on Unemployment

To the extent that a disemployment of factors does not induce any net decline of employment in the economy as a whole, it simply represents the

---

6 This might also be true for the final goods component: a rapid rise in demand for a sector's product would be likely to increase relatively both domestic production and employment in the sector and imports of final goods (and their ratio to total output in consumption).

reallocation of factors. This reallocation, far from being a cost, is the principal goal of liberalization. A net decline of employment, on the other hand, represents a discharge of a resource without its reassignment to another activity – hence a short-term cost to the economy.

A method for precisely distinguishing the net impact of liberalization from the impact of other independent influences obviously did not exist, any more than it did for the disemployment effect. Indeed, in only three country studies – Chile, Spain, and Yugoslavia – have approximating methods been attempted.

In Chile the method used is in fact identical with that described earlier, comparing actual employment values with simulated values. Most of the exportables subsectors mentioned earlier as recording improvements in employment were parts of the agricultural sector, so that for this sector as a whole a large positive effect on employment is identified. When agriculture (as well as mining) is added to manufacturing, the effect on employment as a whole is found to be positive. This holds even when attention is restricted to tradeables; it holds even more strongly when nontradeables (in which, again, a positive employment effect is estimated) are added to the observation.

In Spain, the analytical approach – again an extension of the method used to derive disemployment effects – adds export growth, as a positive impact, to the negative impact of displacement by imports. This method, probably the only feasible one, is very approximate;[7] the results are nevertheless suggestive. It appears that the net impact of the policy differs little from the gross effect for the first two liberalization episodes, declining only from 4.9 to 3.8 percent of industrial employment in the first and from 2.4 to 1.7 percent in the second. In other words, export expansion was too little to counterbalance increased imports. In the third episode (1977–80), on the other hand, the small negative gross effect is turned into a small positive net impact. (For this episode an alternative method of analysis was added.)[8]

In the study of Yugoslavia, the changes in trade shares, extensively used in other country studies for the analysis of the gross employment effect, are

7 Its shortcomings are, first, that it identifies changes in trade flows with the policy: export expansion, as well as the increase of imports, are the representation of liberalization policy. This overlooks the possibility that changes in trade flows might have been independent of the policy. Second, the method obscures the potential absorption of labor displaced from import-competing activities in nontradeable sectors rather than in export expansion. The latter factor would introduce a downward bias to the estimate of the net employment effect reached in this fashion, whereas the error due to the former factor could be either way.

8 A model is estimated in which unemployment in the economy is explained by several factors (such as changes in aggregate demand or in employers' taxes) other than trade policy; these factors were found to explain some 95 percent of the increase of unemployment during this period – leaving very little residual role to liberalization policy or anything else.

instead employed in the evaluation of the net effect. A positive correlation is found, during the liberalization period, between sectoral rates of growth of imports and employment. But sectors in which imports grew most are precisely those in which exports, too, grew substantially. This must be due to the particular form taken by the trade liberalization policy which, in spite of going some way toward neutrality, was still highly discriminatory: as a rule, those sectors in which protection from imports was reduced substantially were also granted particularly high subsidies (in the form of favorable exchange rates) for their exporting activity. Thus, by and large, export expansion more than made up for the displacement of production by increased imports, although this was not true for the economy as a whole in the last year (1967) of the liberalization period.

In the other country studies, evaluation of the net effect of liberalization on employment is more informal, partly because data are sparse and partly because of an *a priori* impression that the net unemployment effect could not be very important in view of actual unemployment levels. Most often, inferences in this sphere are based on "before, after, and during" observations, with note taken of those changes in employment and unemployment clearly arising from strong macroeconomic policies and processes.

In this rough manner – and the authors of many studies reiterate that both quality and quantity of data are inadequate to support firm inferences – most country studies do try to evaluate the employment effect of the policy.

In Argentina's first liberalization episode the unemployment ratio increased slightly in the first year (1967) of the episode, but then fell substantially to reach in 1969 a significantly lower level than before the liberalization. The share of the tradeables sector in total employment fell during the episode, but its absolute level in fact slightly increased. In the second episode (1976–80) the pattern repeated itself. Employment in tradeables this time declined not only as a proportion of the total but also, slightly, in absolute terms; this, however, is undoubtedly ascribable to developments other than the liberalization – primarily massive appreciation of the real rate of foreign exchange.

In Brazil's liberalization episode (1965–73) unemployment was exceptionally low in comparison with its habitual level. Industrial employment grew particularly quickly, almost doubling from the beginning of the episode to its conclusion. These developments, the author notes, should not be assigned to the liberalization but to expansionary fiscal and monetary policies.

For the period covering the first Greek episode (1953–5) no employment data at all are available. During the two decades covered by the second episode (1962–82), unemployment was never a serious issue.

In Indonesia employment as a whole grew more slowly during the second liberalization episode (1966–72) than in previous years; but employment in manufacturing – presumably the sector hardest hit by the economy's openness – grew faster during the period.

During Korea's two liberalization episodes (1965–7 and 1978–9) the economy's aggregate unemployment ratio kept declining (excluding 1979 which, with 1980, was a period of recession, after which the unemployment ratio resumed its long-term decline). The trend of the unemployment rate does not seem to change during the liberalization episodes. Hence the author's conclusion is that liberalization was immaterial for this purpose: it definitely did not lead, as far as the aggregate magnitudes are concerned, to any net creation of unemployment.

In the study of Peru's liberalization episode (1979–80) the author concludes similarly, from data of aggregate changes in unemployment and "underemployment," that no impact on employment could be detected immediately following the implementation of liberalization. Some time later, in 1983–4, a recession developed from sources that could not be reasonably connected with the liberalization process.

In the first liberalization episode of the Philippines (1960–5) the level of aggregate unemployment remained much the same as during the years preceding or following the liberalization. A slight increase in the share of industrial unemployment in the total (from 16 to 28 percent) did occur, on the other hand, toward the end of the period (in 1964 and 1965). Since manufacturing was the sector most exposed to the increased import competition, the authors hypothesize that some slight relationship may be detected. In the second episode (1970–4) no evidence exists to associate unemployment with the liberalization. The aggregate unemployment ratio fell substantially during the period (from 6.7 percent on the eve of liberalization to 3.2 percent in its final year). For both episodes the authors warn, again, that the quality of the data casts any inferences in doubt.

No employment data exist for the period of Portugal's first liberalization episode (1970–4). For the second episode (1977–80), the limited data available indicate a largely unchanged rate of increase of employment and, similarly, a stable (around 8 percent) ratio of unemployment.

In Singapore's liberalization episode (1968–73), unemployment is clearly not an issue. Employment increased steadily, with an aggregate increase over the five-year period of about 35 percent. Unemployment during the period was eliminated as a serious phenomenon: the unemployment ratio went down – again steadily – from 7.3 to 4.5 percent (having been at a peak of close to 9 percent in the mid-1960s).

Data on unemployment in Sri Lanka are confined to the "organized" sector (estimated to constitute only about one third of the total labor market). In the first episode (1968–70), the indication is that employment in manufacturing slightly increased. In the second episode (1977–9), all the available evidence points to a substantial reduction of unemployment. This is partly explained by (temporary or permanent) outmigration of labor; but employment actually increased substantially – by about 23 percent in manufacturing and close to 10 percent in the total "organized" sector – as did production. Particularly noteworthy is the increase of employment (and production) in the sectors of garments and of textiles, in which substantial export expansion more than offset displacement of small firms by import competition. The authors of the country study warn that adding the "unorganized" sector might conceivably change these optimistic findings, but there is no evidence to indicate that such bias is in fact present.

In Turkey, the unemployment ratio (excluding agriculture) remained very low throughout the first liberalization episode (1970–3) at around 1 percent of the labor force; there is no evidence of a relationship with liberalization. During the second episode (1980–4) the unemployment ratio did go up (from 9.4 percent in 1979 to 12.4 percent in 1984). But the fact that public sector employment declined during this period by 10 percent, whereas private sector employment actually increased by about 15 percent, suggests that the (rather modest) increase in unemployment should be ascribed to the contractionary fiscal policy rather than to liberalization. In fact, since 1983 both the trends of increasing aggregate unemployment and increasing share of the private sector in aggregate employment started to reverse themselves.

Finally, in Uruguay's liberalization episode (1974 onwards), fluctuations in the unemployment ratio are noted but no trend, and specifically no changes that could clearly be associated with the liberalization. The first step of liberalization was taken in the fall of 1974, and the unemployment ratio (in Montevideo) fell slightly between 1973 and 1975 (from close to 9 percent to about 8 percent). An intensification of the policy in the fall of 1978 was followed by a decline in the ratio from some 10 percent in 1978 to almost 8.5 percent in 1979. From this rough evidence, liberalization does not appear to have led to any noticeable unemployment.

The clear conclusion indicated by the data and analyses of the country studies is that, by and large, liberalization attempts have not incurred significant transition costs by way of unemployment. A suspicion of some slight negative impact of liberalization on employment is detected only in Argentina 1 and 2, Philippines 1, and Spain 1 and 2. In Chile 2, the analysis indicates a substantial impact of liberalization on the structure of employment: a significant decline in manufacturing, matched by an increase in agriculture and nontradeables. But even here no net unemployment should be attributed to the policy of liberalization.

This impression is strengthened by looking at table 6.1, some of the evidence in which is referred to in the discussion of findings of the country studies. In this table, data on the *absolute* size of employment in manufacturing are presented for those liberalization episodes for which data are available. Since liberalization almost always involves, in a developing economy, the reduction of protection of manufactures, the presumed

Table 6.1 Employment in manufacturing during periods of liberalization (thousands)

Episodes	Employment		
	a	b	c
Argentina 1 (1967–70)	1,836	1,847	1,914
Argentina 2 (1976–80)	1,863	2,099	2,132
Brazil (1965–73)	1,780	2,182	3,397
Chile 2 (1974–81)	515	487	351
Korea 2 (1978–9)	2,000	2,196	2,099
Peru (1979–80)	675	717	736
Philippines 1 (1960–5)	1,456	1,647	1,825
Philippines 2 (1970–4)	2,056	2,313	2,596
Singapore (1968–73)	61	139	210
Sri Lanka 1 (1968–70)	74	108	97
Sri Lanka 2 (1977–9)	112	134	155
Turkey 1 (1970–3)	485	551	651
Turkey 2 (1980–4)	799	829	—

—, not applicable.
a, last year before liberalization episode; b, average during liberalization episode; c, first year after liberalization episode.

negative employment consequences should show up first and most in these data. In the event, a review of the table indicates only a single instance – Chile 2 – in which employment in manufacturing declined during the liberalization period.

Arguably, the absence of impact might be due to the way liberalization attempts have actually been carried out: many episodes were long drawn out, and so no transition costs were to be expected. But even if we confine our attention to *strong* episodes of liberalization, or to the even narrower group of *strong and fast* episodes, our former inference would not change. The few indications of some negative impact of the liberalization policy on employment are roughly equally spread in all categories of liberalization episodes (classified by strength and by speed). Of the 13 episodes classified as "strong" and "fast," in only two (Argentina 2 and the Philippines 1) is some weak impact indicated. Chile's second episode – by far the most intense liberalization experience, combining the most comprehensive scope with a short time span for completion – created no net unemployment. A rigorous statistical analysis of the relationship between the intensity of liberalization and its impact on unemployment is obviously not feasible: no numerical representation of either of the variables is available. But observation of the qualitative data strongly suggests that no such relationship would have been found.

In sum, it appears warranted to infer that liberalization attempts that fall within the range of the large number of observed post-World War II experiences are unlikely to do much harm to employment.

Unemployment and Sustainability of Liberalizations

Does the existence of unemployment contribute materially to the fate of a liberalization policy? Partly, the answer is indicated in the earlier analysis: if liberalization does not tend to lead to unemployment, unemployment, in turn, is less likely to affect the course of liberalization. But this is only one component. Unemployment could coincide with liberalization through completely unrelated developments, or through a contractionary macro-economic policy which is sometimes part of a package of policies that includes liberalization. Such unemployment, though not following from the liberalization policy, may affect the fate of the attempt.[9]

The appearance of unemployment during a period of liberalization may contribute to the reversal of the policy in two ways. First, the public, including policymakers, may (rightly or, more probably, wrongly) ascribe the emergence of unemployment to the liberalization and therefore be inclined to abort the policy. Second, if there is a general perception that any further liberalization would aggravate the unemployment situation, this would again encourage policy reversal.

In the judgment of the authors of the country studies – arrived at through impressionistic evaluation, since quantitative analysis is clearly not feasible or even appropriate – the fate of liberalization has rarely been determined by, or even significantly affected by, unemployment. Only two country studies mention a – rather weak – relationship. In the Yugoslavia study, the author concludes that the policy reversal in 1968 largely arose out of the public perception that the liberalization led to a slowdown of growth (rather than to unemployment). In Israel, the author suggests that a recession in 1965–6, in the middle of the country's second liberalization episode, led the government, not to reverse, but to delay expansion of the liberalization. The other side of the coin is seen in Chile's second liberalization episode (1974–81), in which the public – unable to disentangle the effects of the liberalization from those of exchange rate or stabilization policies – blamed liberalization for creating unemployment more than it deserved. Yet the policy was not reversed. Even in a case where unemployment might legitimately be ascribed to liberalization (Spain 3), the policy was only partially reversed, this time because the effect was swamped in the public perception by the much larger increase in unemployment overall, for which causes other than the liberalization were clearly responsible.

So unemployment, according to the collective evidence of the country studies, has had almost no impact on the course of a liberalization policy. Setting aside for the moment the inference of the individual country

9 The significance of the existence of unemployment at the inception of an episode was discussed in chapter 4.

studies, we may check this finding by looking afresh at the unemployment data (table 6.2). Data (unfortunately available for only about half the episodes) are presented for (a) the year before liberalization, (b) the average for the liberalization period, (c) the last year of the liberalization episode, and (d) the first year following the episode.

It should be emphasized that these data should *not* be considered as providing evidence of the effect of liberalization on unemployment: as has been stated repeatedly, liberalization was rarely the only change from one period to another (specifically, it was quite often undertaken in conjunction with stabilization policies). The data may, however, be used to test a possibility of the reverse causality – in other words, to test the hypothesis that the emergence of unemployment during liberalization, and particularly towards its end, has led to policy reversal.

The data indicate no increase in unemployment in ten of the liberalization episodes covered; in eight episodes, unemployment does increase significantly (mostly for reasons other than the liberalization). Of the latter, in three (Chile 2, New Zealand 2, and Turkey 2) liberalization proceeded undeterred; in one (Israel 2), the process was temporarily delayed. Only in four episodes – Colombia 1, Philippines 1, Spain 3, and Yugoslavia – was the liberalization policy reversed (in the Philippines and

Table 6.2 Unemployment during episodes of liberalization (percentage of labor force)

Episodes	Unemployment			
	a	b	c	d
Argentina 1 (1967–70)	5.6	5.1	4.9	n.a.
Chile 2 (1974–81)	4.8	12.3	12.4	22.5
Colombia 1 (1964–6)	7.9	8.7	10.1	12.2
Colombia 2 (1968–82)	8.8	10.0	9.4	9.4
Israel 1 (1952–5)	9.1	8.8	7.4	7.8
Israel 2 (1962–8)	3.6	5.4	6.1	4.5
Israel 3 (1969–77)	6.1	3.4	3.9	n.a.
Korea 1 (1965–7)	9.9	7.0	6.3	5.2
Korea 2 (1978–9)	4.1	3.5	3.8	5.3
New Zealand 3 (1982–4)	3.7	4.8	4.9	—
Peru (1979–80)	7.1	6.9	6.8	7.0
Philippines 1 (1960–5)	6.3	8.0	8.2	9.4
Philippines 2 (1970–4)	6.9	6.5	4.7	5.0
Singapore (1968–73)	8.1	6.2	4.8	4.7
Spain 2 (1970–4)	1.1	2.1	2.9	3.9
Spain 3 (1977–80)	5.3	9.1	11.5	14.4
Turkey 2 (1980–4)	9.4	11.7	12.7	—
Yugoslavia (1965–7)	5.6	6.6	7.1	8.0

n.a., not available; —, not applicable.
a, last year before liberalization episode; b, average during liberalization episode; c, last year of liberalization episode; d, first year after liberalization episode.

Spain, only partially), and only in the Yugoslavia episode does the author conclude that unemployment was an important agent. In the study of Spain, the authors are emphatic in denying an impact of unemployment on liberalization. But even if we ignore the inferences of the country authors and assume *post hoc, ergo propter hoc*, reversal could be attributed to unemployment in only a very few episodes. Thus, the earlier inference that liberalization has not generally led to significant unemployment is joined by the conclusion that, by and large, an emergence of unemployment, for whatever reason, has not determined the fate of the liberalization policy.

7

Production and Growth

The central finding – one which would have been highly
surprising were it not for our earlier inference of the absence
of damaging effects of liberalization on employment – is
that, right from the beginning, liberalization clearly tends to
accelerate economic growth. Moreover, this applies
particularly to the strong liberalization experiences – where
short-term losses of production might rather have been
expected – and is particularly noticeable in an economy in
which the trade regime has been highly restrictive for many
years. The positive impact on growth is also prominent in
sustained liberalization episodes (in others, it is hardly ever
observed). Here the causality must run both ways: a
sustained policy would encourage growth, and growth
acceleration would help a liberalization policy to survive.

In view of the prevalence of devaluation (and, as we shall
see later, of *real* currency depreciation), the share of
tradeables in the economy should be expected to increase
following a liberalization package. The emerging growth of
tradeables has indeed been considerably greater than the
growth of nontradeables in the episodes classified as strong
and in those with prior severe restrictions. But even on
nontradeables the impact of liberalization does not seem to
be negative, beyond the year immediately following
introduction of the policy (in which the rate of growth does
fall, although it remains positive). Once more, it is primarily
in the strong liberalization episodes that growth of the
tradeables sector accelerates strongly. Commonly taxed in a
regime of protection and restrictions, this sector appears to
rebound forcefully when the trade regime is liberalized.

Among tradeables activities, liberalization seems

particularly to encourage production in the agricultural sector. Its strong reaction from the outset seems to belie the presumption that agricultural production can be expanded only with a substantial time lag. Growth of manufacturing (the sector that generally loses most protection) is slower than that of agriculture. But even manufacturing growth does *not* fall below the pre-liberalization rate, except in the first year following the liberalization (in which, once more, it remains positive).

Do trade liberalization policies have a negative short-term impact on economic activity? What factors influence economic performance during trade liberalization? Specifically, are there common characteristics of the episodes of trade liberalization that systematically correlate with a rise or fall in gross domestic product (GDP), or with patterns of change in sectoral output?

To identify any associations between attributes of trade liberalization and economic activity, we compare first aggregate and then sectoral performance, using the evidence provided by the country studies.[1] The studies yielded comparable data for 31 liberalization episodes for GDP growth rates and for 29 episodes for sectoral growth.

Data of real GDP and sectoral growth rates for complete calendar years are used, each episode comprising seven years: the three immediately preceding, and the four following and including, the year in which trade reforms were put into effect. The year in which liberalization was launched is classified as the first post-liberalization year, in an attempt to capture any large changes in output that were an immediate outcome of the new policies. The attributes under which trade liberalization episodes are classified are those established in chapter 3 (tables 3.1, 3.2, and 3.3). We have collapsed in this chapter the "fast," "slow," and "partially sustained" episodes into other categories (table 7.1).[2]

Trade Liberalization and Aggregate Product

Investigating the relationship between trade liberalization and economic performance is complex because initial economic conditions, policies

1 Simple nonparametric statistics are used here. But see appendix A2 for a statistical testing of several other hypotheses.
2 All episodes classified in chapter 3 as "partially sustained" have been grouped here with the "collapsed" episodes except for all Spain's episodes, which have been classified as "sustained."

Table 7.1 Classification of trade liberalization episodes[a]

Episode	Attributes					
	Strong	Weak	Sustained	Collapsed	Severe restriction	Moderate restriction
Argentina 1		X		X	X	
Argentina 2	X			X	X	
Brazil	X			X	X	
Chile 1	X			X	X	
Chile 2	X		X		X	
Colombia 2	X			X[c]		X
Greece 1	X		X		X	
Greece 2		X	X			X
Indonesia 2	X		X		X	
Israel 2	X		X			X
Israel 3	X		X			X
Korea 1		X	X			X
Korea 2		X	X			X
New Zealand 2[b]		X	X		X	
New Zealand 3		X	X		X	
Pakistan 1		X		X[c]		X
Pakistan 2		X		X[c]		X
Peru	X			X[c]	X	
Philippines 1	X			X[c]	X	
Philippines 2		X		X[c]		X
Portugal 1		X		X[c]		X
Portugal 2[b]		X		X[c]	X	
Singapore	X		X			X
Spain 2		X	X[c]			X
Spain 3	X		X[c]			X
Sri Lanka 1		X		X	X	
Sri Lanka 2	X		X		X	
Turkey 1		X		X	X	
Turkey 2	X		X		X	
Uruguay	X		X		X	
Yugoslavia	X			X	X	
Total	17	14	16	15	18	13

[a] Includes only those episodes for which comparable data are available.
[b] For these episodes data are available only for GDP growth rates.
[c] These episodes are classified as *partially* sustained in chapter 3.

pursued concurrently with the trade liberalization, and external developments differ vastly from episode to episode. We should expect, *ceteris paribus*, to find that liberalization might improve economic performance more in a country that implemented trade liberalization at a low level of economic activity than in a country that introduced trade reforms at a high level of economic activity. Economies that followed expansionary fiscal and monetary policies are likely, on the whole, to perform better in the immediate post-liberalization period than those whose macroeconomic policies were less expansionary. And the effects of trade liberalization that coincide with large changes in the terms of trade, or in autonomous capital inflows, are likely to be unpredictable and difficult to isolate.

Obviously, it is impossible to test for the "pure" effects of trade liberalization on economic activity with our limited observations. But illuminating regularities do emerge from the data, some of which are predictable – such as that the economic performance of countries with severe trade restrictions before liberalization improves considerably after trade reform. Other patterns are more surprising, though consistent with our other finding of a minimal effect of liberalization on unemployment.

Data on the behavior of GDP (tables 7.2 and 7.3) show the average annual GDP growth rate in all episodes for the three years preceding liberalization to be 4.4 percent; for the three years following the year of trade liberalization, it is 5.6 percent. Furthermore, the growth rate for the first full year after implementation ($T + 1$) is 5.4 percent – considerably higher than the average rate of the pre-liberalization period (PtL). In addition 23 episodes are associated with a higher average annual GDP growth rate for the three years following the year of trade liberalization than for the three years immediately preceding it.[3] Some of these increases

Table 7.2 Summary of gross domestic product performance (real annual rate of growth)

Type of episode	PtL	T	T+1	T+2	T+3	AVG-T	AVG
All episodes	4.4	4.7	5.4	5.3	6.0	5.6	5.3
(number of episodes)						(31)	(31)
Strong	3.5	4.9	4.8	5.2	6.2	5.4	5.3
(number of episodes)						(17)	(17)
Weak	5.6	4.4	6.2	5.4	5.7	5.7	5.4
(number of episodes)						(14)	(14)
With severe restrictions	2.9	4.0	3.9	4.3	4.4	4.2	4.1
(number of episodes)						(18)	(18)
With moderate restrictions	6.6	5.6	7.6	6.6	8.2	7.5	7.0
(number of episodes)						(13)	(13)
Sustained	4.7	6.1	5.4	5.8	6.8	6.0	6.0
(number of episodes						(16)	(16)
Collapsed	4.1	3.2	5.5	4.6	5.2	5.1	4.6
(number of episodes)						(15)	(15)

PtL, average of three years up to liberalization; T, year of liberalization; T+1, one year after liberalization; T+2, two years after liberalization; T+3, three years after liberalization; AVG-T, average of three years after T; AVG, average of T plus three years after liberalization.

3 If the trade liberalization year is included in the average of the post-liberalization GDP growth rates, then the number of episodes associated with a higher post-liberalization rate is 21 (table 7.3).

Table 7.3 Performance of gross domestic product (real annual rate of growth)

Episode	PtL	T	T+1	T+2	T+3	AVG-T	AVG
Argentina 2 (1966–80)	6.70	2.60	4.40	8.50	5.40	6.10	5.23
Brazil (1965–73)	2.90	−0.60	6.50	−3.10	6.90	3.43	2.43
Chile 1 (1956–61)	3.23	2.70	5.10	4.80	9.30	6.40	5.48
Chile 2 (1974–81)	2.30	1.20	7.90	2.80	0.53	3.74	3.11
Colombia 2 (1968–82)	−1.50	8.50	−12.90	3.50	9.86	0.15	2.24
Greece 1 (1953–5)	3.87	2.67	4.93	6.59	6.50	6.01	5.17
Greece 2 (1962–82)	4.90	13.06	3.10	6.81	8.70	6.20	7.92
Indonesia (1966–72)	6.13	0.58	10.07	7.54	9.25	8.95	6.86
Israel 2 (1962–8)	0.80	2.72	1.41	10.89	6.83	6.38	5.46
Israel 3 (1969–77)	9.80	10.10	11.40	9.80	9.10	10.10	10.10
Korea 1 (1965–7)	5.77	12.60	7.90	11.00	12.30	10.40	10.95
Korea 2 (1978–9)	6.97	5.80	12.70	6.60	11.30	10.20	9.10
New Zealand 2 (1962–81)	13.80	3.31	6.36	−6.20	6.36	2.17	2.46
New Zealand 3 (1982–4)	4.02	5.84	6.57	5.54	−2.16	3.32	3.95
Pakistan 1 (1959–65)	4.32	4.66	0.48	2.78	3.29	2.18	2.80
Pakistan 2 (1972–8)	2.15	1.47	4.34	5.23	5.92	5.16	4.24
Peru (1979–80)	5.48	1.61	7.53	7.71	4.11	6.45	5.24
Philippines 1 (1960–5)	0.30	3.78	3.07	3.14	0.74	2.32	2.68
Philippines 2 (1970–4)	5.37	0.90	4.90	4.50	6.30	5.23	4.15
Portugal 1 (1970–4)	5.32	4.84	5.72	5.23	8.48	6.48	6.07
Portugal 2 (1977–80)	5.88	7.55	6.39	9.49	11.48	9.12	8.73
Singapore (1968–73)	1.60	5.30	3.20	4.50	4.90	4.20	4.48
Spain 2 (1970–4)	10.10	14.27	13.50	13.65	12.61	13.25	13.51
Spain 3 (1977–80)	6.67	4.89	5.54	8.59	8.06	7.40	6.77
Sri Lanka 1 (1968–70)	3.30	3.72	2.50	0.16	1.48	1.38	1.97
Sri Lanka 2 (1977–9)	3.57	7.57	4.25	3.50	−0.52	2.41	3.70
Turkey 1 (1970–3)	2.80	4.87	8.69	6.28	5.47	6.81	6.33
Turkey 2 (1980–4)	5.69	5.28	9.00	6.00	4.10	6.37	6.10
Uruguay (1974–82)	2.90	−1.07	4.10	4.64	3.25	4.00	2.73
Yugoslavia (1965–7)	−4.96	3.37	5.28	1.62	2.75	3.22	3.26
	7.90	1.40	5.00	0.90	3.50	3.13	2.70
Average	4.45	4.69	5.45	5.26	6.00	5.57	5.35

PtL, average of three years up to liberalization; T, year of liberalization; T+1, one year after liberalization; T+2, two years after liberalization; T+3, three years after liberalization; AVG-T, average of three years after T; AVG, average of T plus three years after liberalization.

Source: International Monetary Fund, 1989, *International Financial Statistics* (IMF on-line data base), November

in the GDP rates are dramatic: for example, Uruguay's turnaround of annual GDP growth rate from −5.0 percent before to 3.2 percent for three years following the trade liberalization. Thirteen episodes had increases in their GDP rates of 2 percentage points or more. In contrast, of the eight episodes with lower post-liberalization GDP growth rates, in only three was the decline of this rate more than 2 percentage points: Korea 2 in which the annual average GDP growth rate declined from 13.8 percent before to 2.2 percent for the three years after the year of trade liberalization; Yugoslavia, in which the growth rate declined from 7.9 percent prior to liberalization to 3.1 percent after liberalization; and New Zealand 3 in which this rate went from 4.3 percent to 2.1 percent.

Finally, while all episodes are associated with *average* annual positive growth rates of GDP in the post-liberalization era, two episodes register negative rates (Chile 2 and Uruguay) in pre-liberalization (PtL). Further, only two episodes had negative GDP growth rates in the year of liberalization (Argentina 2 and Turkey 2), and only one in the following year (Chile 2). This evidence appears to dispel the notion that trade liberalization policies incur short-term economic costs in the guise of a general loss of production. On the contrary, a clear inference emerges from the evidence that trade liberalization is positively associated with a general economic expansion.

The inference is supported by further examination of the data. The figures reveal that trade liberalization episodes classified as "strong" (having a major first step of liberalization) are associated with dramatic increases in GDP growth rates from the very first year of implementation. A quite different pattern emerges for the "weak" episodes: these are associated with a post-liberalization GDP growth rate that does not differ statistically from the pre-liberalization rate. Of the 17 episodes classified as strong, 14 are associated with higher average post-liberalization growth rates of GDP than in the three years preceding it, while only nine of the 14 weak episodes register higher post-liberalization episodes. In total, the 17 strong episodes have an average annual pre-liberalization rate of GDP of 3.5 percent, for the year immediately following the implementation of trade liberalization their aggregate average annual rate increases to 4.8 percent, and their three-year annual average following (AVG-T) is 5.4 percent. For the weak episodes we find no difference in the corresponding average annual GDP rate of 5.6 percent before liberalization and 5.7 percent after it.

These results are surprising: forceful policies would be expected to lead to higher short-term losses, not higher growth rates. Particularly unexpected is the finding that growth speeds up immediately in the year following the implementation ($T + 1$).

Conditions prevailing in the countries before and during implementation may furnish an explanation. Economies with highly restrictive and interventionist trade policies before liberalization are likely to grow more slowly than the rest, and strong liberalization measures are more likely to be undertaken in such severely restricted economies. Low economic growth could help secure political and public impetus for drastic policy changes.

The evidence presented earlier in this study lends credence to this hypothesis. Seventeen liberalization episodes have been classified as being strong and 18 as having highly restrictive trade regimes at the time that the new trade policies were implemented; 12 of these showed both characteristics. The average annual growth rate of GDP before liberalization (PtL) for the "highly restricted" category was a low 2.9 percent; for economies with moderate restrictions, the rate was 6.6 percent (this difference is statistically significant at the 5 percent level).

Indeed, trade liberalization implemented in economies with highly restricted import regimes is associated with visible improvements in their average annual GDP growth rates, from 2.9 percent prior to liberalization to 4.2 percent for the average of the three years following its introduction. For the economies with moderate restriction the changes in the rate of GDP growth following trade liberalization are less striking, from 6.6 percent prior to liberalization to 7.5 percent after its introduction. Furthermore, of the 16 episodes classified as sustained, ten fall in the "strong" classification. This qualitative evidence reinforces findings presented in other parts of this study; that forceful attempts at trade liberalization are undertaken in the presence of slow economic growth and severe trade restrictions and are likely to succeed because they are associated with improved economic performance. The average annual growth rate of GDP in the sustained episodes went from 4.7 percent prior to liberalization to 6.0 percent for the three years following it, while for the failed ones the corresponding rates are 4.1 percent to 5.1 percent.

The accelerated GDP growth rate appears immediately, in the very year of implementation of the liberalization policies, in the "strong," "severe restriction," and "sustained" episodes. Indeed, for these episodes, the improvement in the first year accounts for a good deal of the increase in the average growth rate during the four-year span of the post-liberalization period. For episodes classified as "weak" and to a lesser extent for episodes classified as "collapsed" or as having "moderate import restrictions" at the time that trade liberalization was launched, the rates of GDP growth do not differ significantly before and after liberalization. For all of them, the year of trade liberalization is associated with a sharp fall in the GDP growth rate.

Economies that grew faster before the implementation of trade liberalization policies continue to do so. However, the difference between the growth rates in the fast-growing and the slow-growing groups of countries narrows in the post-liberalization period. Economies with low pre-liberalization growth rates are more likely to have had severe trade restrictions in the pre-liberalization period, and to have undertaken strong trade liberalization policies.

In conclusion, the evidence suggests that trade liberalization policies, far from being associated with an absolute decline, or even a slower growth, of GDP, are positively associated with accelerated growth and that the acceleration begins in the very first year of implementation. Most of the acceleration is accounted for by countries in which the episodes of trade liberalization were strong and survived; and these episodes were mostly evident in economies with severe trade restrictions before liberalization.

Sectoral Performance under Trade Liberalization

In investigating the sectoral origins of the growth pattern just discussed, we focus on the performance of large and analytically relevant segments of the economy.

Tradeables and Nontradeables

Data on the performance of the tradeables and nontradeables sectors for 29 episodes (tables 7.4 and 7.5) show accelerated growth in both sectors after the liberalization, somewhat more for the nontradeables sector. Of the 29 episodes with data, 19 have higher growth rates of their tradeables sector following the introduction of trade liberalization than before, and 20 have higher growth rates for the nontradeables sector (tables 7.6 and 7.7). The increase of the tradeables sector's growth rates in the post-liberalization period of ten episodes is by 2 percent or more (Greece 1 and 2, Indonesia 2, Pakistan 1, Peru, Singapore, Spain 2, Sri Lanka 2, Turkey 2, and Uruguay). Only five episodes are associated with deceleration of 2 percent or more of the tradeables sector's growth rate following the introduction of trade liberalization (Argentina 1, Israel 2, Korea 2, Pakistan 2, and Yugoslavia).

Table 7.4 Summary of tradeables sector performance (real annual rate of growth)

Type of episode	PtL	T	T+1	T+2	T+3	AVG-T	AVG
All episodes	4.6	4.4	5.7	4.4	6.0	5.4	5.1
(number of episodes)						(29)	(29)
Strong	3.9	4.8	4.9	4.6	5.6	5.0	5.0
(number of episodes)						(17)	(17)
Weak	5.7	3.7	6.9	4.1	6.4	5.8	5.3
(number of episodes)						(12)	(12)
With severe restrictions	2.8	3.5	3.6	3.7	4.6	3.9	3.8
(number of episodes)						(16)	(16)
With moderate restrictions	6.9	5.5	8.4	5.3	7.7	7.1	6.7
(number of episodes)						(13)	(13)
Sustained	5.5	6.1	6.1	5.2	7.4	6.2	6.2
(number of episodes)						(15)	(15)
Collapsed	3.8	2.5	5.4	3.5	4.4	4.4	4.0
(number of episodes)						(14)	(14)

PtL, average of three years up to liberalization; T, year of liberalization; T+1, one year after liberalization; T+2, two years after liberalization; T+3, three years after liberalization; AVG-T, average of three years after T; AVG, average of T plus three years after liberalization.

Table 7.5 Summary of nontradeables sector performance (real annual rate of growth)

Type of episode	PtL	T	T+1	T+2	T+3	AVG-T	AVG
All episodes	4.7	5.0	5.7	6.2	5.6	5.8	5.6
(number of episodes)						(29)	(29)
Strong	4.0	4.2	5.4	5.5	4.6	5.2	4.9
(number of episodes)						(17)	(17)
Weak	5.7	6.1	6.0	7.1	6.9	6.7	6.5
(number of episodes)						(12)	(12)
With severe restrictions	3.4	2.8	4.5	4.8	3.3	4.2	3.8
(number of episodes)						(16)	(16)
With moderate restrictions	6.4	7.6	7.2	7.9	8.4	7.8	7.8
(number of episodes)						(13)	(13)
Sustained	5.2	6.3	5.5	6.3	5.4	5.7	5.9
(number of episodes)						(15)	(15)
Collapsed	4.2	3.5	5.9	6.1	5.7	5.9	5.3
(number of episodes)						(14)	(14)

PtL, average of three years up to liberalization; T, year of liberalization; T+1, one year after liberalization; T+2, two years after liberalization; T+3, three years after liberalization; AVG-T, average of three years after T; AVG, average of T plus three years after liberalization.

In the category of "strong" episodes, the pattern of change shows the tradeables sector growing much faster than the nontradeables sector in the post-liberalization period. Moreover, while the growth rate of the tradeables sector picks up immediately in the year that the policies were implemented, for the nontradeables sector this is a year of practically no change in rate. Almost the reverse is true of "weak" episodes, in which the growth rate of the tradeables sector shows no measurable change in the four years following liberalization, and in fact exhibits a large drop in the year of implementation, whereas the growth rate of the nontradeables sector accelerates in that year, as well as over the entire post-liberalization period.

Indeed, while the aggregate average annual growth rate of the tradeables sector of all episodes classified as "strong" is 3.9 percent prior to liberalization, it gets to 4.8 percent in the year of liberalization and reaches an average annual growth rate in the post-liberalization era of 5.0 percent. For the weak episodes, the corresponding pre-liberalization rate is 5.7 percent, that of the year of trade liberalization drops to 3.7 percent, and it averages out at an annual rate in the post-liberalization era of 5.8 percent, about the same as in pre-liberalization.

The "strong" episodes include *all* trade liberalization episodes in which the real exchange rate depreciated. Therefore the evidence is consistent with the inference of economic theory that real devaluation should favor differentially the expansion of the tradeables sector of the economy. The

Table 7.6 Tradeables sector performance (real annual rate of growth)

Episode	PtL	T	T+1	T+2	T+3	AVG-T	AVG
Argentina 1 (1967–70)	7.14	2.66	3.02	9.29	6.14	6.15	5.28
Argentina 2 (1976–80)	3.85	−0.46	6.16	−5.78	7.72	2.70	1.91
Brazil (1965–73)	3.74	0.90	0.52	4.20	7.05	3.92	3.17
Chile 1 (1956–61)	3.86	−2.23	11.53	1.08	1.13	4.58	2.88
Chile 2 (1974–81)	0.38	6.59	−16.63	5.28	10.61	−0.25	1.46
Colombia 2 (1968–82)	3.96	4.44	6.18	5.33	4.40	5.30	5.09
Greece 1 (1953–5)	1.60	22.81	0.14	7.91	5.32	4.46	9.05
Greece 2 (1962–82)	6.72	−6.51	15.51	4.49	10.13	10.04	5.91
Indonesia 2 (1966–72)	0.47	3.94	−0.52	7.82	5.38	4.23	4.16
Israel 2 (1962–8)	10.91	10.72	11.60	5.62	1.05	6.09	7.25
Israel 3 (1969–77)	6.89	7.41	5.45	6.98	8.34	6.92	7.05
Korea 1 (1965–7)	7.05	2.33	11.92	1.63	8.94	7.50	6.21
Korea 2 (1978–9)	12.31	11.74	8.59	−7.19	10.79	4.06	5.98
New Zealand 3 (1982–4)	2.86	4.65	2.49	1.00	5.78	3.09	3.48
Pakistan 1 (1959–65)	1.76	−0.18	5.04	4.43	6.17	5.21	3.87
Pakistan 2 (1972–8)	4.77	1.35	4.25	5.24	−1.26	2.74	2.40
Peru (1979–80)	−9.95	5.40	0.89	1.61	0.71	1.07	2.15
Philippines 1 (1960–5)	5.77	−0.14	4.88	4.44	6.49	5.27	3.92
Philippines 2 (1970–4)	5.45	5.44	6.17	4.89	9.55	6.87	6.51
Portugal 1 (1970–4)	6.54	8.33	3.84	8.93	12.53	8.43	8.41
Singapore (1968–73)	14.16	18.62	19.95	18.92	17.86	18.91	18.84
Spain 2 (1970–4)	6.63	5.53	7.49	10.66	9.30	9.15	8.25
Spain 3 (1977–80)	3.26	1.90	2.92	−1.58	1.95	1.10	1.30
Sri Lanka 1 (1968–70)	2.37	6.99	3.43	4.43	0.53	2.80	3.85
Sri Lanka 2 (1977–9)	1.92	4.90	7.27	3.13	2.50	4.30	4.45
Turkey 1 (1970–3)	4.60	2.44	11.30	1.49	−1.30	3.83	3.48
Turkey 2 (1980–4)	1.61	−2.01	3.42	5.72	3.94	4.36	2.77
Uruguay (1974–82)	5.33	−1.65	11.16	7.39	9.77	9.44	6.67
Yugoslavia (1965–7)	8.81	0.57	8.61	−0.52	1.60	3.23	2.57
Average	4.65	4.36	5.74	4.37	5.97	5.36	5.11

PtL, average of three years up to liberalization; T, year of liberalization; T+1, one year after liberalization; T+2, two years after liberalization; T+3, three years after liberalization; AVG-T, average of three years after T; AVG, average of T plus three years after liberalization.

Source: International Monetary Fund, 1989, *International Financial Statistics* (IMF on-line data base), November

behavior of the tradeables and nontradeables sectors associated with episodes in the "sustained" and "initially severely restricted" classifications lends support to this inferred relationship. The growth rates of the tradeables and nontradeables sectors accelerate equally in the sustained episodes. In the collapsed episodes, however, the nontradeables sector's annual growth rate increases from 4.2 percent in the pre-liberalization period to 5.9 percent in the post-liberalization era (1.7 percentage points),

Table 7.7 Nontradeables sector performance (real annual rate of growth)

Episode	PtL	T	T+1	T+2	T+3	AVG-T	AVG
Argentina 1 (1967–70)	4.17	2.74	5.53	7.86	4.56	5.98	5.17
Argentina 2 (1976–80)	3.23	−0.47	6.68	−1.05	6.34	3.99	2.88
Brazil (1965–73)	2.98	2.27	3.88	8.27	4.51	5.55	4.73
Chile 1 (1956–61)	2.07	0.78	9.89	2.76	−0.16	4.16	3.32
Chile 2 (1974–81)	1.33	−0.37	−8.39	1.57	9.43	0.87	0.56
Colombia 2 (1968–82)	6.06	4.61	6.24	7.10	8.65	7.33	6.65
Greece 1 (1953–5)	7.59	6.64	4.42	5.98	11.23	7.21	7.07
Greece 2 (1962–82)	5.89	5.58	6.68	9.60	8.68	8.32	7.64
Indonesia 2 (1966–72)	1.39	0.72	4.93	5.19	10.35	6.82	5.30
Israel 2 (1962–8)	10.44	14.17	11.60	12.92	9.69	11.40	12.10
Israel 3 (1969–77)	5.27	14.04	7.95	9.55	10.43	9.31	10.49
Korea 1 (1965–7)	6.43	9.72	11.72	12.53	15.63	13.29	12.40
Korea 2 (1978–9)	10.08	13.52	4.14	−3.45	0.63	0.44	3.71
New Zealand 3 (1982–4)	5.10	4.66	−0.55	3.71	2.01	1.72	2.46
Pakistan 1 (1959–65)	2.67	4.33	3.18	6.56	5.53	5.09	4.90
Pakistan 2 (1972–8)	5.52	0.44	8.60	11.22	11.71	10.51	7.99
Peru (1979–80)	−1.07	2.31	5.10	4.49	0.79	3.46	3.17
Philippines 1 (1960–5)	4.92	2.10	4.95	4.54	5.99	5.16	4.40
Philippines 2 (1970–4)	5.18	4.09	5.15	5.67	7.13	5.98	5.51
Portugal 1 (1970–4)	5.14	6.63	9.42	10.12	10.32	9.95	9.12
Singapore (1968–73)	9.66	13.53	12.12	12.24	11.75	12.04	12.41
Spain 2 (1970–4)	6.71	4.47	4.27	7.20	7.20	6.22	5.79
Spain 3 (1977–80)	3.69	3.93	2.21	1.35	1.43	1.66	2.23
Sri Lanka 1 (1968–70)	5.31	8.65	7.43	4.04	1.00	4.16	5.28
Sri Lanka 2 (1977–9)	3.87	3.63	9.00	8.85	8.29	8.71	7.44
Turkey 1 (1970–3)	6.77	8.45	6.75	10.53	8.94	8.74	8.67
Turkey 2 (1980–4)	2.82	−0.22	4.75	4.10	4.19	4.35	3.21
Uruguay (1974–82)	−1.52	1.20	7.38	3.23	−29.32	−6.24	−4.38
Yugoslavia (1965–7)	6.05	1.95	−0.39	2.75	5.22	2.53	2.38
Average	4.75	4.97	5.68	6.19	5.59	5.82	5.61

PtL, average of three years up to liberalization; T, year of liberalization; T+1, one year after liberalization; T+2, two years after liberalization; T+3, three years after liberalization; AVG-T, average of three years after T; AVG, average of T plus three years after liberalization.

Source: International Monetary Fund, 1989, *International Financial Statistics* (IMF on-line data base), November

while the tradeables sector's annual growth rate goes from 3.8 percent to 4.4 percent respectively, or about one third of the nontradeables sector's growth acceleration. This evidence supports other findings of this study that effective trade liberalization results in the expansion of the tradeables sector and is consistent with the fact that most collapsed episodes are not associated with the sustained depreciation of the real exchange rate.

In the "initially severely restricted" category, the rate of growth of the tradeables sector accelerated in the post-liberalization period; in the "moderate restrictions" category it remained almost unchanged. The six episodes that fall into both the "sustained" and the "initially severely restricted" classifications[4] are associated with accelerated growth for the tradeables sector, from an annual average of 1.9 percent before liberalization to an annual average of 4.4 percent in the post-liberalization era. This must be at least partly due to the fact that sustained episodes are associated with an effective real devaluation, and to the presumption that severe trade restrictions must have had a negative effect on the tradeables sector, which "strong" liberalization policies tend to reverse.

The evidence thus suggests that trade liberalization policies with strong initial steps, which tend to survive, and which are implemented in economic environments of severe trade restrictions are related to accelerated growth for the tradeables sector compared with the nontradeables sector; and that this higher growth rate is apparent from the very first year of the trade liberalization. The tradeables sector, which is usually "taxed" under protection – and highly so under a trade regime of severe restrictions – seems to rebound strongly once the protection and restrictions are lifted.

Manufacturing and Agriculture

In examining the two major (largely tradeables) activities – manufacturing and agriculture – the focus, as before, is on the short-term impact of liberalization on output. In the context of our conclusions about differential effects on tradeables and nontradeables sectors, the question arises as to the role of manufacturing and agriculture in sustaining the liberalization policies.

The performance of manufacturing output immediately following the implementation of strong liberalization policies, which expose the sector to international competition, may provide an indication of the distributive and, possibly, economic costs of the policies. We know that in the vast majority of episodes manufacturing was the protected sector before liberalization and the relatively "disprotected" sector immediately following the implementation of strong open-trade policies. In agriculture, inevitably, the opposite must have been true. We expect to find in "strong" and "sustained" liberalization episodes an initial shrinkage of protected sectors and a relative expansion of the formerly disprotected sectors. Thus the agricultural sector would be likely to grow in the post-liberalization period relative to the manufacturing sector, unless it is affected by its

4 The six episodes for which data on tradeables and nontradeables sectors are available are as follows: Chile 2, Greece 1, Indonesia, Sri Lanka, Turkey, and Uruguay.

alleged tendency to respond to changes in relative prices only with a substantial time lag.

The evidence from 29 liberalization episodes rebuts some of these expectations, and fulfills others. The summarized data for manufacturing (table 7.8) and agriculture (table 7.9) show the growth rate of the former gaining only after the second year following the implementation of

Table 7.8 Summary of manufacturing sector performance (real annual rate of growth)

Type of episode	PtL	T	T+1	T+2	T+3	AVG-T	AVG
All episodes	6.7	5.3	6.9	6.9	8.0	7.3	6.8
(number of episodes)						(29)	(29)
Strong	5.6	3.5	6.0	5.8	6.6	6.2	5.5
(number of episodes)						(17)	(17)
Weak	8.4	7.8	8.2	8.4	9.9	8.8	8.6
(number of episodes)						(12)	(12)
With severe restrictions	4.8	2.1	4.7	4.9	6.5	5.4	4.6
(number of episodes)						(16)	(16)
With moderate restrictions	9.1	9.2	9.6	9.4	9.7	9.6	9.5
(number of episodes)						(13)	(13)
Sustained	7.0	7.7	6.6	7.7	9.3	7.9	7.8
(number of episodes)						(15)	(15)
Collapsed	6.5	2.7	7.2	6.1	6.5	6.6	5.6
(number of episodes)						(14)	(14)

PtL, average of three years up to liberalization; T, year of liberalization; T+1, one year after liberalization; T+2, two years after liberalization; T+3, three years after liberalization; AVG-T, average of three years after T; AVG, average of T plus three years after liberalization.

Table 7.9 Summary of agricultural sector performance (real annual rate of growth)

Type of episode	PtL	T	T+1	T+2	T+3	AVG-T	AVG
All episodes	2.8	2.9	5.5	2.8	3.9	4.1	3.8
(number of episodes)						(29)	(29)
Strong	2.7	4.7	5.3	5.1	3.9	4.8	4.8
(number of episodes)						(17)	(17)
Weak	2.9	0.4	5.7	−0.4	4.1	3.1	2.4
(number of episodes)						(12)	(12)
With severe restrictions	1.8	4.8	4.8	5.0	3.5	4.5	4.5
(number of episodes)						(16)	(16)
With moderate restrictions	4.0	0.5	6.3	0.1	4.5	3.6	2.9
(number of episodes)						(13)	(13)
Sustained	2.8	3.4	8.4	2.5	6.3	5.7	5.2
(number of episodes)						(15)	(15)
Collapsed	2.8	2.3	2.4	3.2	1.4	2.3	2.3
(number of episodes)						(14)	(14)

PtL, average of three years up to liberalization; T, year of liberalization; T+1, one year after liberalization; T+2, two years after liberalization; T+3, three years after liberalization; AVG-T, average of three years after T; AVG, average of T plus three years after liberalization.

liberalization policies. The year of implementation, on the other hand, saw a fall in the manufacturing growth rate, from an annual pre-liberalization average of 6.7 percent to 5.3 percent. In the post-liberalization period as a whole, the average annual rate of growth of manufacturing was 7.3 percent – slightly higher than before the liberalization. The evidence therefore supports the prediction that trade liberalization may have an immediate retarding impact on manufacturing growth rate. But once resources are reallocated, the growth rate rebounds – taking off after the second year – to surpass the pre-liberalization level. And even though the manufacturing growth *rate* decelerates in the year of the implementation, growth itself remains in general positive: the sector's output keeps increasing, even right after the launching of liberalization.

The average annual growth rate of the manufacturing sector in the pre-liberalization period is negative for Indonesia 2 (−1.4 percent) and for Peru (−2.1 percent), and in the post-liberalization period is negative for Argentina 2 and Chile 2 (−1.4 percent and −1.9 percent respectively) (table 7.10). Characteristically, of the 29 episodes on hand, trade liberalization causes a negative growth rate for manufacturing in seven episodes for the year it is introduced (Brazil, Chile 1 and 2, Pakistan 2, Sri Lanka 2, Turkey 2, and Yugoslavia) and three in the following year (Argentina 2, Chile 2, New Zealand 3). In general we find that, of the 29 episodes, 17 are associated with higher average annual growth rate in manufacturing in the post-liberalization era than in the pre-liberalization era. In some cases the acceleration of the growth rate is substantial, for example, in Brazil, Greece 2, Indonesia 2, Korea 1, Singapore, and Turkey 2. The largest declines of this rate are observed in Argentina 1, Chile 1 and 2, Israel 2, Korea 2, Philippines 1, and Turkey 1. The evidence from the performance of manufacturing in the initial period of trade liberalization suggests that the sector suffers a setback at first, but for the episodes classified as "strong" or "sustained" and for those launched under conditions of severe import restrictions a rapid recovery of high growth rate is observed from the year following the introduction of trade liberalization.

Inferences about the growth of the agricultural sector also confirm the expectations of economic theory, and challenge the widely held notion of a lagging response of agricultural output to changes in relative prices and economic conditions. The evidence from the 29 episodes is that agriculture grew faster during the post-liberalization years than in the pre-liberalization years, increasing from 2.8 percent before liberalization to an average of 4.1 percent following it – albeit with the large annual swings customary for the sector. In no year did the sector's aggregate growth rate fall below its pre-liberalization level, nor did it decline in the year of implementation, and in the second year it increased significantly.

Of the 29 episodes, 17 are associated with higher average growth rates for agriculture in the post-liberalization period than in the pre-

Table 7.10 Manufacturing sector performance (real annual rate of growth)

Episode	PtL	T	T+1	T+2	T+3	AVG-T	AVG
Argentina 1 (1967–70)	9.14	1.51	6.50	10.83	6.31	7.88	6.29
Argentina 2 (1976–80)	3.31	7.81	−10.52	10.19	−3.79	−1.37	0.92
Brazil (1965–73)	3.83	−3.33	14.01	1.63	15.35	10.33	6.92
Chile 1 (1956–61)	12.07	−2.11	13.51	1.68	1.76	5.65	3.71
Chile 2 (1974–81)	2.70	−2.55	−25.47	6.02	13.69	−1.92	−2.08
Colombia 2 (1968–82)	5.75	3.59	6.18	7.29	8.31	7.26	6.34
Greece 1 (1953–5)	9.84	15.31	11.28	9.55	10.62	10.48	11.69
Greece 2 (1962–82)	6.37	5.27	8.25	12.69	10.22	10.39	9.11
Indonesia 2 (1966–72)	−1.37	1.97	3.31	8.80	14.22	8.78	7.08
Israel 2 (1962–8)	14.61	12.94	11.60	9.02	4.17	8.26	9.43
Israel 3 (1969–77)	7.95	8.74	7.62	6.06	9.34	7.67	7.94
Korea 1 (1965–7)	12.33	19.95	17.11	22.77	27.03	22.30	21.72
Korea 2 (1978–9)	16.48	20.00	9.37	−1.12	7.16	5.14	8.85
New Zealand 3 (1982–4)	2.64	7.64	−0.45	1.47	8.85	3.29	4.38
Pakistan 1 (1959–65)	6.65	4.72	3.97	11.33	11.28	8.86	7.83
Pakistan 2 (1972–8)	7.49	−3.54	10.68	7.45	0.57	6.23	3.79
Peru (1979–80)	−2.07	3.90	5.97	−0.58	−2.65	0.91	1.66
Philippines 1 (1960–5)	7.73	2.11	3.39	5.10	6.81	5.10	4.35
Philippines 2 (1970–4)	6.57	8.49	6.70	6.20	14.00	8.97	8.85
Portugal 1 (1970–4)	8.32	9.39	7.78	12.40	14.59	11.59	11.04
Singapore (1968–73)	15.89	20.72	22.44	21.26	18.70	20.80	20.78
Spain 2 (1970–4)	7.56	7.73	11.04	4.39	3.38	6.27	6.64
Spain 3 (1977–80)	2.83	2.23	2.40	2.60	−2.30	0.90	1.23
Sri Lanka 1 (1968–70)	5.30	9.69	9.23	5.90	3.30	6.14	7.03
Sri Lanka 2 (1977–9)	2.62	−0.59	7.81	4.64	0.83	4.43	3.17
Turkey 1 (1970–3)	11.97	3.08	8.45	6.88	12.10	9.14	7.63
Turkey 2 (1980–4)	4.40	−5.83	7.17	4.99	8.20	6.79	3.63
Uruguay (1974–82)	0.41	2.11	6.33	2.64	5.45	4.81	4.13
Yugoslavia (1965–7)	4.47	−7.10	15.32	−1.53	3.70	5.83	2.60
Average	6.75	5.31	6.93	6.92	7.97	7.27	6.78

PtL, average of three years up to liberalization; T, year of liberalization; T+1, one year after liberalization; T+2, two years after liberalization; T+3, three years after liberalization; AVG-T, average of three years after T; AVG, average of T plus three years after liberalization.

Source: International Monetary Fund, 1989, *International Financial Statistics* (IMF on-line data base), November

liberalization period, with the highest acceleration observed in Chile 2, Greece 1 and 2, Pakistan 1, Spain 2 and 3, and Uruguay (table 7.11). Largest deceleration following the introduction of trade liberalization is found in Brazil, Israel 2 and 3, Korea 1 and 2,[5] Pakistan 2, and Portugal 1. Furthermore, we observe that episodes classified as "sustained," "strong,"

5 Korea, however, provides high protection to its agriculture sector, unlike many other developing countries.

Table 7.11 Agricultural sector performance (real annual rate of growth)

Episode	PtL	T	T+1	T+2	T+3	AVG-T	AVG
Argentina 1 (1967–70)	1.00	4.29	−5.43	5.48	5.61	1.89	2.49
Argentina 2 (1976–80)	3.57	4.53	2.51	2.76	3.50	2.92	3.33
Brazil (1965–73)	4.62	5.29	−12.17	7.42	−2.75	−2.50	−0.55
Chile 1 (1956–61)	1.28	−3.66	6.60	−2.26	0.36	1.57	0.26
Chile 2 (1974–81)	−6.47	26.76	4.37	−1.61	10.62	4.46	10.04
Colombia 2 (1968–82)	3.02	5.17	6.88	3.40	2.44	4.24	4.47
Greece 1 (1953–5)	−1.33	25.90	−2.58	6.99	2.66	2.36	8.24
Greece 2 (1962–82)	3.05	−13.08	20.39	−0.37	9.97	10.00	4.23
Indonesia 2 (1966–72)	0.72	4.79	−1.69	6.94	1.92	2.39	2.99
Israel 2 (1962–8)	4.07	5.75	11.61	−2.50	−7.28	0.61	1.90
Israel 3 (1969–77)	5.71	3.07	−2.00	10.45	−9.70	−0.42	0.46
Korea 1 (1965–7)	5.96	−1.94	10.83	−4.96	2.41	2.76	1.59
Korea 2 (1978–9)	5.79	−3.95	6.72	−21.96	21.97	2.24	0.69
New Zealand 3 (1982–4)	2.38	−1.69	6.50	2.13	0.34	2.99	1.82
Pakistan 1 (1959–65)	1.02	−1.03	5.21	3.18	5.20	4.53	3.14
Pakistan 2 (1972–8)	3.66	3.47	1.67	4.18	−2.12	1.24	1.80
Peru (1979–80)	1.63	3.65	−5.24	10.33	3.09	2.73	2.96
Philippines 1 (1960–5)	4.77	−1.00	5.90	4.30	6.40	5.53	3.90
Philippines 2 (1970–4)	4.40	2.23	4.91	3.78	6.15	4.95	4.27
Portugal 1 (1970–4)	2.79	6.00	−6.10	−0.36	6.04	−0.14	1.40
Singapore (1968–73)	7.07	6.68	4.45	2.45	10.55	5.82	6.03
Spain 2 (1970–4)	1.92	−0.86	10.58	0.18	3.70	4.82	3.40
Spain 3 (1977–80)	3.82	−4.30	6.67	4.06	8.85	6.53	3.82
Sri Lanka 1 (1968–70)	1.45	5.85	1.13	3.63	−0.59	1.39	2.51
Sri Lanka 2 (1977–9)	1.55	10.40	5.42	1.99	3.12	3.51	5.23
Turkey 1 (1970–3)	0.97	5.22	11.83	0.25	−9.88	0.73	1.86
Turkey 2 (1980–4)	0.92	1.68	0.07	6.41	−0.12	2.12	2.01
Uruguay (1974–82)	7.01	−7.72	44.47	27.44	35.90	35.94	25.02
Yugoslavia (1965–7)	4.47	−7.10	15.32	−1.53	−3.70	3.36	0.75
Average	2.79	2.91	5.48	2.83	3.95	4.09	3.80

PtL, average of three years up to liberalization; T, year of liberalization; T+1, one year after liberalization; T+2, two years after liberalization; T+3, three years after liberalization; AVG-T, average of three years after T; AVG, average of T plus three years after liberalization.

Source: International Monetary Fund, 1989, *International Financial Statistics* (IMF on-line data base), November

and launched under "severe restrictions" are associated with highly improved performance of the agricultural sector in the post-liberalization period. In the case of "severe restrictions" the average annual growth rate of agriculture jumps from 1.8 percent before to 4.5 percent after with a 4.8 percent increase for the first and second year of liberalization. This evidence and that of the "strong" episodes, in which agriculture's annual growth rate jumps from 2.7 percent before to 4.8 percent after, suggest the degree to which this sector may respond to a favorable policy environment and the extent to which "severe restrictions" on imports have retarded its growth.

Furthermore the hypothesis that trade liberalization policies have a differential short-term impact on the growth rates of manufacturing *vis-à-vis* agriculture is reinforced by the evidence about characteristics of the policies. Under "strong" liberalization, for example, the annual growth rate of manufacturing declines substantially in the year of implementation from its pre-liberalization level: from 5.6 percent to 3.5 percent. For each year after the year trade liberalization is introduced, the growth rate rebounds to a level higher than before liberalization. Correspondingly, for the agricultural sector, "strong" liberalization episodes are associated with large and immediate acceleration of its growth rate, which is maintained for the entire post-liberalization period. Agriculture's growth rate under "strong" episodes is 2.7 percent before liberalization, 4.7 percent in the year of implementation, and 4.8 percent in the four years following the liberalization.

In the category of "sustained" liberalization episodes, the increase of agriculture's growth rate following the liberalization again noticeably outstrips that of the manufacturing sector – further evidence that sustained liberalization policies cause resources to reallocate to agriculture from once protected activities, found primarily in manufacturing, and from the nontradeables sector. More importantly, reallocation seems to take place sooner than has been generally believed – which may help to explain our finding that trade liberalization policies do not bring large unemployment in their wake.

The findings about the performance of manufacturing and of agriculture strongly confirm the contention that trade restrictions inflicted heavy damage on the tradeables sector. First, comparisons of the growth rate of manufacturing and agriculture in the category of "severe restrictions" reveal that trade restrictions tend to favor manufacturing. We see that removal of these restrictions tends to slow the manufacturing growth rate while speeding up the agricultural rate. Moreover, the growth rates of both manufacturing and agriculture in the pre-liberalization period (PtL) in the instances of moderately restrictive trade regimes are substantially higher – by a statistically significant amount – than the corresponding rates in the severely trade-restrictive instances. This suggests that heavy trade restrictions (mostly extensive use of QRs) may inflict long-term damage on the profitability of the *entire tradeables* sector, including manufacturing activities, which QRs usually shield from international competition (see chapter 10).

Conclusions

Far from supporting the presumption that the implementation of trade liberalization brings measurable economic losses, the evidence suggests that these policies are correlated with accelerated economic expansion. "Strong" liberalization episodes are particularly associated with large relative expansion of the tradeables sector. These strong episodes – which we have seen are likely candidates for survival – are also associated with stable output growth in the year of implementation of the liberalization policy.

The effects of trade liberalization policies on the manufacturing sector are as expected: a deceleration of its growth rate in the first year of implementation, followed by rapid acceleration. The growth rate of agriculture exhibits a sizable increase following the introduction of trade liberalization (albeit with considerable year to year fluctuations) and never falls below its pre-liberalization levels in episodes classified as either "strong," "sustained," or "initially highly restrictive." The view that agricultural output responds with long lags finds little support from the present analysis. Finally, we may infer that severe trade restrictions seem to do harm in the long term, at least to the tradeables sector – including the very manufacturing sector that they are designed to shield from international competition.

8

Income Distribution

Paucity of data and absence of an appropriate analytical framework hamper investigation of the impact of liberalization on income distribution. The inferences of the present chapter are thus partial and inconclusive – at best, indicative. Nevertheless, they are significant in view of the scarcity of other wide-scope findings.

The main representations of income distribution surveyed here are distribution by income level, the share of wages in national income, and the relative change of low versus high wages. Our earlier conclusion about the weak impact of liberalization on employment suggests that the most important potential source of short-term deterioration of income distribution, following trade liberalization, is absent.

No clear pattern emerges. The presumption that liberalization is bound to worsen income distribution, making the poor poorer, is not borne out. Nor does it come out that the lower income deterioration of income distribution, following trade liberalization, is absent.

From the other side, practically no country's experience suggests that a deterioration of income distribution, *per se*, has helped kill off a liberalization policy. Changes in incomes of individuals, or of specific sectors, must have helped determine the fate of the policy; but, apparently, no comprehensive change in the pattern of income distribution has been involved.

A major anxiety for policymakers contemplating trade liberalization might be the potential effects on income distribution. Scarce data and the difficulty of disentangling cause and effect bedevil any attempt to verify these effects empirically. Since the findings available from country studies (reported in the second section) are for this reason fragmentary and at best indicative, it seems worth examining first what *a priori* reasoning and the available indirect evidence can contribute.

Determinants of the Distributional Impact

Several indicators of income distribution may serve to evaluate any distributional impact. Three would probably be of general concern.

Distribution by income levels   Most people would judge a more equal income distribution (overlooking any conceptual difficulties in defining it) as superior to a less equal distribution. We shall therefore refer to an equalization of income distribution as an "improvement," and to its opposite as a "deterioration."

Functional distribution of income   Here the share of labor *vis-à-vis* capital (perhaps specifically of land as a component of capital) attracts most attention. An increase of the labor share would generally be regarded as an "improvement," mostly, as by the former criterion, for equity reasons: it is generally assumed that average family income is lower when derived from labor than from capital, so that a relative increase of labor income would be presumed to distribute income more equally. Partly, this probably often serves as an independent criterion: the derivation of income from labor is judged to be more "justified" than the drawing of income from the provision of capital services.

Personal distribution of income   A liberalization policy, like any other change in relative prices and remunerations, would make some people richer and others poorer. If the status quo is held in any esteem, any change would be deplored on the grounds that some people must be incurring a "human cost" by becoming poorer. But this view is rather esoteric: most people, for instance, would regard the reduction of incomes derived from the appropriation of quota rents (a change which may conceivably be classified under the former heading as "functional" allocation) as an "improvement." Be that as it may, perhaps the only useful point that can be made in this connection is that a liberalization policy must lead to some personal redistribution of income if it is at all effective.

A priori – or with the help of some knowledge that sheds an indirect light on the issue – the following considerations may be suggested with regard to the impact of trade liberalization on one or more of the distributional criteria.

1 In the long run, trade liberalization could affect the share of labor in national income via its influences on the rate of growth of labor and of

capital, on changes in technology, and on changes in factor intensities in the productive activities. The first two impacts would probably be minimal, but the impact on factor intensities would be more influential. Liberalization, by removing or relaxing the (almost universal) anti-export bias, tends to increase the (absolute and relative) share of export activities and lower the share of import-substituting activities. Available empirical evidence strongly suggests that exportable activities, in a developing country contemplating trade liberalization, would be more labor intensive than importable activities (see NBER, 1981–3). Hence, liberalization should lead to increased demand for labor, and thus for increased wages and a higher share of labor in aggregate income.

2 In addition, trade liberalization should lessen disparities *among* wages. This may be a medium-term proposition, since in the long run rewards for identical labor are presumably equal in all activities. But in the concrete world wage disparities (beyond the reward for the human-capital component) are common. Specifically, agricultural wages are normally lower – often much lower – than wages in the urban sector. In a developing country, where manufacturing is generally protected at the expense of agriculture, relaxation of protection would tend to promote agriculture and, in relative terms, discourage manufacturing: this, we have seen in chapter 7, has indeed been most often the case. Thus, by promoting the low-wage sector and relatively contracting the high-wage sector, liberalization should contribute to the intersectoral equalization of wages.

3 A real devaluation often accompanies trade liberalization. By increasing the relative price of tradeable versus nontradeable activities, devaluation should lead to a relative increase of the rewards to factors engaged in the tradeables sector – in which primary activities and manufacturing are normally assumed to be much more heavily represented than services. To the extent that wages in services in developing countries are higher than wages in the aggregate of primary production and manufacturing, this would provide another channel through which a package of liberalization with devaluation would tend to equalize incomes among wage earners.

4 In the short run, undoubtedly the principal impact of the liberalization policy on income distribution would be expected to arise from its potential effect on unemployment: unemployed labor, even where some unemployment compensation is available, would suffer the heaviest income loss. In fact, from our extensive survey, this impact turns out to be rather weak. *Net* unemployment originating from trade liberalization is, we have inferred, small or nonexistent in almost all liberalization experiences. It is, of course, conceivable – even likely – that structural changes in the economy would tend to lead to changes in the incidence of unemployment: some previously employed labor will be laid off and stay unemployed, whereas previously unemployed workers will find new employment. But not much could be said about the ranking of two different personal structures of unemployment.

5 Often a trade liberalization goes hand in hand with a stabilization policy. In these instances, government subsidies will be a prime target in the reduction of budgetary expenditures. Since subsidies presumably tend to equalize the distribution of (disposable) income, cutting them is likely to make income distribution less equal. Another target for cuts will be government wages and salaries. While these cuts would lower the share of labor in aggregate income, the wages they reduce are likely to be particularly high in relation to wages in other sectors. It is not clear whether this, or the equally likely strategy of raising taxes, will work for or against a more equal distribution of income.

6 The relaxation of QRs, without their replacement by tariffs, would benefit directly the "average" consumer at the expense of recipients of quota profits from the rationed imports – presumably improving income distribution. When QRs are replaced by tariffs, the loss of incomes by those who had been appropriating the quota rents would be matched by the gains of the "average" recipient of government expenditures or (if the added tariff revenues replace other taxes) by the "average" taxpayer. Once more, this is likely to be assessed as a move toward a better distribution of income.

7 Finally, the removal, or relaxation, of QRs on imports is frequently associated with the relaxation of price controls and rationing in the domestic market. The latter may be presumed to have worked toward real-income equalization: rationing final consumption goods may be likened to the distribution of equal amounts of rationing coupons to each household, which are added to money income as a determinant of real income. The relaxation of controls and rationing may hence be presumed to lead to a *deterioration* of income distribution.

The Evidence

The fragmentary empirical evidence gathered in the country studies mainly points out associations over time. It refers to the three criteria of distribution mentioned at the outset, most often to the first two: the distribution by income levels and the share of wages in national income. In addition, changes in relative *sectoral* wages are often cited.

In Argentina 1 (1967–70), the share of wages in the national income slightly increased, even when adjusted for the proportion of wage earners in total employment: the share of wages in income was 50.7 percent in 1960–6, before the liberalization: 57.8 percent during 1967–70, the liberalization period; and 57.0 percent in the following years 1971–2. Wages in the tradeables sector declined relative to wages in the nontradeables sector during the liberalization – presumably an indication of *deterioration* of income distribution.

In Argentina 2 (1976–80) the share of wages declined – from 43 percent in 1975, on the eve of liberalization, to 31 percent during the liberalization period (these figures, it should be noted, are not comparable with those mentioned earlier for the first episode). The authors of the country study maintain that the substantial fall in real wages is not related to the liberalization process: it is the product of a radical political change, where the new regime replaced one in which trade unions were dominant. In this episode, too, the relative wage in the tradeables sector versus the nontradeables sector declined – a trend consistent with the large fall in the real exchange rate that characterized this experience.

For Brazil's liberalization (1965–73) the relevant data are scarce. In the earlier years of liberalization real wages in the urban industrial sector declined, but they soon recovered. They still show a decline for the liberalization period as a whole: their level went from 120.4 in 1962–4 (1965–7 = 100) to 113.7 in the liberalization years 1965–73 and to 137.1 in the later years 1974–6.

In Chile a partial indication, related to sectoral relative wages, exists for the country's second liberalization (1974–81). The ratio of wages in manufacturing to the wages in three other major sectors changed as follows:

	Ratio of wages in manufacturing to wages in		
	Agriculture	Mining	Services
1962–73	4.15	0.52	1.11
1974–9 (liberalization years)	4.96	0.52	1.41

The relative increase in wages in manufacturing versus wages in agriculture presumably indicates a deterioration of income distribution. This finding is somewhat surprising in view of the substantial decline of employment in manufacturing and increase of employment in agriculture that characterizes this liberalization experience.

In Colombia's second liberalization episode (1968–82) the main evidence refers again to sectoral wage levels. Income distribution improved during this episode as a result of a relative increase in the domestic terms of trade of the agricultural sector. Relative wages had been very low in agriculture – on average, 33 percent of wages in manufacturing and somewhat below wages of unskilled labor in construction. From 1971 to 1980 (roughly the period of liberalization) agricultural wages increased substantially – owing, the author maintains, to the reduction of the anti-export bias. Within the manufacturing sector, there must also have been corresponding changes in the direction of equalization: of the 13 (out of a total of 28) manufacturing activities with above-average wages, only two (tobacco and glass) were producers of exportables as against nine import-substituting activities.

The share of aggregate wages in total value added increased during the second half of the 1960s, fell in the first half of the 1970s, and increased again in the second half of the 1970s. Thus no general trend change of this share is apparent during the long period of liberalization.

For Greece's second liberalization experience (1962–82) some partial indicators are mentioned. The share of wages in aggregate income increased substantially during this long period – from 33.7 percent to 47.7 percent – but this may, partly at least, reflect the large relative decline of agriculture (a sector in which wages are a minor component) from 25.7 percent to 18.2 percent of total income. The share of income from property and entrepreneurship declined from 37.5 percent to 34.5 percent; thus, in relation to this, wages indeed increased very significantly. A supporting indication is the fact that wages, in the stricter sense, increased over the liberalization period by 2.5 percent whereas salaries – presumably the higher component of labor income – increased by only 1.8 percent. A similar indication is that differences in average earnings between manufacturing and other sectors, as well as among activities within the manufacturing sector, declined over the period.

Real wages in Indonesia's second liberalization experience (1966–72) appear to be strongly and positively associated with the liberalization: a dramatic fall, by more than half, before the liberalization (from 1955 to 1965) turned into just as dramatic an increase, by about two thirds, during the years of the liberalization (from 1965–72). The author of the country study assigns this increase in real wages not just to the general expansion of economic activity but also to an increase in the share of labor in income, arising from the relative growth of labor-intensive activities.

In Israel's first liberalization episode (1952–5), a worsening of income distribution appears when this is measured by the share of the bottom two-fifths in total disposable income. This is a period of major changes in crucial economic variables – the size of the labor force, the stock of capital, factor productivity, and nonearned income from abroad. Nevertheless, the author of the country study assigns the deterioration of income distribution, at least partly, to the relaxation of rationing and price controls which had worked before, during the "austerity" period, to equalize real incomes.

In both of Korea's liberalization episodes (1965–7 and 1978–9) income distribution as measured by factor shares remained largely unchanged – showing no trend despite some fluctuations. The share of labor in total income generated in the business sector was practically equal (around 60 percent) during the first liberalization episode to its share during the several years preceding or following it. This was true also for the second episode (during which the labor share was slightly lower, at 58 percent).

Relative sectoral changes of wages in Pakistan's two liberalization periods (1959–65 and 1972–8) are shown in table 8.1 (data for both countries are taken from the country studies). "Manufacturing" here refers to the subsector of "large-scale" manufacturing – a sector in which wages are presumably particularly high. An increase of relative wages in the agricultural sector would thus be deemed a trend toward equalization of incomes (at least among wage earners). This, indeed, appears to be the trend in the country's experience. During the first liberalization episode wages increased much more in agriculture than in manufacturing, whereas following the liberalization they increased only slightly more. During the second episode, the relative increase of wages in agriculture was minor, and no different from the years preceding the liberalization; but it should be contrasted with a major fall of this relative wage in the years immediately following the liberalization period.

The authors of the country study also note that redistribution of income was a prime motive for Bhutto's introduction of the second liberalization. But this, apparently, was not so much concerned with distribution by factor shares, or by income levels, as with distribution among specific sectors or groups.

Similar data are presented, in table 8.1, for the two liberalization episodes of the Philippines (1960–5 and 1970–4). The inferences in this case are different for the two experiences. In the first liberalization the relative wages in agriculture declined substantially in comparison, with only a milder decline in the years preceding it, and with no trend change in the years following the liberalization. In the second liberalization period, on the other hand, wages in agriculture increased, in relative terms, in contrast with a large relative deterioration in the following years. If the two

Table 8.1 Sectoral changes in wages (percent, for whole period)

		Manufacturing	Agriculture
Pakistan			
1960–5	(liberalization)	8.8	29.9
1965–71		20.0	26.9
1971–8	(liberalization)	19.0	26.2
1978–81		32.6	8.7
Philippines			
1957–9		11.7	2.4
1959–65	(liberalization)	−7.9	−25.7
1965–9		6.0	6.8
1969–74	(liberalization)	−34.8	−24.8
1974–80		14.5	−4.0

liberalization episodes are combined, it may be seen that the relative wage in agriculture fell during both the liberalization years and others, but the fall was more moderate during the liberalization experiment.

Another available indicator, for the country's second episode, is the share of aggregate wages in aggregate income: during this period, real wages in the economy fell very substantially (by roughly 40 percent), while per capita income increased. Thus, by this yardstick, this liberalization experience is characterized by a substantial deterioration of income distribution.

In Portugal's first liberalization episode (1970–4) labor's share in aggregate value added increased substantially – from 49.9 percent to 54.5 percent. However, this was totally due to the increase of the labor share in the *nontradeable* activities. Also, it occurred in a period characterized by a substantial increase in the economy's aggregate capital-to-labor ratio – although the impact of the latter change on the share of labor in income is not self-evident.

For Singapore's liberalization (1968–73) no direct evidence is available, but changes in economic structure would have some implications. In the first few years following the introduction of liberalization, labor-intensive activities relatively expanded, whereas in later years a relative increase of sectors intensive in both capital and skill was manifested – as would normally be expected in an open economy in which both physical and human capital expand fast.

In Sri Lanka's second episode (1977–9), a changing pattern of income redistribution appears following the implementation of liberalization. First, immediately following the introduction of the policy, income distribution deteriorated: the share of labor in aggregate income declined, while the share of property incomes increased. In addition, changes in subsidies – especially food subsidies, primarily for rice growing – accompanying the liberalization eroded the disposable income of lower income families. A reduction of the level of several social services had much the same effect. In subsequent years, on the other hand, in an environment in which all incomes grew rather fast, incomes grew particularly fast in the lower income group, so that its share in aggregate income increased in comparison with the years before the liberalization.

In Spain's three liberalization episodes the share of labor in income increased persistently on each occasion – though not much more than when liberalization was absent. During the first episode (1960–6), labor income as a share of aggregate net income at factor cost increased from 49.0 percent to 53.1 percent, whereas the share of capital income dropped slightly, from 17.0 percent to 16.3 percent – the discrepancy being accounted for by the large relative decline of "mixed" income (essentially income from agriculture) from 16.8 percent to 13.1 percent. During the years of the second liberalization (1970–4), the share of labor income jumped from 55.5 percent to 62.4 percent, while the share of capital income dropped from 16.0 percent to 12.9 percent and that of agricultural income from 8.4 percent to 6.5 percent. This should be contrasted with the inter-liberalization years 1966–70 in which the relative change in the share of labor versus capital was only slight: labor income's share increased from 53.1 percent to 55.5 percent. Finally, from 1975 to 1982 (a period which includes the third liberalization episode of 1977–80) the share of labor income abruptly rose again, to around 73 percent. Although comparability is not complete, a trend of increase of the share of labor income with liberalization does seem to be indicated.

In the first liberalization experience of Turkey (1970–3), which consisted primarily of a devaluation, many other policy changes, in the judgment of the study's authors, must have overshadowed any potential impact of the devaluation on income distribution. One significant impact of the liberalization must have been a substantial fall of the quota rents appropriated by the holders of import licenses. In the country's second liberalization episode (1980–4), several bits of evidence indicate a deterioration of income distribution. Real wages declined sharply, substantially more than aggregate spending – a fact which very probably indicates a fall of labor income relative to capital income. With the tightening of the budget, income-relief programs have been contained. Another budgetary measure was a substantial reduction of the real level of government salaries – although, to repeat, it is not clear *a priori* whether such a change tends to increase or lower the inequality in income distribution.

Finally, in Yugoslavia's liberalization (1965–7) the partial evidence is ambiguous, partly because the definitions of functional incomes in this economy differ from those of other countries. The share of "capital" tended to decline during the liberalization, but workers' incomes are assigned as a reward for both "labor" and "capital," with possible changes in the methods of allocation. For the years 1963 and 1968, within which the liberalization falls, measures of dispersion show a deterioration of income distribution. This is shown by the Gini coefficient or by a comparison of the rate of increase of income of the bottom 40 percent of income recipients with that of the top 10 percent. The income distribution of *earning* families, however, became more equal during these years. The deterioration of income distribution was thus a function of the creation of substantial unemployment, particularly in an economy in which unemployment compensations were very few.

An issue of specific concern in Yugoslavia is the income distribution among its various republics. It appears that in the short run liberalization favored the poorer republics. In the longer term, however, the opposite was true: the policy package of which trade liberalization was a component included a reduction of the transfer of savings from the richer to the poorer regions.

No general inference emerges from this survey of country experiences. In several instances a deterioration of income distribution with liberalization seems to have occurred: Argentina 2; Israel 1; Philippines 1 and perhaps 2; Turkey 2; Yugoslavia. In almost an equal number of experiences, an improvement is suggested: Colombia 2; Greece 2; Indonesia 2; both episodes of Pakistan; and all three liberalization episodes of Spain. In other liberalization experiences, either no evidence is available or the existing evidence suggests a mixed outcome.

In sum, while there is no evidence that lower income groups derive particular advantage from liberalization (beyond sharing in any general impetus to growth) nor is there any confirmation for the oft-repeated contention that liberalization is bound to lead to a deterioration of income distribution, deepening the poverty of the poor.

Furthermore, deterioration of income distribution *per se* has not, it seems, been instrumental in killing off a liberalization in any country but Yugoslavia (where inequality of income distribution was increased by unemployment, which did play a part in aborting the policy). While liberalization must have affected the pattern of income distribution, therefore, a reciprocal impact seems to be absent.

Part III

Policies, Performance, and Sustainability

9

The Long-term Perspective

Over the long run, the post World War II experience
distinguishes two groups of countries: the "liberalizers" –
countries that have pursued a clear course of liberalization,
continuous or with interruptions – and the
"nonliberalizers" – countries in which the trend toward
liberalization has been slight, or volatile, or absent. The
liberalizers include Chile, Greece, Indonesia, Israel, Korea,
New Zealand, Singapore, Spain, and Uruguay; the
"nonliberalizers" are Argentina, Brazil, Colombia, Pakistan,
Peru, the Philippines, Portugal, Sri Lanka, Turkey, and
Yugoslavia.
   The countries that have persevered in their attempts to
liberalize have several characteristics in common. They tend
to be smaller and (a related attribute) poorer in natural
resources than the others. Furthermore, small resource-poor
economies tend to be long-term liberalizers; among large
resource-rich economies a long-term liberalization course is
the exception. Liberalizers also tend to have a higher level
of per capita income and education than nonliberalizers.
   Perhaps the clearest distinction concerns the political
regime. A *stable* regime, of whatever shade, clearly
distinguishes the liberalizing countries from the others – to
the point that stability of the political regime may be
considered a necessary (though not sufficient) condition for
maintaining a long-term course of stabilization.
   In terms of economic performance and policies,
liberalizing countries are characterized by a much faster
growth of exports, generally lower budgetary deficits and
(less clearly) budgetary expenditures, and, clearest of all,

long-term stability of the real rate of foreign exchange. (The absence of fluctuations of the exchange rate is what matters here: the trend change of the rate does not seem to differ much between the two groups of countries.)

Some *negative* findings are also of interest. The aggregate size of the economy in terms of *income* does not seem to distinguish one group from another. Even more surprising, the weight of the manufacturing sector does not seem to be relevant: the share of manufacturing, whether in aggregate product or in aggregate exports, does not seem to differ consistently between the liberalizing countries and the rest.

Most of part III is concerned with what makes for durability or what causes collapse of an episode of liberalization. The present chapter, however, addresses the issue of the determinants of the *long-term* course of the liberalization policy.

Country Patterns

Over the long term, certain patterns emerge from the trade policy experiences of the 19 countries analyzed:

1 *Continuous uninterrupted progress* characterizes the experiences of Greece, Israel, Korea, and Singapore. In Greece and Israel, substantial liberalization has moved the trade regime from highly restrictive to fairly liberal. In Korea and Singapore, the change has been less substantial, either because the regime in the end has remained fairly restricted (Korea), or because trade restrictions were not very severe in the first place (Singapore).

2 *Clear, though not continuous progress*: Chile, Indonesia, New Zealand, Spain, and Uruguay manifest this pattern.[1] In all these countries, trade regimes toward the end of the period are significantly more liberal than at the beginning; the extent of Chile's liberalization has surpassed any other country's experience. But for all of them, the process has been interrupted by a reversal at some point.

3 *Slight or volatile trend* describes the experiences of Colombia, Pakistan, the Philippines, Sri Lanka, Turkey,[2] and Yugoslavia. In these seven

---

1 At the time of writing, the experiences of New Zealand and Uruguay have become more durable and persistent than the liberalization indices of chapter 2 would suggest.

2 In Turkey, the trade regime latterly is much more liberal than it was in the 1950s. But the difference originates from a sharp process of liberalization that has started only recently, and is still going on.

countries, the long-term trend is still toward a liberalized trade regime. But the trend has less significance, either because it is slight (as, say, in Pakistan) or because, as in most countries in this category, it is the outcome of substantial changes in both directions.

4 *Purely cyclical movement* is the pattern of Argentina, Brazil, Peru, and Portugal. In the experiences of these countries, liberalization attempts have been made and have collapsed, once or more often. No general trend is apparent, and the trade regime has remained, over the long run, roughly equally restrictive – in fact (with the exception of Portugal) highly restrictive. Three of the four countries are in Latin America and, in turn, half the Latin American countries studied in this project belong in this category. This "stop–go" process of liberalization thus character- izes, to some extent, the trade regimes in Latin America but not in the rest of the developing world.

Only in one of the 19 countries – Peru – is the long-term trend toward a *more* restrictive trade regime. Thus, among countries which have at- tempted some liberalization and have thus become subjects of this study, the long-run tendency in the last three decades has been toward a more liberalized trade policy. In other countries, this general inference does not necessarily apply: indeed, for African countries at any rate, casual observation suggests that the long-term movement during the last genera- tion must have been toward further restriction, although a turn toward liberalization may have been made in most recent years.

Policies and Attributes

What attributes, if any, distinguish countries that have moved *over the long run* to more liberalized trade from those that have not? To examine what makes a long-term movement toward liberalization durable, we compare two groups of countries. The first group encompasses the first two categories mentioned above, that is, the nine countries that have exhibited a significant long-term trend toward liberalization (whether monotonic or not). This group includes Chile, Greece, Indonesia, Israel, Korea, New Zealand, Singapore, Spain, and Uruguay. The other group, of ten "nonliberalizing" countries, consists of Argentina, Brazil, Colom- bia, Pakistan, Peru, the Philippines, Portugal, Sri Lanka, Turkey and Yugoslavia.

Potential explanations of a country's long-term commercial policy trend may be classified under three headings: (a) *country attributes* (these are exogenous data, at least at the time trade policies are undertaken or contemplated); (b) policies (including the general policy framework) followed in the countries concerned; (c) *economic performance*.

Country Attributes

Size   In a large country (in terms of territory, population, or both) international trade and specialization are likely to matter less than in a small country. The forces working toward greater specialization through freer trade – hence to a long-term policy of trade liberalization – would thus be weaker in the larger country.

Natural resources   Abundant natural resources (often, of course, a reflection of territorial size) may also work against trade liberalization since dependence on trade would tend to be weaker. Specifically, a country rich in natural resources, presumably able to export them even with a policy strongly biased against exports, may be less inclined to change this policy.

The structure of exports   Similarly, an economy starting with a more diversified export structure would probably be more receptive to reducing an anti-export bias (that is, elasticity of supply of aggregate exports would be higher). In particular, a country that exports more manufactures and services than products based on natural resources is likely to be more responsive and more inclined to open up the economy.

The structure of product   Even if exports are not diversified, an economy with a highly diversified production structure may be expected to be more responsive to policies and policy changes. And, once again, the share of manufacturing in the total product is likely to be particularly important.

Income level   It is often argued that only better-off economies can "afford" to liberalize their trade, while the really poor countries may be expected to pursue an interventionist policy. The logic is not transparent, but may be related to diversification: the richer economy is presumably more highly diversified and better able to respond to changes in prices or policies. The income level is also related to the characteristics of the labor force.

Characteristics of the labor force   A better educated and more skilled labor force would presumably be more mobile among activities and correspondingly responsive to market factors and policy changes. Strong unionization, conversely, would tend to lessen mobility and raise transition costs, eroding a country's ability to persevere in a liberalization policy.

Aggregate income of the economy   Adam Smith's old dictum, that the size of the market limits the extent of specialization, obviously does not define market size in terms of size of population: large but poor populations constitute small markets. Probably the best yardstick for the economic "size" is the country's aggregate income – a product of the size and richness of its population. Economies with higher incomes would be expected to have a higher degree of *intra*-economy specialization and trade when they are closed, and would thus, all things being equal, gain less from international trade. These economies might therefore be less inclined to liberalize, feeling that the cost of staying largely closed may not be high.

Sectoral intensity of locations   As another important influence on sectoral mobility and transition costs, this is also likely to affect the inclination to persevere in liberalization. If specific locations within the country tend to be based largely on a single activity ("one-industry towns"), a policy leading to movement among sectors would tend to require greater geographical mobility: the policy may thus be more strongly resisted than in an economy in which workers could move among sectors without major locational disruptions. This reinforces the effect of territorial size: in very small territories, geographical mobility may be a lesser consideration than otherwise.

Availability of capital inflows   Balance-of-payments considerations are crucial to the fate of a liberalization policy (see chapter 11). The long-term availability – through outright grants or good credit standing in international financial markets – of substantial inflows of foreign capital alleviates the constraining effects of balance-of-payments developments, and this would strengthen the policy.

Policy Attributes

Political stability   Since commercial policies are crucial in almost any economy, long-term perseverance in pursuing any given strain of commercial policy is likely to depend on the absence of violent and radical changes in the nature of the political regime and in the basic approach of policymakers.

Existence of multinational commitments   Liberalization policies may be expected to persist in countries that pursue them within the framework of an international commitment, either general or specific to the country involved, rather than unilaterally.

Real exchange rate "policy"   Strictly speaking, there is no policy determining the *real* exchange rate: the real exchange rate is affected by a combination of policies, shocks, and processes, and is the "reduced form" of all of these. But whether classified as a "policy" or as a "performance" variable, this magnitude may be expected to influence the long-term outcome for a trade liberalization. Its movement must, in turn, be partly related to the following two policy variables.

The budgetary deficit   Large budget deficits are likely to be associated, causally, with more rapid inflations and with balance-of-payments difficulties. An economy in which these phenomena are common would be less likely to be committed to a long-term course of trade liberalization.

Budgetary expenditures   The size of fiscal expenditures could be relevant to the fate of liberalization in at least two ways. One is that the larger expenditures are likely – though this is not certain – to lead to relatively higher budgetary deficits. The other is that a large government sector may reflect a general inclination to rely less on the market and on market signals than on government intervention. The existence of a large government sector is also likely to weaken the responsiveness to market changes that should follow liberalization and to strengthen resistance to such policies. In this regard, the size of public sector enterprises is at least as relevant as the size of expenditures recorded in the budget of the central government.

Economic Performance

Two representations of economic performance may seem, *a priori*, to be relevant to the fate of liberalization.

Economic growth   Although a relationship should be expected, its direction here is not entirely clear cut. On the one hand, a fast-growing economy is getting richer, and the argument that higher income might support long-term durability of liberalization may then apply. But on the other hand, in a country that seems to be doing well with present policies, pressures for policy change would be less likely.

Export growth   Here, the probabilities are unambiguous: an economy in which exports grow fast is more likely to sustain a trade liberalization policy. Fast export growth is likely to be perceived as fulfilling one of the principal expectations of trade liberalization. It is also likely to establish quickly a strong vested interest in the continuation of the policy. And, finally, strong export performance is likely to relieve balance-of-payments constraints, making the resort to import suppression less likely.

Clearly, in any testing of possible relationships between these two (or any other) performance variables and the long-term course of trade liberalization, a problem of simultaneity, or two-way causality, must be present. This problem will be discussed later.

The Empirical Evidence

In the following, we shall where possible test the hypotheses listed above against the data provided in the country studies. For most variables quantitative representation is feasible and available; where this is not so, suggestive evidence will be used instead.

Table 9.1 Country attributes

	1	2	3 Share of manufactures (%)	4	5	6	7
	Size of territory (×1000 km²)	Natural resources	In exports	In GDP	Aggregate annual income (billion US$)	Per capita annual income (US$)	Ratio of capital inflow to imports (US$)
Long-term liberalizers							
Chile	756	Rich	6.9	19.3	1.73	228	n.a.
Greece	132	Poor	9.9	14.3	3.41	410	16.4
Indonesia	1,920	Rich	n.a.	12.1	6.91	73	17.3
Israel	21	Poor	n.a.	n.a.	1.88	891	30.5
Korea	99	Poor	11.3	17.9	3.58	143	14.4
New Zealand	270	Rich	n.a.	n.a.	3.43	1,445	23.3
Singapore	1	Poor	4.8	13.0	0.68	419	4.8
Spain	505	Poor	37.6	27.0	9.65	317	11.9
Uruguay	177	Rich	n.a.	23.1	1.45	571	n.a.
Mean	431	n.a.	n.a.	18.1	3.64	500	16.9
Median	177	n.a.	n.a.	17.9	3.41	410	16.4
Other countries							
Argentina	2,785	Rich	n.a.	33.9	12.12	588	n.a.
Brazil	8,541	Rich	8.2	33.1	16.91	233	n.a.
Colombia	1,141	Rich	4.1	16.5	3.53	224	n.a.
Pakistan	804	Poor	n.a.	12.0	3.44	75	n.a.
Peru	1,289	Rich	n.a.	20.0	1.85	191	n.a.
Philippines	300	Rich	n.a.	17.6	4.47	163	n.a.
Portugal	92	Poor	53.2	30.0	2.29	260	7.6
Sri Lanka	66	Poor	14.9	6.1	1.33	134	n.a.
Turkey	782	Poor	n.a.	13.7	4.90	178	n.a.
Yugoslavia	256	Poor	37.6	24.5	n.a.	n.a.	n.a.
Mean	1,606	n.a.	n.a.	20.7	5.65	227	n.a.
Median	793	n.a.	n.a.	18.8	3.53	191	n.a.

n.a., not available.
Columns 3, 4, 5, and 6, 1960 or thereabouts.
Column 7, average for the period 1960–80, or most of it.

Table 9.1 presents the "country attributes" for which quantitative data or qualitative evaluations are available. The data suggest several inferences, some supporting and some rejecting the hypotheses postulated above.

Comparison of the *territorial size* of the countries (column 1) points to a systematic difference between the long-run liberalizers and the others, in the expected direction. Among the nine "liberalizers," over half are definitely small countries in terms of geographical size. Only one (Indonesia) could be called large, whereas three others (Chile, New Zealand, and Spain) are roughly medium sized. Among the ten other countries, on the other hand, only two (Portugal and Sri Lanka) could be classified as small, whereas two (Argentina and Brazil) are definitely large, and the rest medium sized.

Column 2 indicates the availability in the economy of natural resources, including ample land and climatic conditions suitable for specific agricultural products, as well as minerals. Since no obvious quantitative index exists for the "abundance" of resources, a qualitative judgment as to whether the country is "rich" or "poor" in resources is presented in the table. It appears that this factor does not systematically distinguish liberalizing countries from the rest.

The economy's *aggregate income* also appears to have little bearing on the long-term fate of liberalization. On average, the nonliberalizing countries do record a higher aggregate income when the process of liberalization starts (data are for around 1960). But the average is heavily weighted by Brazil and Argentina. The median size of income in the two categories of countries is almost identical. From the individual country studies, it appears that in Singapore a firm conviction that a small country must be open to world trade and specialization has impelled the introduction and sustained the long-term persistence of liberalization. But other small countries have not pursued that route, whereas at least two countries with relatively large markets (Spain and Indonesia) are among the long-term liberalizers. In sum, the size of the local market is apparently not one of the attributes that in practice distinguish the liberalizing countries from others.

Per capita income – an indication (neither well defined, nor feasibly measured) of the country's "level of development" – seems more relevant. By and large, the liberalizers have higher per capita income, though there are clearly overlaps and contradictions. Thus Argentina, a richer country at the *eve* of liberalization, is a nonliberalizer, whereas poor countries like Indonesia or Korea are liberalizers. On the whole, however, the inference that countries with higher starting income levels are more likely to pursue a course of liberalization than poor countries does seem to be warranted.

An increased *share of manufacturing* is, presumably, one of the manifestations of development (up to a certain threshold). Yet it does not seem to have any obvious bearing on the long-term course of the trade regime. Neither the share of the manufacturing sector in the economy's total product nor its share in the country's exports appear, from the data of table 9.1, to differ much between the two groups. In fact, of the nine countries that did follow a long-term policy of liberalization, only two (Spain and Israel) could be considered as above average in their level of industrialization on the verge of the period of liberalization. Among the nonliberal-izers, however, one finds such relatively industrialized economies as Argentina, Brazil, and Portugal.

For some of the *labor force* characteristics that hypothetically have a bearing on the long-term durability of liberalization no comparable data were available. Data on the degree of unionization may be found in many of the country studies, but they are not sufficient to provide for a cross-country comparison; and the existing data on the "single industry" phenomenon are too sparse to test the relevance of that variable.[3] The general level of education of the population, which probably applies roughly to the labor force, is one of the attributes more amenable to quantification. We have used two alternative measures as indicators: the ratios (of the relevant age group) of enrollment in secondary school and of enrollment in tertiary education.[4] Ranking the 19 country studies by these ratios shows a rather similar outcome for both alternatives: the group of "liberalizers" ranked slightly higher than the other group.[5] Some relation-ship, in the expected direction, may thus be indicated. This would be consistent with our former observation about the role of per capita income – a magnitude that must be positively correlated with the level of education. Indonesia provides again a strong exception to the (weak) rule: it is a clear liberalizer despite a level of education that is about the lowest among the countries studied.

Our evaluations of the *policy attributes* discussed previously are pre-sented in table 9.2. The assessment of the stability of the *political regime* (column 1) is based on the political histories in the respective country studies. As such, it is probably the most subjective of the evaluations, and a

3 A set of data on this variable has been constructed in the country study of Brazil. There, the phenomenon of regional preponderance of new activities has been found to be quite widespread.

4 The level of primary education – as measured by the ratio of enrollment – does not seem to differentiate much among countries. Data were derived from the World Bank *World Development Report* (1987). They refer to 1965 – about a midpoint in the period relevant for the present study. The use of alternative dates – primarily the adoption of a much later year – would have changed materially the absolute numbers, and to some extent also the ranking.

5 The mean (and median) rank, for 19 countries, is 10. For the "liberalizers," the mean was 7.8 and the median 7 for the ratio of secondary education. For tertiary education, the mean was 8.4 and the median 8.

Table 9.2 Policy attributes and measures of performance

	1 Political regime	2 Average annual change	3 Trend coefficient as percentage of mean[a]	4 Standard error	5 Variance of trend regression	6 Deficit as percentage of GDP	7 Expenditures as percentage of GDP	8 Annual rate of growth of GDP (%)	9 Annual rate of growth of exports (%)
Long-term liberalization									
Chile	Stable	-6.1	-4.4	0.28	0.86	4.7	20.3	3.8	7.1
Greece	Stable	1.4	1.2	0.09	0.73	2.4	17.2	6.2	10.8
Indonesia	Stable	-0.7	0.3	0.09	0.02	2.1	14.9	5.9	6.2
Israel	Stable	0.7	-1.9	0.09	0.82	n.a.	18.6	6.8	10.7
Korea	Stable	-1.4	-3.4	0.07	0.67	0.4	10.6	8.5	24.5
New Zealand	Stable	n.a.	n.a.	n.a.	n.a.	n.a.	n.a.	2.9	4.7
Singapore	Stable	-1.9	-2.5	0.10	0.56	1.7	20.4	9.2	11.8
Spain	Stable	-2.1	-3.1	0.08	0.89	1.1	10.1	8.2	11.2
Uruguay	Stable	n.a.	n.a	n.a.	n.a.	1.2	15.0	n.a.	n.a.
Mean		-1.4	-2.0	0.11	0.65	1.9	15.9	6.4	10.9
Median		-1.4	-2.5	0.09	0.73	1.7	16.1	6.5	10.8
Other countries									
Argentina	Unstable	-4.8	-2.2	0.21	0.38	4.0	22.4	3.5	5.8
Brazil	Stable	1.9	6.6	0.38	0.55	4.3	134.1	7.4	6.0
Colombia	Stable	0.8	-0.5	0.11	0.05	-0.3	9.8	5.5	4.9
Pakistan	Unstable	0.7	1.5	0.16	0.30	7.9	20.6	2.8	6.3
Peru	Unstable	-0.7	-0.3	0.14	0.02	n.a.	n.a.	4.1	1.3
Philippines	Stable	1.4	1.4	0.18	0.22	0	9.5	5.7	6.4
Portugal	Unstable	-3.0	-4.1	0.28	0.76	n.a.	n.a.	5.6	7.0
Sri Lanka	Unstable	3.6	4.3	0.25	0.60	n.a.	n.a.	6.7	0.5
Turkey	Unstable	n.a.	n.a	n.a.	n.a.	4.8	28.8	6.0	n.a.
Yugoslavia	Stable	-0.7	-1.8	0.14	0.29	n.a.	n.a.	n.a.	13.2
Mean		0.1	0.5	0.23	0.35	3.5	17.4	5.3	5.7
Median		0.7	-0.5	0.18	0.30	4.1	16.8	5.6	6.0

n.a. not available.

Columns 6 and 7, 1960 or thereabouts.

Columns 2, 3, 4, 5, 8, and 9, average for the period 1960–80, or most of it.

[a] Coefficient *b* of the regression lines in which the real exchange rate is a function of time.

word of caution is in order. Our guideline was continuity, where "continuity" implies commitment by any government to the undertakings of its predecessors, even though it may change specific policies. Whether or not the regime was democratic was immaterial in this context. Since the classification is based on *ex post* histories, it does not necessarily indicate whether, at the inception of the relevant period, expectations for continuity predominated. Furthermore, our classification refers to limited periods in which liberalization either was carried out or could potentially be undertaken. Thus Chile, Indonesia, the Philippines, and Uruguay, despite post-World War II histories that include some notable upheavals, are classified as "stable" because their political regimes were stable during the periods in which the long-term course of liberalization was determined.

Granting these caveats, the result is nevertheless striking. All nine countries that followed a long-term course of liberalization are found to have had stable political regimes. Looked at differently, of the 13 countries with stable political regimes, only four have not been liberalizers; whereas *all* six countries with "unstable" regimes have failed to sustain liberalization in the long term. This evidence implies that a stable regime is both an impetus for perseverance in a trade liberalization policy and a necessary (though not a *sufficient*) condition for its long-term survival.[6]

Columns 2 through 9 of table 9.2 provide quantitative representations of several policy instruments by averaging the data for 1960–80, or those segments of the period for which data are available in the country studies. (The average is not given for Turkey or Uruguay, where data are recorded only for relatively short periods.)

Observing, first, the real exchange rate, no clear difference between the two groups of countries can be distinguished when long-term *trends* of performance are observed. In terms of average changes of the exchange rate,[7] the liberalizers have, if anything, done somewhat worse than the others, but not enough to matter. Similarly, the trend movement of the rate over time in each country among the liberalizers (column 3) appears to be slightly, but not significantly, below that of the others.

When the *variance over time* of the level of the real exchange rate is observed, however (column 4), the contrast between the two groups is obvious. With the exception of Chile the standard error in the liberalizing group is low (and surprisingly uniform). In the other group, it is highly varied among countries, and remarkably higher: in none of them is it as

6 It should be stressed that no *direct* causality is implied. It is conceivable, for instance, that a "stable" regime does not lead to a greater desire for liberalization, or greater resistance to countervailing forces, but to a greater ability and inclination to follow *other* policies whose existence makes trade liberalization sustainable.

7 The "exchange rate" refers throughout to the price of foreign currency in units of local currency. A currency devaluation (or depreciation) is an *increase* of the rate; an appreciation is a *fall* of the rate.

low as the highest measure for countries in the liberalizing group (excluding Chile). Once more, the inference is reinforced by observing the measure of variance around the trend line (that is, a measure that abstracts from trend line changes in estimating the variance of the series). This is represented in column 5, which shows the variance R^2 of the regression estimate of the trend line. The position of individual countries sometimes differs substantially, when judged by this indicator, from what it is when represented by the standard error; but for the two categories of countries, the contrast is still remarkable.

The performance of the real rate of foreign exchange therefore clearly does differentiate liberalizers from nonliberalizers. But it is not the direction or extent of the trend change that matters so much as its stability. In other words, liberalizers have tended to keep the level of the real exchange rate fairly even over the long run, whereas nonliberalizers have tended to let it suffer from spasms. The indications are therefore that *predictability* of the level of this crucial price is a significant ingredient of a policy that sustains trade liberalization in the long term.[8]

Data on the level of the *budgetary deficit* (column 6) are less complete; the observations and inferences are correspondingly tentative. With this qualification the finding seems clear: the liberalizing countries have tended to maintain a significantly smaller budgetary deficit than the nonliberalizers. This inference becomes even more evident if we note that the high average budgetary deficit recorded for Chile reflects primarily the long stretch of time – up to 1974 – in which Chile was definitely a nonliberalizing economy.

A difference in the share of *budgetary expenditures* between the two categories of countries also emerges (column 7) but is much less remarkable, especially since a large variance exists *within* each category. Thus, no clear inference is drawn on the relevance of this factor for the long-term fate of liberalization policy.

We now move to the observation of *performance variables*, two of which have been mentioned in the preceding discussion. First, the *rate of growth of income* (column 8) differs somewhat between the two groups of countries but the divergence is too slight – particularly given the rather small number of observations – to allow a conclusion that a meaningful association exists.[9]

---

8 A recent study by Cavallo, Cottani, and Khan (forthcoming) finds strong associations of the national product, exports, and investment with *stability* of the real exchange rate; mostly, these are stronger than the associations of the performance variables with the *level* of the exchange rate.

9 This should *not* read as a statement of no association between liberalization and rate of growth of income. As chapter 7 has recorded, a positive association of the two does appear to be the rule.

Observation of the other performance criterion – export growth – leaves no such doubt. A remarkable contrast can be seen here between the two groups (column 9): export growth is nearly twice as large in the liberalizing group. Among the nonliberalizers only Yugoslavia shows a rate of growth of exports above the average (or median) for the group of liberalizers; all the rest are far below it. Furthermore, in all the liberalizing countries, exports grew faster – usually much faster – than GDP growth (that is, the share of exports in product has been rising); for the group as a whole, export growth approached twice the size of GDP growth. For the nonliberalizers, on the other hand, the two growth rates were, on average, rather similar.

This strong association of export performance and long-term liberalization does not unequivocally imply *causality*. Good export performance (arising, presumably, from appropriate policies) may have made liberalization easier to sustain for the reasons discussed earlier. But conceivably causality ran in the other direction: persistence of trade liberalization, implying a long-term and credible reduction of the anti-export bias of a restrictive trade regime, may have led to a large export expansion. Most likely (though this cannot be deduced from the data) both chains of causality were present, each reinforcing the other.

10

Replacement and Relaxation of Quantitative Restrictions

Extensive QRs are commonly a basic ingredient of a highly restrictive trade regime. Their relaxation is the most common – often virtually the sole – element of trade liberalization, and particularly of a "strong" liberalization. Even in sustained episodes, substantial tariff reductions have tended to come quite a long time after QRs were relaxed.

QRs are generally removed gradually, starting with the liberalization of noncompeting imports (usually raw materials and intermediate goods, as well as most capital goods). Imports of final, especially consumer, goods are freed at a later stage. Two sectors that tend to be last in line are the textile and the automotive industries.

Ten episodes consisted of a *major* relaxation of QRs: almost all of them have survived in the long term. By contrast, for other intense liberalization policies – where QRs were not radically interfered with – sustainability was more of an exception. Clearly, liberalization of a highly restrictive trade regime is likely to survive when it starts with a major relaxation of QRs, and to fail otherwise. But this does not imply that the removal of QRs is sufficient for success. Specifically, in the liberalization episodes in question a formal devaluation was common, generally leading to a real currency depreciation. Undoubtedly, too, the strong acceleration of economic growth characteristic of these episodes had much to do with their sustainability. The lesson is significant: the most radical liberalizations, in which transitory adjustment costs might have been expected to be high, on the contrary demonstrate a remarkable increase of economic growth in the very first few years following the introduction of liberalization.

Since QRs are an important element in virtually all protective regimes, most of the programs we have studied have involved relaxation of QRs. A mere change in the form of QRs may constitute a step toward liberalization, and some programs have, indeed, amounted to nothing more than a shift from QRs to tariff protection.

In this chapter we shall consider the role of QR relaxation in trade liberalization, its relationship to tariffs and other features that play a part in the effectiveness of a liberalization policy and its chance of survival.

The Significance of Quantitative Restriction Protection

In principle, any degree of QR has a corresponding tariff level: the counterpart of a zero quota would be a prohibitive tariff; the counterpart of a less restrictive quota would be a tariff level permitting the same level of imports, or of domestic production, as the quota.[1] The *form* of a protection system – whether it is conducted through tariffs (or other price instruments) or through QRs – is of great importance, however, for a number of reasons.

1 To start with, QRs are a particularly arbitrary instrument of protection. Tariffs, admittedly, involve *ad hoc* decisions (for instance, specification and valuation of goods). But these decisions entail relatively marginal consequences and, once made, are likely to be applied in future transactions. In the case of QRs, on the other hand, arbitrary decisions are of the essence. They may vary greatly between one mechanism of administration of QRs and another – an important variable for the operation of an economy. But however rigorously general standards are observed in applying a QR system, *ad hoc* decisions will inevitably bulk larger than under a tariff system.

2 Certain adverse consequences flow from the above. Since decisions about imports cannot be made freely by the individual economic agent (importer or producer), availability of imported goods cannot be taken for granted. This is particularly crucial for the process of production, although fluctuations in the availability of imported consumer goods (and services) are also a source of loss to the economy. Producers would

1 The "tariff equivalent" of a given quota would be uniquely defined under circumstances of perfect competition on the domestic market. Otherwise, levels of equivalence would differ according to whether equality of *imports* or of *domestic production* is sought (see Bhagwati, 1965; McCulloch, 1973).

often find themselves without production inputs, replacement parts, or capital goods which, in the short run, are indispensable for the production process. Such a bottleneck is bound to lead to unplanned idleness of complementary factors of production (labor, capital) and to a loss of output.

3 *Per contra*, producers (and consumers) where future availability is not assured will tend to overstock; in some cases material and machinery required for plant expansion may be hoarded years in advance of installation, incurring interest costs and maintenance and storage charges, as well as running the risks of physical wear and tear and obsolescence.

4 QR systems, unlike tariffs, do not normally[2] allow scope for the internal reallocation of imports: the direction of imported goods and services is most often in the hands of the holder of the import quota title. This inhibits the efficient distribution of imports, particularly of intermediate and capital goods used in the production process, and makes it unlikely that resources will be rationally allocated to the productive activities that yield the highest marginal product.

5 Often – though not inevitably – QRs are associated with monopolies and barriers to entry which insulate firms from competition, whether domestic or foreign.

6 Whether import quotas are transferable directly or not, the holder of a quota enjoys a title that enables him to collect a scarcity rent.[3] Under a tariff system (and with an equivalent tariff), this rent accrues as a tax to the government. Put differently, under a QR system the government would have to impose other alternative taxes. This would normally lead to an undesirable impact on income distribution as well as to an economic excess burden due to the other forms of taxation – which in many instances may also include taxation through inflation.

7 "Rent seeking" is inseparable from the arbitrary and discrete decisions involved in almost any QR scheme, and where there is latitude for administrative discretion, corruption is seldom absent. The phenomenon of rent seeking would be found even when clearly defined rules are formulated, and it entails real economic costs (see Krueger, 1974). Real resources are diverted to secure the right to import. In the extreme case (under the assumption of perfect competition in rent-seeking activities), the real resources spent in this way would be equal to the size of rents

2 Except in the rare instances where the QR system allows transfers of the imported goods, and these transfers are generally practiced: in such cases, quota profits would obviously be generated but goods would be allocated just as under an equivalent tariff.
3 A comprehensive system of price controls, in which no extra profits are allowed anywhere in the process, may conceivably leave all the economic rents with the final consumers. Such a system would have its own damages; in any case, it is not enforceable in the long term in an otherwise market economy.

that would otherwise originate in the system of restrictions – which would amount to a rather significant economic loss.

8 A particular disadvantage of a QR scheme is that it masks the implied prices of the restricted imports so that the degree of protection it affords is unknown, fortuitous, and unplanned. Similarly, with a tariff, the degree of protection is given; with a QR, which is disconnected from movements in foreign and domestic prices, this degree becomes variable.

The disadvantages of QR systems listed above must add up to a very substantial loss in terms of reduction of the economy's real income, distortion of income distribution, and corruption. Nevertheless, QRs are the favorite form of restriction in the countries studied in this project. Why should this be so in view of the obvious economic and social losses they involve? There are several answers.

1 QRs were often resorted to originally not for protection but as a means of allocating foreign exchange in a balance-of-payments crisis when the use of price mechanisms was thought impracticable. Direct foreign exchange allocations were made instead, and these became built in as part of a protective system.

2 Often, the use of quantity allocations is chosen in preference to the price mechanism to encourage more equal distribution of income: QRs, combined with a domestic rationing system and controls of domestic prices, are presumed to direct specific imported goods to households which would not consume them under price rationing. In principle, this would obviously not apply where QRs are introduced for protection but only when imports of noncompeting goods and services are concerned.

3 Advocates of protection prefer quantity over price regulation because it makes the import level more predictable (especially when imports are completely prohibited). While the level of a prohibitive tariff may in principle be estimated, its impact on imports would not be as certain as that of direct administrative prohibition. And there will always be a lingering suspicion that it could be evaded. Also, the imposition of an inordinately high tariff might not seem feasible. Moreover, the incidence of tariff protection changes with changes in the levels of foreign or domestic prices or of the formal exchange rate. QRs are immune from this.

4 Discrimination, *ad hoc* decisions, and, in general, absence of universal rules may be seen by both policymakers and beneficiaries as desirable rather than a source of loss.

5 A mechanism of regulation through QRs, once in place, confers substantial power on the administration which may then become reluctant to dismantle it. QRs may thus be perpetuated beyond the need that originally called them into being.

Removal of Quantitative Restrictions

In the overwhelming majority of country experiences, QRs were a major element of import regulation on the eve of a liberalization episode. The few exceptions were liberalization policies that followed earlier stages of liberalization in which the bulk of QRs had been removed.

We have likewise noted that, in almost all the instances in which QRs had been prevalent before liberalization, relaxation of QRs was an important element of liberalization. The three exceptions are Brazil (in which the major policy element was export promotion), Philippines 2 (in which liberalization consisted primarily of a formal devaluation), and Turkey 1 (which also primarily involved a formal devaluation). Remember that a devaluation may be considered here as an element of liberalization precisely because it leads to the effective relaxation of QRs. Thus, even though the liberalization policies in the Philippines and Turkey did not explicitly specify any change in the machinery, regulation, coverage, or intensity of QRs, these episodes should still be considered liberalizations in which relaxation of QRs was the major element. Thus Brazil stands as practically the only exception.

In about half the episodes, we recall, the relaxation of QRs was not just one element in the policy of liberalization but its heavily predominant component: Chile 1, Greece 1, Indonesia 1 and 2, Israel 1 and 2, Korea 1, New Zealand 1 and 3, Pakistan 1 and 2, Philippines 1, Singapore, Spain 1, Sri Lanka 1 and 2, and the second, ongoing, liberalization attempt in Turkey.

While relaxation of QRs appears, thus, to be the major (or exclusive) policy element in most liberalization experiences, this does *not* necessarily imply that the relaxation involved was itself major (obviously when it was not and it was nevertheless the major policy element, liberalization as a whole must have been a weak experiment).

In 11 episodes, not only was the relaxation of QRs the principal element of liberalization policy but the liberalization programs were themselves of major proportions. These are listed in table 10.1 and will be given particular attention in the analysis that follows.

Relaxation of Quantitative Restrictions and Changes of Tariffs

Relaxation of QRs has often been accompanied by tariff reductions but sometimes, with the intention of offsetting the initial loss of protection, it has been matched by tariff *increases*. Israel's second liberalization episode (1962–8) presents a classic case. This is probably the only instance in which the principle of full replacement of QRs by their equivalent tariffs was clearly adopted, and a period of some six years was devoted to a gradual

Table 10.1 Attributes of episodes with major relaxation of quantitative restrictions

Episode	Intensity	Sustainability	Change in tariff levels	Impact in real exchange rate
Chile 2	Strong–fast	Sustained	Lowered	Depreciation
Greece 1	Strong–fast	Sustained	Lowered	Depreciation
Indonesia 2	Strong–fast	Sustained	No change	Depreciation
Israel 1	Strong–fast	Sustained	No change	Depreciation
Israel 2	Strong–slow	Sustained	Raised	Depreciation
Philippines 1	Strong–fast	Partially sustained	Raised	Depreciation
Singapore	Strong–fast	Sustained	Raised	No change
Spain 1	Strong–slow	Partially sustained	Raised	Appreciation
Sri Lanka 2	Strong–fast	Sustained	Raised	Depreciation
Turkey 2	Strong–fast	Sustained	No change	Depreciation
Uruguay	Strong–slow	Sustained	Lowered	Depreciation

The classification system is explained in chapter 3.

transformation, involving a separate study of each item to determine the tariff equivalent of the quota. In other instances, the substitution of tariff equivalents has been less comprehensive and more rough and ready. These compensating increases of tariffs were practiced in Peru, Philippines 1, Singapore, Spain 1, and Sri Lanka 2. In all cases the relaxation of QRs was substantial, and in all but Singapore's episode a *devaluation* was undertaken and an increase of the *real* rate of exchange materialized. Thus the impact on imports of QRs was compensated for, not only by increasing tariff levels, but also by raising the real price of foreign exchange.

Has the relaxation of QRs been followed, in time, by the reduction of tariffs? Of 17 liberalization episodes where liberalization was confined first to the relaxation of QRs, four were soon reversed: these were the first attempts of Chile, Indonesia, New Zealand, and Sri Lanka. In Peru's liberalization, a major tariff reduction followed on the heels of the pervasive relaxation of QRs, but the whole experiment collapsed shortly thereafter. In five instances no tariff reduction at all took place, even after a long delay: Indonesia 2, Pakistan 1 and 2, the Philippines 1, and Sri Lanka 2. In Turkey 2, which is still in process, with QRs being gradually relaxed, a tariff reduction stage may have started.[4] In several countries the liberalization process has been persistent and consistent but very long

---

4 Some tariff changes were made in Turkey in 1984. Mostly tariffs were lowered but some have been increased, partly as compensation for removals of QRs. Altogether, some general tariff reduction has been implemented.

drawn out, with tariff reduction following the relaxation of QRs after a long delay. This characterizes the experience of Israel, in which tariff reduction started in the third liberalization phase (1969–77); New Zealand, where the persistent liberalization process started with the second episode (1962–81), and tariff reductions were introduced at the conclusion of the third episode, in the mid-1980s; and Korea, in which tariff reductions were part of the second liberalization episode (1978–9). In the case of Spain, tariff reductions did follow the relaxation of QRs in all episodes, and in the last two episodes were implemented at the same time as the QR relaxation, although the liberalization process has not been as consistent. Finally, in Greece 1 and Uruguay tariff reduction was part of the episode and in Singapore and Chile 2 tariff reductions followed quickly on the relaxation of QRs, and liberalization has become for all of them a permanent fixture.

Thus we see that where the liberalization process started with a relaxation of QRs it has either (a) been reversed (though less frequently than in other episodes); (b) not been followed at all by tariff reductions but has persisted, on its own, with no reversal; (c) been followed by tariff reductions only after a long time; or (d) on two occasions, been followed by tariff reductions with only a short interval. In short, where the initiation of a liberalization has been confined to the relaxation of QRs, it is only exceptionally that speedy tariff reduction follows.

Removal of Quantitative Restrictions and the Industrial Structure

The general pattern of removal of QRs is as follows.

1 Goods regarded as not competing with domestic production are liberalized first. "Competing" imports may never come to be liberalized at all.
2 Where removal of QRs remains incomplete, most consumer goods continue to be highly restricted. The major exceptions are goods deemed to be "essential," such as certain foodstuffs or medical supplies.
3 Raw materials, capital goods, and semiprocessed goods needed by industry are seldom viewed as competitive with local production. Where they are (for instance, for some metals or chemicals) they tend to be last in the queue for liberalization.
4 In general, no distinction is made between agricultural and manufactured products. (Exceptions are Greece 1, where manufactures as a whole tended to remain protected – though less than before – and Israel 2, where agricultural products were excluded from the process of removal of QRs.)
5 Finally, two subsectors stand out as being most often last in the order of liberalization. One is automobiles or the automotive industry in general (including other transportation equipment or parts), which are often regarded as luxuries to be restricted until late in the process, especially

when there is a domestic automotive industry. The other activity most often relegated to the end of the line is textiles – another sector that is often specially favored – which the government is reluctant to expose to competing imports.

It is not clear how beneficial the partial removal of QRs on the lines just described is likely to be. Had it involved tariffs, their reduction on primarily noncompeting intermediate and capital goods, while not affecting consumer prices, actually *increases* effective protection of the end product, and dispersion of protection, and aggravates loss in the economy.[5] The relaxation of QRs has a similar effect, but QRs are a source of loss in other ways owing to the scarcity and uncertainties they generate in the markets for imported intermediate and capital goods. The relaxation of QRs thus tends, on this score, to increase production and contract waste and losses in the economy. Undoubtedly, the replacement of QRs by *equivalent tariffs* on intermediate and capital goods would be bound to improve economic performance, but even without the impositions of such compensating tariffs the process, at this stage, may still be beneficial.

Episodes of Radical Relaxation of Quantitative Restrictions

Of the 11 episodes where there was a radical relaxation of QRs (see table 10.1) the most far reaching was probably that of Chile 2, where QRs were eliminated practically altogether within a short time. (The same was true for Singapore, but in that country the intensity of QRs before liberalization had been relatively moderate.) In terms of the intensity of the change, probably the most radical policy next to that of Chile was that of Greece 1, where a widespread network of QRs was mostly eliminated overnight. Spain 1 signaled a turning point away from QRs to a commercial policy based on price intervention. In Israel, a broad elimination of QRs was achieved in two liberalization episodes, both of them gradual and quite far apart. Liberalization in other instances – in Indonesia 2, Philippines 1, and Sri Lanka 2 – left more of the QR system intact. In the remaining instances, Turkey 2 and Uruguay, liberalization through relaxation of QRs is still in process.

Column 2 of table 10.1 indicates the intensity of the policies undertaken in these ten episodes. It should not be surprising that all the episodes in this group are characterized as strong, since QRs were the keystone of the original protective regime. What does not necessarily follow is that in the large majority of these episodes relaxation has also been fast: most often,

---

5 A process of tariff reduction that starts with the contraction of tariffs on intermediate and capital goods has not been observed in any episode. If for no other reason, this is simply due to the fact that tariffs in these categories are typically low or nonexistent to start with. Even when they are high, various systems of exemption make them low in effect.

most of the changes were implemented within a relatively short time – from an overnight change, for Greece 1, to implementation within a year or two.[6] Only in Spain 1, Israel 2, and Uruguay was implementation slow, with Israel 2, as noted before, furnishing the sole instance of an almost complete removal of QRs carried out by following predetermined rules that were implemented gradually over a substantial stretch of time.[7]

Column 3 of table 10.1 indicates the degree of *sustainability* of the ten episodes in question. The emerging pattern is remarkably clear: virtually universal survival, with the single exception of Philippines 1 in which the policy has been merely partially sustained.

The positive relationship between sustainability and the intensity of liberalization policies was noted in chapter 3. The near perfect record of sustainability of the episodes of liberalization under consideration – which obviously diverges from the mixed results of liberalization experiences as a whole – is then compared in particular with other strong policy episodes in which the element of a major removal of QRs was absent. A comparison of table 10.1 with table 3.1 (chapter 3) shows eight such other episodes altogether. Five of these episodes are characterized as both strong and fast: Argentina 2, Chile 1, Peru, Spain 3, and Yugoslavia. All have totally collapsed. Except for Spain 3 which has been partially sustained, the other three – Brazil, Colombia 2, and Israel 3 – were strong and slow. Of these, only Israel 3 has been fully sustained; in this instance QRs had practically been removed at an earlier stage. The episode of Colombia 2 was partially sustained; in Brazil the policy collapsed. The record here is not as bad as in the highly intensive (strong and fast) category of liberalization experiences, but is still mixed (especially if Israel 3 is ignored).

Altogether, the contrast is striking. In half of the 19 liberalization episodes classified as strong, a major relaxation of QRs was undertaken. These have been almost universally sustained; for the rest, survival has been the exception. Thus the positive relationship between intensity of liberalization and their sustainability can be assigned to the powerful association of the two in the category of QR-relaxing episodes. Without this category, the relationship would be *negative*. In short, a liberalization policy is likely to survive if it starts with a stage of a radical relaxation of QRs; it is likely to fail without it.

6 In Philippines 1 liberalization had actualy been planned, and pre-announced in 1960, as a rather *slow* process. It was accelerated dramatically in 1962 in an attempt to increase its chance of survival.

7 The "gradualism" here means moving from one *good* to another – removing restrictions entirely from each – rather than following intermediate steps in reducing the intensity of restriction of the imports of each good. Neither in this nor any other experience has a serious relaxation of QRs been undertaken through gradual steps to reduce the intensity of restrictions over a wide range of goods.

This inference cannot be ascribed to a coincidence of relaxation of QRs with other measures of trade policy. Column 4 of table 10.1 indicates the nature of *tariff* policy in the 11 episodes in question. In several instances no significant changes at all were made in the tariff system while the QRs were being relaxed. In four, tariffs were actually increased: these were instances of at least a partial replacement of QRs by tariffs. Only in four episodes – Chile 2, Greece 1, Singapore, and Uruguay – were tariff reductions adopted simultaneously with or soon after the relaxation of QRs. The element of tariff reduction thus cannot possibly explain the pattern in which a radical relaxation of QRs is closely associated with the sustainability of a trade policy.

More often than not, radical contraction of QRs has been followed by tariff reduction. The clearest case is that of Israel where, in the second liberalization episode (1962–8), a stage of elimination of QRs was explicitly meant to serve as an opening stage – to be followed by a stage of tariff reduction (which in fact has constituted the country's third liberalization episode (1969–77)). In other instances, tariff reductions followed without being part of a well-defined predetermined process. Sometimes, as has been noted – in Chile 2, Greece 1, Singapore, and Uruguay – tariffs were lowered simultaneously with or soon after the relaxation of QRs. In the experience of Singapore, tariff reductions started within a relatively short time. In the second Turkish episode, tariff reductions are beginning. In other instances, however, no stage of tariff contraction has been undertaken. In the Philippines 1 episode, we recall, liberalization was partially reversed. The liberalization episodes of Indonesia 2 and Sri Lanka 2 have survived for a long time – especially the former – without a follow-up stage of tariff reductions.

No clearly consistent pattern is found in the circumstances preceding major relaxation of QRs. In four cases – Chile 2, Indonesia 2, Israel 1, and Turkey 2 – the liberalization policies were undertaken following a perception of economic collapse (see table 4.1). In the case of Uruguay there was a balance-of-payments crisis, while in three other instances – Israel 2, Singapore, and Sri Lanka 2 – the balance of payments was favorable. It should be noted, though, that most of those instances in which a perception of total collapse was evident prior to liberalization belong to the category under consideration here, Argentina's second episode (1976–80) being the only exception.

While the record of sustainability of the strong QR-relaxing episodes under consideration is almost perfect – and fully accounts for the sustainability of strong liberalization experiences in general – it should *not* be inferred that a major relaxation of QRs would, by itself, guarantee survival. The foreign exchange rate policy (discussed in detail in chapter 13) was mostly conducted in the "right" way during these episodes. In most of the instances, a formal devaluation was undertaken, usually of sizable proportions: the episodes of Indonesia 2 and Singapore are the only exceptions.[8] As far as the *real* rate of foreign exchange is concerned, Singapore is the single exception to a pattern in which a depreciation, very often substantial, was the norm.

Finally, it should be observed that the liberalizations in question have led to remarkable growth. This topic has been dealt with extensively in chapter 7, but one point bears emphasis here. If the rate of growth of the economy during the first three years following the launching of a liberalization policy is compared with growth in the two years preceding liberalization, the group of strong episodes beginning with radical relaxation of QRs stands apart. The (unweighted) average *increase* of the growth rate in this group is 2.4 percent, and the median is 3.0 percent, compared with the other nine strong liberalization episodes in which the average increase is only 0.7 percent and the median is 1.0 percent. The growth performance during the weak episodes was even less impressive. The lesson is of great significance. Episodes with the most radical liberalizations, in which transitory adjustment costs might have been expected to be high, demonstrate on the contrary a remarkable increase of economic growth in the years immediately following the liberalization.[9] Undoubtedly, this also helps to explain the universal sustainability of liberalization policies launched in this form.

Changes in the Administrative Machinery of Quantitative Restrictions

In relaxing QRs, changes in the administration of the system were usually introduced. The administrative schemes devised are too varied and intricate to allow useful generalizations about the superiority of one system to another, except to note that, the more simple, universal, and predictable the regulations applied are, the smaller is the damage to the economy. Three points of detail should be noted.

1 Import quotas may be auctioned rather than assigned to importers by discretion. This was, indeed, a component of the New Zealand 2 policy.

8 In Philippines 1 a formal devaluation was indeed undertaken at the point when liberalization was greatly accelerated. Some devaluation had also been effected earlier via a mechanism of multiple exchange rates.

9 The study of Singapore investigates the effect of the tightness of QRs on production. In an intersectoral analysis in which production is dependent on several explanatory variables, one of which is the tightness of the sector's QRs, a highly significant relationship is found: the looser the restriction, the *higher* is the level of production (normalized in a given manner) of the sector. Similar findings were inferred for the levels of employment and of exports of the sector.

The shift from administrative allocation to auctioning, while retaining some of the excess damage yielded by a system of QRs, nevertheless accomplishes a substantial part of what a complete shift to tariffs would have achieved.

2 In the process of relaxation of restrictions, a stage found in some of the experiences is a switch from a "positive" to a "negative" list of imports. In the first case, all imports are prohibited except for goods or categories of goods that appear on the (positive) list. In the second case, all imports are admitted that do not appear on the negative list. Such a switch was found, for instance, in Korea 1, Pakistan 2, (in 1983, five years after the conclusion of the episode as it is defined here), Spain 2, and Turkey 2. In principle, of course, the positive and negative lists could be made exact counterparts, but even so the negative list would have the advantage of leaving future, as yet undeveloped, products free of restriction. More important, perhaps, the shift from positive to negative indicates a change in attitude: in one scheme everything is presumed to be prohibited unless specifically allowed, whereas in the other the reverse is true. A more tangible advantage of a negative list is that it facilitates the planning (and announcement) of *future* relaxation of controls, by relating the expected changes to the existing list of restrictions.

3 Wherever the administrative machinery of a QR system has been dismantled, QRs have not been reinstated. This must partly reflect the fact that the QR machinery would only have been dismantled in the context of a serious commitment to relaxation of QRs – the kind of policy that tends to insure sustainability. But it is also likely that where regulatory machinery is dismantled altogether there is less incentive, indeed a practical impediment, for the reintroduction of controls.

11

Liberalization and the Balance of Payments

In this chapter we look at the balance-of-payments position at the time when the liberalization policy is introduced; at the impact effect of the policy on the balance of payments (the change during the first year or so after the launching of the policy); and at the balance-of-payments performance at the conclusion of the episode.

First, trade liberalization appears more likely to be launched while the balance of payments is deteriorating than otherwise. In such circumstances the policy is likely to be part of a stabilization package. In any case, the initial balance-of-payments position does not seem to be consistently related to the eventual fate of a liberalization policy.

The *impact* effect of liberalization on the balance of payments appears commonly to be *favorable*. The level of foreign exchange reserves tends to increase, often replacing a prior trend of declining reserves. Exports, too, commonly react favorably, to a significant degree: either they grow much faster or, often, a decline is reversed. Imports also generally tend to increase following liberalization; but their trend appears to be closely associated with that of exports so that no balance-of-payments deterioration is evident. With so many improvements, it is not surprising that the longer-term sustainability of liberalization does *not* seem to be obviously related to the performance of the balance of payments immediately following the liberalization.

Further balance-of-payments performance does, however,

appear to be intimately related to the fate of a liberalization policy. Episodes of liberalization in which foreign exchange reserves keep rising, or at least do not fall, are most likely to be fully sustainable, whereas policy reversal is almost bound to follow a falling trend of reserves. The association, if anything, is even stronger with the trend of exports: survival of liberalization attempts accompanies a favorable export trend; dismal export performance is overwhelmingly connected with abortion of the policy. For imports, the pattern of relationship naturally follows: when imports rise while exports fall, liberalization tends to collapse; but when imports rise alongside exports, trade liberalization is sustainable.

That a strong relationship is likely to exist between the design, implementation, and fate of liberalization policy and a country's balance of payments may be taken for granted. A broad picture of some of its manifestations has already been outlined in chapter 4's depiction of clusters and trends. The relationship may be classified by posing three questions.

1 What is the balance-of-payments position when a liberalization policy is launched?
2 What, in turn, is the likely impact of the implementation of liberalization *on* the balance-of-payments performance?
3 What is the balance-of-payments position if and when liberalization is aborted, and is it likely to be typically different from the experience of liberalization attempts that are sustained?

Balance-of-payments position and performance are obviously manifested and represented by a variety of indicators, and no two episodes could conceivably be evaluated by precisely the same set of such variables. In a multi-episode synthesis such as the present one, however, we must select the strategic indicators that may be expected to play a major role and to draw much attention in most circumstances. We have selected three indicators: the level of foreign exchange reserves, export performance, and import performance. The first is the closest single representation of the overall balance-of-payments position, as well as being a variable whose movements will be of considerable concern to policymakers. Exports and imports, on the other hand, are important both as the crucial components of balance-of-payments performance and as representations of major structural changes in the economy.

The data used here differ from those provided, for somewhat different purposes, in the individual country studies. Both the inception of a liberalization policy and its reversal may be – and often was – the consequence of rather *short-term* developments; that is, of the performance of the relevant economic variables just a short time before the analyzed event. For this reason, longer-term averages may often conceal the relevant evidence. Rather than using annual data over several years (which, when tested, yielded only blurred and weak findings), we have used here monthly data for the three indicators.[1]

This form of empirical verification requires one other change from the procedures used elsewhere in the study. So far, the liberalization episodes have been defined as covering complete calendar years, as determined by the individual country authors. For the present purpose of examining short-term developments, we need to pinpoint the month in which a liberalization episode starts. Most often, the nature of the change, and its description in the country study, specify rather accurately the required point of time;[2] but where events lasting for several months indicate the launching of an episode, the midpoint of such a period has been selected as a reasonable approximation. In the small number of episodes where the evidence gives no clue to a precise turning point, the midpoint of the calendar year (June) has been selected arbitrarily as the start of the episode.[3]

---

1 The data are drawn from IMF, *International Financial Statistics*. Some of the data are seasonally adjusted, but most often they are not; since nothing in the analysis will rely on the performance during a single month, or even just two or three months, however, this is unlikely to distort the analysis appreciably. But to reduce any "noise" created by seasonality and random variations, we have used three-month moving averages rather than the original data. Another potential distortion is our use of current-price estimates: in principle, constant-prices estimates would be preferable, since quantity rather than value changes of exports and imports (but not of foreign exchange reserves!) would presumably be most relevant to decisions of policymakers. But monthly estimates of trade at constant prices are quite rare for the countries and periods on hand, and in any case the use of current-prices estimates for such brief periods is unlikely to lead to radical misreading of emerging patterns. One other limitation of monthly data is the scarcity of monthly records of transactions in services. Thus export and import figures used here inevitably refer only to trade in *goods*.

2 This, naturally, is more frequent in the strong–fast episodes than in others.

On a single occasion, this emphasis on a *point* of time has led us to define a somewhat different period for the liberalization episode. The first episode of the Philippines started very timidly in mid-1960. Only in January 1962, however, was a clear-cut policy (a major devaluation) actually undertaken. In the present context, this seems to be a preferable date for the "launching" of liberalization, and the episode is hence designated here as lasting from 1962 to 1965.

3 No attempt to determine a turning point has been made for the *end* of a liberalization episode. Unlike most beginnings, most reversals of liberalization policies appear in a more gradual fashion: liberalization episodes tend to fade away rather than face sudden death. Thus complete calendar years will still serve here to indicate the end of a liberalization period.

In the following three sections, most of the quantitative evidence will consist of the monthly data just described. These will be presented through time series figures in which the relevant turning points – beginnings or ends of liberalization episodes – will be indicated.

The Balance of Payments when Liberalization is Undertaken

A prudent policymaker might feel that the balance of payments should be healthy before a liberalization is launched, to allow for an ensuing rundown of foreign reserves if imports expand much more quickly than exports. Where this thinking has influenced decisions, we would expect to see a high initial level of foreign exchange reserves, sometimes deliberately accumulated. The expected balance-of-payments deterioration would then merely imply a slowdown of foreign exchange reserves accumulation rather than an actual decline.

But a favorable balance-of-payments position might equally lead to complacency and a reluctance to initiate policy changes. A policy shift as radical as a serious liberalization might be more likely to be undertaken when existing policies are perceived to be failing – as they certainly would be when the balance of payments is seen to be in trouble. Both initial positions for the balance of payments – healthy and unhealthy – are well represented in the 36 episodes (see chapter 4, table 4.1).

Figures 11.1–11.31 show, for all episodes for which we have data, the levels of the three variables concerned: foreign exchange reserves, exports of goods, and imports of goods. Data are presented for the year to a year and a half preceding and following the launching of liberalization; the date of launching is indicated by a vertical line.

Examining, first, the level of foreign exchange reserves, we note that about two thirds of the episodes start from a position in which these reserves had either been falling noticeably or had been stable at a level so low that there is practically no room for (gross) reserves to fall any further. This would indicate, in turn, that such liberalization policies must have been accompanied, at least at the time of launching, by an attempt at real devaluation, and are thus likely to be part of a package of stabilization policies which would include a nominal devaluation and restrictive demand policies.

No relationship can be established between the level of foreign exchange reserves on the eve of liberalization and the likelihood of the policy's eventual survival. The mix of opening positions is roughly equal in all three categories (classified by sustainability) of liberalization episodes, except that the (relatively smaller) category of "partially sustained" policies happens to include no single case in which foreign exchange reserves had been increasing before liberalization. This is a significant finding: the initial

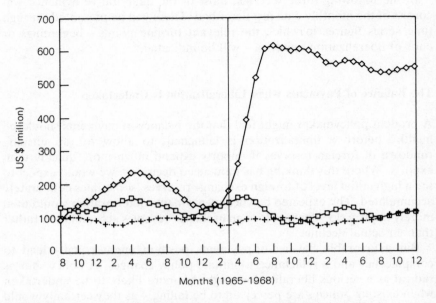

Figure 11.1 Balance of payments at the launching of liberalization: Argentina 1 (1967–1970): □, exchange reserves; +, exports; ◇, imports.

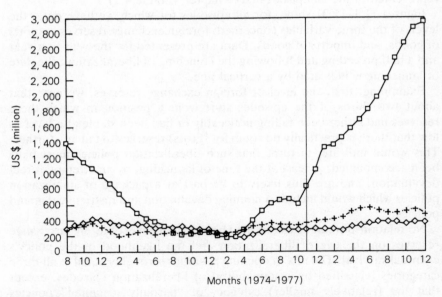

Figure 11.2 Balance of payments at the launching of liberalization: Argentina 2 (1976–1980): □, exchange reserves; +, exports; ◇, imports.

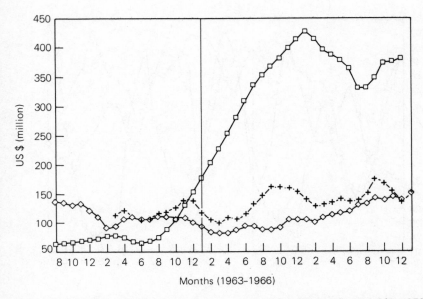

Figure 11.3 Balance of payments at the launching of liberalization: Brazil (1965–1973): □, exchange reserves; +, exports; ◇, imports.

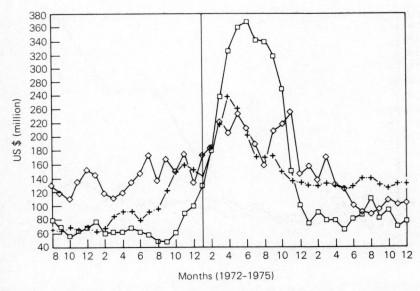

Figure 11.4 Balance of payments at the launching of liberalization: Chile 2 (1974–1981) : □, exchange reserves; +, exports; ◇, imports.

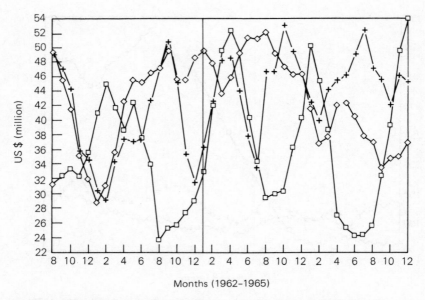

Figure 11.5 Balance of payments at the launching of liberalization: Colombia 1 (1964–1966): □, exchange reserves; +, exports; ◇, imports.

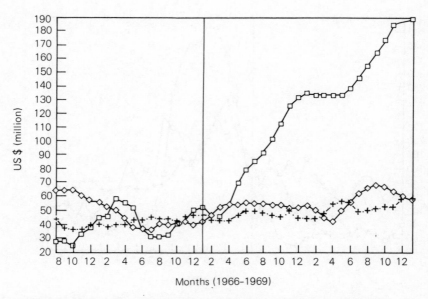

Figure 11.6 Balance of payments at the launching of liberalization: Colombia 2 (1968–1982): □, exchange reserves; +, exports; ◇, imports.

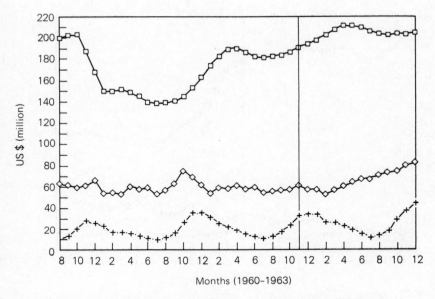

Figure 11.7 Balance of payments at the launching of liberalization: Greece 2 (1962–1982): □, exchange reserves; +, exports; ◇, imports.

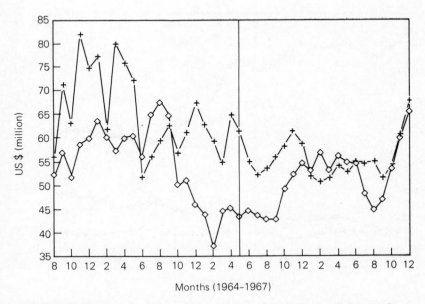

Figure 11.8 Balance of payments at the launching of liberalization: Indonesia 2 (1966–1972): +, exports; ◇, imports.

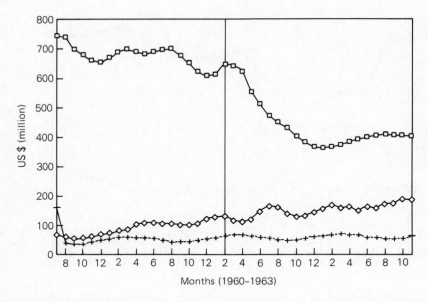

Figure 11.9 Balance of payments at the launching of liberalization: Israel 2 (1962–1968): □, exchange reserves; +, exports; ◇, imports.

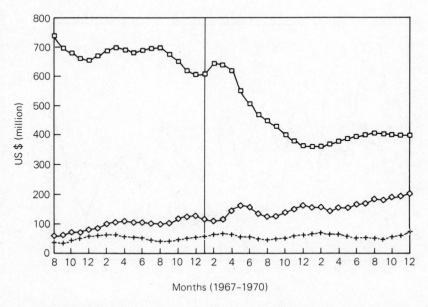

Figure 11.10 Balance of payments at the launching of liberalization: Israel 3 (1969–1977): □, exchange reserves; +, exports; ◇, imports.

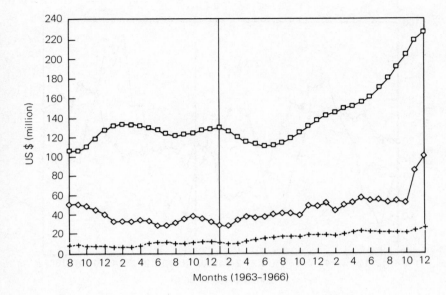

Figure 11.11 Balance of payments at the launching of liberalization: Korea 1 (1965–1967): □, exchange reserves; +, exports; ◇, imports.

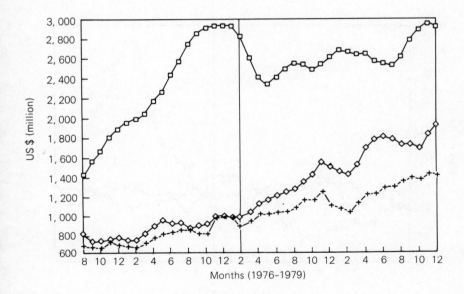

Figure 11.12 Balance of payments at the launching of liberalization: Korea 2 (1978–1979): □, exchange reserves; +, exports; ◇, imports.

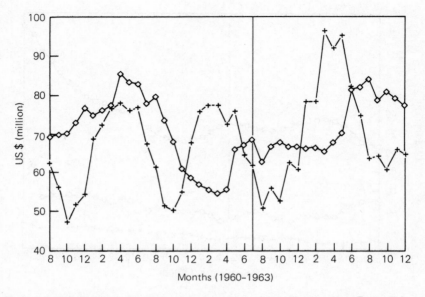

Figure 11.13 Balance of payments at the launching of liberalization: New Zealand 2 (1962–1981): +, exports; ◇, imports.

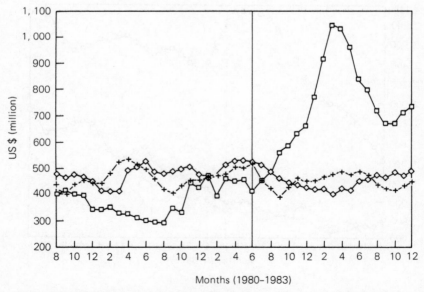

Figure 11.14 Balance of payments at the launching of liberalization: New Zealand 3 (1982–1984): □, exchange reserves; +, exports; ◇, imports.

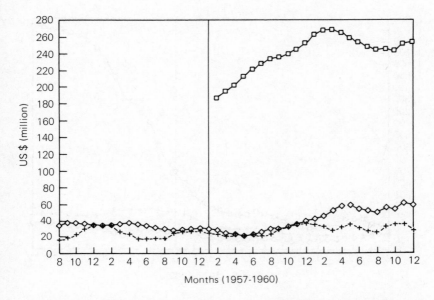

Figure 11.15 Balance of payments at the launching of liberalization: Pakistan 1 (1959–1965): □, exchange reserves; +, exports; ◇, imports.

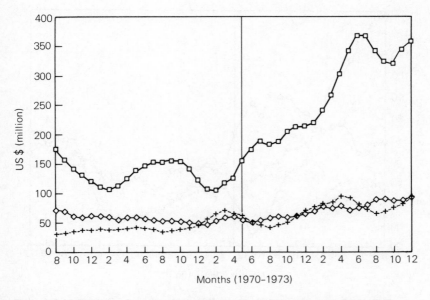

Figure 11.16 Balance of payments at the launching of liberalization: Pakistan 2 (1972–1978): □, exchange reserves; +, exports; ◇, imports.

152

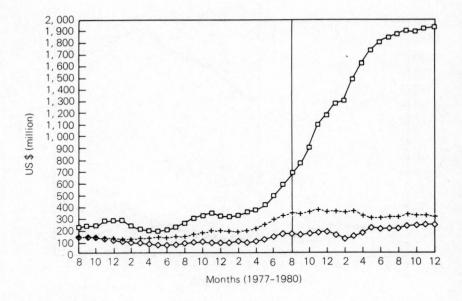

Figure 11.17 Balance of payments at the launching of liberalization: Peru (1979–1980): □, exchange reserves; +, exports; ◇, imports.

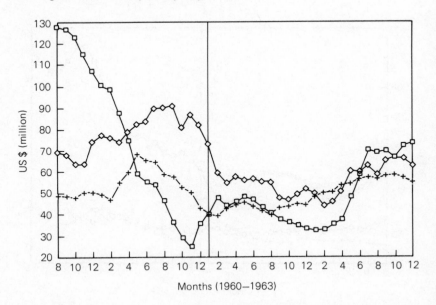

Figure 11.18 Balance of payments at the launching of liberalization: Philippines 1 (1962–1965): □, exchange reserves; +, exports; ◇, imports.

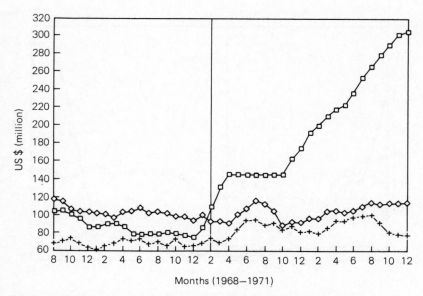

Figure 11.19 Balance of payments at the launching of liberalization: Philippines 2 (1970–1974): □, exchange reserves; +, exports; ◇, imports.

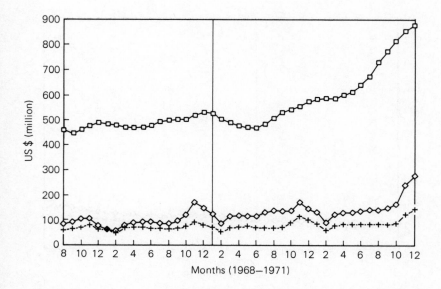

Figure 11.20 Balance of payments at the launching of liberalization: Portugal 1 (1970–1974): □, exchange reserves; +, exports; ◇, imports.

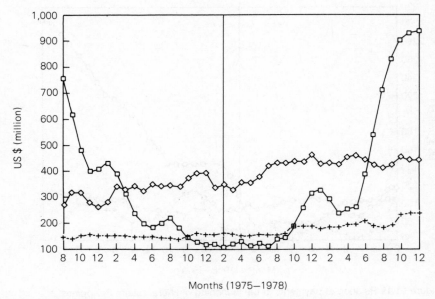

Figure 11.21 Balance of payments at the launching of liberalization: Portugal 2 (1977–1980): □, exchange reserves; +, exports; ◇, imports.

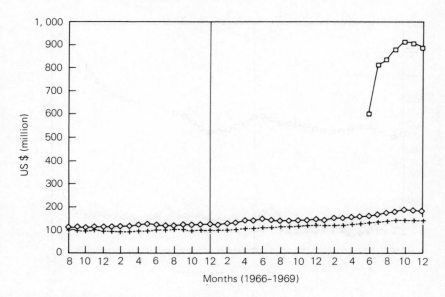

Figure 11.22 Balance of payments at the launching of liberalization: Singapore (1968–1973): □, exchange reserves; +, exports; ◇, imports.

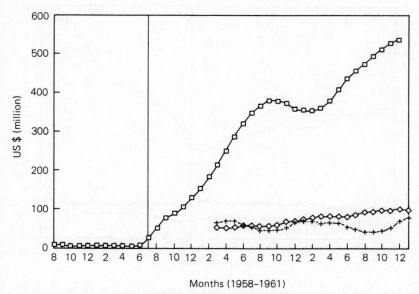

Months (1958–1961)

Figure 11.23 Balance of payments at the launching of liberalization: Spain 1 (1960–1966): □, exchange reserves; +, exports; ◇, imports.

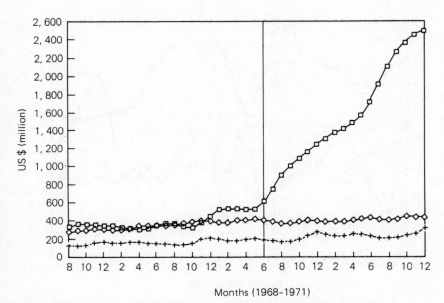

Months (1968–1971)

Figure 11.24 Balance of payments at the launching of liberalization: Spain 2 (1970–1974): □, exchange reserves; +, exports; ◇, imports.

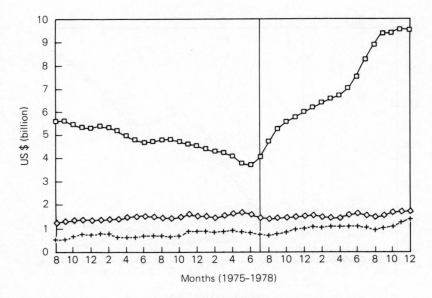

Figure 11.25 Balance of payments at the launching of liberalization: Spain 3 (1977–1980): □, exchange reserves; +, exports; ◇, imports.

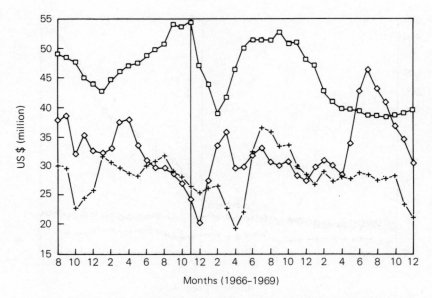

Figure 11.26 Balance of payments at the launching of liberalization: Sri Lanka 1 (1968–1970): □, exchange reserves; +, exports; ◇, imports.

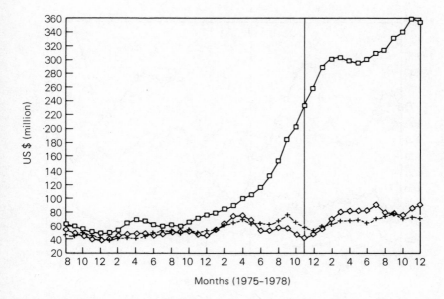

Figure 11.27 Balance of payments at the launching of liberalization: Sri Lanka 2 (1977–1979): □, exchange reserves; +, exports; ◇, imports.

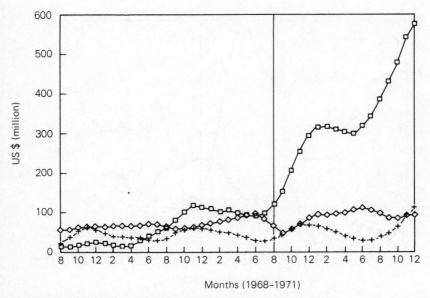

Figure 11.28 Balance of payments at the launching of liberalization: Turkey 1 (1970–1973): □, exchange reserves; +, exports; ◇, imports.

158

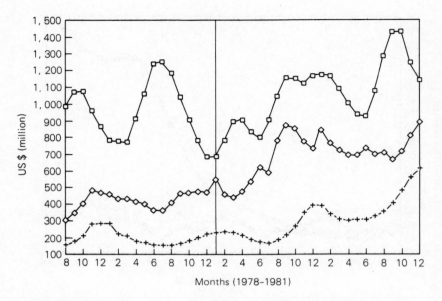

Figure 11.29 Balance of payments at the launching of liberalization: Turkey 2 (1980–1984): □, exchange reserves; +, exports; ◇, imports.

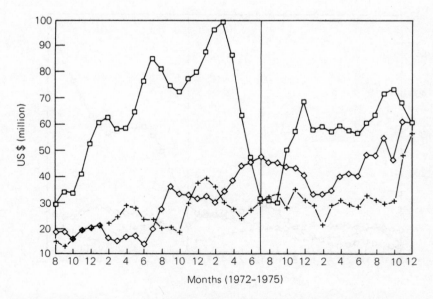

Figure 11.30 Balance of payments at the launching of liberalization: Uruguay (1974–1982): □, exchange reserves; +, exports; ◇, imports.

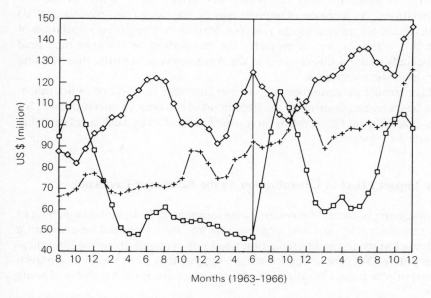

Figure 11.31 Balance of payments at the launching of liberalization: Yugoslavia (1965–1967): □, exchange reserves; +, exports; ◇, imports.

position of the balance of payments (judged by the level of foreign exchange reserves or changes therein) does not appear to have a role in the eventual fate of the policy.

Turning our attention to exports, the outcome is somewhat surprising. An opening position in which foreign exchange levels were deteriorating might have been expected to be one in which export performance too was deteriorating. But of all liberalization episodes, in only two (Argentina 2 and Indonesia 2) were exports actually declining before liberalization (although the Indonesian trade data, reflecting only *legal* exports, are not quite reliable as an indicator). Export performance before the liberalization episode does seem to have some association with its survival: in most of the instances in which exports were initially increasing, policy did survive. But since exports were seldom in decline preceding the launching of liberalization, this association is rather weak – unlike, as we shall see, the role played by *post*-liberalization longer-term export performance in deciding the fate of liberalization.

For import performance prior to liberalization, no regularity could be discerned. Imports are about as likely to have been increasing, on the eve of liberalization, as to have been falling or to have exhibited no time trend of much significance. Falling or low foreign exchange reserves are equally likely to be associated with increasing as with declining imports. Presumably, the causation may run either way, giving rise to either of the two associations. An increase of imports may be the cause (exclusive or partial) of declining foreign exchange reserves, leading to a negative association of the two variables; or, conversely, the exhaustion of reserves may lead (especially under a QR regime) to the contraction of imports, thus yielding the opposite association.

Like export performance, import performance on the eve of liberalization bears no relationship to the likelihood of the policy's survival. Nor, for that matter, can we establish on *a priori* grounds why such a relationship should be expected.

The Impact Effect of Liberalization on the Balance of Payments

In observing balance-of-payments developments following the launching of liberalization, the *post hoc, ergo propter hoc* fallacy should be avoided: a process following the liberalization need not originate from the liberalization policy. Yet, the evidence would suggest that the change in environment, of which the liberalization policy was a part, must have played some role.

We see, first (figures 11.1–11.31), that in most episodes levels of foreign exchange reserves tended to increase following the launching of liberalization policies. In several instances no trend is apparent. Only in Korea 2 and Israel 3 did foreign exchange reserves actually decline; and in the case of Israel 3 no impact effect could conceivably be attributed to liberalization since that episode was launched by a very gradual process of tariff reduction.[4]

In most of these instances, accumulation of foreign exchange reserves replaced a balance-of-payments deterioration preceding the liberalization. Thus these liberalizations (often part of a stabilization package) normally improved rather than damaged the balance of payments. With this almost universal pattern, it inevitably appears that the *impact* effect of liberalization on the balance of payments does not seem to have played a role in determining the eventual fate of the policy: the eventual survival of a liberalization policy seems unrelated to whether or not the balance of payments improved immediately after the liberalization was launched. This "negative" finding is of substantial significance, for *later* balance-of-payments developments, as we shall see, were crucial for the fate of liberalization attempts.

---

4 Basically the balance-of-payments deterioration in Israel at that time was partly the direct result of a just concluded war and partly the consequence of a strong revival of economic activity after a deep recession and its impact on the size of imports.

A clear pattern of response also emerges for *export* performance:[5] in about two thirds of the episodes, it showed a definite rising trend in the period immediately following the launching of the policy.[6] In no case did exports actually decline. In most cases, the rising trend was an improvement over export performance before liberalization. In only three episodes had exports actually been falling before liberalization (in Argentina 2, Chile 2, and Indonesia 2); and of these, in two (Argentina and Chile) exports started to expand following the liberalization, whereas in the third (Indonesia) the falling trend of exports was halted rather than reversed (and may merely reflect a shift from illegal to legal exports). Moreover, in ten liberalization episodes the expansion followed a pre-liberalization stagnation of exports, whereas in only two cases (Philippines 1 and Uruguay) did the reverse occur – a change from a rising pre-liberalizing trend to stagnation following it. It thus seems clear that export performance generally improves following the introduction of a liberalization policy (mostly, again, in conjunction with a stabilization policy).

In most instances in which the foreign exchange position improved, export performance too appears to have improved, most often in the form of a reversal from contraction to expansion of exports. A very strong association thus seems to exist between the improvement of export performance and the overall improvement of the country's balance of payments following the launching of a liberalization policy.

But the evidence is not so clear about whether the impact effect of liberalization on export performance is significant in determining the policy's eventual fate. Export performance tends to improve less often following liberalization in episodes that are eventually reversed than in those that partially or fully survive. But the difference is too small to permit more than a suspicion that the impact effect of liberalization on exports may influence its eventual survival.[7]

The pattern of response of *imports* to the introduction of liberalization roughly resembles that of exports. In about half of the liberalization episodes, imports tended to increase following the liberalization. In most

5 Here, only the *immediate* response of exports is examined: the next chapter is devoted to a more extensive analysis of the impact of liberalization on export performance.

6 On occasion this must have been at least partly due to a shift from unrecorded to recorded exports following a devaluation. See chapter 12 for a discussion.

7 A caveat should be entered here that applies also to the role of the performance of foreign exchange reserves in determining sustainability. Since our "liberalization episodes" include, by definition, only those in which liberalization survived for at least two years, a bias is introduced into the observations: it is conceivable that inadequate export or balance-of-payments performance immediately after the introduction of liberalization did appear occasionally and that it *was* important in leading to an abortion of the policy within a short time – short enough to prevent such a case from being studied as a liberalization episode in our analysis.

of the other episodes no trend appears, either upward or downward, whereas in only four episodes did imports actually tend to decline. Put differently: in about half the episodes no change in trend from the period just preceding the liberalization policy appears to have taken place. In the other half, however, almost all trend changes were *upward* – either a change from a stagnant level of imports to a rising one, or a reversal of a downward trend to stability or to an upward trend.

Particularly noticeable for the impact increase of imports were the liberalization experiences in which the relaxation of QRs was major. For three of the 11 episodes, the required data were not available. Of the other eight, in six a very strong increase of imports is evident following the liberalization. The two exceptions were Philippines 1, in which imports fell substantially, and Israel 2, in which only a "normal" increase of imports was evident (but in this case, it should be noticed, the implementation of the removal of QRs was a rather long process). This relationship may be expected: the existence of a comprehensive system of QRs must lead to a large pent-up demand for imports, with a "correction" taking place once the restrictions are removed.

In almost all instances in which imports demonstrated an upward trend following the liberalization, exports did the same (the only exception being New Zealand 3 in which no trend is discernible). Probably because of this strong association, no relationship that would signify an effect of imports on foreign exchange reserves seems to have existed between the trend increases of imports and the changes in the reserves analyzed earlier. Such an association of the two would of course require the predominance of cases with changes of opposite signs of these two magnitudes (increased imports associated with falling foreign exchange reserves, and vice versa). In effect, however, we have seen that very few episodes occur either of falling exchange reserves or of falling imports, so that not much coincidence of the two variables in the required direction is possible. Imports did exhibit an upward trend in the only two instances in which foreign exchange reserves were falling (Israel 3 and Korea 2). But besides being a minor exception, in Israel at least the increased imports bore practically no relation to the introduction of a new stage of liberalization policy. Thus the notion that trade liberalization may be aborted by its impact on the balance of payments through the ensuing import expansion finds no support in the pattern of actual experience: no *single* case of liberalization represents a response along these lines.[8]

As with the behavior of foreign exchange reserves and of exports, the impact response of imports appears to bear no relation to the final fate of a liberalization attempt: the incidence of the various trends of change is roughly similar in the various categories of survival.

8 But recall, again, the bias involved in our delineation of liberalization episodes.

In sum, the *impact* effect of liberalizations on the balance of payments and on its major elements seems not to have been crucial in determining the durability of trade liberalization experiences.

Balance-of-payments Performance and Policy Reversals

Whereas no relationship could be established between the immediate balance-of-payments performance and the fate of a liberalization, examination of the eventual performance of the balance of payments shows a clear relationship. As in the previous analysis, the basic data (drawn from IMF, *International Financial Statistics*, and presented in a diagrammatic form in figures 11.32–11.63) are *monthly* data of the three balance-of-payments variables involved, using a three months moving average to smooth out accidental fluctuations. Each country figure terminates with the end of the respective liberalization episode, that is, the end of the calendar year specified by the respective author as the last year of the episode.[9]

Table 11.1 cross-classifies all liberalization episodes by two dimensions. One is the performance ("increase," "no trend," or "decrease") of the analyzed variable (foreign exchange reserves, exports, and imports)

Table 11.1 Sustainability of liberalization episodes and external performance

Category of liberalization episode	Trend change of performance variable before end of episode			
	Increase	No trend	Decrease	Total
Foreign exchange reserves				
Sustained	6	5	2	13
Partially sustained	2	3	3	8
Collapsed	0	3	8	11
Total	8	11	13	32
Exports				
Sustained	6	7	0	13
Partially sustained	3	3	2	8
Collapsed	0	3	7	10
Total	9	13	9	31
Imports				
Sustained	8	4	1	13
Partially sustained	2	4	2	8
Collapsed	7	2	1	10
Total	17	10	4	31

9 This is obviously not identical with the treatment accorded earlier to the *introduction* of a liberalization episode, for the reasons discussed in note 3.

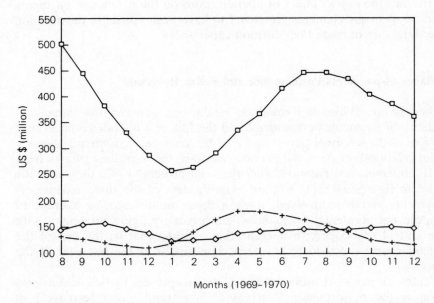

Figure 11.32 Balance of payments at the close of liberalization: Argentina 1 (1967–1970):
□, exchange reserves; +, exports; ◇, imports.

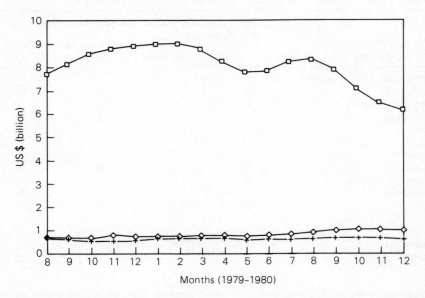

Figure 11.33 Balance of payments at the close of liberalization: Argentina 2 (1976–1980):
□, exchange reserves; +, exports; ◇, imports.

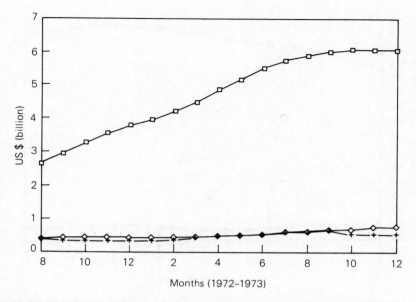

Figure 11.34 Balance of payments at the close of liberalization: Brazil (1965–1973): □, exchange reserves; +, exports; ◇, imports.

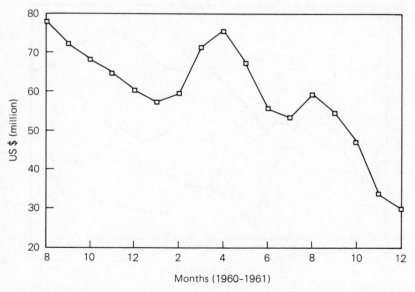

Figure 11.35 Balance of payments at the close of liberalization: Chile 1 (1956–1961): □, exchange reserves.

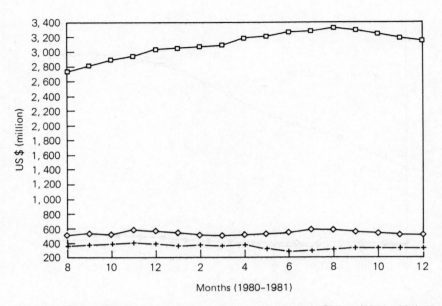

Figure 11.36 Balance of payments at the close of liberalization: Chile 2 (1974–1981): □, exchange reserves; +, exports; ◇, imports.

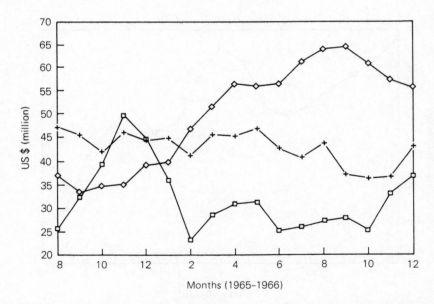

Figure 11.37 Balance of payments at the close of liberalization: Colombia 1 (1964–1966): □, exchange reserves; +, exports; ◇, imports.

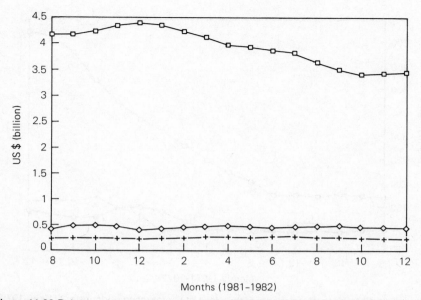

Figure 11.38 Balance of payments at the close of liberalization: Colombia 2 (1968–1982): □, exchange reserves; +, exports; ◇, imports.

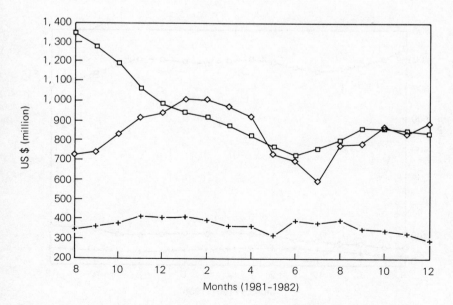

Figure 11.39 Balance of payments at the close of liberalization: Greece 2 (1962–1982): □, exchange reserves; +, exports; ◇, imports.

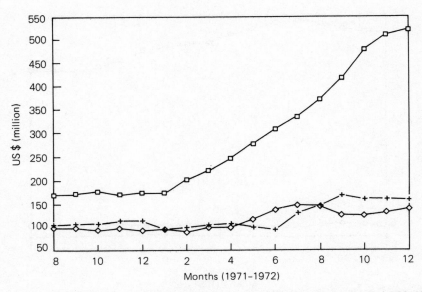

Figure 11.40 Balance of payments at the close of liberalization: Indonesia 2 (1966–1972): □, exchange reserves; +, exports; ◇, imports.

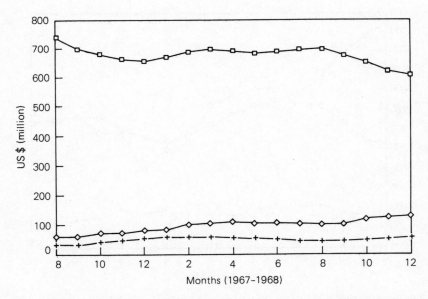

Figure 11.41 Balance of payments at the close of liberalization: Israel 2 (1962–1968): □, exchange reserves; +, exports; ◇, imports.

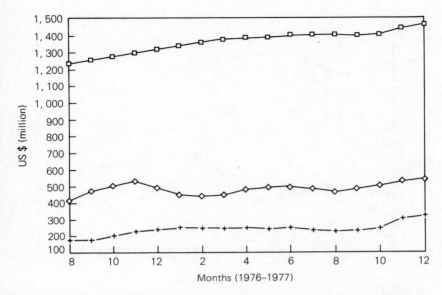

Figure 11.42 Balance of payments at the close of liberalization: Israel 3 (1969–1977): □, exchange reserves; +, exports; ◇, imports.

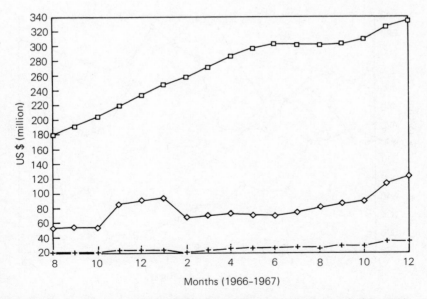

Figure 11.43 Balance of payments at the close of liberalization: Korea 1 (1965–1967): □, exchange reserves; +, exports; ◇, imports.

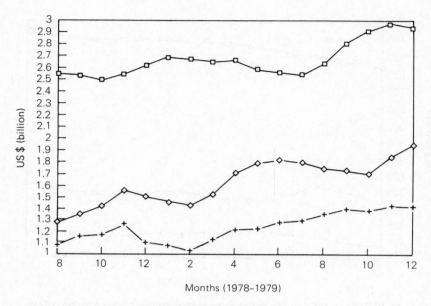

Figure 11.44 Balance of payments at the close of liberalization: Korea 2 (1978–1979): □, exchange reserves; +, exports; ◇, imports.

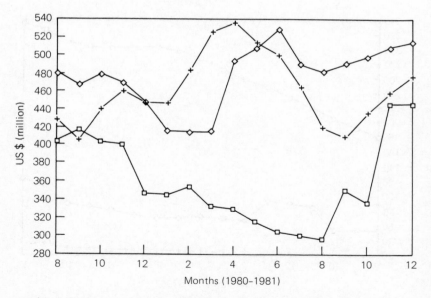

Figure 11.45 Balance of payments at the close of liberalization: New Zealand 2 (1962–1981): □, exchange reserves; +, exports; ◇, imports.

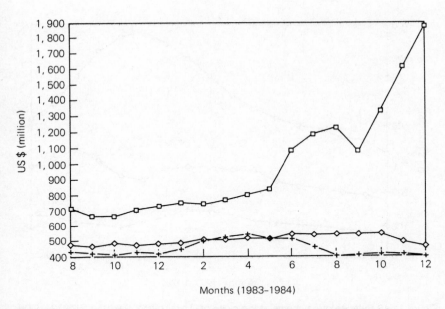

Figure 11.46 Balance of payments at the close of liberalization: New Zealand 3 (1982–1984): □, exchange reserves; +, exports; ◇, imports.

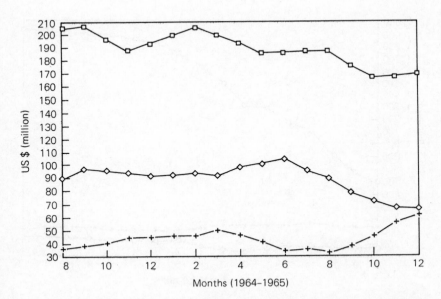

Figure 11.47 Balance of payments at the close of liberalization: Pakistan 1 (1959–1965): □, exchange reserves; +, exports; ◇, imports.

172

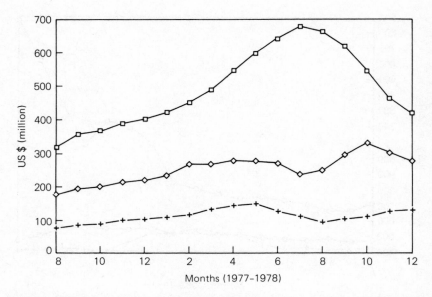

Figure 11.48 Balance of payments at the close of liberalization: Pakistan 2 (1972–1978): □, exchange reserves; +, exports; ◇, imports.

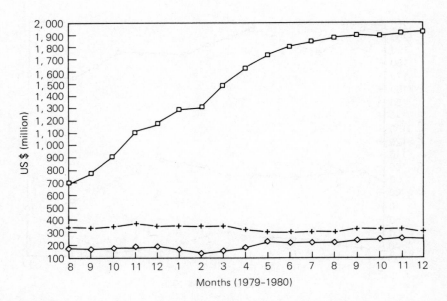

Figure 11.49 Balance of payments at the close of liberalization: Peru (1979–1980): □, exchange reserves; +, exports; ◇, imports.

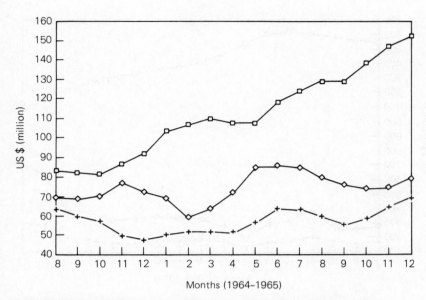

Figure 11.50 Balance of payments at the close of liberalization: Philippines 1 (1962–1965): □, exchange reserves; +, exports; ◇, imports.

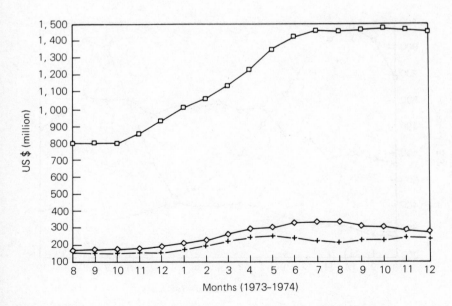

Figure 11.51 Balance of payments at the close of liberalization: Philippines 2 (1970–1974): □, exchange reserves; +, exports; ◇, imports.

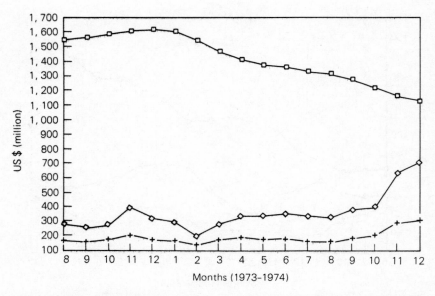

Figure 11.52 Balance of payments at the close of liberalization: Portugal 1 (1970–1974): □, exchange reserves; +, exports; ◇, imports.

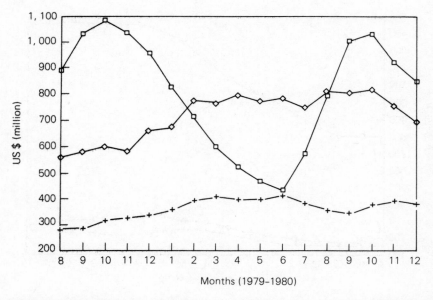

Figure 11.53 Balance of payments at the close of liberalization: Portugal 2 (1977–1980): □, exchange reserves; +, exports; ◇, imports.

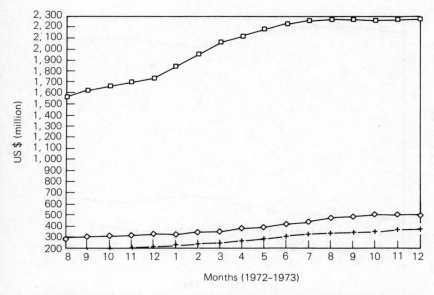

Figure 11.54 Balance of payments at the close of liberalization: Singapore (1968–1973): □, exchange reserves; +, exports; ◇, imports.

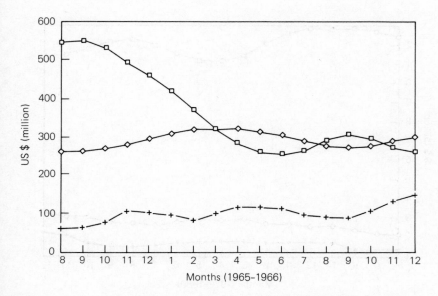

Figure 11.55 Balance of payments at the close of liberalization: Spain 1 (1960–1966): □, exchange reserves; +, exports; ◇, imports.

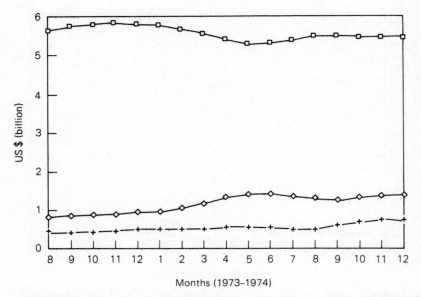

Figure 11.56 Balance of payments at the close of liberalization: Spain 2 (1970–1974): □, exchange reserves; +, exports; ◇, imports.

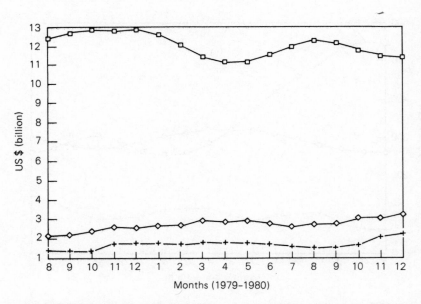

Figure 11.57 Balance of payments at the close of liberalization: Spain 3 (1977–1980): □, exchange reserves; +, exports; ◇, imports.

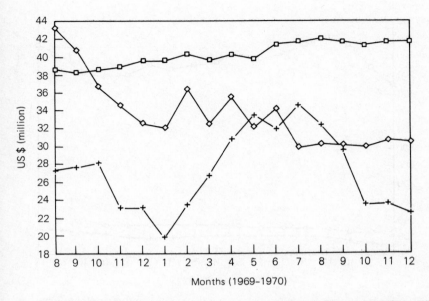

Figure 11.58 Balance of payments at the close of liberalization: Sri Lanka 1 (1968–1970): □, exchange reserves; +, exports; ◇, imports.

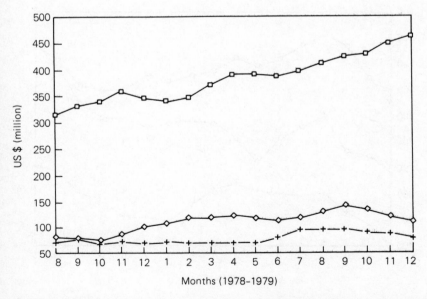

Figure 11.59 Balance of payments at the close of liberalization: Sri Lanka 2 (1977–1979): □, exchange reserves; +, exports; ◇, imports.

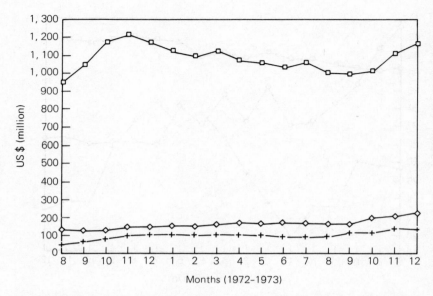

Figure 11.60 Balance of payments at the close of liberalization: Turkey 1 (1970–1973): □, exchange reserves; +, exports; ◇, imports.

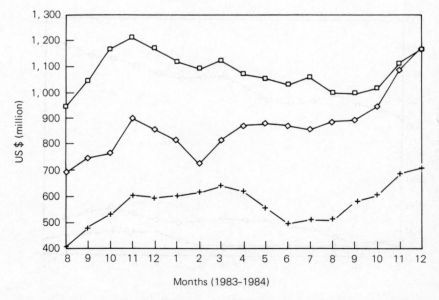

Figure 11.61 Balance of payments at the close of liberalization: Turkey 2 (1980–1984): □, exchange reserves; +, exports; ◇, imports.

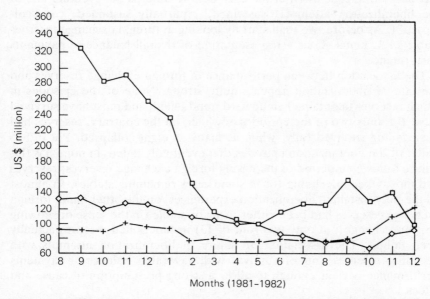

Figure 11.62 Balance of payments at the close of liberalization: Uruguay (1974–1982): □, exchange reserves; +, exports; ◇, imports.

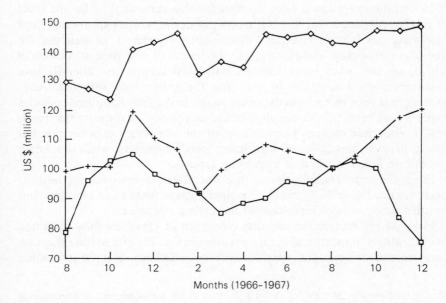

Figure 11.63 Balance of payments at the close of liberalization: Yugoslavia (1965–1967): □, exchange reserves; +, exports; ◇, imports.

just before the conclusion of the episode; the other is the eventual fate of the liberalization attempt ("sustained," "partially sustained," or "collapsed"). As before, we shall start by looking at foreign exchange reserves (table 11.1, panel A) as a representation of overall balance-of-payments performance.[10]

The association between performance of foreign exchange reserves and the fate of liberalization appears quite strong. None of the episodes in which reserves maintained an upward trend failed, and most have survived fully. But only two of the episodes in which, on the contrary, reserves had been falling survived fully, while as many as eight collapsed. Put differently: of the liberalization episodes that eventually failed, in none has this failure followed a period of increasing foreign exchange reserves; reserves had mostly been declining (or in some cases remaining stable). In almost all the fully sustained liberalization experiences, on the other hand, foreign exchange reserves had been either rising or stable (in the sense of showing no trend change); in only two (out of 13) instances had reserves actually been falling. The association of failure of liberalization attempts with declining reserves and of survival with favorable balance-of-payments performance is clear enough to allow a strong presumption of cause and effect.

The presumption is reinforced by the association observed for export performance (table 11.1, panel B); if anything, the association with the failure of liberalization is even stronger for this variable than for the level of foreign exchange reserves. Of nine episodes in which exports had kept increasing, six fully survived and three partially survived; in none did the liberalization policy completely fail. In seven of the nine instances in which, on the other hand, exports had been falling, the liberalization experiences collapsed; and in none has the policy fully survived. And, looking at it once more from the other angle, in the fully sustained episodes exports had been (about equally) either increasing or showing no trend, and in none had exports been falling; of the ten policy experiences that failed, in seven this followed a declining trend of exports, while in no case did failure follow a trend of increasing exports.

From the cross-classification of the liberalization episodes for *imports* performance (table 11.1, panel C) a clear pattern once more emerges, but not this time a simple repetition of the earlier inferences.

First, we see that, in the majority (eight out of 13) of the fully sustained liberalizations, imports had been increasing before the end of liberalization (only in one episode had they actually been falling). But an increasing

10 The total number of episodes shown falls short of the actual number of liberalization episodes analyzed in this project, and varies slightly among the panels of table 11.1 owing to incompleteness of the available data.

trend of imports, on the eve of the policy collapse, is equally prevalent in failed episodes.

The contradiction is more apparent than real: imports could rise together with exports; or rising imports could accompany *falling* exports. Where the first association holds, liberalization policy tends to survive: the economy is becoming increasingly open, with a trade balance being roughly maintained. But rising imports accompanying falling exports (both tendencies being due, presumably, to a common factor, such as an expansion of local demand or a fall of the real exchange rate), should be a natural prescription for failure of the liberalization policy. Indeed, in most of the (seven) episodes where collapse followed a rising trend of imports, exports had been falling and the level of foreign exchange reserves had also been dropping. These were clear instances of deterioration of the balance-of-payments performance.

Though the data on which we have based our inferences are different from those provided in the separate country studies, the inferences themselves are commonly and strongly shared with those reached by the authors from their respective country experiences. In most of the relevant cases the individual authors have assigned the collapse of a liberalization episode to a prior deterioration of the external transactions. In 14 of the 19 countries studied in this project, complete or partial reversals of one liberalization attempt or more have taken place (the five exceptions being Greece, Israel, Korea, Singapore, and Uruguay). For eight of the 14 countries (Argentina, Brazil, Chile, Pakistan, Peru, the Philippines, Portugal, and Spain) the authors concluded that a balance-of-payments deficit led to the abortion of the policy; without such a crisis of the balance of payments, liberalization is likely to be sustained even when faced with other economic hardships. In Yugoslavia the balance-of-payments situation is inferred to be significant, but only alongside several other criteria of performance. In the study of Colombia a "razor's edge" inference is suggested: a severe balance-of-payments deficit is detrimental to the sustainability of liberalization; but so also is a large surplus (due usually, in that country, to improvements of the terms of trade), which through its impact on the real exchange rate is likely to lead to the contraction of tradeable activities and to pressures for protection.

Of the five countries in which no reversals of liberalization policies have taken place, in only one, Israel, would such reversal be called for had the fate of liberalization been decided by the balance-of-payments position. This country did appear, in our earlier observations, to be an exception. Indeed, Israel is the only country study in which the authors have concluded explicitly that the balance-of-payments performance has *not* played a role in determining the sustainability of liberalization.

In sum, we conclude that an intimate relationship exists between the balance-of-payments position, in particular the performance of exports, and the longer-term sustainability of a liberalization policy. In the next few chapters we shall see what factors or policies are likely to determine, in turn, the course of performance of the country's external transactions during a liberalization experience.

12

Export Growth and Export Promotion

This chapter provides strong evidence that correlates trade
liberalization with an appreciable increase in the export
growth rate. Strong growth is seen immediately in the year
of liberalization, and even more in later years. This growth,
in turn, correlates with the depreciation of the real exchange
rate. But we found no correlation between export incentive
policies and export growth during or before liberalization.
Striking evidence emerges about the pernicious effects of
severe import restrictions on exports and the extraordinarily
large positive impact their removal has on export growth.

In this chapter we examine exports during trade liberalization. We
investigate whether trade liberalization affects export performance appreciably. In the examination we attempt to discover what empirical regularities link trade liberalization and export growth, what export incentives
contribute to export growth, and how changes in the real exchange rate
relate to changes in export growth.

The Relevance of Export Growth

Why is export growth relevant to trade liberalization? What policy lessons
can we derive if we establish strong empirical regularities in the data? After
all, export growth does not mean improved welfare. Perhaps the most
compelling reason for analyzing export performance during liberalization
is the widespread fear that trade liberalization leads inevitably to the
depletion of the country's foreign reserves. According to this fear, sluggish
export response follows trade liberalization. Does the evidence support
these conclusions? Is there any empirical basis to suspect that trade

liberalization leads to serious balance-of-payments problems? Do exports respond sluggishly, and for a long time, to the improved environment for the tradeables sector?

In chapter 11 we observed the performance of imports and exports as they affect developments in the balance of payments suggesting that trade liberalization is not responsible for balance-of-payments crises. Further emphasized was the importance of accelerating export growth rates for maintaining external stability after liberalization. In this chapter we analyze in more detail export performance before and after liberalization highlighting the empirical relation between exports and trade liberalization.

Considerable speculation exists that the supply response of developing countries for exports is sluggish in the short run. Empirical support for this claim would diminish immediate welfare gains from a trade liberalization. The change in relative prices of the liberalization policies would not generate growth in exportables. They would simply produce rents for export producers in the short run. No resource reallocation to the export sector would be observed after trade is liberalized. But in chapter 7 we find higher GDP growth, in general, and of the tradeables, agricultural, and manufacturing sectors, in particular, after liberalization compared with before. These higher post-liberalization rates point to the potential for a strong increase in exports, which in turn suggests that trade liberalization does not necessarily lead to a balance-of-payments crisis.

Thus our interest in trade liberalization focuses on export growth, the contribution of export incentives and the real exchange rate (RER) to that growth, and the factors associated with trade liberalization leading to a balance-of-payments crisis and therefore to a reversal of liberalization.

Definition and Data

Evidence linking export performance and trade liberalization covers 31 episodes. Real export growth rates included are based on annual export data in constant terms (except for the first trade liberalization of Greece, for which export growth rates were calculated from data in current US dollars). Export growth rates were calculated in three ways: first, for each of the three years before the year of the trade liberalization; second, for the year of the trade liberalization; and third, for each of the three years following the year of the liberalization. We present aggregate data on export growth rates for the 31 episodes, and for groups of episodes according to the liberalization's intensity (strong or weak), the conditions before liberalization (severely restricted trade regime or moderately restricted trade regime), and, finally, according to the outcome of liberalization (survived or failed) (table 12.1). For these classifications we present

Table 12.1 Classification of trade liberalization episodes[a]

| Episode | Attributes | | | | | |
	Strong	Weak	Sustained	Collapsed	Severe restriction	Moderate restriction
Argentina 1		X		X	X	
Argentina 2	X			X	X	
Brazil	X			X	X	
Chile 1	X			X	X	
Chile 2	X		X		X	
Colombia 2	X			X[b]		X
Greece 1	X		X		X	
Greece 2		X	X			X
Indonesia 2	X		X		X	
Israel 2	X		X			X
Israel 3	X		X			X
Korea 1		X	X			X
Korea 2		X	X			X
New Zealand 2		X	X		X	
New Zealand 3		X	X		X	
Pakistan 1		X		X[b]		X
Pakistan 2		X		X[b]		X
Peru	X			X[b]	X	
Philippines 1	X			X[b]	X	
Philippines 2		X		X[b]		X
Portugal 1		X		X[b]		X
Portugal 2		X		X[b]	X	
Spain 1	X		X[b]		X	
Spain 2		X	X[b]			X
Spain 3	X		X[b]			X
Sri Lanka 1		X		X	X	
Sri Lanka 2	X		X		X	
Turkey 1		X		X	X	
Turkey 2	X		X		X	
Uruguay	X		X		X	
Yugoslavia	X			X	X	
Total	17	14	16	15	19	12

[a] Includes only those episodes for which comparable export data are available.
[b] These episodes are classified as *partially* sustained in chapter 3.

the export growth rates for the seven years in the analysis, the average annually compounded growth rate before liberalization, and two comparable average rates after liberalization – one including the year when the trade liberalization took place and the other excluding it.

We present these two-part post-liberalization averages in order to isolate the probable effects of capital flight before the liberalization. In many cases, as overvalued official exchange rates prevail on the eve of trade liberalization, exports are underinvoiced in anticipation of official devaluation or to sell proceeds from exports in the black market of foreign exchange. Underinvoicing will become less compelling following trade liberalization if the official exchange rate is devalued substantially. Moreover, illegally accumulated holdings of foreign exchange will probably be partially repatriated with the realization of the anticipated devaluation. As a result, unusually high recorded exports may be observed in the year of trade liberalization – higher than in the year before liberalization even if the real export level does not change.[1] As a result, to gauge trade liberalization's true effect on real export growth, we contrast average real export growth rates between the periods of pre- and post-liberalization, excluding the year of liberalization, and distinguish them from capital movements.

To prevent a few large exporters in our sample – such as Korea or Brazil – from distorting the average rates of export growth, we computed the rates for all the aggregates using simple averages unweighted by export size. But we may have introduced another bias: the aggregates may be affected disproportionately by few episodes with uncharacteristically high or low (or negative) export growth rates. But our analysis in appendix A2 does not establish any such bias in our findings.

To analyze the relation between export growth rates and export incentives, and export growth rates and changes in the RER we constructed quantitative indices of the trade liberalization episodes for these four variables (table 12.2). Specifically, export incentives must be in place when the real effective exchange rate of exports (REERx) is devalued more than the formal RER. Again, we divided the seven years of data into three periods: the three years before the trade liberalization, the trade liberalization year, and the three years after liberalization. To capture changes in the relative intensity of export promotion within and between periods, we assume that if the difference between the REERx and RER was increasing in any period with REERx > RER, then the period has relatively intensified export incentives. If the difference was decreasing, the period has relatively reduced export incentives. For REERx < RER the periods are reversed. Finally, if we observe no noticeable changes between these two variables within the period, we classify the period as unchanged with respect to export incentives.

In one episode – Sri Lanka 2 – the export incentive policies before liberalization disappear during the liberalization and reappear after it. In

1 These capital inflows are welcomed for balance-of-payments purposes and should be counted as important benefits of trade liberalization.

Table 12.2 Trade liberalization and export incentives: some qualitative characteristics[a]

Beginning of episode	Export incentives in place[b]	Relative change in export incentives[c]	RER at trade liberalization[d]
Argentina 1 1967			
Periods: Before[e]	No	*	—
During	No	*	Deprec.+
Post	No	*	—
Argentina 2 1976			
Periods: Before	No	*	—
During	No	*	Deprec.+
Post	No	*	—
Brazil 1965			
Periods: Before	n.a.	n.a.	—
During	Yes	+	Apprec.
Post	Yes	+	—
Chile 1 1956			
Periods: Before	No	Unchanged	—
During	No	Unchanged	Deprec.+
Post	No	Unchanged	—
Chile 2 1974			
Periods: Before	Yes	*	—
During	Yes	*	Deprec.+
Post	Yes	*	—
Colombia 2 1968			
Periods: Before	Yes	Unchanged	—
During	Yes	Unchanged	Deprec.
Post	Yes	+	—
Greece 1 1953			
Periods: Before	Yes	+	—
During	Yes	*	Deprec.+
Post	Yes	Unchanged	—
Greece 2 1962			
Periods: Before	Yes	Unchanged	—
During	Yes	+	Deprec.
Post	Yes	+	—
Israel 2 1962			
Periods: Before	Yes	+	—
During	No[f]	*	Deprec.+
Post	No[f]	Unchanged	—

Table 12.2 *(cont'd)*

Beginning of episode	Export incentives in place[b]	Relative change in export incentives[c]	RER at trade liberalization[d]
Israel 3 1969			
Periods: Before	Yes	+	—
During	Yes	Unchanged	Apprec.
Post	Yes	Unchanged	—
Korea 1 1965			
Periods: Before	Yes	+	—
During	Yes	*	Deprec. +
Post	Yes	Unchanged	—
Korea 2 1978			
Periods: Before	Yes	Unchanged	—
During	Yes	Unchanged	Deprec.
Post	Yes	Unchanged	—
New Zealand 2 1962			
Periods: Before	No	Unchanged	—
During	No	Unchanged	Unchanged
Post	Yes	+	—
Pakistan 1 1959			
Periods: Before	Yes	n.a.	—
During	Yes	n.a.	n.a.
Post	Yes	+	—
Pakistan 2 1972			
Periods: Before	Yes	+	—
During	No	*	Deprec.+
Post	No	*	—
Peru 1979			
Periods: Before	Yes	+	—
During	Yes	*	Deprec.+
Post	Yes	Unchanged	—
Philippines 1 1960			
Periods: Before	Yes	Unchanged	—
During	Yes	+	Deprec.+
Post	Yes	*	—
Philippines 2 1970			
Periods: Before	Yes	Unchanged	—
During	Yes	+	Deprec.+
Post	Yes	+	—

Table 12.2 *(cont'd)*

Beginning of episode	Export incentives in place[b]	Relative change in export incentives[c]	RER at trade liberalization[d]
Singapore 1968			
Periods: Before	Yes	Unchanged	—
During	Yes	Unchanged	Apprec.
Post	Yes	Unchanged	—
Spain 1 1960			
Periods: Before	No	n.a.	—
During	No	n.a.	Deprec.+
Post	No	*	—
Spain 2 1970			
Periods: Before	No	+	—
During	No	+	Unchanged
Post	Yes	+	—
Spain 3 1977			
Periods: Before	No	*	—
During	No	*	Deprec.
Post	Yes	+	—
Sri Lanka 1 1968			
Periods: Before	No	Unchanged	—
During	Yes	+	Deprec.+
Post	Yes	+	—
Sri Lanka 2 1977			
Periods: Before	Yes	+	—
During	No	*	Deprec.+
Post	Yes	+	—
Turkey 1 1970			
Periods: Before	Yes[g]	n.a.[g]	—
During	Yes	Unchanged	Deprec.+
Post	Yes	Unchanged	—
Turkey 2 1980			
Periods: Before	Yes	n.a.	—
During	Yes	n.a.	Deprec.+
Post	Yes	Unchanged	—
Yugoslavia 1965			
Periods: Before	Yes	+	—
During	Yes	+	Deprec. +
Post	Yes	*	—

Table 12.2 *(cont'd)*

—, not applicable; n.a., not available.

[a] These qualitative indices were determined from the real exchange rate (RER) and real effective exchange rate for exports (REERX) measured by the authors of each of the country studies. Therefore the index of export incentives here may not coincide with the same authors' determination of the presence or absence of export incentive policies in the country because their conclusion was based on the presence or absence of policies, such as QRs on exports, which the price measure of REER and RER does not ordinarily reflect, and because the authors have not explicitly and exclusively compared the relative values of the REERX and RER.

[b] We have solely determined the presence of export incentive policies on whether REERX > RER. In these cases in which we had additional information about the REER for nontraditional exports and for manufacturing we used these data instead.

[c] For the before and post-liberalization periods, and by comparing each period's beginning and end, if we find that the difference between the REERX and RER has not changed then we note it as Unchanged; if this difference is positive and growing or is negative and being reduced then we note it as +; if this difference is positive and being reduced or is negative and growing then we note it as *.

[d] In this column we indicate the status of the RER at the year of trade liberalization with respect to its value the year before that. We distinguish the following cases: depreciation (Deprec.), depreciation by more than 10 percent (Deprec. +), appreciation (Apprec.), and Unchanged.

[e] The period before liberalization refers to the three years preceding the year of trade liberalization, the period *during* refers to the year of trade liberalization only, and the *post*-liberalization period refers to the three years following the year of trade liberalization.

[f] In these cases REERX = RER.

[g] In this episode the data for the REERX were available only for the year preceding trade liberalization.

addition, there may be either increased or reduced export incentives relative to the exchange rate for the same period.

Finally, we defined another index – a strong devaluation of the RER – to see whether the devaluation of the RER in the year of the liberalization correlates with changes in the export growth rate. A strong devaluation exists if the RER is devalued by 10 percent or more during the year of liberalization. As is shown in the next section, most liberalizations had a strong devaluation, suggesting that capital flight before liberalization was a possibility in many instances.

These qualitative indices – taken largely from individual country studies – are constructed from the authors' quantitative estimates of the REERx and RER. Because of these definitions and classifications, categorizing episodes here as having or not having export incentive policies is somewhat different from the way these episodes are classified in chapters 5 and 13.

Liberalization and Exports

The findings in this section are simple comparisons of averages and, when the data permit, statistical tests of differences in means among periods and episodes.[2] These periods and episodes are classified according to the indices of table 12.2 and the groups of episodes established in chapter 3 (see table 12.1). No modeling or elaborate econometric methods were tried to establish causation between export growth rates and the variables used here. Our intention is to search for empirical regularities associated with trade liberalization that will lead to hypotheses about how trade liberalization affects export growth.

The export growth rates of the 31 episodes remove any doubt of the correlation between export growth and trade liberalization (table 12.3). While the average annual export growth rate for the 31 cases for the three years before liberalization is only 4.4 percent, the corresponding rate for the three-year post-liberalization period is 10.5 percent and for the four-year post-liberalization period is 11.0 percent. Furthermore, we reject

Table 12.3 Summary of export performance (annual real rate of growth)

Typology of episodes	Years before liberalization				Year of liberalization and after					
	1	2	3	Annual rate for period	1[a]	2	3	4	Annual rate for period[b]	Annual rate for period[c]
All episodes	5.1	6.5	1.6	4.4	12.6	11.8	9.6	9.9	11.0	10.5
Number of episodes				(31)					(31)	(31)
Episodes With previous severe restrictions	2.9	5.9	−3.8	1.7	10.0	13.4	12.3	9.0	11.2	11.6
Number of episodes				(19)					(19)	(19)
With previous moderate restrictions	8.9	7.2	9.1	8.4	13.2	12.4	5.1	12.2	10.7	9.9
Number of episodes				(12)					(12)	(12)
With strong start	3.9	9.0	−1.1	3.9	12.4	17.3	10.8	8.6	12.3	12.3
Number of episodes				(17)					(17)	(17)
With weak start	6.1	3.8	4.0	4.6	9.9	8.1	8.3	12.2	9.6	9.5
Number of episodes				(14)					(14)	(14)
Sustained	9.6	8.6	0.5	6.2	12.0	18.3	15.8	10.3	14.1	14.8
Number of episodes				(16)					(16)	(16)
Collapsed	−0.1	4.6	2.0	2.1	10.5	7.6	3.1	10.2	7.9	7.0
Number of episodes				(15)					(15)	(15)

[a] This is the year of liberalization.
[b] This is the post-liberalization average annual real export growth rate, which includes the year of liberalization.
[c] This is the annual average real export growth rate after liberalization which excludes the year of trade liberalization.

2 For details of statistical testing performed with these and other data of this project, see appendix A2.

that the mean export growth rates before and after liberalization are equal at a p level of less than 0.5 percent, indicating significant differences of means in *all* cases.[3] This extraordinarily strong empirical regularity is manifested in several ways. For example, the average export growth rate of eight episodes was negative before liberalization: Argentina 2, −1.2 percent; Chile 2, −1.6 percent; Pakistan 1, −2.3 percent; Pakistan 2, −3.4 percent; Philippines 2, −3.0 percent; Portugal 2, −7.3 percent; Turkey 2, −4.4 percent; and Uruguay, −11.3 percent (table 12.4). The corresponding post-liberalization averages show only Pakistan 2 with a negative growth rate of −3.0 percent for the three-year average and −3.9 percent for the four-year average, and Spain 1 with −2.2 percent for the three-year average.

Similarly, of the 31 episodes, 24 had higher average export growth rates following the liberalization (the three-year average) than before liberalization. In several cases the change is dramatic. For example, in Argentina's second episode the export growth rate went from −1.2 percent before liberalization to 16.1 percent for the three-year period following the year of liberalization. In Chile's second episode, the corresponding averages were −1.6 percent before and 13.6 percent after liberalization; and Turkey's second episode also, −4.4 percent before and 46.4 percent for the three years after the year of trade liberalization, would offer further evidence of the strong correlation between export growth and trade liberalization if we overlook capital flight. Trade liberalization not only correlates with export growth, but this growth appears immediately, from the first year of trade liberalization. The average export growth rate of the 31 episodes jumped to 12.6 percent in the year of liberalization, from 5.1 percent in the year before. More qualitative evidence of the quick improvement in the export performance is that, for the year before liberalization, 11 episodes had negative growth rates while, for the year of liberalization, the number of episodes with negative growth rates dropped to five.

Further strengthening the correlation between trade liberalization and export growth is the size of the change and the continuous strong export growth rate observed in the second year of liberalization (11.8 percent). The evidence so far empirically refutes the claim that exports respond sluggishly to trade liberalization. On the contrary, exports appear to grow in the first two years of the liberalization at more than twice their former pace.

Is export growth related to the intensity of the trade liberalization? Evidence suggests that strong trade liberalization seems to accompany remarkably higher export growth rates during liberalization. Exports increase from an annual average growth rate of 3.9 percent before liberalization for the 17 strong episodes to 12.3 percent during the three-

3 See appendix A2.

Table 12.4 Export performance (annual real rate of growth)

Episodes	T−3	T−2	T−1	PtL	T	T+1	T+2	T+3	AVG	AVG-T
Argentina 1 (1967–70)	−6.4	9.8	9.8	4.4	−1.2	−1.4	16.1	7.2	5.2	7.3
Argentina 2 (1976–80)	16.8	2.2	−22.7	−1.2	31.5	42.2	5.2	0.7	19.9	16.1
Brazil (1965–73)	−7.2	28.8	−14.1	2.5	4.0	11.7	−2.9	15.2	7.0	8.0
Chile 1 (1956–61)	−23.6	15.3	13.3	1.7	−7.3	1.9	0.7	16.4	3.0	6.4
Chile 2 (1974–81)	8.6	−13.0	−0.4	−1.6	49.4	7.9	25.4	7.4	22.5	13.6
Colombia 2 (1968–82)	6.5	−1.7	8.7	4.5	8.3	4.7	0.9	−0.2	3.4	1.8
Greece 1 (1953–5)	−21.7	13.3	17.6	3.1	7.5	17.8	20.4	3.8	12.4	14.0
Greece 2 (1962–82)	−3.5	1.7	9.3	2.5	8.2	2.5	7.7	8.8	6.8	6.3
Indonesia 2 (1966–72)	−6.0	11.9	3.1	3.0	−1.1	−0.2	10.5	14.0	5.8	8.1
Israel 2 (1962–8)	44.4	23.1	12.5	26.7	15.3	20.5	6.0	10.4	13.0	12.3
Israel 3 (1969–77)	12.2	9.0	26.9	16.0	7.6	7.5	19.0	14.9	12.2	13.8
Korea 1 (1965–7)	12.6	7.4	23.6	14.5	40.6	52.3	35.7	41.6	42.6	43.2
Korea 2 (1978–9)	10.6	35.5	27.9	24.7	13.8	−0.3	10.0	19.0	10.6	9.6
New Zealand 2 (1962–81)	17.4	3.1	−6.4	4.7	0.6	14.0	18.1	−6.3	6.6	8.6
New Zealand 3 (1982–4)	−7.7	13.1	6.8	4.1	3.3	−1.1	9.3	9.7	5.3	6.0
Pakistan 1 (1959–65)	26.3	−13.2	−20.0	−2.3	10.0	49.1	−23.8	4.8	10.0	10.0
Pakistan 2 (1972–8)	−3.3	7.1	−13.9	−3.4	−6.4	−21.6	−5.3	17.8	−3.9	−3.0
Peru (1979–80)	−14.4	17.0	19.6	7.4	44.7	−2.7	−9.8	16.0	12.0	1.2
Philippines 1 (1960–5)	−6.2	9.9	−1.0	0.9	8.1	−3.7	9.7	23.8	9.5	9.9
Philippines 2 (1970–4)	−1.5	−3.9	−3.5	−3.0	23.1	9.0	−13.5	11.6	7.5	2.4
Portugal 1 (1970–4)	8.9	5.0	10.0	8.0	12.0	1.2	5.9	7.8	6.7	5.0
Portugal 2 (1977–80)	1.7	−22.8	−0.7	−7.3	9.0	3.0	21.4	10.1	10.8	11.5
Spain 1 (1960–6)	1.0	3.1	11.0	5.0	51.4	1.2	−7.1	−0.6	11.2	−2.2
Spain 2 (1970–4)	−4.6	18.4	15.5	9.8	17.4	13.0	12.2	9.0	12.9	11.4
Spain 3 (1977–80)	0.9	−1.4	10.0	3.2	8.5	10.7	6.4	0.6	6.6	5.9
Sri Lanka 1 (1968–70)	6.1	−6.0	6.2	2.1	2.1	−2.6	3.1	0.1	0.7	0.2
Sri Lanka 2 (1977–9)	−13.4	20.1	2.2	3.0	−13.3	9.5	13.8	3.6	3.4	8.9
Turkey 1 (1970–3)	9.3	−1.8	8.1	5.2	8.0	7.4	29.7	15.6	15.2	17.6
Turkey 2 (1980–4)	−17.7	14.1	−9.6	−4.4	4.2	85.5	40.0	13.7	35.8	46.4
Uruguay (1974–80)	−12.9	−19.5	−1.3	−11.3	20.4	13.9	28.2	6.8	17.3	16.3
Yugoslavia (1965–7)	17.0	15.0	8.4	13.5	11.1	12.6	5.2	4.9	8.4	7.6
Average	1.6	6.5	5.1	4.4	12.6	11.8	9.6	9.9	11.0	10.5

T−3, three years prior to liberalization; T−2, two years prior to liberalization; T−1, one year prior to liberalization; PtL, average of the three years prior to liberalization; T, year of liberalization; T+1, one year after liberalization; T+2, two years after liberalization; T+3, three years after liberalization; AVG, average of T plus the three years after liberalization; AVG-T, average of the three years after liberalization.

Sources: Papageorgiou, Michaely, and Choksi (eds), 1990, *Liberalizing Foreign Trade*; World Bank, 1988–9, *World Tables*

and four-year post-liberalizations. Of the 17 episodes, only four – Israel 2 (from 26.7 percent to 12.3 percent), Israel 3 (from 16.0 percent to 13.8 percent), Peru (from 7.4 percent to 1.2 percent), and Yugoslavia (from 11.1 percent to 7.6 percent) – show export growth rates declining after liberalization. Characteristically, while four episodes show negative export growth rates before liberalization – Argentina 2, −1.2 percent; Chile 2, −1.6 percent; Turkey 2, −4.4 percent; and Uruguay, −11.3 percent – all episodes show positive growth rates after liberalization.

Overwhelming nonparametric evidence about the export performance of a pre-liberalization trade regime, replete with severe import restrictions, supports the claim that such restrictions impede severely not only imports but exports as well. Conversely, removing these trade barriers is correlated with impressive export growth. The average annual export growth rate of the 19 episodes with severe trade restrictions before liberalization was 1.7 percent. But this rate exploded to 11.6 percent for the three years after liberalization and to 11.2 percent for the four years after liberalization. Five export growth rates before liberalization were negative; none after. The post-liberalization export growth rate was less than before liberalization in only three episodes: Peru (where this rate fell from 7.4 percent before liberalization to 1.2 percent after liberalization); Sri Lanka 1 (from 2.1 percent to 0.2 percent); and Yugoslavia (from 13.5 percent to 7.6 percent). These data reinforce trade liberalization's strong association with export growth, while severe import restrictions – particularly nontariff barriers – retard export growth severely.

The evidence here also suggests, as does evidence from the data used in chapter 11, that export growth and sustained liberalization are highly correlated. For example, annual export growth for the 16 episodes that were sustained is 6.2 percent before liberalization, but it jumps after liberalization to 14.8 percent. In 13 of the 16 sustained episodes, export growth rates are higher after liberalization than before. The export growth rate of all sustained episodes rose to 12.0 percent in the first year and to 18.3 percent in the second year of liberalization compared with 9.6 percent in the last year before liberalization. But export performance during the failed episodes suggests a lack of continuous export drive. The export growth rate for the year of liberalization increases materially – to 10.5 percent – but the following years' rates drop to 7.6 and 3.1 percent.

In sum, the picture shows the strong correlation between trade liberalization and rapid export growth, and that the stronger the liberalization is, the more impressive is the export growth. In addition, the evidence indicates that severe trade restrictions impede exports as much as they impede imports; and good export performance and sustainability of the trade liberalization are strongly correlated. Finally, exports grow immediately following liberalization, with no apparent sluggishness in export responsiveness.

The Relevance of Export Promotion

The next question deals with how incentive policies affect export growth and how the RER changes when the liberalization is introduced. To answer these questions we look at 27 episodes according to the following: first, the presence or absence of export promotion policies; second, the relative changes in the intensity of these policies; and third, the evolution of the RER during the year of liberalization (table 12.2).[4]

4 These definitions of export incentives policy are not the same as those in chapter 5.

These data show 18 episodes with export incentive policies before liberalization, and eight episodes without. For the year of liberalization, 17 episodes are with incentive policies and 10 are without, while, for post-liberalization, 21 episodes are with such policies and seven are without. Thus most episodes are associated with sufficiently strong export incentive policies for the REERx to be more devalued than the RER. Only four episodes have no noticeable export incentive policies at any time: Argentina 1 and 2, Chile 1, and Spain 1. But in 15 episodes noticeable export incentive policies are observed for the seven years covered here – Chile 2, Colombia 2, Greece 1 and 2, Israel 3, Korea 1 and 2, Pakistan 1, Peru, Philippines 1 and 2, Singapore, Turkey 1 and 2, and Yugoslavia. The remaining eight episodes are characterized by fluctuations between the presence and absence of export policies for this period (before and after liberalization).

The most frequent development of the RER at liberalization was depreciation. In 21 episodes the RER depreciated, and 17 of these depreciations were "strong" by our definition (a depreciation of at least 10 percent or more). The exchange rate appreciated in only three episodes; it remained unchanged in two (in one case the data are incomplete). Thus the common attributes of trade liberalization episodes are the presence of export incentive policies and a depreciation of the RER when trade liberalization was implemented.

Statistical testing of the export growth data and the classification of these episodes shows how strong depreciation of the RER accelerates export growth. Although the statistical results are not very strong, they correlate export growth and strong depreciation of the RER. But no statistically meaningful correlation was found between export growth and the presence or absence of export incentive policies. No clear pattern emerges about whether export incentive policies enhance export growth or retard it on the basis of the export growth rates for the seven years of each liberalization as well as the subperiods.[5] One explanation for this result may be the limited sample of our study and its dominance by the depreciation of the RER. But as far as this evidence goes, a general impact of maintaining export promotion at the time of liberalization (in addition to the liberalization itself, and to the real depreciation associated with it) is absent.

5 See appendix A2. It is established, however, that low pre-liberalization report performance correlates with the *introduction* of export incentive policies.

13

Accompanying Policies: the Role of the Real Exchange Rate

Experience shows a strong relationship between the *immediate* behavior of the real exchange rate, following the launching of liberalization, and the survivability of the experiment: the policy is likely to be sustained when the exchange rate increases, and to collapse when it falls. An increase of the real exchange rate appears to be almost a necessary condition for at least partial survival of a liberalization policy. The same relationship appears between the behavior of the real exchange rate *during* the life of the liberalization episode and its eventual fate. Similarly, an increase of the real exchange rate toward the *close* of a liberalization episode appears clearly associated with survival of the policy, and a fall with the policy's collapse. In all time dimensions the behavior of the real exchange rate is clearly related to the sustainability of liberalizations.

This relationship helps explain the positive association between the *strength* of a liberalization policy and its chance of being sustained: in most of the "strong" episodes, the real exchange rate *increased* following the launching of the liberalization policy.

Not surprisingly, the movements of the nominal and of the *real* rates of exchange appear to be closely related: a nominal devaluation when liberalization is introduced seems almost a necessary condition for a real devaluation. In achieving a *persistent* increase of the real exchange rate, a *substantial* initial nominal devaluation would make an important contribution. Contractionary fiscal or monetary policy appears to be important (though not so vital) for achieving a real devaluation. The absence of both would be likely to prevent an increase of the real exchange rate.

We now move from discussing the direct elements of a trade liberalization policy to concentrate on *accompanying* policies. Liberalization is the focus of our study, and therefore other policy measures undertaken at the same time are, for our purposes, accompanying policies, even when (as quite frequently) the liberalization was by no means the centerpiece of the policy package as a whole. In this chapter we shall discuss the behavior of the real exchange rate: the intention is to investigate the connection between patterns of change of the real exchange rate and the sustainability of a liberalization.

Changes in the Real Exchange Rate

The *real* exchange rate (as distinct from the *nominal* rate) is not strictly a policy "instrument" but the outcome of combinations of policies and market forces, together with exogenous factors and processes. But at the same time, while the government cannot directly determine the real exchange rate, it very often does formulate a target rate – and in this sense does have some control – over this variable.[1]

Estimates of the "real" exchange rate are provided in all 19 country studies. Despite the variety of methods, and uneven reliability of the data, these estimates provide a sufficient basis of evidence for our analysis; the principal methods employed in constructing them are briefly described in the annex to this chapter.

Figures 13.1–13.29 present the estimates of the real exchange rates available from the country studies. In each country figure the liberalization episode is indicated by vertical lines.[2] The following discussion will be based on the evidence suggested by these figures.

The figures representing the time series of the real exchange rate give a general indication about the direction of change of the rates. Three time segments would seem *a priori* to be relevant for the fate of a liberalization policy: the direction of change *immediately after* the launching of a

---

1 The question whether a given variable is or is not a policy "instrument" is, of course, common to many policy elements; and the answer is very often ambiguous. Thus, for instance, the money supply may be regarded as an "instrument" or, alternatively, as the outcome of such "instruments" as the discount rate or the bank reserve requirements; or government revenues may be treated as an "instrument" or, alternatively, as the outcome of such "instruments" as various tax schedules; and so on.

2 See chapter 11 for discussion of the demarcation of the period of liberalization.

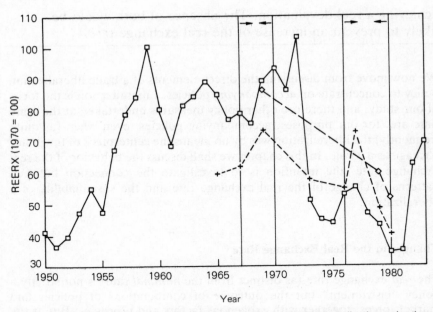

Figure 13.1 The real effective export exchange rate: Argentina. Liberalization episodes are between arrows; □, REERX; +, REERX (traditional); ◇, REERX (nontraditional).

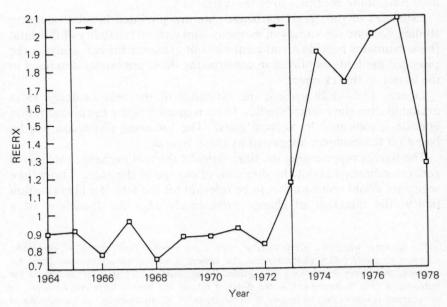

Figure 13.2 The real effective export exchange rate: Brazil. Liberalization episodes are between arrows.

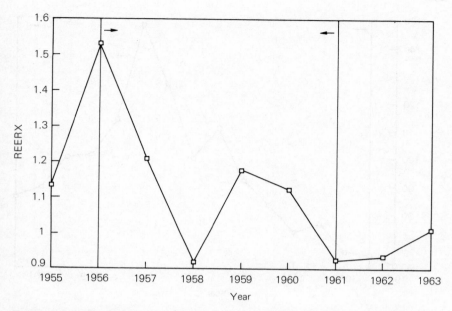

Figure 13.3 The real effective export exchange rate: Chile 1. Liberalization episodes are between arrows.

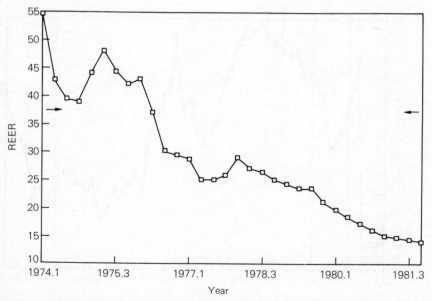

Figure 13.4 The real effective exchange rate: Chile 2. Liberalization episodes are between arrows.

200

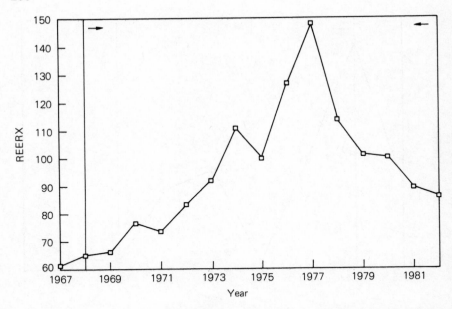

Figure 13.5 The real effective export exchange rate: Colombia. Liberalization episodes are between arrows.

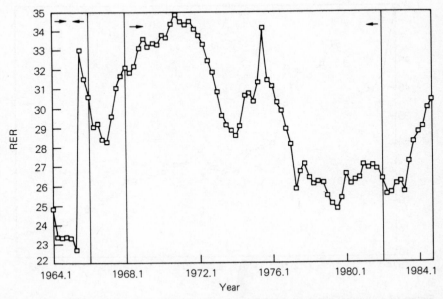

Figure 13.6 Real exchange rate: Colombia quarterly. Liberalization episodes are between arrows.

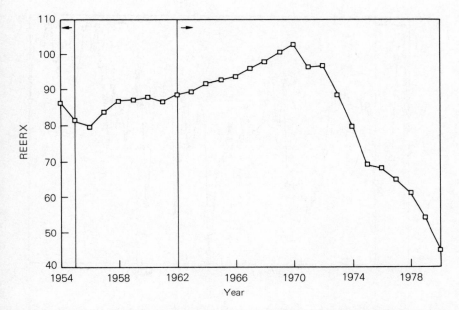

Figure 13.7 The real effective export exchange rate: Greece. Liberalization episodes are between arrows.

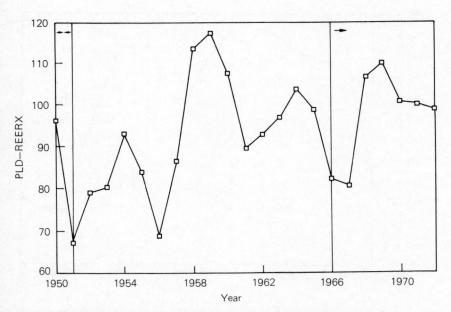

Figure 13.8 Price-level-deflated real effective export exchange rate: Indonesia. Liberalization episodes are between arrows.

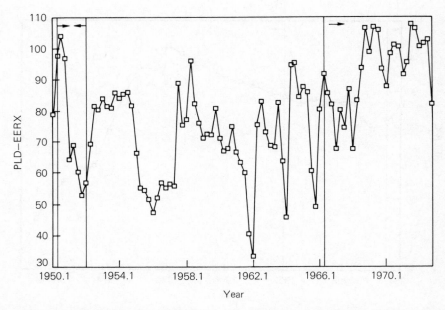

Figure 13.9 Price-level-deflated effective export exchange rate (rubber): Indonesia quarterly. Liberalization episodes are between arrows.

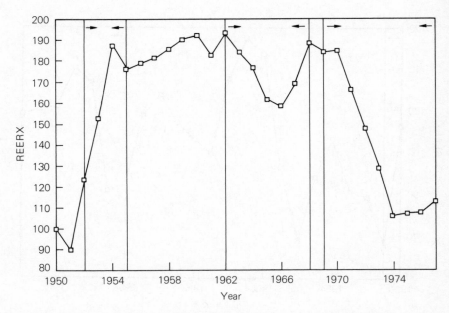

Figure 13.10 The real effective export exchange rate: Israel. Liberalization episodes are between arrows.

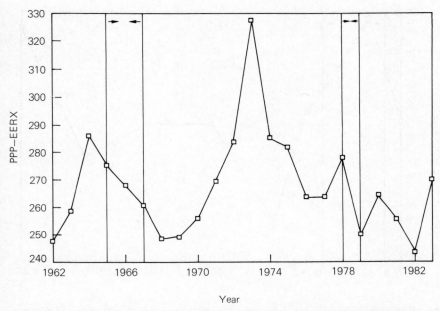

Figure 13.11 Purchasing-price-parity-adjusted effective exchange rate: Korea annual. Liberalization episodes are between arrows.

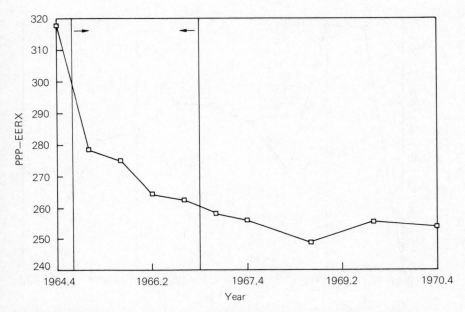

Figure 13.12 Purchasing-price-parity-adjusted effective exchange rate: Korea biannual. Liberalization episodes are between arrows.

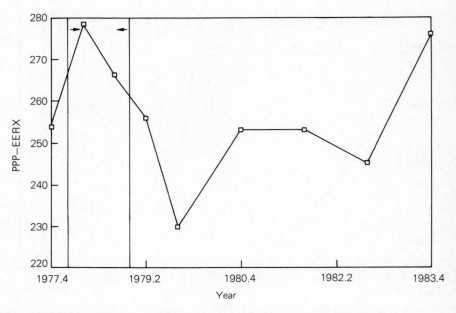

Figure 13.13 Purchasing-price-parity-adjusted effective exchange rate: Korea biannual. Liberalization episoles are between arrows.

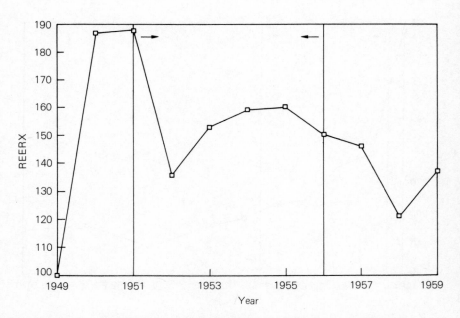

Figure 13.14 The real effective export exchange rate: New Zealand. Liberalization episodes are between arrows.

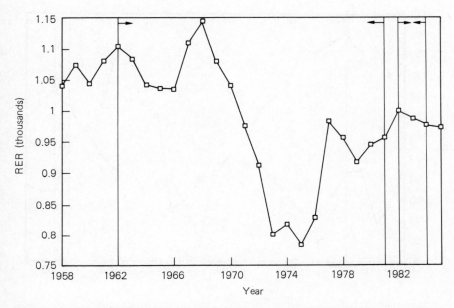

Figure 13.15 The real exchange rate: New Zealand. Liberalization episodes are between arrows.

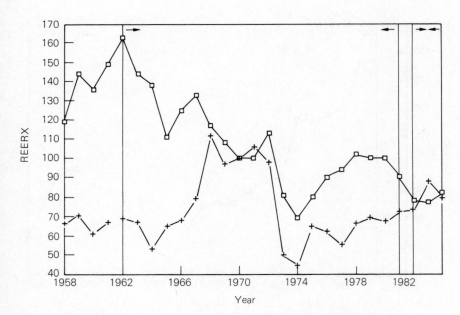

Figure 13.16 The real effective export exchange rate by export: New Zealand. Liberalization episodes are between arrows; □, REERX (sheep); + REERX (wool).

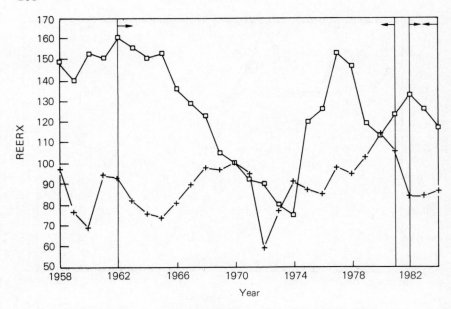

Figure 13.17 The real effective export exchange rate by export: New Zealand. Liberalization episodes are between arrows; □, REERX (beef); +, REERX (dairy).

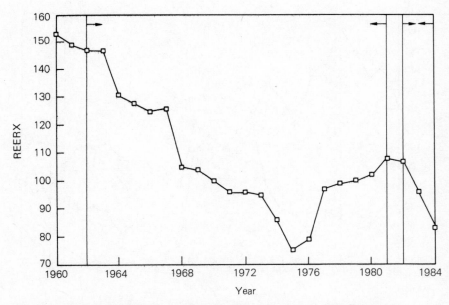

Figure 13.18 The real effective export exchange rate by export: New Zealand. Liberalization episodes are between arrows; □, REERX (other manufacturing).

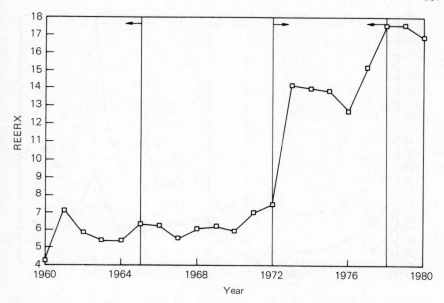

Figure 13.19 The real effective export exchange rate: Pakistan. Liberalization episodes are between arrows.

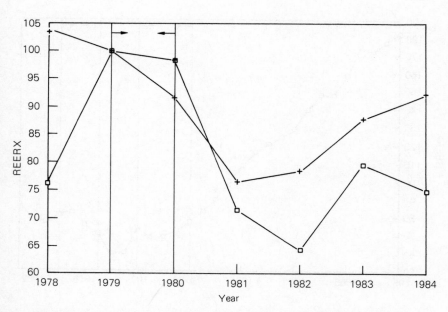

Figure 13.20 The real effective export exchange rate: Peru. Liberalization episodes are between arrows; □, REERX (traditional); +, REERX (nontraditional).

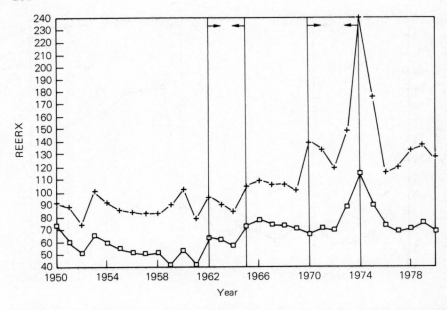

Figure 13.21 The real effective export exchange rate: Philippines. Liberalization episodes are between arrows; □, REERX (traditional); +, REERX ("new").

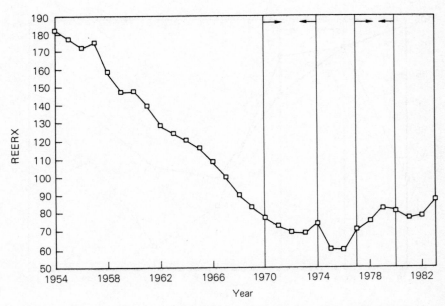

Figure 13.22 The real effective export exchange rate: Portugal. Liberalization episodes are between arrows.

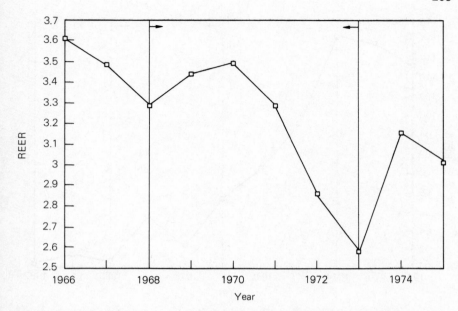

Figure 13.23 The real effective exchange rate: Singapore. Liberalization episodes are between arrows.

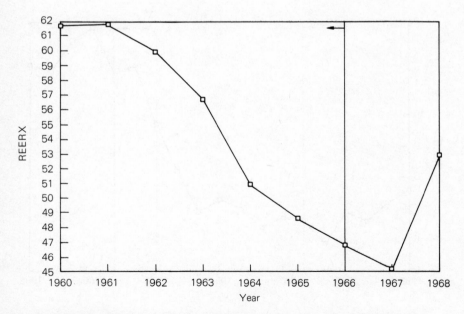

Figure 13.24 The real effective export exchange rate: Spain 1. Liberalization episodes are between arrows.

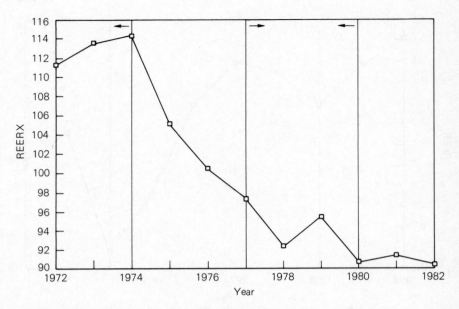

Figure 13.25 The real effective export exchange rate: Spain 2 and 3. Liberalization episodes are between arrows.

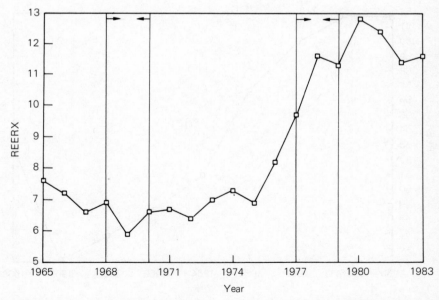

Figure 13.26 The real effective export exchange rate: Sri Lanka. Liberalization episodes are between arrows.

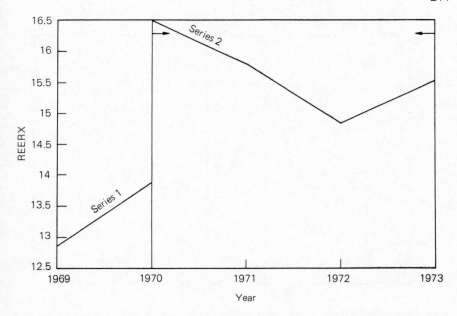

Figure 13.27 The real effective export exchange rate: Turkey. Liberalization episodes are between arrows.

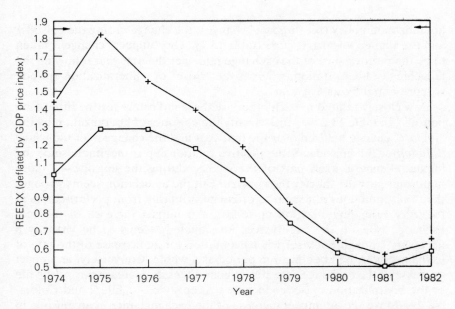

Figure 13.28 The real effective export exchange rate: Uruguay. Liberalization episodes are between arrows; □, REERX (traditional); +, REERX (nontraditional).

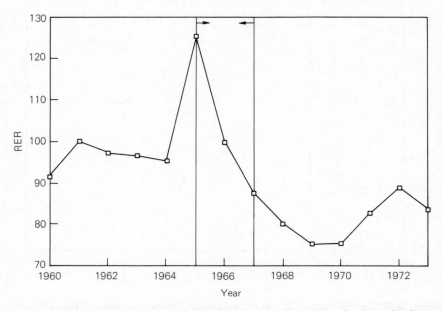

Figure 13.29 The real exchange rate (definition 2): Yugoslavia. Liberalization episodes are between arrows.

liberalization policy (the "impact" change); the change *during* the episode; and the change toward its *close* (table 13.1). The "impact" change is taken to be the performance of the exchange rate over the first year following the launching of liberalization, whereas the "close" of a liberalization episode is represented by its last year.

How closely related to each other are these indicators for the three time periods? In table 13.2 we cross-classify the episodes of liberalization by the *"impact"* change realized over the first year and the change over the *whole duration* of the episode. Some positive relationship is inevitable since the impact change is itself part of the change during the episode – a more important part the shorter the episode. But the association seems stronger than that (and does not seem to originate primarily from performances in the very brief liberalization episodes). An impact increase of the real exchange rate, in the experiences investigated, seems to be virtually a necessary (though not a sufficient) condition for an increase of the rate of exchange over the liberalization period as a whole. Conversely, an impact decrease of the exchange rate almost guarantees its decrease during the life of the liberalization episode. In only two episodes – Chile 2 and Colombia 2 – do we see an impact increase of the exchange rate in an episode in which the exchange rate went down over its duration as a whole. It should

Table 13.1 Directions of change in the real exchange rate in episodes of liberalization

Episode		Impact change	Trend change during the episode	Change toward the close of the episode
Argentina 1	(1967–70)	Decrease	Decrease	Stable
Argentina 2	(1976–80)	Decrease	Decrease	Stable
Brazil	(1965–73)	Increase	No trend	Increase
Chile 1	(1956–61)	Increase	No trend	Decrease
Chile 2	(1974–81)	Increase	Decrease	Decrease
Colombia 1	(1964–6)	Decrease	Increase	Increase
Colombia 2	(1968–82)	Increase	Decrease	Stable
Greece 1	(1953–5)	Increase	Increase	Stable
Greece 2	(1962–82)	Stable	Decrease	n.a.
Indonesia 1	(1950–1)	Decrease	Decrease	Decrease
Indonesia 2	(1966–72)	Increase	Increase	Stable
Israel 1	(1952–5)	Increase	Increase	Increase
Israel 2	(1962–8)	Increase	No trend	Stable
Israel 3	(1969–77)	Stable	No trend	Stable
Korea 1	(1965–7)	Stable	Decrease	Decrease
Korea 2	(1978–9)	Increase	No trend	Decrease
New Zealand 1	(1951–6)	n.a.	n.a.	n.a.
New Zealand 2	(1964–81)	Stable	Decrease	Stable
New Zealand 3	(1982–4)	Stable	No trend	Stable
Pakistan 1	(1959–65)	Stable	No trend	Stable
Pakistan 2	(1972–8)	Increase	Increase	Increase
Peru	(1979–80)	Decrease	Decrease	Decrease
Philippines 1	(1960–5)	Increase	Increase	Stable
Philippines 2	(1970–4)	Increase	Increase	Increase
Portugal 1	(1970–4)	Decrease	Decrease	Decrease
Portugal 2	(1977–80)	Increase	Increase	Increase
Singapore	(1968–73)	Stable	Decrease	Decrease
Spain 1	(1960–6)	Decrease	Decrease	Decrease
Spain 2	(1970–4)	Decrease	No trend	Increase
Spain 3	(1977–80)	Decrease	Decrease	Decrease
Sri Lanka 1	(1968–70)	Decrease	Decrease	Decrease
Sri Lanka 2	(1977–9)	Increase	Increase	Increase
Turkey 1	(1970–3)	Increase	No trend	Stable
Turkey 2	(1980–4)	Increase	Increase	Increase
Uruguay	(1974–82)	Increase	Decrease	Stable
Yugoslavia	(1965–7)	Increase	No trend	Decrease

Based on figure 13.1.

be noted, though, that in quite a few episodes an impact increase of the exchange rate resulted, eventually, in no significant upward or downward trend of the rate over the whole length of the liberalization episode.

In table 13.3 we similarly cross-classify the episodes by exchange rate movements at the *close* of the episode and *during* the liberalization period as a whole. The association is again obvious (and again supersedes the

Table 13.2 Relationship between the impact change in the real exchange rate and its trends during liberalizations

Trend change during the episode	Impact change		
	Increase	Stable	Decrease
Increase	Greece 1	Colombia 1	Israel 1
	Pakistan 2		
	Philippines 1		
	Philippines 2		
	Portugal 2		
	Sri Lanka 2		
	Turkey 2		
No trend	Brazil	Greece 2	Spain 2
	Chile 1	Israel 3	
	Indonesia 2	New Zealand 3	
	Israel 2	Pakistan 1	
	Korea 2	Uruguay	
	Turkey 1		
	Yugoslavia		
Decrease	Chile 2	Korea 1	Argentina 1
	Colombia 2	New Zealand 2	Argentina 2
		Singapore	Indonesia 1
			Peru
			Portugal 1
			Spain 1
			Spain 2
			Sri Lanka 1

association of the whole with the part). With a single exception (Brazil's liberalization, in which no trend is discerned for the exchange rate movement during the episode), all increases of the exchange rate at the close of the period occurred in episodes in which the exchange rate moved upward, as a trend, throughout the period. For decreases of the exchange rate this is also generally true: in no single instance did an increase in the rate during the period end up in a fall of the rate at the close of the episode, or vice versa.

Despite these close associations, the movement of the exchange rate is consistent *throughout* (on impact, during the episode, and toward its close) only in the minority of the episodes for which the required data are available: a consistent increase in six episodes (Israel 1, Pakistan 2, Philippines 2, Portugal 2, Sri Lanka 2, and Turkey 2) and a consistent decrease in five others (Indonesia 1, Peru, Portugal 1, Spain 1, and Sri Lanka 1); in two instances (Israel 3 and Pakistan 1) no trend change was

Table 13.3 Relationship between trends in the real exchange rate during and toward the close of episodes

Trend change during the episode	Change toward the close		
	Increase	Stable	Decrease
Increase	Colombia 1	Greece 1	
	Israel 1	Philippines 1	
	Pakistan 2	Spain 2	
	Philippines 2		
	Portugal 2		
	Sri Lanka 2		
	Turkey 2		
No trend	Brazil	Indonesia 2	Chile 2
		Israel 2	Korea 2
		Israel 3	Yugoslavia
		New Zealand 3	
		Pakistan 1	
		Uruguay	
Decrease		Argentina 1	Chile 2
		Argentina 2	Indonesia 1
		Colombia 2	Korea 1
		New Zealand 2	Peru
			Portugal 1
			Singapore
			Spain 1
			Spain 3
			Sri Lanka 1

evident in either of the three time criteria. In the other 21 episodes the record was mixed (though a *decrease* in one time indicator and an *increase* in another is observed in only four of these – Korea 2, Spain 2, Chile 1, and Yugoslavia). Thus, despite the close association, there is still room to analyze separately the possible association of each of the indicators of exchange rate movements with other phenomena.

The Real Exchange Rate and Sustainability

An increased real exchange rate following a liberalization might be expected to contribute to the policy's sustainability, for at least two reasons. First, a higher real exchange rate, amounting to a higher relative price of tradeables versus nontradeables, should promote all tradeable activities. It should thus lead to the expansion of exportable activities, as well as of some import-substituting sectors (the least protected or those from which the least protection has been removed), and to a weaker downward pressure on the other import-substituting sectors. The liberalization policy might thus generate stronger support, or encounter weaker resistance. Second, when – as most often – a liberalization takes the form of reduction of protection of import-competing activities, the absence of a real increase of the (formal) exchange rate would turn an equilibrium balance-of-payments position into one of disequilibrium, stimulating pressure for reversal of the policy.

In tables 13.4, 13.5 and 13.6 the episodes of liberalization are cross-classified by the exchange rate performance – increase, stable, decrease – over the three time dimensions of the episode and the degree of sustainability of the episode – "sustained," "partially sustained," and "collapsed."

The relationship of the *impact* movement of the exchange rate[3] to sustainability (table 13.4) seems quite clear. In most of the 18 instances in

Table 13.4 Relationship between the impact change in the real exchange rate and sustainability of liberalizations

Sustainability	Exchange rate change		
	Increase	Stable	Decrease
Sustained	Chile 2	Colombia 1	
	Greece 1	Greece 2	
	Indonesia 2	Israel 3	
	Israel 1	Korea 1	
	Israel 2	New Zealand 2	
	Korea 2	New Zealand 3	
	Sri Lanka 2	Singapore	
	Turkey 2		
	Uruguay		
Partially sustained	Colombia 2		Spain 1
	Pakistan 2		Spain 2
	Philippines 1		Spain 3
	Philippines 2		
	Portugal 2		
Collapsed	Brazil		Argentina 1
	Chile 1		Argentina 2
	Turkey 1		Peru
	Yugoslavia		Portugal 1
			Sri Lanka 1

3 The estimates of the real exchange rate are sometimes quarterly, in which case the delineation of the "first year of liberalization" may be fairly accurate. Often, however, only annual observations are provided; for obvious reasons, an element of error in the identification of the appropriate year is then introduced.

Table 13.5 Relationship of real exchange rate trends during episodes and sustainability of liberalizations

Sustainability	Exchange rate change		
	Increase	No trend	Decrease
Sustained	Greece 1 Israel 1 Sri Lanka 2 Turkey 2	Greece 2 Indonesia 2 Israel 2 Israel 3 Korea 2 New Zealand 3 Uruguay	Chile 2 Korea 1 New Zealand 2 Singapore
Partially sustained	Pakistan 2 Philippines 1 Philippines 2 Portugal 2	Pakistan 1 Spain 2	Colombia 2 Spain 1
Collapsed	Colombia 1	Brazil Chile 1 Turkey 1 Yugoslavia	Argentina 1 Argentina 2 Indonesia 1 Peru Portugal 1 Sri Lanka 1

Table 13.6 Relationship of changes in real exchange rate toward the close of episodes and sustainability of liberalizations

Sustainability	Exchange rate change		
	Increase	Stable	Decrease
Sustained	Israel 1 Sri Lanka 2 Turkey 2	Greece 1 Indonesia 2 Israel 2 Israel 3 New Zealand 2 New Zealand 3 Uruguay	Chile 2 Korea 1 Korea 2 Singapore
Partially sustained	Pakistan 2 Philippines 2 Spain 2	Colombia 2 Pakistan 1 Philippines 1	
Collapsed	Brazil Colombia 1	Argentina 1 Argentina 2 Turkey 1	Chile Indonesia 1 Peru Portugal 1 Spain 3 Sri Lanka 1 Yugoslavia

which the exchange rate increased, on impact, the liberalizations were either fully or at least partially sustained; only four eventually collapsed. In the seven liberalizations in which the rate remained stable, all episodes were fully sustained. But of the eight episodes in which the exchange rate decreased, *none* was fully sustained and five collapsed. Put differently: in most of the liberalization episodes that were fully sustained, the exchange rate increased; in *none* did it decrease. Among the partially sustained episodes, those in which the exchange rate increased again form a majority. The collapsed episodes, on the other hand, are approximately evenly divided between those with a rise or fall of the exchange rate.

The inference is clear: the liberalization is likely to be sustained when the exchange rate increases on "impact," and to collapse when it falls. An "impact" increase of the real rate appears to be almost a prerequisite for survival of any liberalization policy.

The same association is apparent in the performance of the real exchange rate *during* the episode of liberalization[4] (table 13.5).[5] The relationship of this variable to sustainability is perhaps not as strong as for the "impact" effect but is obvious nonetheless. In eight of the nine instances in which the exchange rate increased during the episode, the latter was fully or partially sustained. When no trend change was evident, the record is mixed. Half of the 12 episodes during which the exchange rate fell, however, ended in collapse. From the other angle, in the large majority of the "sustained" and "partially sustained" episodes the exchange rate either increased or, at least, manifested no trend change. But in over half of the collapsed episodes the exchange rate fell, and all but one of the rest were episodes with no trend change of the exchange rate.

For performance of the real exchange rate at the *close* of the episode (table 13.6) the conclusion to be drawn from the data is almost identical with that reached for the other two variables. A clear relationship exists between the performance of the real exchange rate toward the close of the liberalization episode and the latter's fate: an increase of the exchange rate is associated with the survival of liberalization, and a fall of the rate with its collapse.

---

4 In the short liberalization episodes this performance must be closely related to the "impact" (first year change and the closing (last year) change of the exchange rate. When the episode is as short as two years, the change "during" the period is of course nothing but the aggregate of the other two changes.

5 Table 13.5 differs slightly from table 13.4 in classifying an exchange rate performance as "no trend" rather than "stable." The two are obviously not synonymous. In several instances with no trend change, fluctuations – sometimes very substantial – were observed. Performances of no trend change but with varying degrees of stability of the exchange rate should certainly not be considered as identical – as witness, for instance, in the discussion of the last chapter. But in the present context this factor is ignored, to avoid the creation of boxes with very few observations.

All three periodical indicators of performance of the real exchange rate – at the *beginning* of, *during*, and at the *close* of an episode – are therefore clearly related to the sustainability of liberalization: a rise of the exchange rate, in all these periodical dimensions, tends to be associated with the survival of a liberalization policy. Somewhat surprisingly, perhaps, the relationship appears strongest for the *impact* movement of the exchange rate. Authors of various country studies have noted the fall of the real exchange rate *during* and toward the *close* of the liberalization episode as a major factor contributing to failure. This has been assigned the heaviest weight in the investigations of the second liberalization episode of Argentina (1976–80) and the first episode of Chile (1956–61).

The 12 instances mentioned earlier in which the real exchange rate moved consistently either upward or downward reinforce the conclusion. In the six episodes showing consistent upward movement of the rate, the policy was sustained either fully or at least partially; in the six where a consistent *fall* was observed, all but two collapsed.[6]

The Real Exchange Rate and the Balance of Payments

A key to interpreting the strong association between the pattern of change of the real exchange rate and the sustainability of liberalization might be the impact of the exchange rate on the balance of payments, whose strong association with the fate of liberalization has already been noted (chapter 11).

In a rough attempt to discover patterns of association, table 13.7 cross-classifies episodes in a matrix whose two dimensions are the direction of change of the real exchange rate and the direction of change of the foreign exchange reserves, both being the "impact" changes following liberalization.[7] In table 13.8 this procedure is repeated for the last year of each episode.[8]

Table 13.7 does not indicate any association of the impact changes in the exchange rate and in foreign exchange reserves – not surprising in view of the almost universal increase in foreign exchange reserves following the

---

6 The dependence of success of liberalization on the behavior of the real exchange rate is obviously not a surprising finding. It has been highlighted in the volume of Krueger (1978) synthesizing the multicountry experience in the study directed by J. Bhagwati and A. Krueger.

7 Not *all* episodes are presented: unavailability of data on either the real exchange rate or foreign exchange reserves lowers the number of observations to 24 (of the total of 36) in table 13.7 and to 27 in table 13.8.

8 A more thorough analysis of the causal effect would require the use of a full model in which the exchange rate would be just one of several explanatory variables. The construction and testing of such a model is beyond the scope of the present study.

Table 13.7 Relationship between the impact changes in the real exchange rate and movements of foreign exchange reserves

Reserves change	Exchange rate change		
	Increase	Stable	Decrease
Increase	Brazil	Greece 2	Argentina 1
	Chile 2	New Zealand 3	Argentina 2
	Colombia 2		Peru
	Israel 2		Portugal 1
	Pakistan 2		Spain 1
	Philippines 2		Spain 2
	Portugal 2		
	Sri Lanka 2		
	Turkey 1		
	Turkey 2		
	Yugoslavia		
No change	Israel 1	Colombia 1	Sri Lanka 1
	Philippines 1		Korea 1
	Uruguay		
Decrease	Korea 2	Israel 3	

Table 13.8 Relationship between changes in the real exchange rate toward the close of episodes and movements of foreign exchange reserves

Reserves change	Exchange rate change		
	Increase	Stable	Decrease
Increase	Brazil	Indonesia 2	Korea 1
	Israel 1	Philippines 1	Korea 2
	Philippines 2	Turkey 1	Singapore
	Sri Lanka 2	Israel 3	
No change	Pakistan 2	Argentina 1	Peru
	Spain 2	Colombia 2	
	Turkey 2	Israel 2	
		New Zealand 3	
Decrease	Colombia 1	Argentina 2	Chile 1
		Israel 2	Chile 2
		Pakistan 1	Portugal 1
		Uruguay	Spain 3
			Sri Lanka 1
			Yugoslavia

launching of liberalization. Some pattern can, however, be discerned from the performance of the two variables toward the *close* of the liberalization episode. When the foreign exchange rate increased, foreign exchange reserves either increased or manifested no change, except in Colombia 1 where reserves fell while the exchange rate increased. A reduction of the exchange rate, on the other hand, is mostly associated with a declining level of foreign exchange reserves.[9] It may thus be inferred that the performance of the foreign exchange rate toward the end of a liberalization episode could have affected the fate of liberalization through its impact on the balance of payments.

The relationship of export performance to the real exchange rate – its positive response both to an upward trend and to stability of the exchange rate – has been mentioned on various occasions in this study. In the present context we shall only add the indications that a classification along the lines we have been pursuing here provides about possible associations.

As with strong exchange reserves, no relationship of the exchange rate with the *impact* effect on exports following liberalization can be expected. Of the 31 episodes for which data for both variables are available, in *none* did exports fall; in about two thirds of the instances exports increased, whereas in the rest no significant change was manifested. The cross-classification of the exchange rate movement *during* the liberalization episode and export performance at the *close* of the episode's last year (table 13.9) does, however, indicate a relationship in the expected direction (though again it is not overwhelming). Where exports declined (in five episodes altogether), so did the real rate of exchange, whereas such a decrease was evident in only two of the nine instances in which exports increased.[10] Put differently: in most instances in which the exchange rate increased, exports either increased or stayed unchanged, whereas in about half of the episodes in which the exchange rate decreased, so did the size of exports.

The same, not very strong, relationship emerges from the depiction in table 13.10 of the relationship of both performance variables during the last year of the episode. The outcome is somewhat puzzling. If the pattern of change of the real exchange rate affects the fate of liberalization through

9 The *numbers* alone are probably misleading here. In six cases a fall of both variables is observed, whereas in three others the exchange rate fell while exchange reserves increased. These three should be viewed as an "exception," however. They include Korea's two liberalization episodes and the episode of Singapore. It is most probable that in the case of these two economies causation ran the opposite way: a strong balance-of-payments (and exports) performance, *not* originating from *current* real depreciation, must have led to a real appreciation.

10 These two were, again, the episodes of Korea 1 and of Singapore – where, we have argued before, causality must have run from the balance-of-payments performance to the exchange rate movement.

Table 13.9 Relationship between the real exchange rate trends during the episode and changes in exports at its close

	Exchange rate change		
Exports change	Increase	No trend	Decrease
Increase	Philippines 1 Philippines 2 Turkey 2	Indonesia 1 Israel 2 Korea 2 Spain 2	Korea 1 Singapore
No change	Israel 1 Pakistan 2 Portugal 2 Sri Lanka 2	Brazil Greece 2 Israel 3 New Zealand 3 Pakistan 1 Turkey 1 Uruguay Yugoslavia	Chile 2 Colombia 2 Portugal 1 Spain 1
Decrease	Colombia 1		Argentina 1 Argentina 2 Peru Sri Lanka 1

Table 13.10 Relationship between changes in the real exchange rate and in exports toward the close of episodes

	Exchange rate change		
Exports change	Increase	Stable	Decrease
Increase	Philippines 2 Spain 2 Turkey 2	Indonesia 2 Israel 2 Philippines 1	Korea 1 Korea 2 Singapore
No change	Brazil Israel 1 Pakistan 2 Sri Lanka 2	Colombia 2 Israel 3 New Zealand 3 Pakistan 1 Turkey 1 Uruguay	Chile 2 Portugal 1 Yugoslavia
Decrease	Colombia 1	Argentina 1 Argentina 2	Peru Spain 3 Sri Lanka

its impact on the balance of payments (or on the specific element of exports), the relationship between the exchange rate and the sustainability of liberalization should be *weaker* than its relationship with balance-of-payments performance, since the latter is only one element (even though it may be the most important) in determining the fate of liberalizations. Yet, on the contrary, the exchange rate movement appears to be more strongly associated with the sustainability of liberalizations than with the performance of foreign exchange reserves, or of exports. The difference may not be meaningful, in view of the quite small number of observations and the method used for drawing inferences, but if it is, indeed, real, it must indicate that the behavior of the real exchange rate affects the fate of liberalizations through additional channels to its impact on the balance of payments. One such channel could be a possible effect of the real exchange rate on the economy's growth (beyond its effect on export performance). Another may be the fact – only partly represented in balance-of-payments performance – that a real devaluation, by encouraging import-competing activities (including those from which protection is fully or partly removed by liberalization), lessens resentment against a liberalization policy. Also the movement of the real exchange rate represents the outcome of a whole set of policies (parts of which – say, the restrictiveness of budgetary or monetary policies – may affect the credibility of the whole policy package) which, in turn, may influence the fate of the policy beyond the impact on the balance of payments.

The Real Exchange Rate and Attributes of Liberalizations

What connection is there between the performance of the real exchange rate and the *intensity* of a liberalization policy? We examine this association by, once more, cross-classifying the liberalization episodes by the indicator of exchange rate performance and by categories of the intensity of liberalization, as defined in chapter 3 ("strong–fast," "strong–slow," "weak–fast," and "weak–slow").

In table 13.11 this is done for the *impact* change of the exchange rate. An association of the two variables does indeed emerge, but it is only the *strength* of the liberalization that seems to matter; speed does not seem to be relevant in this context. In the large majority of the 19 "strong" episodes – whether "fast" or "slow" – the real exchange rate *increased* following the launching of liberalization, it decreased in only three, and remained unchanged in the other three. In the 15 "weak" episodes, the exchange rate appears to have been almost equally likely to increase, decrease, or remain unchanged (once more, with not much distinction between "fast" and "slow" episodes). It does seem that "strong" introduc-

Table 13.11 Relationship between the impact change in the real exchange rate and the intensity of liberalizations

| | Exchange rate change | | |
Intensity	Increase	Stable	Decrease
Strong–fast	Chile 1	Singapore	Argentina 2
	Chile 2		Peru
	Greece 1		
	Indonesia 2		
	Israel 1		
	Philippines 1		
	Sri Lanka 2		
	Turkey 2		
	Yugoslavia		
Strong–slow	Brazil	Israel 3	Spain 1
	Colombia 2	New Zealand 3	
	Israel 2		
	Uruguay		
Weak–fast	Philippines 2	Colombia 1	Argentina 1
	Portugal 1		Indonesia 1
	Turkey 1		Portugal 1
			Sri Lanka 1
Weak–slow	Korea 2	Greece 2	Spain 2
	Pakistan	Korea 1	
		New Zealand 2	
		Pakistan 1	

tions of trade liberalization are commonly accompanied by an increase of the real exchange rate.

In table 13.12, the cross-classification is repeated using the movement over the period of liberalization *as a whole*. Here, almost the only inference that may be drawn is that the highly intensive liberalizations – "strong" and "fast" – are more likely than others to be accompanied by an increasing rather than a declining trend of the real exchange rate. But, again, this association is rather weak. The emerging inference is that it is mainly the impact performance of the exchange rate, and much less so its persistent performance throughout the episode, that is likely to be associated with the strength of a liberalization experiment.

Is there any relationship between the behavior of the real exchange rate and the circumstances in which the policy was introduced? An association seems to exist (table 13.13) but it is surprisingly weak. In *all* categories of

Table 13.12 Relationship between real exchange rate trends during the episode and the intensity of liberalizations

| | Exchange rate change | | |
Intensity	Increase	No trend	Decrease
Strong–fast	Greece 1 Israel 1 Philippines 1 Sri Lanka 2 Turkey 2	Chile 1 Indonesia 2 Yugoslavia	Argentina 2 Chile 2 Peru Singapore
Strong–slow		Brazil Israel 3 New Zealand 3 Uruguay	Colombia 2 Spain 1
Weak–fast	Colombia 1 Philippines 2 Portugal 2	Israel 2 Turkey 1	Argentina 1 Indonesia 1 Portugal 1 Sri Lanka 1
Weak–slow	Pakistan 2	Greece 2 Korea 2 Pakistan 1 Spain 2	Korea 1 New Zealand 2

circumstances, increases of the exchange rate outweighed decreases – more so for the "crisis" and "collapse" categories than for those regarded as being undertaken under "favorable circumstances." This certainly conforms with *a priori* expectations. Yet, no difference seems to emerge between the experience in the categories designated as "severe deterioration" and "partial deterioration," in almost all of which a balance-of-payments problem was evident, and the category of "favorable circumstances," in which episodes with no serious balance-of-payments (or any other) difficulty were present.

Whatever relationship is revealed here, it disappears completely when the performance of the exchange rate during the liberalization period *as a whole* is examined (table 13.14): liberalization episodes starting from severe or comfortable circumstances, with or without balance-of-payments deteriorations, seem to have been equally likely to demonstrate an increase, a decrease, or no significant trend change at all of the real exchange rate.

Quite in line with these observations is the way that the real exchange rate performs in a context of stabilization. The real exchange rate would be

Table 13.13 Relationship between the impact change of the real exchange rate and the circumstances of launching the liberalization

| | Exchange rate change | | |
Circumstances	Increase	Stable	Decrease
Full crisis	Chile 2 Indonesia 2		Argentina 2
Collapse	Chile 1 Israel 1 Turkey 2		
Severe deterioration	Uruguay Yugoslavia		Argentina 1 Spain 1 Spain 2
Partial deterioration	Brazil Philippines 2 Portugal 2 Sri Lanka 2 Turkey 1		Colombia 1 Portugal 1 Sri Lanka 1
Favorable circumstances	Colombia 2 Greece 1 Israel 2 Korea 2 Pakistan 2 Philippines 1	Greece 2 Israel 3 Korea 1 New Zealand 2 New Zealand 3 Pakistan 1 Singapore	

expected to increase more often in episodes launched within the framework of a stabilization policy than in others. This occurs (though not in any remarkable way) for the *impact* change of the exchange rate in the ten episodes concerned: the rate increased in seven of these but in only half of the other episodes. But when the exchange rate performance *throughout* the episode is examined, this difference disappears, and perhaps is even slightly reversed: in only two of the 11 "liberalization-cum-stabilization" episodes is an upward trend of the exchange rate evident, whereas the ratio is somewhat higher (one third) among other liberalization episodes.

Finally, a close association was observed between the change of the real exchange rate and the intensity of removal of QRs (chapter 10). In all but two of the 11 episodes in which a major removal of QRs was undertaken an *impact increase* of the exchange rate is observed. But here, too, the association becomes weaker – though it still exists – when the movement of the rate *throughout* the liberalization episode is examined. In only five

Table 13.14 Relationship between real exchange rate trends during episodes and the circumstances of launching the liberalization

Circumstances	Exchange rate change		
	Increase	No trend	Decrease
Full crisis		Indonesia 2	Argentina 2
			Chile 2
Collapse	Israel 1	Chile 1	
	Turkey 2		
Severe deterioration		Uruguay	Argentina 1
		Yugoslavia	Spain 1
Partial deterioration	Philippines 2	Brazil	Portugal 1
	Portugal 2	Turkey 1	Sri Lanka 1
	Sri Lanka 2		
Favorable circumstances	Colombia 1	Greece 2	Colombia 2
	Greece 1	Israel 2	Indonesia 1
	Pakistan 2	Israel 3	Korea 1
	Philippines 1	Korea 2	New Zealand 2
		New Zealand 3	Peru
		Pakistan 1	Singapore
		Spain 1	

of the episodes is an increase in the rate still recorded, whereas in most of the rest no significant trend change is observed – Singapore is the only exception, in which the real exchange rate actually declined during the liberalization episode.

Policy Determinants of the Real Exchange Rate

How far can the impact movements of the real exchange rate be associated with major policy variables? Three obvious candidates for examination are the nominal exchange rate, fiscal policy, and monetary policy.

Table 13.15 summarizes the behavior of the three policy variables concerned against the *impact* (first-year) behavior of the real exchange rate ("increased," "stable," and "decreased").

Obviously, there is quite a close relationship between the movements of the *nominal* and the *real* rates of exchange. A nominal devaluation seems to be almost a necessary condition for a real devaluation: of 16 liberalization episodes in which the real rate increased, in 14 a nominal devaluation was also present (the two exceptions being the episodes of Brazil and

Table 13.15 Macroeconomic policies accompanying the launching of liberalizations by category of change of the real exchange rate

Episodes of liberalization by impact change of the RER	Nominal devaluation 1	Fiscal policy 2	Monetary policy 3
Increased RER			
Brazil		+	+
Chile 1	✓	+	+
Chile 2	✓	+	+
Colombia 2	✓	0	0
Greece 1	✓	+	0
Indonesia 2		+	+
Israel 1	✓	+	+
Israel 2	✓	−	−
Pakistan 2	✓	0	0
Philippines 1	✓	+	0
Philippines 2	✓	0	0
Portugal 2	✓	0	0
Sri Lanka 2	✓	+	+
Turkey 1	✓	−	−
Turkey 2	✓	+	+
Yugoslavia	✓	0	+
Stable RER			
Greece 2		0	0
Israel 3		0	0
Korea 1		0	+
Korea 2		0	0
New Zealand 2		0	0
New Zealand 3		0	0
Pakistan 1		0	0
Singapore		0	0
Uruguay		0	0
Decreased RER			
Colombia	n.a.	n.a.	n.a.
Argentina 1	✓	+	−
Argentina 2	✓	+	−
Indonesia 1	n.a.	n.a.	n.a.
Peru		−	0
Portugal 1		0	0
Spain 1	✓	+	+
Spain 2		0	0
Spain 3	✓	−	+
Sri Lanka 1	✓	−	+

n.a., not available.

+, contraction; 0, no change; −, expansion.

Indonesia 2).[11] Conversely, in the clear majority of episodes in which the nominal rates increased, so did the real rate. The number of exceptions, however, precludes a statement that a nominal devaluation is also, empirically speaking, a sufficient condition for a real devaluation.

It should be noted (this is not recorded in the table) that a *persistent* increase of the real rate, throughout the liberalization episode, was maintained only in eight of the 14 instances in which an impact increase of the rate followed a nominal devaluation (and in neither of the two instances in which the real rate increased, on impact, without a nominal devaluation). This is one of the indications of the significance of the other policy measures, which will be noted shortly. In the more limited group of seven episodes in which *major* nominal devaluations were undertaken when liberalization was launched – Greece 1, Israel 1, Philippines 1 and 2, Sri Lanka 2, Turkey 1 and 2 – an impact increase of the real exchange rate was realized, needless to say, in all cases. But beyond this, with only one exception (Turkey 1, in which both fiscal and monetary policies were expansionary), an upward trend change of the real rate *throughout* the liberalization episode was established. This may indicate that in achieving a persistent increase of the real exchange rate a substantial initial nominal devaluation would be an important contributory element.

For fiscal and monetary policies, a contractionary direction is closely associated with an increase in the real exchange rate. In nine of the 12 instances in which fiscal policy was tight, an impact increase of the exchange rate is also observed; the ratio is similar for instances in which monetary policy was tight. In all of the eight instances in which either fiscal or monetary policy (or both) were expansionary, a nominal devaluation is observed – but the real rate increased in only three of them, and actually decreased in the other five. And of the first three, the increase of the exchange rate continued throughout the episode in only one, Turkey 1, in which a major nominal devaluation launched the liberalization experiment. Where *all* the policy elements were "right" – a nominal devaluation was accompanied by both tight fiscal and monetary policies – an increased real exchange rate normally followed: this was true for four out of five such instances (the exception being Spain 1, where an increase of the rate closely after the launching of liberalization turned into a slight decrease by the end of the episode's first year). In three of these four, the increase in the exchange rate actually persisted through the whole liberalization episode.

The number of observations, and the nature of the data, make it impossible to tell which of the two demand policy measures – tight fiscal policy or tight monetary policy – is more crucial for the realization of an

---

11 Technically, the real rate could increase without the nominal rate through a relative decrease of home prices (of nontradeables) over world prices (of tradeables).

increase in the real exchange rate. The evidence suggests, though, that while neither would be essential in the same sense that a nominal devaluation is, both are important – and certainly, that the absence of both would be likely to prevent an increase of the real exchange rate. In chapter 14 we shall turn again to these policy elements, examining directly their relationship with the fate of liberalization.

Annex: Country Study Estimates of the Real Exchange Rate

The "real" exchange rate is a medium of representation of some change over time of a *relative* price. Different uses of the concept would call for different definitions. For most of the purposes required here, the relative price sought is that of tradeables versus nontradeables.[12] That is,

$$\dot{c} = \frac{P^t_1/P^t_0}{P^h_1/P^h_0} - 1$$

where $\dot{c}$ is the change in the country's real exchange rate from period 0 to period 1, and P^t_0 and P^t_1 are the domestic price levels of tradeables in periods 0 and 1 respectively, and P^h_0 and P^h_1 are the domestic price levels of nontradeables in periods 0 and 1 respectively.

Under certain conditions, a starting position of balance-of-payments equilibrium will remain an equilibrium level if no change occurs in the real exchange rate. These conditions include, primarily, the absence of a change in the country's terms of trade (that is, in the relative price of exports to imports); the absence of a bias, for or against tradeables, in technological changes and changes in demand patterns in the economy; and the absence of changes of autonomous capital inflows.

Only a few of the country studies have adopted this definition because a crucial element in the methods of estimation is the foreign exchange prices of the country's exports and imports. This is needed, first, to establish the numerator in the definition of the real exchange rate change; but it is also required in order to estimate the denominator. Rarely, if ever, does one find a direct estimate of the prices of nontradeables; but if foreign exchange prices of tradeables, the current rate of exchange, and the overall price level in the country concerned are available, the price level of

12 Here and elsewhere in this study the "exchange rate" (in whatever form – "nominal," "real," "formal," etc.) is understood as the *price of foreign exchange* in units of domestic currency (pesos for a dollar in a Latin American country etc.). This is the most common convention; but it is not applied universally. An *increase* of the exchange rate is a *currency depreciation*, and a reduction of the rate, a currency appreciation. An increase of the real exchange rate would thus be a real depreciation of the *currency*.

nontradeables may be derived by using some (estimated or guessed) proportions of tradeables and nontradeables in the total. In fact, in only few countries were the foreign exchange prices of tradeables available for the relevant periods, so that other approximations had to substitute for the "ideal" measure. In many country studies the definition discussed above was replaced by a definition such as

$$\dot{c} = \frac{R_1}{R_0} \bigg/ \frac{P_1/P_0}{P^*_1/P^*_0}$$

where R is a nominal exchange rate, P stands for some indication of the overall price level in the home country (such as the consumer price index or the index of wholesale prices), and P^* represents the price level (mostly the index of wholesale prices) in one major trading partner (most often, the United States) or a weighted (by home-trade flows) average of several important trade partners.

The nominal exchange rate, in this formulation, could represent either the *formal* rate of exchange, or the *effective* rate – where elements such as tariffs, export subsidies, export taxes, and the like are added to or subtracted from the formal rate. In the studies involved, either of these definitions would be found. Another issue, significant particularly when the effective rather than the formal rate is used, is whether the rate employed is the one which applied to export transactions, import transactions or, perhaps, some average of both. In most of the studies, only one rate is provided – for tradeables as a whole. Where separate rates are shown for exports and imports, we have chosen to use the former. Most often, when the two rates diverge following the liberalization, the export rate would increase relative to the import rate. The liberalization act will often include tariff reductions, leading to a fall in the *effective* exchange rate for imports,[13] whereas the export rate would increase, by an increase in subsidies or a reduction of export taxes. A formal devaluation, often undertaken on such occasions, would of course tend to increase both the import and the export exchange rates. For the purpose of our present analysis, the movement of the export rate seems to be more relevant – although a single representation of all tradeables would have been better.

---

13 Where a reduction of QRs tends to be offset by increasing tariffs and the quota profits are not recorded properly in the estimate of the effective exchange rate for imports, the estimated change in this rate following the liberalization will have an upward bias. This is a deficiency which cannot feasibly be removed.

14

The Role of Macroeconomic Policies

Fiscal and monetary policies tended to move from restrictive, when the liberalization was launched, to expansionary, toward the end of an episode. During most of the life of the episode, fiscal policy seems more inclined than monetary policy to retain its original restrictive direction; this tenacity seems to require a tight policy at the outset of the episode. Episodes that start with highly distressed circumstances are likely to be accompanied upon launching by a restrictive fiscal policy, and to retain this feature during most of the life of the episode.

The nature of the fiscal policy (and to a lesser extent monetary policy) upon the launching of liberalization bears some relationship to the fate of the latter. Practically no liberalization attempt introduced when fiscal policy was expansionary has managed to stay fully sustained. The relationship is even stronger at the *close* of liberalization episodes: at that stage, a sustained liberalization episode is likely to be accompanied by either restrictive or, at least, "neutral" fiscal and monetary policies. When macroeconomic policies are expansionary toward the close of an episode, on the other hand, the liberalization tends either to collapse totally or, at best, to be partially sustained.

Restrictive accompanying macroeconomic policies are thus important for the sustainability of trade liberalization but not, apparently, at the expense of dampening economic growth. True, growth is slower in the year immediately following liberalization; but the "distress" circumstances that often herald such policies also imply slower economic growth *before* the liberalization. Hence, in terms of *change* in the period immediately following a liberalization, the growth performance in episodes with contractionary macroeconomic policies is no worse than in other liberalization episodes. Moreover, the acceleration of growth in later years is even *stronger* in the episodes that start with restrictive macroeconomic policies. Thus, no tradeoff between sustainability of trade liberalizations and a favorable impact on growth is implied in the practice of accompanying fiscal and monetary policies.

Macroeconomic policies pursued concurrently with trade reforms will obviously affect those reforms, and this potential is the main topic of the present chapter. But trade reforms may also affect macroeconomic policies, principally through their impact on government revenues. We look at this side of the coin before embarking on the enquiry into the role of macroeconomic policies in the fate of trade liberalizations.

The Effect of Liberalization on Government Revenues

An act of liberalization could affect (net) government revenues directly[1] principally through the following impacts.

1 When QRs are replaced by tariffs, quota profits appropriated by holders of licenses turn into government revenues except on the rare occasions on which quotas have been auctioned before liberalization.
2 The reduction of tariff rates *per se* would lead to a decline of tariff revenues if the size of the imports remained the same.
3 When protection is reduced, however, the imports concerned will increase, raising tariff revenues. In other words, it is not clear whether the elasticity of revenues from import duties to changes in tariff rates is positive or negative. Revenues must increase, by definition, in one case, which is probably not insignificant – when a prohibitive tariff is lowered to a subprohibitive level. By the same token, the higher and more restrictive the tariff is, the higher the probability that a tariff reduction will result in a higher revenue.
4 On the infrequent occasions when some low tariffs are raised (normally tariffs on imports of intermediate inputs and capital goods), tariff revenues will be likely to increase. The demand for these imports,

---

1 Indirect effects of liberalization, via impacts on total production and its allocation, or on total consumption, are not discussed here; they are probably not assessable in any case.

particularly intermediate inputs, must be quite inelastic in the short and medium run.

5 When a liberalization involves an export promotion policy through subsidies, (net) government revenues from trade taxes should fall.

6 Likewise, a reduction of the anti-export bias, which liberalization would normally aim to achieve, may be effected through a reduction of export *taxes*. Here, too, the direction of change of government revenues will be ambiguous: the consequent increase of exports may bring higher revenues from export taxes. But trade taxes are normally imposed on traditional exports, whose supply elasticity – at least in the short run – may be expected to be low.

7 Finally, a real devaluation, whether as an integral part of a liberalization or as an accompanying policy, is bound to increase government revenues from trade taxes by raising the local currency value of given imports. It sometimes also replaces export subsidies, which leads either to an increase of (net) revenues, or to the imposition (or increase) of trade taxes on traditional exports – yielding again an increase of government net revenues from trade taxes.

The direction in which a liberalization might push government revenues from trade taxes is therefore not predictable on *a priori* grounds; effects are likely to differ from case to case. The evidence of the country studies, summarized below, offers some clue, but it is too fragmentary to afford definite conclusions.

Separation of the effect on government revenues of trade liberalization from the impact of other changes would require a full-fledged study, beyond the scope of the country studies. In fact, the authors found the investigation of the subject feasible in only 13 episodes. Two (the second liberalization episode of Indonesia and the Peruvian episode) were quite closely studied. In the Indonesian episode liberalization led to a very substantial *increase* of revenues from trade taxes. The engines of this increase were the shift from reliance on QRs to protection through tariffs – particularly for "nonessential" goods subject to relatively high tariffs – and, less important, a shift from illegal trade channels to legal trade. The outcome was dramatic: revenues from trade taxes, in real terms, more than doubled between 1965 – the year before liberalization – and 1966; and doubled again in 1967.

In the Peruvian episode net government revenues were again increased substantially by the liberalization, primarily via replacement of QRs by tariffs, reduction of prohibitive tariffs to subprohibitive levels, and reduction of subsidies to nontraditional exports (only partly offset by a reduction of export taxes on traditional exports). The net increase thus assigned to liberalization is substantial: for 1981 – the year just following the liberalization episode – it is estimated to be roughly US$250 million (over 1 percent of gross domestic product).

The 11 other instances are more casually evaluated. In Argentina the first liberalization episode was accompanied by a tax reform, making it impossible to distinguish changes in tax revenues brought by the trade liberalization policy. In the second liberalization episode liberalization is (cautiously) credited with a substantial increase of revenues from trade taxes. A fall in export taxes was much more than offset by increases of revenues from import tariffs, so that the combined value of the two in US dollars approximately tripled from 1976 to 1980. In Greece's first liberalization episode, a substantial increase of revenues from tariffs again followed the introduction of the policy – not surprising, given the major removal of QRs accompanied by the doubling of the nominal exchange rate. The authors of the New Zealand study assign a major fiscal deterioration to the impact on revenues (only partly offset by auctioning of import quotas) of New Zealand's second liberalization phase, which consisted primarily of export promotion. In Portugal's first liberalization episode, a comparison is made with the years *following* the episode: the policy reversal led to a decline of tariff revenues – implying that revenues had increased as a result of the trade liberalization. In the country's second episode, on the other hand, a reduction of tariff levels was accompanied by lower imports, so that tariff revenues declined. In Singapore (where liberalization largely consisted of tariff reductions), revenues from trade taxes in total government revenues had all along been much below the level common in developing economies. An increase of tariff revenues, though temporary, was observed in Spain's first liberalization episode. In Sri Lanka's second liberalization episode, in which relaxation of QRs was a major component, revenues from trade taxes increased substantially – though again temporarily – following introduction of the policy. In Turkey's first trade liberalization episode, the effect of a substantially higher nominal exchange rate more than offset the impact of both lower imports and lowered tariff rates, to produce an increase of tariff revenues (not just nominally but as a share of aggregate revenues). In Uruguay's trade liberalization, revenues from trade taxes at first declined sharply owing to the virtual elimination of the substantial export taxes; but within two years the increase of revenues from import tariffs was enough to offset this loss. Finally, in Yugoslavia an increased level of tariff revenues is also apparent. First, with a shift from QRs to tariffs, revenues from the latter approximately tripled. At later stages no further trend is seen.

None of the individual observations provides conclusive evidence about the way a trade liberalization might be expected to affect revenues from trade taxes. Obviously, much depends on the policy mix. Nevertheless, the weight of the evidence suggests that in most patterns in which trade liberalization has been practiced it has led to an increase of net revenues. At least, liberalization seems generally not to have pushed revenues downward, as is sometimes feared; nor has it been identified as a source of concern in the concrete experiences of trade liberalization.

The Effects of Macroeconomic Policies on Liberalization

Characterization of Policies

We now move to the examination of the impact on trade liberalization of macroeconomic policies, in particular fiscal and monetary policy as elements of aggregate demand management.

The ambiguity involved in the definition, interpretation, and estimation of any policy instrument is particularly in evidence here. To start with, the indicators are various. For the fiscal policy instrument they could be the size of budgetary deficits (and there may be various definitions of the "deficit"), the size of government expenditures, or levels of tax rates – to mention only some of the more obvious indicators. For the monetary instrument, they could be the quantity of money (and, again, there are various definitions of "money"), the level of the rate (or rates) of interest, credit supply (or some specific element of credit), the monetary base, or the rules set by the monetary authority (such as required reserve ratios of the commercial banks), again to name a few.

Second, even granted agreement on an indicator, no universal inferences can normally be drawn from either given *levels* or given *changes* in them; usually, both would be involved. Thus, for instance, a deceleration of the rate of increase of money supply might, *prima facie*, indicate contraction, but could still be regarded as expansionary where the downward change started from a very high rate of expansion. Similar considerations would apply to the size of credit supply or to the fiscal deficit. The final judgment would also differ between countries and time scales.[2] We have therefore not attempted to construct universal indicators but will for the most part adopt the conclusions and evaluations of the authors of the country studies.

Clearly, no quantitative index of the nature of fiscal or monetary policy can be established. We therefore propose to confine ourselves to characterizing the application of policy instruments in a tentative way, as "restrictive," "expansionary," or "neutral."[3]

2 Yet another difficulty is that the level of an indicator may be determined either exogenously, by policymakers, or endogenously. Thus, for instance, money supply could increase either as a result of direct determination and manipulation by the monetary authority or, alternatively, following a capital inflow from abroad (which may, in turn, have originated from a *restrictive* monetary policy). Or, to cite another example, tax revenue could increase as a consequence of increased tax rates or an increase of income levels. The very definition of "policy" may thus be ambiguous.

3 "Neutral" is a shorthand description: it does not imply that the policy instrument in question was somehow unimportant in the designated period but simply that it was applied in neither a restrictive nor an expansionary direction. Likewise, as noted earlier, "neutrality" does not necessarily imply stability: very often, it applies to instances with substantial variation over the analyzed period. The term should be understood as roughly indicating the average for the period.

As usual, we shall observe the policy instrument at or about the time of the launching of liberalization, during the episode, and close to its conclusion. The designations of policy directions are presented in table 14.1. In some episodes where the data are insufficient, indicators will be missing, either partly or for all three phases.

Consistency of Policies

Before searching for possible connections of demand policies with any attributes or measures of performance of liberalization programs, we shall briefly examine the degree to which these policies were *persistent*, over the life of the episode, and *consistent* in the conduct of the two major components – fiscal policy and monetary policy.

Table 14.2 presents, by way of a matrix, the association between the direction of the fiscal policy on impact, when liberalization is implemented, and its trend throughout the lifetime of the episode.[4] It appears that, though no one-to-one relationship can be established, a considerable positive association does nevertheless exist. In particular, if a fiscal policy is restrictive over the whole program, a tight policy on its introduction will be found. (The only exception is Spain 2, which was marked by a restrictive fiscal policy even though its initial thrust was expansionary.) In general, the direction of fiscal policy, whether restrictive or expansionary, was determined at the outset.

This persistence is not so apparent when the directions of fiscal policy on impact and at the close (that is, during the last year) of liberalization are compared (table 14.3). An originally restrictive policy still seems to have less chance than an originally expansionary policy of ending up expansionary; but the difference is slight. Most originally tight policies became expansionary by the end of an episode. What remains true (though only three episodes are involved) is that all episodes that ended up with a restrictive fiscal policy also started that way.

In short, the fiscal policy undertaken at the launching of a liberalization program tends to determine the policy followed throughout, except that this ceases to apply in the concluding phase. It would therefore seem that the two points at which fiscal policy might usefully be studied are at impact and at close.[5]

As to monetary policy, table 14.4 examines the relationship between its impact and the continuing trend. Table 14.5 sets out the general trend and the state of policy at the close of the episode. Here, a strong association is apparent. Very few liberalization programs have been accompanied by a

---

4 See the discussion in chapter 11 of potential shortcomings in such a distinction when liberalization episodes are short.

5 Alternatively, the policy undertaken *during* the episode might replace the impact policy, but in view of the relationship just observed the outcome should not be much different.

Table 14.1 Directions of fiscal and monetary policies in episodes of liberalization

	Fiscal policy			Monetary policy		
	1	2	3	4	5	6
Episode	On impact	During the episode	At the close of the episode	On impact	During the episode	At the close of the episode
Argentina 1 (1967–70)	Restrictive	Restrictive	Expansionary	Expansionary	Expansionary	Expansionary
Argentina 2 (1976–80)	Restrictive	Restrictive	Expansionary	Restrictive	Expansionary	Expansionary
Brazil (1965–73)	Restrictive	Restrictive	n.a.	Restrictive	Expansionary	Expansionary
Chile 1 (1956–61)	Restrictive	Neutral	Expansionary	Restrictive	n.a.	Expansionary
Chile 2 (1974–81)	Restrictive	Restrictive	Restrictive	Restrictive	Neutral	Restrictive
Colombia 1 (1964–6)	n.a.	n.a.	n.a.	n.a.	n.a.	n.a.
Colombia 2 (1968–82)	Restrictive	Neutral	Expansionary	n.a.	n.a.	Expansionary
Greece 1 (1953–5)	Restrictive	Restrictive	Restrictive	Neutral	Neutral	Neutral
Greece 2 (1962–82)	n.a.	Expansionary	Expansionary	n.a.	Neutral	Neutral
Indonesia 1 (1950–1)	n.a.	n.a.	n.a.	n.a.	n.a.	n.a.
Indonesia 2 (1966–72)	Restrictive	Restrictive	Restrictive	Restrictive	Restrictive	Neutral
Israel 1 (1952–5)	Restrictive	Restrictive	Neutral	Restrictive	Neutral	Neutral
Israel 2 (1962–8)	Expansionary	Neutral	Neutral	Expansionary	Neutral	Expansionary
Israel 3 (1969–77)	Restrictive	Expansionary	Expansionary	Restrictive	n.a.	Expansionary
Korea 1 (1965–7)	Neutral	Neutral	Neutral	Expansionary	Expansionary	Expansionary
Korea 2 (1978–9)	Neutral	Neutral	Expansionary	Expansionary	Expansionary	Expansionary
New Zealand 1 (1951–6)	n.a.	n.a.	n.a.	n.a.	n.a.	n.a.
New Zealand 2 (1964–81)	Neutral	Neutral	Neutral	Neutral	Neutral	Neutral
New Zealand 3 (1982–4)	Neutral	Neutral	Expansionary	Expansionary	Restrictive	Restrictive
Pakistan 1 (1959–65)	Neutral	Neutral	Neutral	Restrictive	Neutral	Neutral
Pakistan 2 (1972–8)	Expansionary	Expansionary	n.a.	Restrictive	Neutral	Neutral
Peru (1979–80)	Expansionary	Expansionary	Expansionary	Expansionary	Expansionary	Expansionary
Philippines 1 (1960–5)	Restrictive	Neutral	Expansionary	Expansionary	Neutral	Expansionary
Philippines 2 (1970–4)	Restrictive	Expansionary	Expansionary	Expansionary	Neutral	Restrictive
Portugal 1 (1970–4)	n.a.	n.a.	n.a.	Expansionary	Neutral	Neutral
Portugal 2 (1977–80)	Expansionary	Expansionary	Expansionary	Restrictive	Restrictive	Expansionary
Singapore (1968–73)	Neutral	Neutral	Neutral	Neutral	Neutral	Neutral
Spain 1 (1960–6)	Restrictive	Restrictive	Expansionary	Restrictive	Expansionary	Expansionary
Spain 2 (1970–4)	Expansionary	Restrictive	n.a.	Neutral	Expansionary	Neutral
Spain 3 (1977–80)	Expansionary	Expansionary	Expansionary	Neutral	Neutral	Neutral
Sri Lanka 1 (1968–70)	Expansionary	Expansionary	n.a.	Neutral	Neutral	n.a.
Sri Lanka 2 (1977–9)	Restrictive	n.a.	n.a.	Restrictive	n.a.	n.a.
Turkey 1 (1970–3)	Expansionary	Expansionary	Expansionary	Expansionary	Expansionary	Expansionary
Turkey 2 (1980–4)	Restrictive	Neutral	Neutral	Restrictive	Expansionary	Neutral
Uruguay (1974–82)	n.a.	n.a.	n.a.	Restrictive	Neutral	n.a.
Yugoslavia (1965–7)	—	—	—	Restrictive	Restrictive	Restrictive

n.a., not available. —, not applicable.

Table 14.2 The persistence of fiscal policy: relationship between its direction on impact and during liberalization episode

Direction during the episode	Impact direction		
	Restrictive	Neutral	Expansionary
Restrictive	Argentina 1 Argentina 2 Brazil Chile 2 Greece 1 Indonesia 2 Israel 1 Spain 1		Spain 2
Neutral	Chile 1 Colombia 2 Philippines 1 Turkey 2	Korea 1 Korea 2 New Zealand 2 New Zealand 3 Pakistan 1 Singapore	Israel 2
Expansionary	Israel 3 Philippines 2, 3		Pakistan 2 Peru Portugal 2 Spain 3 Sri Lanka 1 Turkey

persistently restrictive monetary policy: most of the episodes are characterized by either an expansionary or a "neutral" policy. But, whether predominantly expansionary or neutral, there is no marked change toward the close.

As with fiscal policy, the two points – impact and closing – merit attention, with the proviso that for monetary policy it is the latter rather than the former that also indicates the policy trend throughout most of the episode.[6]

Turning to the issue of consistency of policies, tables 14.6 and 14.7 set out the relationship between fiscal and monetary policy at points of impact and closure. The figures indicate considerable correspondence when liberalization is launched. In most instances in which fiscal policy was

6 In other words, the two time dimensions here are (a) the impact policy and (b) the policy followed later, including the close of the episode, whereas for fiscal policy the dissection was (a) the impact policy and the policy followed during most of the episode and (b) the policy implemented toward the close of the episode.

Table 14.3 The persistence of fiscal policy: relationship between its direction on impact and toward the close of the liberalization episode

Direction during the episode	Impact direction		
	Restrictive	Neutral	Expansionary
Restrictive	Chile 2 Greece 1 Indonesia		
Neutral	Israel 1 Turkey 2	Korea 1 New Zealand 2 Pakistan 1 Singapore	Israel 2
Expansionary	Argentina 1 Argentina 2 Chile 1 Colombia 2 Israel 3 Philippines 1 Philippines 2 Israel 3 Spain 1	Korea 2 New Zealand 2	Peru Portugal 2 Spain 3 Turkey 1

Table 14.4 The persistence of monetary policy: relationship between its direction on impact and during the liberalization episode

Direction during the episode	Impact direction		
	Restrictive	Neutral	Expansionary
Restrictive	Indonesia 2 Portugal 2 Yugoslavia		New Zealand 3
Neutral	Chile 2 Israel 1 Pakistan 1 Pakistan 2 Turkey 2	Greece 1 New Zealand 1 Singapore Spain 3	Israel 2 Philippines 1 Philippines 2 Portugal 1
Expansionary	Argentina 1 Brazil Spain 1 Uruguay	Spain 2	Argentina 1 Korea 1 Korea 2 Peru Turkey 1

Table 14.5 The persistence of monetary policy: relationship between its direction during the liberalization episode and towards its close

	Direction during the episode		
Direction toward the close	Restrictive	Neutral	Expansionary
Restrictive	New Zealand 3 Yugoslavia	Chile 2 Philippines 2	
Neutral		Greece 1 Greece 2 New Zealand 2 Pakistan 1 Pakistan 2 Portugal 1 Singapore Spain 3 Turkey 2	Spain 2
Expansionary	Portugal 2	Israel 2 Philippines 1	Argentina 1 Argentina 2 Brazil Korea 1 Korea 2 Peru Spain 1 Turkey 1

Table 14.6 The consistency of policies: relationship between the direction of impact fiscal policy and monetary policy

	Direction during the episode		
Direction toward the close	Restrictive	Neutral	Expansionary
Restrictive	Argentina 2 Brazil Chile 1 Chile 2 Indonesia 2 Israel 1 Israel 3 Spain 1 Sri Lanka 2 Turkey 2	Pakistan 1	Pakistan 2 Portugal 2
Neutral	Greece 1	New Zealand 2 Singapore	Spain 2 Spain 3
Expansionary	Argentina 1 Philippines 1 Philippines 2	Korea 1 Korea 2 New Zealand 3	Israel 2 Peru Turkey 1

restrictive, so was monetary policy; and vice versa. Exceptions, however, are not rare. Correspondence appears closer (table 14.7) in the closing phase of liberalization episodes, when both fiscal and monetary policies tend to be expansionary or neutral.

The two tables, 14.6 and 14.7, illustrate how fiscal and monetary policies develop. Upon the launching of liberalization both tend to be restrictive, with only three episodes in which both instruments are expansionary. Toward the end of the liberalization episodes this trend is reversed: both policy instruments then tend toward expansion. In several episodes both policies are neutral toward the end; in only a single episode (Chile 2) are they both restrictive at this stage.

It would have been interesting to observe the eventual development of policies in episodes in which both fiscal and monetary policies were restrictive when liberalization was launched. Unfortunately, for half of the ten episodes in this category the necessary evidence is missing for the period close to the episode's end. Of the remaining five, only in Chile 2 was the restrictive combination practiced also at the end of the episode, whereas on three occasions an expansionary combination is found (the fifth episode being characterized by "neutral" policies). In the few instances in which evidence is available for either fiscal or monetary policy (but not both), that policy is also mostly found to be expansionary. The rule seems to be, on the other hand, that where both policies were expansionary when

Table 14.7 The consistency of policies: relationship between the direction of fiscal and monetary policies toward the close of episodes

Direction of monetary policy	Direction of fiscal policy		
	Restrictive	Neutral	Expansionary
Restrictive	Chile 2		New Zealand 3 Philippines 2
Neutral	Greece 1	Israel 1 New Zealand 2 Pakistan 1 Singapore Turkey 2	Greece 2 Spain 3
Expansionary		Korea 1 Israel 2	Argentina 1 Argentina 2 Chile 1 Colombia 2 Korea 2 Peru Philippines 1 Portugal 2 Spain 1 Turkey 2

the liberalization program started, they remained so at its conclusion (the episode of Israel 2 being a partial exception, among the three in this group, where only a "neutral" fiscal policy accompanied an expansionary policy at the close of the episode).

In conclusion, the drift over time of policies, and the less than full consistency of the two, preclude a clear-cut categorization of liberalization experiences by the nature of macroeconomic policies. Fiscal policy does tend to be similar during the episode to what it was when the episode was launched; but monetary policy tends to be similar during the period to what it would be at its close. Persistent and consistent combinations of the two policies, in either restrictive or expansionary directions, are infrequent. Thus no strong inferences about the *impact* of a given nature of policies on performance, or on the fate of liberalizations, should be expected from the evidence on hand: at best, suggestive inferences may emerge.

Relationships of Macroeconomic Policies with Attributes and Circumstances of the Liberalization

All the liberalization programs launched under severe pressure ("full crisis" or "perception of collapse"(see table 4.1)) have been characterized on *impact* by both restrictive fiscal and restrictive monetary policies. Of the 18 episodes classified as having started with "favorable circumstances," only one – Israel 3 – exhibits this combination. At the other extreme are the three episodes characterized by an expansionary combination of fiscal and monetary policies. Two of these (Israel 2 and Peru) started in "favorable circumstances," whereas in the third (Turkey 1) there was only a partial deterioration. The association of a restrictive tendency in macroeconomic policies with economic crisis is thus as plain as it is predictable.

We have seen that fiscal policy during the liberalization episode tends to be similar in direction to that of the policy followed on impact. Thus, episodes starting in critical circumstances tend to exhibit a continuing restrictive fiscal policy, while those launched under favorable circumstances almost universally exhibit an expansionary fiscal policy. The same is not true for monetary policy, nor does either fiscal or monetary policy at the close of an episode appear to be related in any coherent fashion to the economic and political circumstances obtaining when liberalization was introduced.

Of the 11 episodes distinguished by a major removal of QRs (earlier identified as likely to be sustainable and to result in favorable economic performance), six belong to the group in which *both* fiscal policy and monetary policy were restrictive, on impact. Of the other five episodes of major QR removal, in only one (Israel 2) were both policies expansionary; in three others the policy combination was partly restrictive; in the remaining episode, that of Uruguay, evidence about directions of macro-economic policies could not be established. In practically all these episodes the real exchange rate also exhibited an upward movement following the liberalization (short lived only in Israel 2, where macroeconomic policies were expansionary). It should be noted, however, that in almost all these instances a nominal devaluation too accompanied the launching of liberalization. In short, mostly restrictive fiscal and monetary policies combined, in these instances, with nominal devaluations to produce a rising trend in the real exchange rate.

Macroeconomic Policies and Sustainability of Liberalizations

Fiscal and monetary policies may be expected to participate in determining the fate of liberalization in the same way as the behavior of the real exchange rate. An expansionary macroeconomic policy would tend to contribute to a trade deficit and a balance-of-payments deterioration, and thus to a pressure for reversal of liberalization; and to the encouragement of the nontradeables sector at the expense of tradeables activities, thus promoting antagonism to the policy among producers of tradeables. On the other hand, an expansion of aggregate demand may lower unemployment, thus weakening another potential resistance to the liberalization.

Since fiscal and monetary policies combine to determine the behavior of the real exchange rate, much of their impact on the liberalization policy must have been captured when the real exchange rate was analyzed. We shall nevertheless try now to observe directly the relationship, if any, of macroeconomic policy and the sustainability of trade liberalization.

To examine any more direct relationship that might exist, liberalization episodes are cross-classified according to the nature of the *impact* fiscal policy and the eventual fate of the liberalization (table 14.8). Some relationship does seem to exist. In particular, no liberalization attempt except Israel 2 has been fully sustained when accompanied by an expansionary fiscal policy upon its launching. But the relationship is not impressive; in particular, no general difference seems to appear, in terms of the impact fiscal policy, between the partially sustained liberalizations and those that collapsed completely.

If anything, the relationship between the impact monetary policy (table 14.9) and the sustainability of liberalization seems to be even weaker than it is for fiscal policy – perhaps because the trend of monetary policy during the episode is further from its pattern at the launching of the episode than is the case with fiscal policy.

Tables 14.10 and 14.11 cross-classify the nature of fiscal and monetary policies toward the close of the liberalization episodes. A mere counting of cases appears to show no close relationship, but closer examination reveals distinct patterns. By and large, a *sustained* episode is accompanied by

Table 14.8 Impact fiscal policy and sustainability of liberalizations

Sustainability	Direction of fiscal policy		
	Restrictive	Neutral	Expansionary
Sustained	Chile 2 Greece 1 Indonesia 2 Israel 1 Israel 3 Sri Lanka 2 Turkey 2	Korea 1 Korea 2 New Zealand 2 New Zealand 3 Singapore	Israel 2
Partially sustained	Colombia 2 Pakistan 1 Philippines 1 Philippines 2 Spain 1		Pakistan 2 Portugal 2 Spain 2 Spain 3
Collapsed	Argentina 1 Argentina 2 Brazil Chile 1		Peru Sri Lanka 1 Turkey 1

Table 14.9 Impact monetary policy and sustainability of liberalizations

Sustainability	Direction of fiscal policy		
	Restrictive	Neutral	Expansionary
Sustained	Chile 2 Indonesia 2 Israel 1 Israel 2 Sri Lanka 2 Turkey 2 Uruguay	Greece 2 New Zealand 2 Singapore	Israel 2 Korea 1 Korea 2 New Zealand 3
Partially sustained	Pakistan 1 Pakistan 2 Portugal 2 Spain 1	Spain 2 Spain 3	Philippines 1 Philippines 2
Collapsed	Argentina 2 Brazil Chile 1 Yugoslavia		Argentina 1 Peru Portugal 1 Turkey 1

Table 14.10 Fiscal policy toward the end of the episode and sustainability of liberalizations

	Direction of fiscal policy		
Sustainability	Restrictive	Neutral	Expansionary
Sustained	Chile 2	Israel 1	Greece 2
	Greece 1	Israel 2	Israel 3
	Indonesia 2	Korea 1	Korea 2
		New Zealand 2	New Zealand 3
		Singapore	
		Turkey 2	
Partially sustained		Pakistan 1	Colombia 2
			Philippines 1
			Philippines 2
			Portugal 2
			Spain 1
			Spain 3
Collapsed			Argentina 1
			Argentina 2
			Chile 1
			Peru
			Turkey 1

Table 14.11 Monetary policy toward the end of the episode and sustainability of liberalizations

	Direction of monetary policy		
Sustainability	Restrictive	Neutral	Expansionary
Sustained	Chile 2	Greece 1	Israel 2
	New Zealand 3	Greece 2	Korea 1
		Israel 1	Korea 2
		New Zealand 2	
		Singapore	
		Turkey 2	
Partially sustained	Philippines 2	Pakistan 1	Colombia 2
		Pakistan 2	Philippines 1
		Spain 2	Portugal 2
		Spain 3	Spain 1
Collapsed	Yugoslavia	Portugal 1	Argentina 1
			Argentina 2
			Brazil
			Chile 1
			Peru
			Turkey 1

either a restrictive or a "neutral" fiscal policy; and the same is true for monetary policy. But where fiscal and monetary policies are expansionary, the program is only partially sustained or totally collapses. There are some special exceptions, notably the later stage liberalization policies in Greece, Israel, Korea, and New Zealand – countries in which the liberalization was a long-running policy, presumably well established by the time the latest stage was undertaken. Under such circumstances the nature of the macroeconomic policies is not material in determining the durability of liberalizations (we also have to note that in none of these instances – except, perhaps, Israel 3 – did expansionary fiscal and monetary policy bring, at the relevant times, any substantial inflation).

We now consider the few episodes in which fiscal and monetary policies were persistent over time or consistent in their application (or both). In three episodes – Chile 2, Greece 1, and Indonesia 1 – fiscal policy was restrictive at impact, during the episode, and toward the close of the episode. In all three, the liberalization policy was fully sustained. This applies also to the single episode of Korea 1, in which a "neutral" fiscal policy was applied persistently. Of the five episodes, on the other hand, in which an expansionary policy persisted, three – Peru, Sri Lanka 1, and Turkey 1 – totally collapsed, while two (Portugal 2 and Spain 3) were partially sustained.

As to *monetary policy*, we see that of the three episodes with persistently restrictive policy two – Chile 2 and Indonesia 2 – were fully sustained, while the third, in Yugoslavia, collapsed. Of the two in which policy was persistently "neutral" one, Singapore, was fully sustained, and the other, Spain 3, partially sustained. Four of the six episodes, on the other hand, where an expansionary policy was pursued, totally collapsed (Argentina 1 and 2, Peru and Turkey 1), while the other two (Korea 1 and 2) were fully sustained. The evidence is less clear cut than in respect of fiscal policy, but still reveals some relevance of the policy for the fate of liberalization.

Restrictive fiscal and monetary policies were applied *consistently* on impact in ten liberalization episodes. In six of these the policy was fully sustained, and in one partially sustained. In the other three (Argentina 2, Brazil, and Chile 1) it collapsed. Of the three episodes in which, on the other hand, an expansionary policy was applied consistently, the liberalization survived in one (Israel 2) and collapsed in the other two (Peru and Turkey 1). By itself the indication again is not unequivocal. But comparing it with our earlier observations about the separate relevance of impact fiscal policy and impact monetary policy, it does seem that a *consistent* pursuit of fiscal and monetary policies together, on impact, is more closely connected with the eventual fate of liberalization than each of the policies separately. Not incidentally, of course, in all three instances in which the liberalization policy collapsed, fiscal and monetary policies were consistently expansionary toward the close of each episode; in the other seven instances, policies at this stage were predominantly either restrictive or "neutral."

Macroeconomic Policies and Balance-of-payments Performance

It will be recalled (chapter 11) that the *impact* reaction of both foreign exchange reserves and exports to the launching of a trade liberalization policy was almost uniformly positive. Balance-of-payments performance toward the *close* of liberalization episodes, on the other hand, has been quite varied, and is therefore worth study in the context of macroeconomic policies. Tables 14.12 and 14.13 group liberalization episodes according to the direction of fiscal or monetary policy at their closing stage. In each

Table 14.12 Fiscal policy and the balance of payments toward the end of liberalization episodes

Direction of fiscal policy	1 Change of reserves	2 Change of exports
Restrictive		
Chile 2	No change	No change
Indonesia 2	Increase	Increase
Neutral		
Israel 1	No change	No change
Israel 2	Decrease	Increase
Korea 1	Increase	Increase
Pakistan 1	Decrease	Increase
Singapore	Increase	Increase
Turkey 2	No change	Increase
Expansionary		
Argentina 1	Decrease	Decrease
Argentina 2	Decrease	Decrease
Chile 1	Decrease	Increase
Colombia 2	Decrease	No change
Greece 2	Decrease	No change
Israel 2	Increase	No change
Korea 2	Increase	Increase
New Zealand 3	No change	No change
Pakistan 2	Decrease	No change
Peru	No change	Decrease
Philippines 1	Increase	Increase
Philippines 2	Increase	Increase
Portugal 2	Increase	No change
Spain 1	Decrease	No change
Spain 3	Decrease	Decrease
Turkey 1	Increase	No change

Table 14.13 Monetary policy and the balance of payments toward the end of liberalization episodes

Direction of fiscal policy	1 Change of reserves	2 Change of exports
Restrictive		
Chile 2	No change	No change
New Zealand 3	No change	No change
Philippines 2	Increase	Increase
Yugoslavia	Decrease	No change
Neutral		
Greece 2	Decrease	No change
Israel 1	No change	No change
Pakistan 1	Decrease	Increase
Pakistan 2	Decrease	No change
Portugal 1	No change	No change
Singapore	Increase	Increase
Spain 2	No change	No change
Spain 3	Decrease	Decrease
Turkey 2	No change	Increase
Expansionary		
Argentina 1	Decrease	Decrease
Argentina 2	Decrease	Decrease
Brazil	No change	No change
Chile 1	Decrease	Increase
Colombia 2	Decrease	No change
Israel 2	Decrease	Increase
Korea 1	Increase	Increase
Korea 2	Increase	Increase
Peru	No change	Decrease
Philippines 1	Increase	Increase
Portugal 2	Increase	No change
Spain 1	Decrease	No change
Turkey 1	Increase	No change

table, directions of changes of foreign exchange reserves and of exports, at this stage, are recorded.

Some regularity does seem to appear: in general, foreign exchange reserves are more likely to fall when fiscal policy is expansionary than when it is either restrictive (a very small category or observations – three altogether) or "neutral" (table 14.12). But the evidence seems to be rather weak, and is much more convincing when *export* performance is examined. There, of the eight instances of a restrictive or "neutral" fiscal policy for which export data are available, in six the trend of exports is increasing, while in two it is stable. Of the 15 episodes where fiscal policy is expansionary, in only three did exports tend to increase; in eight they were stable; while in the other four episodes they actually declined. Examination of episodes in which fiscal policy was *persistent* – applied in roughly the same direction both when liberalization was launched, during its lifetime, and toward its close – reinforces these observations. Of three episodes (for which data are available) in which fiscal policy was persistently restrictive or "neutral," exports grew in two and were stable in the third. Of four episodes in which fiscal policy was consistently expansionary, on the other hand, one shows a growth in exports and two show an actual fall. The inference is that an expansionary fiscal policy has tended to prevent, while a restrictive or "neutral" policy has encouraged, export growth.

No such relationship appears from the data on monetary policy (see table 14.13). This is somewhat surprising but does accord with our earlier observations about the sustainability of liberalization, which seemed to be more strongly related to the conduct of fiscal than of monetary policy.

Macroeconomic Policies and Growth

Now that we have looked at the role that restrictive macroeconomic policies seem to have played in sustaining liberalization, it is worth considering whether, in the short run, this has been achieved only at the cost of constraining economic growth. No fully satisfactory answer is possible within the scope of this project, but a "stylized facts" impression may be gained by a brief look at the record of the relevant episodes.

Table 14.14 presents average growth records in two categories of episodes: those in which both monetary and fiscal policies were restrictive on impact (ten episodes altogether); and all other episodes for which data

Table 14.14 Growth rates by category of macroeconomic policies

	1	2	3	4	5	6	7
			Percentage annual rate of increase of GDP				
Category of episodes	Year before liberalization $(t-1)$	First year of liberalization (t)	Second year $(t+1)$	Third year $(t+2)$	Fourth year $(t+3)$	Four-year average $(t$ to $t+3)$	Average for 1960–80[a]
1 Consistently restrictive impact fiscal and monetary policies							
(a) Mean	2.4	4.0	3.8	7.0	7.8	5.8	6.8
(b) Median	2.8	2.7	5.8	5.6	6.9	5.5	6.3
2 Other episodes							
(a) Mean	5.1	5.5	5.3	5.3	6.2	5.5	5.7
(b) Median	5.4	4.8	5.5	5.2	6.4	4.7	6.2

[a] These are *not* averages for the countries concerned, since countries are weighted by their number of liberalization episodes.

are available (23 altogether).[7] The growth record is presented (along the lines of the investigation pursued in chapter 7) for the following periods: the year preceding liberalization; the first year of the episode; the three subsequent years, separately; the average for the four years following the introduction of liberalization; and the average for the years 1960–80 (as some representation of "normal" growth rates).

It appears that, on average, countries in the "restrictive" group grew substantially less in the year in which liberalization was launched than did other countries. But the starting position of the two groups was also different: growth rates in the "restrictive" group in the year before liberalization were only about half what they were in other episodes. This seems to reflect the relationship of restrictive macroeconomic policies with a situation of economic distress on the eve of the launching of a liberalization policy. Be that as it may, the *change* from the year preceding liberalization to the following year was about the same – rather small – in both categories of episodes.

Following the first year of liberalization, growth appears to accelerate in the "restrictive" category, but less noticeably so elsewhere. In sum, the average growth rate for the four-year period following liberalization appears to be roughly similar in the two categories of episodes. This would remain true if we confined our observation to the subgroups (six of the ten episodes) in which a restrictive fiscal policy was maintained during the episode (as well as being restrictive on *impact*). Similarly, we observe that in the small group of episodes in which expansionary fiscal and monetary policies were applied consistently, on impact, growth rates were also similar to those found in the "restrictive" group (although an averaging of three observations is probably of questionable usefulness).

Thus, as far as this evidence goes, the accompaniment of a trade liberalization policy by restrictive macroeconomic policies did not tend to produce a short- or medium-term reduction in growth rates when liberalization policies were undertaken. We can tentatively conclude that the reinforcing of trade liberalization by restrictive fiscal and monetary policies tend to increase the sustainability of liberalizations without imposing a cost of restraining.

7 Some further subclassifications might have been tried, but the number of observations would become too small.

15

Liberalizations of the Goods Market and of the Capital Market

Appropriate sequencing of two forms of liberalization – of the goods market and of the (external) capital market – involves allocative efficiency and macroeconomic impact. No empirical verification is offered on the first aspect, but *a priori* reasoning suggests that it would be more efficient to implement trade liberalization first, introducing capital market liberalization only when adjustment to trade liberalization is largely over.

As far as the limited empirical inferences go, they tend to suggest the following macroeconomic events and implications. First, an opening of the capital market tends (here the evidence is strongest) to lead to a short-term capital *inflow* rather than an outflow. This, in turn, tends to lead to a real currency *appreciation*. With time, both tendencies are reversed: short-term capital starts flowing out of the economy, and a process of currency depreciation is on its way. The fluctuations of the real rate of exchange may be quite dramatic, as indeed they were in three countries ("the Southern Cone") of the four (Argentina, Chile, Israel, and Uruguay) studied in this context.

These fluctuations of capital inflows are likely to jeopardize trade liberalization on two scores. First, the appreciation of the exchange rate, following the capital market liberalization, depresses tradeable activities, whereas a real depreciation, encouraging tradeables, is required to sustain a trade liberalization. In addition, when the capital inflow turns to an outflow, the government is likely to resort again to controls of imports to alleviate an emerging balance-of-payments problem. A capital market liberalization undertaken before trade liberalization, and the adjustment to it, are well advanced is thus likely to make trade liberalization unsustainable.

Sequencing Liberalizations in Two Markets

A principle stated at the outset and followed faithfully so far is that the present project is confined to the study of *trade* liberalization. Restrictions in other markets, such as the domestic labor or capital markets, may have played their part in the outcome of trade liberalization but they have not been studied for their own sake. The present chapter deviates from this principle in one important respect.

Three major markets are involved in a country's economic relationship with the outside world; three forms of *external* liberalization are hence possible. First – the subject of the present study – is the market for goods and (nonfactor) services. Second is the labor market. Completely free movements of labor – out of the country and, primarily, into it – are still the exception, and "liberalizations" of the *external* labor market have been rare, whether in conjunction with trade liberalization or independently. This potential form of liberalization would thus not be of much importance, or relevance, in the context of a study of trade liberalization.[1]

Third is the capital market. Here, liberalizations[2] have been implemented, and their influence on the success or failure of those undertaken in the markets for goods has attracted a great deal of attention in recent years – in particular, with regard to the issue of how best to sequence the two forms of liberalization.

Constraints on external movements of goods and of capital imply a distorted market for both. Liberalization, in each market, would then involve a reduction of distortions in each. Simultaneous liberalization at first glance would seem the most promising course to pursue. But in practice a simultaneous process is not feasible; it may not necessarily even be the most desirable.

---

1 This statement does not imply that external movements of labor have no potential significance. In fact, labor remittances from abroad have on various occasions been a substantial component of foreign exchange receipts; changes in them, through their impact on the balance of payments, may have been important to a trade liberalization's survival.

2 "Liberalization" of the capital market is understood here as the removal of (all or most) restrictions on external capital flows. Our discussion refers strictly to a liberalization of *external* capital market transactions. Logically, such liberalization may not necessarily involve any measure of liberalization of the *internal* capital market. In fact, though, highly restricted internal transactions rarely survive with freedom of external capital movements.

To start with, *processes* of liberalization must be different between the goods and the capital markets, in both duration and form. Normally, the process would be shorter when the capital market is liberalized; the measures of liberalization, being of quite different natures, would not be comparable between the two processes. "Simultaneity" of liberalizations is thus essentially impracticable (nor, indeed, could it be defined) unless both processes take the nature of immediate and total liberalization: a sequencing in time is practically inevitable. Usually, the issue is put in the form of "which comes first." A better formulation is whether the capital market should be liberalized before, during, or after implementation of trade liberalization, or, further, after adjustment required by trade liberalization has been largely completed. In our analysis, we shall understand by "goods market first" a process in which liberalization in the goods market is practically completed, and most of the adjustment is realized, by the time that capital market liberalization is undertaken. Otherwise, it would be a process of "capital market liberalization first."

The sequencing issue has two interrelated aspects: the effects on allocative efficiency, and the macroeconomic impact. *A priori* hypotheses about both aspects will be presented in the next two sections; the empirical evidence (limited to the macroeconomic process) will be presented in the subsequent two sections.

Three of the countries studied have episodes in which the capital market was liberalized in conjunction with trade liberalization: Argentina 2, Chile 2, and Uruguay. In addition, a liberalization of the capital market was implemented in Israel by the end of the country's third liberalization episode (1969–77). The authors of the studies of these countries have investigated the issue separately in special studies for this project;[3] the empirical inferences will largely rely on these four supplementary investigations.[4]

Effects of Alternative Sequencing on Welfare

In an economy in which two distorted markets exist, theory furnishes no guidance as to which should first be freed of distortions – it may not even be desirable to remove distortions in one market while they are present in the other. The two markets in question (goods and capital) do, however, differ enough to permit some deductions about desirable sequencing. The considerations involved are the following.

3 Cottani and García (1989), Favaro and Spiller (1989), Hachette (1989), and Halevi (1987).
4 But references to the issue, based on limited experiences, are also available in several other studies.

1 The assets market adjusts much faster than the goods market. To reduce distortions simultaneously in both markets, capital market opening should therefore be lagged behind liberalization of the goods market (see Frenkel, 1983).
2 The vast movements involved in the capital market's quick response are likely to magnify any error. The slow reaction of the goods market will enable policymakers to correct errors more slowly, when strong responses of the capital market are absent (see Frenkel, 1983).
3 Opening capital markets when trade is highly restricted and the protection system highly dispersed would attract more investment to the wrong activities and increase the overall cost of distortions, but relaxing restrictions on trade flows while the capital market remains constrained should not reinforce distortions (see Frenkel, 1983; Edwards, 1984; Krueger, 1986).

It might be countered that when liberalization of the goods market is first introduced investors would take into account the expected "right" relative prices of goods when the process is fully implemented; hence real investment would *not* be distorted from that moment on (see Lal, 1987). The experiences surveyed do not lend much conviction to this argument. Pre-announced, comprehensive schemes of removal of protection have been rare and full adherence to them even rarer; liberalization attempts are almost as likely to be reversed as to survive. "Correct" anticipation of future prices, based on a recently introduced trade liberalization policy, must therefore be rather unlikely.

A counter-argument may be made in favor of opening the *capital* market first. Over the long term, it may be assumed that with an open capital market some "normal" amount of capital inflow (that is, of foreign investment in the economy) will be forthcoming. This inflow should affect (via a real exchange rate appreciation) the relative prices of tradeables, and hence the profitability of investment in various activities. If trade liberalization takes place before the opening of the capital market, investment would be misdirected in comparison with what it should be when all markets are open. The relevance of this argument depends largely on the relationship of the size of expected capital inflows in the first few years following the opening of the capital market to the "normal" size of such inflows. If the discrepancy is substantial – and experience, as well as *a priori* reasoning, tend to suggest that it is – the argument would lose its significance.

This is not to imply that the capital market opening should follow the goods market opening only after a long delay. Specifically, liberalizing long-term foreign investment shortly after the goods market liberalization is entrenched may substantially increase the responsiveness of the production structure to the new pattern of incentives – in particular, the removal of the anti-export bias.

The weight of the argument seems to be that from the point of view of welfare effects trade flows should be liberalized first, and the capital market later. Since we see no way to test this proposition empirically the argument will have to rest at that.

The Macroeconomic Effects of Alternative Sequencing

Considerations of the macroeconomic effects of opening the capital market while the goods market is still constrained (or not fully adjusted) lead almost invariably to the conclusion that such a sequencing is inferior to its alternative. The considerations themselves – obviously not proposed in the same breath – may, however, be diametrically opposed.

First, expectations of large-scale capital outflows are mentioned as a source of concern (see the not necessarily approving survey in Edwards (1984)). These would presumably originate from several sources. One is pent-up demand for the holding of foreign assets: economic agents, long frustrated from increasing the proportion of foreign assets on their portfolios, would now act. Another could be hoarding of foreign assets arising from the not implausible assumption that the opening of the capital market may be short lived. Another source of outflows may be directly attributable to the consecutive introduction of *trade* liberalization: since sustainability of the latter requires a real exchange rate depreciation, demand for foreign assets would increase in anticipation of this movement (see Rodrik, 1987).

The emergence of capital outflows could, in turn, harm the trade liberalization via potential effects on the balance of payments and on domestic activity and employment. In a regime of a fixed nominal exchange rate (or at least where the exchange rate is prevented from reaching its equilibrium level), the depletion of foreign exchange reserves would be likely, as we have seen, to disrupt the process of trade liberalization,[5] while adverse effects on domestic activity and employment of an increase of the real rate of interest originating from the capital outflow (see Rodrik, 1987) might, again, harm trade liberalization attempts (although we have seen that this is not a common pattern of response). On the other hand, if the nominal exchange rate is *not* fixed, capital outflows may *contribute* to the sustainability of trade liberalization: by leading to a (nominal and real) exchange rate depreciation, they would provide protection to tradeable activities and increase support for the liberalization policy.

---

5 When the foreign exchange rate *is* allowed to reach its equilibrium level, a real *depreciation* should follow. This should then have a favorable impact on the tradeables sector. In this situation – not a very likely outcome with a large-scale outflow of capital – no adverse effects on the level of foreign exchange reserves and on the fate of liberalization should emerge.

The opposite effect – large-scale capital *inflows* – is also cited as a likely outcome of opening the capital market; these too – in their different way – would be likely to weaken the tenacity of a trade liberalization.[6] Capital inflows might emerge because of interest rate differentials when capital markets are opened; the (real) interest rate in the trade-liberalizing developing economy is likely to be higher than those found in the international (developed world) capital markets. For related reasons, capital inflows might be stimulated by pent-up demand for credit from abroad, in an economy with a repressed financial market. The trade liberalization policy itself is another potential source: an economy with newly liberalized trade may attract foreign investors. Or, if the liberalization policy lacks credibility and is widely perceived as likely to be shortly reversed, anticipation of future imposition of restrictions on imports may encourage accumulation and hoarding of imported goods. This, in turn, would increase demand for credit, part of which will be provided by foreign lenders.[7] However, if this is the source of capital inflow, the inflow would at most offset the increased demand for foreign exchange arising from the increase in imports. On this score, therefore, no excess supply of foreign exchange should be expected. A welfare cost, though, would still emerge (Calvo, 1988).

The natural outcome of the emergence of substantial capital inflows would be a real exchange rate appreciation. This would result from a downward movement of the nominal exchange rate (relative to the movement of domestic prices) under a regime of a freely floating exchange rate or, in a fixed exchange rate regime, from the monetary impact of the accumulation of foreign exchange reserves and the increase of the monetary base. (The only exception would be where, in the fixed exchange rate regime, the increase of foreign exchange reserves is sterilized; but such sterilization is rare.)

This movement of the real rate of foreign exchange may be expected to be abrupt. Moreover, it may easily become self-reinforcing (Michaely, 1983). An actual appreciation, lasting for some time (say, several months), is likely to lead to further expectations of an appreciation. With such anticipations, the perceived real rate of interest on borrowing from abroad would be lowered in relationship to the interest rate on domestic borrowing. This, in turn, would lead to further borrowing from abroad, with the ensuing further actual appreciation of the real exchange rate. Naturally, such a process would not last indefinitely and at some point – presumably following some new event – would be reversed. With other modes of forming expectations – specifically with rational expectations – this process would obviously be absent.

6 Most of the following considerations have first been raised by McKinnon (1982). See also Dornbusch (1983), Edwards (1984), Frenkel (1983), and Harberger (1986).
7 A strong relationship may be expected between the size of imports and the size of foreign lending for the financing of imports.

Granting the emergence of capital inflows, and ensuing appreciation of the real exchange rate, several deterimental impacts on the economy should follow. Presumably, capital inflows are likely to be halted or reversed within a few years once the original incentives for these inflows are exhausted – that is, once what is mostly a stock adjustment to the opening of the capital market is completed. Supply of foreign capital is not infinitely elastic. A strong negative response may be expected, in terms of erosion of the economy's creditworthiness, increased interest rates and, beyond a certain range, complete disappearance of the supply of new foreign lending. Moreover, the self-reinforcing process would be reversed, working against a capital inflow and in favor of a capital outflow.

Accepting the likelihood of such a pattern, damage would be expected on two scores. One is a welfare cost. Economic agents will be receiving inconsistent signals, over time. First, an exchange rate appreciation would discourage tradeable activities, shifting resources to the nontradeables sector. Then price movements would be reversed. The important point is that the original appreciation leads to relative prices that cannot be sustained over the longer run, thus leading inevitably to resource movements in and out of nontradeable and tradeable activities. Assuming rigidities in such movements of resources, waste would be involved. The other damage will be inflicted on the *sustainability* of trade liberalization. The reversal of capital movements, from inflows to outflows (or even just a major reduction of inflows), would probably lead to balance-of-payments deterioration (that is, to a loss of foreign exchange reserves) – which is bound to endanger survival of the trade liberalization experiment.

Even if the initial level of capital inflows is sustainable over the long run, trade liberalization is likely to be damaged. The exchange rate appreciation would discourage tradeable activities – in exportables as well as some import substituting. This implies the prevention of emergence of activities that benefit from – and thus have a vested interest in preserving – trade liberalization. Meanwhile, relative prices of formerly protected import-substituting activities would be reduced still more, discouraging such activities further and thus fostering pressure for aborting the policy. In fact, it might be argued that the usually strong anti-export bias before the liberalization argues for an initial excessive depreciation of the real exchange rate to make the policy more credible and sustainable.[8]

The point is sometimes raised that inappropriate macroeconomic policies (primarily, a budgetary deficit), not the opening of the capital market, are to blame for the collapse of trade liberalization.[9] This argument ignores the pattern of performance just outlined, which was not dependent on the

8 This point is made in the special study of Chile by Hachette (1989).
9 This argument is made particularly with reference to the Argentinian experience in the special study by Cottani and García (1989).

existence of a budgetary deficit. But even if that series of events does not transpire, the argument is at best only partly valid. A budgetary deficit is indeed likely to shorten the life of trade liberalization. In principle, however, without an open external capital market the deficit might lead to domestic demand and an expanding trade deficit. With a floating (or properly adjusted) exchange rate, this might lead to a reestablishment of an equilibrium rate. The whole budgetary deficit would then be financed by the inflationary tax derived from the increase in domestic prices. But with an open external capital market the sequence of events is bound to be different: the increase in domestic demand, following the budgetary deficit, would tend to raise the domestic interest rate. This, in turn, would induce a capital inflow, with a consequent appreciation of the real exchange rate. In the new equilibrium the trade deficit would be higher, with the budgetary deficit being partly financed by foreign credit. The effects on the fate of liberalization would be precisely those described before, given the immediate exchange rate appreciation and the eventual change of course of capital flows. In sum, a large-scale budgetary deficit is more likely to lead to the abortion of trade liberalization with a free external capital market than without it.

The main disagreement with the contention that the freedom of capital flows would be detrimental has been voiced by Lal (1987). His argument is based on the presumed existence of rational expectations. With these, the initial reaction of a strong real exchange rate appreciation should not materialize: economic agents would recognize the transitory nature of capital inflows, so that the *eventual* direction and size of capital flows would be influential in determining the immediate level of the foreign exchange rate. In the same vein, even violent fluctuations of relative prices should not lead to any waste if future price levels are anticipated and taken into account in making current decisions about investment and resource allocation: waste would then be involved in movements of resources in and out of activities only if a discrepancy exists between private and social costs of such movements.[10]

A crucial issue to resolve, then, is whether, with the opening of capital markets, the real exchange rate does fluctuate violently, experiencing a large-scale but short-lived appreciation. Empirical evidence on this central question is examined in the following section.

---

10 Lal also argues that if the considerations against opening the capital market were granted, they would imply that such opening should never be undertaken. This argument is not valid, at least in the present context. While the damage caused by the ensuing fluctuations would be expected at any time, the trade liberalization would not be harmed if the capital market were opened only after trade liberalization has been implemented and the goods market had already undergone the necessary adjustment.

Capital Market Opening and the Real Exchange Rate

This section relies primarily on the four special studies on the issue in question. In three of the country experiences studied – Argentina, Chile, and Uruguay – the capital markets were opened while the trade liberalization was in process. In the fourth – Israel – the capital market was liberalized when trade liberalization, and even the process of adjustment to it, were essentially over.

Figures 15.1–15.6 present, in a diagrammatic form, data of the real exchange rate around the relevant time periods. In each figure the broken line represents the time at which the capital market was opened (usually a fairly definite date); the solid line indicates the time (mostly, the quarter) at which large-scale exernal flows of capital started to materialize.

In all four instances these capital movements were *inflows* rather than outflows. Casual recollection of worldwide experience suggests that this has usually been the case.[11] Some reasons why inflows, rather than outflows, should be expected were specified earlier; several others may be suggested.

First – and the evidence supports this assumption – a country would choose to open at a time when the balance of payments is relatively comfortable, and likely to remain so. A quick reversal of the capital market liberalization would not be expected, and a capital outflow motivated by the wish to exploit a transitory opening of the market would thus be unlikely.

Furthermore, the accumulated stock of previously outflowing capital would tend to be repatriated, at least partly. First, exchange control regulations may be assumed to have been less than fully effective in preventing the capital outflow; by and large, those who want to hold capital abroad would do so despite the controls. But in view of the high transaction costs of moving capital in and out, when controls are stringent many economic agents will hoard more foreign assets than are warranted by relative current yields of domestic and foreign assets (including expectations for exchange rate changes). With the removal of controls, these extraordinary transaction costs disappear (completely, if the absence of controls is expected to survive for a long time), and reduction of the size of assets held abroad – that is, a capital inflow – should materialize.

Turning to the real exchange rate, we see from figures 15.1–15.6 that in all four countries large-scale capital inflows started following a period of

---

11 Other than the dramatic capital outflow when external capital movements were allowed in the United Kingdom in 1947 (which led to an immediate reversal of the capital market liberalization, and must have colored perceptions and anticipations for many years), no similar reaction comes to mind.

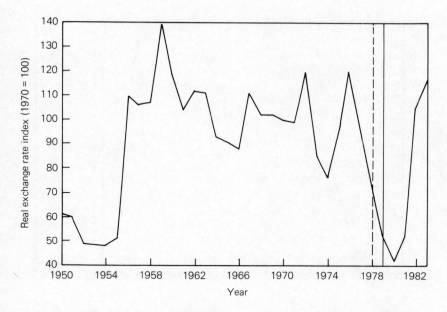

Figure 15.1 The real exchange rate under capital account liberalization: Argentina (annual, 1950–1983).

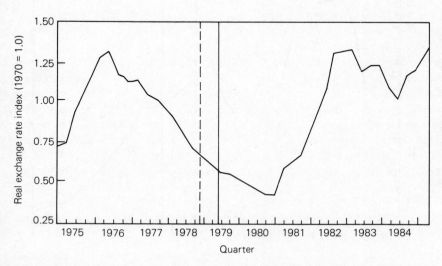

Figure 15.2 The real exchange rate under capital account liberalization: Argentina (quarterly, 1975–1984).

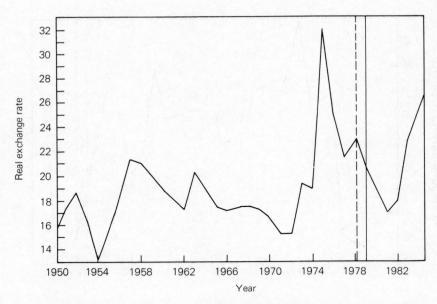

Figure 15.3 The real exchange rate under capital account liberalization: Chile (annual, 1950–1984).

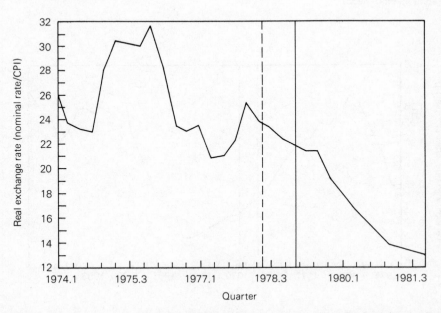

Figure 15.4 The real exchange rate under capital account liberalization: Chile (quarterly, 1974–1981).

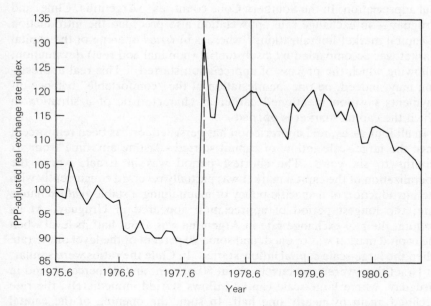

Figure 15.5 The real exchange rate under capital account liberalization: Israel (monthly, June 1975 to March 1981).

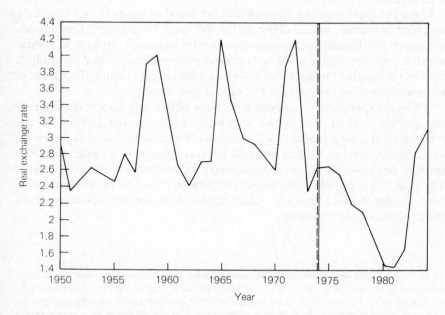

Figure 15.6 The real exchange rate under capital account liberalization: Uruguay (annual, 1950–1984).

real appreciation. In the Southern Cone countries – Argentina, Chile, and Uruguay – an exchange rate appreciation also preceded the introduction of capital market liberalization;[12] whereas in *Israel* opening of the capital market was accompanied by a substantial (nominal and real) devaluation, following which the process of appreciation started.[13] This real appreciation may, indeed, be one manifestation of the "comfortable" balance-of-payments position mentioned earlier as characteristic of a situation in which the capital market is opened.

In all four cases, real appreciation has persisted, or has been reinforced, once the large-scale inflow of capital started – lasting any time from six months to six years. The shortest period was in Israel, where the liberalization of the capital market was partially reversed concurrently with the introduction of a specific policy of maintaining a stable *real* exchange rate; the longest period of appreciation appeared in Uruguay. At its bottom, the real exchange rate in Argentina was about half its level when the capital market was opened, and some 70 percent of the level of the rate when the large-scale capital inflow started. In Chile the ratios were similar. In Israel they were respectively about 80 percent and 90 percent. And in Uruguay, where large-scale capital inflows started immediately, the rate declined again by nearly one half. In sum, the opening of the capital market and the inflow of capital from abroad were followed by a massive exchange rate appreciation.

Once the capital inflow stopped and the trend of the real exchange rate reversed its course, radical depreciation followed. Such violent fluctuations are much too intense to be explained by (unexpected) changes in fundamental economic attributes; a "rational expectations" (and certainly a "perfect foresight") behavior of the real exchange rate should therefore, in all probability, be rejected for the case in question.

All four experiments surveyed here were admittedly undertaken during the second half of the 1970s, a period unique in the history of the international capital markets when unprecedented amounts of capital were available for foreign lending and real interest rates were exceptionally low (mostly *negative*, as far as contemporary expectations were concerned). The doubt thus raised as to whether the pattern of capital flows would have been similar in more "normal" times must qualify any lessons drawn from these particular experiences.

---

12 In Uruguay, the year just prior to the capital market liberalization witnessed a very slight depreciation of the real exchange rate, but this followed a year of a dramatic appreciation.
13 The effective devaluation in Israel, on that occasion, was substantial only for imports; the exchange rate for exports changed very little because of the abolition of a major export subsidy. For most purposes, it should be noted, it is movements of the real formal (rather than effective) exchange rate that are relevant in the present context.

Needless to say, a variety of other economic events, related and unrelated, occurred during the period in which capital inflows took place. An obvious example is the very high fiscal deficits in Argentina at the time. The real exchange rate may thus have appreciated for reasons other than the opening of capital markets and the emergence of capital inflows. This issue has been extensively addressed in the analyses of Argentina, Chile, and Uruguay.

The Argentina study emphasizes the role of the encouragement of exports. The abolition of taxes on the country's major traditional exports gave the latter a large boost. In fact, these exports have been found to respond much more strongly to changes in export taxes than to equivalent changes in the formal exchange rate. This export expansion, accompanied by relatively little liberalization of imports and hence little change in their size, increased the trade surplus and contributed to a real appreciation of the exchange rate. Using a formal model the authors assign equal responsibility for the real appreciation (over 20 percent each) to the export expansion, to the "excessive" expansion of credit, and to the emergence of capital inflows. Capital inflows are thus found to have been an important factor, but not predominant, in bringing on the real exchange rate appreciation during the period under review.[14]

In the analysis of Chile no formal modelling of the real exchange rate appreciation is carried out: this is done instead for the large-scale capital inflows themselves (which in Chile, unlike Argentina, originated chiefly from credit to the private rather than the public sector). But the authors' belief – based, among other things, on the results of other studies – is that capital inflows were the principal contributor to the exchange rate movement.

In the study of Uruguay a formal model is again used to analyze the issue in question. The authors find only two variables to explain the movement of the real exchange rate. The first and most important is the exchange rate in Argentina: owing to very close trade ties of the two countries, and the huge discrepancy in the countries' sizes, prices in Argentina tend to determine those in Uruguay. The other – much less important – factor is the size of capital inflows. Capital inflows were thus only a minor factor in determining the course of the real exchange rate.[15]

14 But our earlier comment about the fiscal impact applies equally to credit expansion: in a closed capital market and in the absence of capital flows, this should not result in a real appreciation. If this is true, a stronger impact should be assigned to the opening of the capital market than the analysis on hand would indicate.

15 It should be noted, though, that the predominant role of Argentina's exchange rate is found in particular for the period 1974–84, and much less so in earlier years. This later period is precisely that of the opened capital market and the existence of heavy capital inflows. It is thus possible that colinearity of the two explanatory variables detracts, in the findings of this analysis, from the true impact of capital inflows.

From the experiences examined here, it seems that the importance of opening the capital market, and the emergence of capital inflows, varies from one country to another.[16] If a general statement is allowed, it is perhaps that capital inflows were an important, but by no means predominant, instigator of the real exchange rate appreciation when the capital markets were opened.

The Sustainability of Trade Liberalizations

How have the experiences of opened capital markets, the emergence of short-term capital inflows, and real exchange rate appreciation affected the fate of *trade* liberalizations?

Of the four experiences under consideration, that of Argentina is the clearest instance of a reversal of trade liberalization related to the capital market liberalization. The real exchange rate appreciation – caused partly by the combination of highly restricted imports with an open capital market – discouraged the emergence of new export activities with trade liberalization. No benefit from the trade liberalization was thus perceived, and no vested interests in such policy were created. With the reversal of capital flows, in early 1982, trade liberalization was thus immediately aborted.

The experience of Uruguay is more ambiguous. As in Argentina the capital market was liberalized at an early stage of the process of trade liberalization. Whether or not the emerging capital inflows played a major role, a substantial appreciation did take place, which lasted for a long time (six years, from 1975 to 1981), by the end of which the rate was just over half its level in 1975 and only one third of its 1972 level. The process of trade liberalization – partly, it may be presumed, because of this real appreciation – was halted in the early 1980s, but it was not reversed (by the mid-1980s, in fact, it was renewed).

In Chile, unlike the two former instances, capital market liberalization was not seriously introduced until the end of the trade liberalization process (in the late 1970s). The emergence of capital inflows did lead, we have seen, to a very significant real appreciation, the discouragement of tradeable activities, and the creation of large-scale unemployment. In this case, no reversal of the trade liberalization process followed – probably partly because of the strong earlier commitment to liberalization of

16 For the fourth case, that of Israel, another study of the relevant period (Michaely, 1983) may shed some indirect light. In an analysis of the changes in the *nominal* (rather than real) exchange rate, the latter appears to appreciate with an increase of foreign exchange reserves at the central bank. These reserves are in turn – during the period concerned – quite closely related to changes in short-term capital inflows.

policymakers and the stability of the political regime. But the absence of reaction against trade liberalization was probably also attributable to the fact that, by the time capital markets were opened, both the implementation of the liberalization policy and much of the adjustment to it had been realized. The benefits of trade liberalization were by then more fully perceived, and the interest in it was much more strongly established.

Finally, the experience of Israel points in the same direction, though less convincingly. Here, too, real appreciation followed the opening of the capital market, but only at the end of a very long and gradual process of trade liberalization. Moreover, the real exchange rate appreciation lasted less than a year and was much smaller (averaging around 10 percent) than in the Latin American experience. Nevertheless, as far as it goes, the Israeli experience would accord with the hypothesis that once trade liberalization has been fully implemented, and time for adjustment to it has been allowed, the opening of the capital market will not affect its fate.

The latter hypothesis – and its corollary that a liberalization of capital markets at an early stage of trade liberalization is likely to make the latter less sustainable – thus find some empirical support. Scattered references to experiences in several other country studies would tend to reinforce this interpretation. But the evidence is rather weak, and its inferences are not clear. More robust and sharply defined empirical conclusions would require a much vaster range of experiences – which are not forthcoming for the simple reason that there has not been much *capital* market liberalization in the developing world. A casual look at the *developed* world would probably support the hypothesis on hand. Specifically, the opening of the capital markets in Europe after World War II came only after the implementation of the main part of trade liberalization – the removal of QRs – and did not hinder the process, which proceeded to its next stage of extensive reductions of tariff barriers to trade.

16
Conclusions

Standing back from the jigsaw puzzle of country study evidence, we begin to perceive the outlines of a coherent picture. True, there are gaps to be filled, and some of the pieces can only tentatively be assigned a place. Equally, some pieces might be assembled differently – the path of change to a durable trade liberalization must depend on many shifting political and economic circumstances. Even so, the research has found enough common characteristics of a successful policy for some general principles to be derived. Indeed, some of the patterns are distinct enough to suggest broad rules for designing a policy.

The salient inferences, grouped under headings related to the primary issues posed at the outset of this volume (though not following them precisely), are summarized below. Arising from these, guidelines for the appropriate design of a policy are suggested. A brief note of remaining gaps to be filled by additional research follows.

The Lessons of Experience

Determinants of the Long-term Course of Liberalization

Some countries appear to have just flirted with liberalization, sometimes more than once, while others have stuck with it with varying degrees of constancy. What distinguishes the long-term "liberalizers" from the others?

A cluster of structural characteristics comes first to mind as having an influence on long-term outcomes. *Geographical size*, for instance, seems to be important: almost all the countries that have persevered in their attempts to liberalize are either small or medium sized; almost all large countries are not among the "liberalizers." Similarly, abundance of *natural resources* seems to make some difference: the "liberalizing" group consists mostly of resource-poor countries, whereas over half the "nonliberalizing" countries are relatively abundant in natural resources. On its own, the difference is not very significant, but taken together with size it affords a clearer inference: economies that are both small and resource poor tend to be "liberalizers"; "nonliberalizers" are more often large and rich in resources. This is not surprising: smaller resource-poor economies would be inclined to liberalize, since they are likely to be larger beneficiaries of free international trade.

The *level of development*, measured by per capita income, also distinguishes liberalizers from non-liberalizers. The former group tends – with some important exceptions – to start out with higher per capita income levels than the others. The fact that the *poorest* countries are barely represented in this study – because they had not even attempted liberalization policies by the time the study was launched – reinforces this observation. Of course, an economy that does not do much trading in any case is unlikely to be strongly tempted to liberalize its foreign trade activities.

But liberalizers do not seem to be distinguished by any particular *economic structure*. In particular, the share of manufacturing, either in production or in exports, seems to be neither here nor there.

Perhaps the most striking finding about determinants of a liberalization's long-term durability is that *political stability*, in our sense of the term, is a necessary – though not sufficient – condition for success. Admittedly, assessing the influence of this variable calls for more qualitative judgment, and allows less quantitative measurement, than its more purely economic confreres. Nevertheless, with all due caveats, the relationship between political stability and the pursuit of a long-term course of *liberalization* is intimate enough and consistent enough to support the contention.

An observation that may feed into this conclusion is that there seems to be a watershed in the life of a trade liberalization experiment: all but one of the liberalization experiments that lasted as much as six years stayed put. Now the chances of a policy surviving are likely to improve the longer it has been in place, but this does not account for the specific length of time identified as the point of no return. Plausibly, a policy that stays on course for six years is indicative of political stability.

To the cluster of *structural* differences between long-term liberalizers and nonliberalizers, a few distinguishing characteristics of *performance* and *policy* may be added. One contrast is glaring: the *export growth* of liberalizing countries is almost double that of the nonliberalizers – in fact, only one nonliberalizer reaches the *average* of the liberalizing category, the rest falling far below it. In all liberalizing economies, exports grew faster, usually much faster, than the national product; for nonliberalizers the two growth rates were roughly similar. The causality may run either way, but the strength of the relationship cannot be doubted.

Probably related is a clear association of the pattern of behavior of the real exchange rate and the long-term course of liberalization. It is not so much the trend of the real exchange rate as its *stability over time* that tends to differentiate the two groups of countries: among the liberalizers, the real exchange rate stayed fairly level over the long run. This would support a hypothesis that the predictability of this crucial price – probably through its contribution to rapid growth of exports – is an element conducive to the durability of a liberalization policy in the long run.

Finally, liberalizers appear to be fiscally prudent: as a rule, their budgetary deficits have been smaller than those of the rest. This finding, of course, is not entirely independent of our observation about the influence of the behavior of the real rate of foreign exchange.

The Influence of Initial Circumstances

Liberalization policies have been launched under a variety of circumstances. Some have been implemented under "distress" – when the economy was suffering severe economic difficulties (usually including balance-of-payments deterioration, rapid inflation, and a slump of production) or was even perceived to have totally collapsed. On occasion, a radical (sometimes violent) change of political regime was also an ingredient. At the other extreme, some liberalizations were launched in placid conditions, with no severe deterioration apparent in any major aspects of economic performance. In between lie those episodes introduced when the economy was under some stress (for instance, when inflation was high) but not so critically as to require fundamental change of economic policies.

Liberalization policies launched under "distress" were almost universally radical: they were strong in the degree of liberalization of the trade system and were usually administered rapidly rather than gradually. These tended mostly to survive over the long run, rather than for just a few years. The performance of episodes undertaken under "placid" conditions was more mixed: more survived than failed, but the proportion is not as impressive as in the "distress" category. Some of these were follow-up episodes, coming in the wake of an earlier liberalization experience that had been sustained, and thus were natural candidates for survival. In such circumstances, even weak liberalization efforts quite often survived. The *least* sustainable liberalizations have proved to be those undertaken under "in between" circumstances – of a flawed yet not completely enfeebled economic performance. Only a few of these have survived in the long run. These policies, it would seem, have neither the urgency and intensity imposed by hardship nor the tenacity fostered by a secure economic background.

Motives and goals, like the initial circumstances to which they were often related, varied greatly. Prominent among the stimuli for policymakers was a shift to the free-market persuasion, whether through ideological conversion or as a result of a change in the balance of political power. The most common goals, severally or in combination, were as follows: improvement of resource allocation, accelerated growth, increased exports, and the reduction of inflation. Whatever the motive or stimulus, none seems to have mattered much to the ultimate sustainability. Similarly, the wish to accommodate pressures by outside entities and organizations (such as the US Government, the World Bank, or the International Monetary Fund), or to join a multicountry agreement (such as the European Economic Community) seems to have played only a subsidiary part in sustaining a liberalization policy. In the instances where outside commitments are a factor, these seem to prevent, or reduce, temporary aberrations and to help determine the *timing* of launching the policy, but they do not seem to shape the long-term course of the policy or seal its eventual fate.

Trade Liberalization and Unemployment

A liberalization policy, by changing relative prices and relative profitability, encourages some activities at the expense of others. Presumably, the shift of resources from the losing to the gaining sectors is uneven, and some unemployment is created.

The country studies are virtually unanimous in concluding that this impact has been very small. Generally, even employment in any large *sector* of the economy has not been reduced by the trade liberalization. The most notable exception is Chile's liberalization of 1974–81, where employment in the manufacturing sector dropped substantially. This decline was more than offset by the encouragement given to employment in agriculture, so that even here no net unemployment resulted from the liberalization. Apparently, much of the adjustment, and shifts of resources among activities, must have been carried out *within* sectors – even when "sectors" are defined in a narrower manner than "manufacturing" or "agriculture" as a whole.

The lessons of experience are limited, of course, by the range of the experience itself. Among the episodes of liberalization studied, none was imposed in one sudden action – conceivably, policies more radical even than that of Chile (1974–80) or of Greece (1953–5) might have produced significant unemployment. Among the actual experiences studied, however, the degree of intensity seems to have made no difference: the impact on unemployment seems to be as inconsiderable in "strong" and "fast" liberalizations as in "weak" and "slow" episodes.

In sum, the expectation that a trade liberalization will bring significant unemployment is *not* borne out. But, does unemployment – whether brought by the liberalization or not – significantly affect the fate of liberalization policies? The answer of experience is once more "no." The presence or absence of unemployment when liberalization is introduced does *not* apparently influence the eventual outcome. More important, the emergence of unemployment during the course of a liberalization experiment does not on the whole seem to matter either: in no case can the termination, or even partial reversal, of a liberalization policy be ascribed to the existence of unemployment – although the latter was evident in several instances.

The relationship of liberalization to unemployment seemed at the outset of this study to be of major concern; it turns out to be an issue of minor importance.

The Short-term Effect on Production

Quite in line with our inference that the impact of liberalization on unemployment is negligible, we have found that, *even in the short run*, liberalization does not lower production and does not inhibit economic growth. On the contrary, liberalization is clearly associated, virtually from its launching, with accelerated economic expansion. This is particularly true for episodes characterized as *"strong"* – precisely those in which, presumably, rigidities and lags in positive responses should have led to a temporary loss of production. Less surprisingly, this immediate economic expansion is also particularly common in sustained liberalization episodes – with causality probably again running both ways.

Liberalization is followed by a significant increase of the share of the tradeables sector in the economy's product – probably because many liberalizations, particularly those that survived, were accompanied by an increase of the real exchange rate. Within the mostly tradeables sector, agriculture and manufacturing have been, predictably, affected differently, since agricultural activities had generally been discriminated against by the pre-liberalization trade regime and would therefore be favored by the liberalization policy. From the outset, liberalization seems to have brought accelerated growth and an increased share of product to the agricultural sector, dispelling the notion that agricultural production responds to changing circumstances only with a substantial time lag. In manufacturing, normally the protected sector, the growth rate does indeed tend to *fall* immediately following the introduction of liberalization. But this fall is temporary: within about a year, the rate of growth regains its pre-liberalization level. Furthermore, even in the first year the rate of growth in manufacturing is still *positive*: no actual decline of production is evident, at least for the sector as a whole.

Intensity and Durability of Liberalization

The evidence of experience is that a liberalization launched by a bold step is more sustainable than one introduced by minor stages over a long time span. A weak, hesitant, and gradual start is more likely to be reversed than to gather momentum and grow.

The country's history of trade restrictions is very relevant in this context: the longer established and tighter the restrictions are, the less likely is the success of the liberalization experiment. Where trade restrictions have been protracted, a strong first move signifying a clear break with the past is particularly important to sustainability; it is also more crucial when a previous trade liberalization experiment has failed. Without a record of failure, a weak and slow beginning stands a chance of long-term survival, particularly if a prior episode has been sustained, even if it was then followed by a long pause.

The Relaxation of Quantitative Restrictions

QRs of imports were pervasive on the eve of liberalizations except, of course, when these followed earlier episodes in which QRs had already been dealt with. Under such circumstances a policy that lowered tariffs while leaving QRs untouched would not make much sense – and indeed was rarely found. Wherever QRs were common, their relaxation was an ingredient – most often a vital first ingredient – of the policy.

No recurrent pattern of events follows the relaxation of QRs. Sometimes the policy was reversed before any other measures were implemented (though less frequently than when liberalizations started in a different fashion). On several occasions the relaxation of QRs persisted over the long run unassisted by further policy measures. On two occasions, tariff reductions followed shortly after the relaxation of QRs; in other instances they were implemented only after several years.

While we cannot therefore reach any general conclusions about the nature or timing of policies that might follow the relaxation of QRs, it clearly emerges that radical removal of QRs is highly conducive to the sustainability of a liberalization policy. It is this component, indeed, that explains the success of strong liberalizations. In fact, whenever a strong opening move consisted primarily of a relaxation of QRs, liberalization nearly always survived; when it did not, survival was the exception. Experience thus strongly suggests that a liberalization policy contemplated in a trade regime in which QRs are pervasive would be likely to be sustained over the long run if it opened with a radical relaxation of QRs; if not, it is likely to fail.

Balance-of-payments Performance and Sustainability

Liberalization policies appear to be strongly associated with balance-of-payments performance: each clearly affects the other.

Liberalizations appear to affect positively both major components of external transactions – exports and imports – as well as the balance of the two. As a rule, export growth has accelerated substantially immediately following the launching of liberalizations, often reversing a previous trend of decline. Imports, too, have usually, though less consistently, increased following the liberalizations. But, interestingly, the increase of imports represented only one side of the process: virtually without exception, it went hand in hand with an increase of exports, and was most often less substantial than the latter. This is reflected in the performance of the balance of payments as a whole: in the large majority of liberalization experiences the level of foreign exchange reserves increased after liberalization was launched. Thus the expected damage of import liberalization – a fast import increase leading to a balance-of-payments deterioration – generally failed to materialize.

Turning to the opposite effect – of the balance of payments on the course of trade liberalization – it should first be noted that the initial position of the balance of payments, on the eve of liberalization, did not influence the fate of the policy. Liberalizations have been undertaken as often under "comfortable" situations as under "distress" – where the latter includes, almost universally, a severe balance-of-payments deterioration – and the likelihood of survival was roughly equal under both sets of initial circumstances. In other words, the balance of payments does not necessarily have to be healthy for the launching of a liberalization policy that would stand a high chance of survival.

For different reasons, the *impact*, that is, the immediate effect, of liberalization on the balance of payments does not appear to matter either: the impact has almost universally been favorable, whether the experiment was sustained or not.

But balance-of-payments developments beyond the immediate period following the introduction of liberalization do seem crucial. Abortions of liberalizations are almost universally preceded by a balance-of-payments deterioration (although the obverse is not true: *any* external deterioration would not necessarily be followed by the reversal of liberalization); in the absence of such deterioration, the liberalization experiment is likely to proceed. Most often, the balance-of-payments deterioration is associated with a decline of exports, or a sharp deceleration of their growth (which may on occasion be due to a fall in world prices rather than a quantity change). The implication is important: it is not, as a rule, the surge of imports that might have been expected from a more liberalized trade regime that damages the balance of payments and consequently disrupts the liberalization policy; rather it is the poor performance of exports.

The Impact of Liberalization on Exports

A more extensive analysis of the impact of trade liberalization on exports reveals even more strongly a clear-cut connection: liberalization leads to a fast and substantial increase of export growth. While it might be suspected that recorded data for the first-year performance of exports, following liberalization, are biased by mis-statements originating in anticipation of devaluation, the second-year performance indicates an even stronger impact; and the aggregate period of the three years following the implementation of liberalization manifests an unmistakable and strong trend of expansion of exports.

The favorable effect on exports is particularly noticeable in the instances of *strong* liberalizations. Similarly, it is more powerful in those instances in which the trade barriers prior to liberalization had been particularly high. Indirectly, this must attest to the discouragement of exports which must be involved in a trade regime in which *import* barriers are pervasive.

It is the relaxation of these import restrictions, accompanied almost invariably by an increase in the real rate of foreign exchange, which accounts for the export expansion. No additional impact, however, can be generally attributable to the introduction, or intensification, of export promotion measures when import liberalization is introduced. Somewhat surprisingly, then, we must conclude that the act of liberalization most relevant to export expansion is that of *import* liberalization – provided that it is accompanied by a real devaluation.

The Role of the Foreign Exchange Rate

In noting the relationship of the *long-term trends* of the real exchange rate and the foreign trade regime, we have seen that stability of the real rate is closely related to the existence of a persistent long-term trend of trade liberalization. The relationship is also close in all three short-term time dimensions of a liberalization episode: *immediately* following introduction; *during* the course of the episode; or toward the *end* of the experiment, whether this end was a reversal or just a pause in a longer-term liberalization process. The liberalization policy was mostly sustained when the real rate increased or remained stable; when it fell substantially, the liberalization experiment was generally doomed.

The real exchange rate is obviously not, by itself, a policy variable but the outcome of several policy measures (as well as some shocks and processes). Fiscal and monetary policies are particularly strong influences on the rate. Nevertheless, manipulations (or fluctuations) of the *nominal* exchange rate must also have strongly affected behavior of the *real* rate. The association is quite close; in particular, when a major nominal devaluation was part of the policy package of which trade liberalization was an element, the real rate of exchange almost always increased too, remaining relatively high during the course of the episode. Though not a sufficient condition, a nominal devaluation does appear to be almost a necessary condition for a real devaluation, and consequently also for the ultimate sustainability of a liberalization policy.

The Role of Fiscal and Monetary Policies

The fate of liberalization policies appears to be clearly related to the conduct of macroeconomic policies. To start with, the impact of the real exchange rate implies relevance – indeed, a trend of increasing real rate seems to be yielded most often by a combination of a nominal devaluation and restrictive fiscal and monetary policies.

The relationship is weaker when the *immediate* macroeconomic policy, followed when the liberalization policy is launched, is observed. The majority of liberalization policies were introduced in a climate of restrictive fiscal and monetary policy. True, such an opening stage seems to be practically prerequisite to establishing a restrictive trend that will persist during the life of the liberalization episode. And, more often than not, once a restrictive direction was introduced into fiscal policy, it was maintained for several years. This, most probably, is the reason why *some* (though weak) relationship is found between the direction of fiscal policy upon impact and the eventual fate of the liberalization policy. But the relationship is much stronger at the close of an episode when, very often, fiscal policy became *expansionary*: expansionary macroeconomic policy was strongly associated with the abortion of trade liberalization.

An important qualification must be made. This close relationship appears primarily in "immature," early stage liberalizations. When the liberalization poilcy had been in place for many years and an "episode" in essence introduced further stages rather than an entirely new initiative (as, for instance, in the histories of Greece, Israel, or Korea), expansionary macroeconomic policies do not appear to matter much: the trade liberalization is sustained despite such policies.

Is the increased likelihood that a liberalization policy will be sustained when macroeconomic policies are restrictive bought at the price of slowed growth? Our earlier observation that long-term sustainability of liberalizations is associated with higher economic growth is probably a sufficient answer, and direct observations bear out this conclusion. Even the *impact* effect on growth is much the same, whether the liberalization is accompanied by a restrictive macroeconomic policy or not. Indeed, in the period beyond the first year following the introduction of liberalization, it even appears that growth tends to accelerate substantially on those occasions in which the impact macroeconomic policy was restrictive, and not in others. This tends to support the earlier inference that a sustainable trade liberalization does not tend to constrain employment, production, and growth. Hence, measures that contribute to the sustainability of trade liberalization do not tend, as a rule, to inhibit economic growth.

The Sequencing of Liberalizations in the Goods and the Capital Markets

Should liberalization of the capital market be introduced *before* a trade liberalization begins? *During* that process? Or *after* the liberalization of the goods market is fully implemented, and perhaps the adjustment to it is largely over?

The weight of current opinion is that the goods market should be liberalized first, and liberalization of the capital market should be added only when much of the adjustment to the former has been completed. The rationale for this view is the expectation that, if the capital market is already open when the goods market liberalization is launched, large-scale capital *inflows* will ensue; the real rate of foreign exchange will decline (that is, a real *appreciation* will follow); import-competing goods for which protection has diminished will be hit harder, while exports and other import-competing activities will be discouraged rather than encouraged; and the liberalization of goods will therefore be less likely to survive. This outcome would be reinforced when the expected reversal of the capital inflow into a substantial *outflow* occurs: the immediate reaction to such sharp deterioration of the balance of payments is likely to be an abortion of the liberalization of goods. Essentially, this pattern depends on the absence of perfect foresight: with accurate prediction, fluctuations of capital flows and real exchange rate should be minor and the damage to liberalization of goods correspondingly minimal.

The lessons on this sequencing issue to be drawn from the experience of the *developing* world must be quite limited, because the experience itself has not been very common: few of the episodes of trade liberalization observed in this study have been accompanied by a liberalization of external capital movements. As far as it goes, the evidence does indicate the absence of foresight. Capital movements have indeed fluctuated substantially, with large-scale inflows being followed, within several years, by substantial outflows. Related, at least partly, to these movements, drastic fluctuations of the real exchange rate are observed – massive appreciations, following the opening of capital markets, turning later into as large depreciations. The predictable impact on tradeable activities followed. But the experience is much too restricted to allow general inferences as to whether these impacts do play a major role in determining the fate of a trade liberalization policy.

Similarly, on the two issues that follow – patterns of tariff reduction and the advantages and disadvantages of pre-announcement – experience has been too meager to afford solid lessons, and we have to rely on *a priori* analysis.

Patterns of Reductions of Tariffs

The experiences studied here do not afford reliable empirical inferences about the potential advantages of one pattern of tariff reductions over another. Only a few experiments followed a consistent pattern; generally, either no rules were clearly defined or one set of rules was quickly replaced by another.

We are left, then, with reasoning from first principles. Such analysis (appendix A1) tells us that the "concertina method" of tariff reductions, by which the system is collapsed downwards through consecutive reductions of the highest tariffs, is superior to uniform schemes of tariff contraction: the ratio of ultimate welfare gains to short-term transitional costs is highest when this scheme is pursued. An "across-the-board" scheme, by which the tariff system is collapsed through equiproportional reductions of all tariffs at each stage, would be the next best.

The collapse of a tariff system toward something that approaches neutrality should best be carried out not just through tariff reductions but also through *increasing* those tariffs originally at the bottom of the ladder. This would definitely be called for when the target for the uniform tariff level is not zero but some positive magnitude; or, if it is zero, when the approach to that level is expected to be protracted. In all the experiences studied the goal set was in fact above zero and the planned approach was indeed quite long (Chile's liberalization of 1974–81 being probably the only exception). Tariffs on intermediate inputs and capital goods warrant special consideration in this context, since these imports are often duty free even in highly restrictive trade regimes. If a satisfactory drawback scheme can be installed for imported inputs used in exports, the imposition of (low) tariffs on inputs is most likely to be warranted; otherwise, the benefit of such a step would be more doubtful.

If the "concertina method" of tariff reductions is adopted, no particular attention need be paid to the industrial structure of production: whether an industry is fully competitive or highly monopolized, tariff reductions should be administered only with a view to the height of the tariff by which the industry is protected. For QRs, similarly, *a priori* analysis tells us that the preferred scheme should be to start by removing QRs in those industries where differentials (quota rents) between the domestic and the international price are highest, whatever the industrial structure. Even when a scheme of equal reductions of all tariff levels rather than the "concertina method" is followed, it is unclear whether such tariff reductions are more beneficial in a competitive or a monopolistic activity.

Pre-announcement of the Policy Course

The planned course of liberalization has been pre-announced in only a few of the episodes, so that we are left once more with *a priori* reasoning.

Transitory costs of a trade liberalization policy may be incurred only to the extent that the event is unexpected: with a policy fully anticipated long enough in advance, no rents would be lost or created with the change, and no unemployment should be forthcoming. Thus, to reap the benefits of a gradual (as opposed to an abrupt) process of liberalization, the process should be pre-announced so that actual future changes may be predicted.

With these advantages, why were pre-announced programs so rare? One obvious reason would be that policymakers lack sufficient information about the concrete regime (for instance, about the actual degree of protection granted to various activities, particularly in a regime where protection through QRs is extensive), and cannot assess potential impacts with any confidence. Such forecasting is in any case fraught with uncertainty, and the designers of the policy might well prefer to await the outcome of one stage before designing another. Political expedience may also be a factor: it might be easier to introduce one phase of a policy without announcing in advance that it is only a preliminary step in a process of radical change, thus alerting potential opponents.

In this context external commitments may become important. An agreement with foreign countries or organizations is likely to make pre-announcement virtually inevitable, and hence more acceptable politically.

The Design of a Trade Liberalization Policy

Our prescriptions for designing a liberalization policy are derived primarily from the inferences yielded by this study, but sometimes they are based on scattered observations of the multicountry experience that were not common enough to yield general inferences and, in a few instances, on *a priori* reasoning.

It is self-evident that no two situations are similar, even in a given country at different points of time; that the specific circumstances of each case must be considered before a policy is designed; and hence that no given set of rules may be articulated that would be ready for application in any concrete case. Nevertheless, some salient principles emerge from the experiences that would probably be relevant to many – even most – instances in which a liberalization policy is contemplated. We believe that the suggested guidelines are of that nature.

We assume here an initial pattern of restrictions that must be most common in economies in which trade liberalization is contemplated.

Tariffs are pervasive and very high, but QRs of trade are widespread and intensive enough to make them, rather than tariffs, the binding constraint on imports. Both forms of protection are tighter in branches of final consumption goods and looser for intermediate inputs. Exports may sometimes be taxed; but also in the absence of such taxes, and even when some export subsidization exists, a strong anti-export bias is implied by the trade regime. External capital transactions are also highly regulated, for both inflows and outflows of capital.

Initial Circumstances

No particular set of opening circumstances should be looked for as a promising springboard for the liberalization policy although, obviously, different macroeconomic settings should call for different *accompanying* policies. Specifically, the launching of a liberalization policy should not wait until foreign exchange reserves are judged to be particularly high, or until exports have demonstrated a rising trend. It should also not have to wait until an economy that suffers from a rapid inflation stabilizes; but a *concurrent* stabilization policy would then be a necessary condition for a successful liberalization.

Political Stability

Political stability is virtually essential for the success and long-term survival of a trade liberalization policy. Planners of the policy would have at best a marginal influence on maintaining such stability, but one implication is still relevant for policy design. Coming back to the specification of appropriate opening circumstances, a reasonably high expectation of future political stability should be an important initial condition for launching a liberalization policy: if radical upheavals are expected, the policy is likely to fail. Specifically, the policy should not be introduced toward the end of the life of a political regime when it may reasonably be suspected that the next regime would be unlikely to feel committed by its predecessor's actions. In democracies, the early days of a new regime would be the appropriate time for launching trade liberalization.

Speed of Implementation

The implementation of a full-fledged liberalization should be gradual, but not drawn out over many years. There is no solid foundation for specifying the precise length of time that would be optimal for implementation, but observations of extreme cases suggest that a period of six to seven years for moving from the initial situation of massive restrictions to something approaching free trade would not be too short. This guideline is based on our inferences about the generally low transition costs of the policy: the general absence of unemployment, due to liberalization, and the widespread acceleration of growth *even in the short run* following the introduction of trade liberalization. While minimizing these transition costs, a liberalization carried out over six or seven years would avoid a long delay in reaping the full benefits of the policy.

A Strong Opening Move: Dismantling Quantitative Restrictions

A second guideline is very clear: the liberalization policy should start with a strong move. "Creeping" liberalizations appear to be doomed (except when they follow earlier strong policies). A strong opening step seems virtually a prerequisite to success, probably because of its importance in signaling a change in economic factors, its credibility, and its influence on the speed with which a vested interest in the liberalization policy is established. The strength of the initial move should be commensurate with the country's past history of trade restrictions. The longer established and more pervasive the restrictions are, or the more the country's history is colored by failed attempts to liberalize, the stronger should be the initial effort.

This opening move should consist primarily, even solely, of dismantling QRs of imports. The mere change of *method* – from protection through QRs to the use of price instruments – should be viewed as a substantial first stage of liberalization. This stage may last two or three years, and should incorporate the following main features.

1 A substantial part of the QRs should be removed forthwith, or very shortly after the policy announcement. Specifically, QRs should be removed not just from intermediate inputs, capital goods, and other noncompeting imports, but also from a wide range of final (mostly consumer) goods that do compete with domestic production.

2 Any remaining QRs should be administered through a *"negative"* list which specifies which goods are subject to QRs, leaving any other good free of restriction, rather than a *"positive"* list scheme in which everything is forbidden unless specifically allowed in a list of freely moving goods. This guideline, admittedly, is one of those based on only a few observations (such as the liberalization process in Korea). Hypothetically, negative and positive lists could be so constructed as to be precisely equivalent. But two important distinctions would remain. First, a negative list would omit, and thus automatically leave free, the import of goods whose import is not yet contemplated; a positive list would automatically prohibit such imports. Second, a shift from a positive to a negative list, even if it changed none of the specifics, would represent a change in attitude, which by itself may make the announced policy more credible.

3 Although primarily a change in *form* of protection, the new rules should not aim to simulate completely the operation of the pre-liberalization system – the tariffs that replace the QRs should not be designed to be precisely "equivalent." More specifically, the tariff system must not be tailored to keep *effective* protection rates unchanged – a forlorn hope in any case. Instead, broad tariff levels should be specified, into one of which any good released from quota restriction would be placed. In this process, a maximum ceiling should be set so that, for goods very highly protected by the QRs, the change in form would inevitably entail reduced protection.

4 Unless the replacement tariff is *transparent*, much of the benefit of shifting from QRs will be lost. This point deserves emphasis: since the shift would presumably be regarded as a transitory step, there might be a temptation to determine the tariff levels in a more haphazard and less transparent fashion than usual. Occasional observations also suggest that at the end of the stage of removal of QRs their administrative machinery should be completely dismantled. The survival of such machinery would always constitute a pressing invitation to revive its functions. And the complete dismantling of the machinery would make the policy more credible, establishing expectations of a permanent rather than a reversible change in the trade regime.

Tariff Reduction

Once QRs are dismantled the stage of tariff reduction should start, and it should be completed within several years. *A priori* reasoning – experience is too scarce here – tells us that, to reap the benefits of a *gradual* process fully, the future course of tariff reductions should be planned and pre-announced. The pattern of tariff changes should be simple and, once more, transparent. The best scheme of gradual tariff reductions would be the "concertina method," by which the tariff system is collapsed downwards through the continuous reductions, in a series of phases, of the highest tariffs. Assuming that the common tariff designated for the end of the process is low but not zero, this process should also include the *raising* of the lowest tariffs and, specifically, the imposition early in the process of (low) tariffs on goods which are tariff free.

Stabilization

When trade liberalization starts from circumstances of rapid inflation, it must be accompanied, or preceded, by a general policy of stabilization of the economy. This would include at least two components: restrictive demand (fiscal and monetary) policies, and a substantial (nominal) devaluation. In the absence of such policies, trade liberalization should not be introduced: it would be bound to collapse, impeding the introduction and imperiling the survival of a subsequent attempt. As should be clear from earlier remarks, it would also be pointless, in the absence of stabilization, to start a process of "creeping" liberalization in the hope that it will pick up when the macroeconomic setting changes.

Devaluation

The strong opening move should be accompanied by a significant devaluation even under "placid" circumstances. This would encourage released resources to shift to the export sector, stimulating export growth and lessening the threat of unemployment; devaluation would also encourage import-competing activities which would be capable of surviving, under a higher real rate of foreign exchange, without a system of protection. In addition, the devaluation would lower the likelihood of the emergence of an imports surplus and a drain on the country's foreign exchange reserves, which might lead to a reversal of the liberalization policy.

Once devaluation (nominal as well as real) has been effected, sustainability of the policy would require that the real exchange rate should neither decline continuously nor fluctuate excessively. In that context, a continuing restrained fiscal policy is important. Large spasms of fiscal deficit before the liberalization process is entrenched are most likely to lead to the policy's failure.

Export Promotion

We have encountered three inferences which are relevant to the issue of export promotion: the positive reaction of exports to import liberalization (cum devaluation) is strong and fast; the addition of export promotion measures does not seem to be generally relevant; and import liberalization does not generally lead to unemployment. The joint outcome of these findings leads to an important policy inference about the design of trade liberalization: it should involve the relaxation of *import* barriers, whereas export promotion should, at most, be subsidiary. This guideline has two manifestations. First, when import liberalization is implemented and is accompanied by a significant real devaluation (which is true in most experiences, and without it liberalization is practically doomed to fail), the introduction, or intensification, of specific export promotion measures would not be essential. Second, a *separate* stage of liberalization involving export promotion, and preceding a stage of relaxation of import barriers, does not seem to be required for the efficiency or sustainability of trade liberalization.

Liberalization of the Capital Market

Liberalization of the capital market should be withheld to a quite late stage. It should not be undertaken before the process of dismantling QRs is complete, and should probably be delayed until well into the stage of tariff reduction. Even then, liberalization of the capital market should be viewed as a more flexible and, unlike liberalization of the goods market, even reversible element of the system. In particular, the possibility of influencing capital inflows through taxation should be established, to prevent damage potentially inflicted by capital inflows through the reduction of nominal and real rates of foreign exchange.

Agenda for Further Research

The experiences investigated have provided us with reasonably reliable answers to most of the questions posed for this study. Some questions, however, still lack an answer, and the credibility of some inferences would be enhanced by further evidence.

Several issues do not promise returns to research within some reasonable time in the future. It seems unlikely, for instance, that further liberalization experiences in the next decade will illuminate the issues of alternative patterns of tariff reductions, or of pre-announcement, or of alternative sequencing of liberalizations in the goods market and the capital market. In those spheres, we shall probably have to be content for some time to come with *a priori* reasoning. But some other directions for further research do seem promising.

One would be an attempt to identify reactions of individual activities in the liberalization process, to investigate the potential benefits of singling out certain activities – in one way or another – in the implementation of trade liberalization. The pattern of research would necessarily differ from that followed here in concentrating on a few selected activities, chosen either because they are important or because some particular attributes might be suspected (the textile and the automobile assembly industries are cases in point). The reactions of such activities may be examined not only when liberalizations are implemented but also on other occasions in which changes in relative prices take place.

Another candidate for further research is the impact of liberalization on income distribution – an area in which the inferences of the present study are not robust. Once more, this would probably require a different research method from ours: a concentration on just a few episodes, in which all pertinent evidence might be thoroughly investigated. Here, too, the study might go beyond experiments of liberalization – for instance, to episodes of substantial changes of the real exchange rate, from which inferences about the impact of liberalization might be borrowed.

Finally, additional research in the near future may add analysis of economies with attributes that fall beyond the range of those dealt with in the present study, specifically of experiences of liberalization in the *least* developed economies, for which no evidence was available at the outset of our study. Several trade liberalizations have been introduced since, in African countries in the mid-1980s. Future research along the lines of the present study, emphasizing the experiences of the least developed economies, may qualify or supplement our inferences in a way that would make it easier to apply the lessons of experience to the design of policies in the poorest countries.

Appendix A1

Issues in the Pattern of Removal of Trade Barriers

"Redundancy" of Tariffs

The country studies noted on occasion that tariff reductions were apparent rather than real, in that they merely removed redundancy in the system – "water in the tariff." Some redundancy is to be expected from time to time – a government may err on the high side when intending to impose a prohibitive tariff or, if circumstances change, a tariff that originally constituted a real restraint may become redundant.

Neither eventuality, however, can account for the massive tariff redundancies observed in some of the countries reviewed. We explore two possible explanations: (a) that the redundancy, not the tariff reduction, is more apparent than real; (b) that a genuine redundancy exists, whose source may have some important implications.

The argument that the redundancy is illusory originates from the observation that goods are not generally homogeneous and identical when they have a common designation. This characteristic can lead to the misperception in two totally different ways. First, the statement that a tariff is "redundant" is often derived from a price comparison: the home price of the good is compared with the foreign price, and the proportional excess of the former over the latter is found to be smaller than the posted tariff rate. But quite often, the same good is not being compared in the two markets: the designation is the same, and some essential features are similar, but vast differences exist between the foreign "good" and the home-produced one. Generally, the latter has less inherent value (as seen by the user) than the former. The price comparison may well therefore involve a misleading bias toward finding an apparent tariff redundancy. A lowering of the "redundant" tariff would then indeed have an economic consequence and would (most often) be an act of trade liberalization.

The second argument is more complicated. The tariff code may distinguish thousands, perhaps tens of thousands, of different "goods." But even with such detailed distinction few "goods" would be genuinely uniform. Normally, a "good" would consist of several, probably many, homogeneous subunits, each with its own cost structure. The implication of this pattern is analyzed with the aid of figure A1.1. Assume, for simplicity, constant marginal (and average) costs of production of each subunit ("branch"); this assumption is immaterial for the outcome. The unit of a product of each branch is defined so that its foreign price is one (say, one dollar). The branches 1 to n are represented in ascending order of domestic costs (for simplicity, again, assume equal quantities – hence values in foreign currency – of production of all branches). The tariff level is meant to prohibit any imports of the good, that is, of all its branches. It is therefore set at level t, which would prohibit imports of n, the product of the highest-cost branch in this activity. For branches 1 to $n - 1$, then, there will inevitably be a positive level, higher or lower, of tariff "redundancy." Any actual estimation, whether it takes an average of all branches or happens to hit upon one of them as a sample, would be likely to record a tariff redundancy in this activity. But lowering the tariff level would *not* be meaningless: branch n at least – and others, depending on the extent of tariff reduction – would become exposed to foreign competition. We may think of a curve SS as the supply curve of the "good," where changes in the quantities supplied originate not from changes in the level of production of

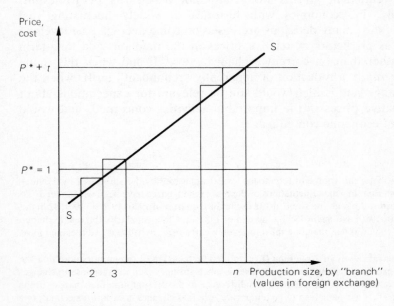

Figure A1.1 Tariff redundancy and production structure.

a homogeneous unit but from the addition, or subtraction, of "branches." What we see, then, is a normal supply response: a price reduction would lower the size of production – a certain level of production was profitable before the tariff reduction, and less of it remains so after the tariff change. If, for any activity, the costs of submarginal units are calculated, the tariff would be found to be "redundant" for them. Only in this sense is tariff "redundancy" present. The more important consideration is that here, too, a tariff reduction would change an economic constraint, and *would* be of economic consequence.

The argument may be extended further. Normally, no thousands or ten of thousands of tariff levels in the tariff code match the number of "goods" in the tariff classification: many goods will be subject to one tariff level. That level may presumably be intended to be prohibitive for *all* goods subject to this tariff. But goods (assuming, now, each "good" to be homogeneous) must differ in their cost levels. Hence, for all "submarginal" goods, a tariff "redundancy" would be found. Once more, the important consideration is that a tariff reduction *would* be a relevant economic change.

One source of genuine redundancy is common – the "change of circumstances" involved in a radical change of the real exchange rate. Many tariff levels contemplated and formulated as "prohibitive" under a given exchange rate would become redundant under a substantially higher exchange rate,[1] and this redundancy would indeed be real. But reduction of such "redundant" tariffs would still not necessarily be irrelevant. Presumably, in economies with histories of widely fluctuating real exchange rates, many decisions are based on some average past levels of the rate, as predictors of relative prices in the medium- and long-term future, rather than on current exchange rates.[2] If and when this is the *modus operandi*, a reduction of apparently "redundant" tariffs when the real exchange rate is high would still be relevant for expectations about future relative prices in the importable activities concerned, and would again be of economic consequence.

1 Not surprisingly, this source of redundancy was emphasized by the authors of the country study of Argentina, in which fluctuations of the real exchange rate have been wide indeed. To cite a few figures: the real rate stood at 132 in the third quarter of 1976 (1970 = 100); 42 in the last quarter of 1980; and again 135 by the end of 1982. In Chile, similarly, the real exchange rate in early 1981 was less than one third its level in early 1974; by 1984, it had regained most of this loss.

2 In the "special" study of Argentina (Cottani and García, 1989), the authors note that the response of exports to changes in export taxes is much stronger than the response to changes in the real exchange rate. They ascribe this difference to the presumption that changes in the real exchange rate are perceived to be temporary, whereas changes in export taxes (and, one would think, in import duties) are expected to be longer term.

Alternative Patterns of Tariff Reform

Methods of Tariff Reduction[3]

Suppose that tariff levels are to be lowered in stages and through some *uniform* scheme.[4] The scheme could have a variety of formulations, but three methods in particular recur in deliberations on alternative routes of tariff reduction.

One is the across-the-board reductions of all tariffs by equal amounts, that is, by an equal percentage of the foreign price of each good, until a final target level (whether zero or otherwise) is reached.[5]

A variant of the across-the-board method reduces tariffs by *proportional* rather than equal amounts: at each stage, tariffs are cut by equal proportions of themselves rather than of the (foreign) prices of the goods.

The third scheme, finally, is the "concertina" method (Corden, 1974) in which the highest tariffs are lowered to a given level, with no change in tariffs below that level; this is then repeated at each stage so that the top level becomes progressively lower. By the last stage all tariffs have been lowered to the target level.

As a method that would most reduce *dispersion* in the tariff system, the concertina method would seem intuitively to be the preferred scheme, since it is the dispersion that distorts the economic system and lowers welfare. Figure A1.2 demonstrates this proposition more formally. Assume two activities A and B, identical except for their tariff level. Specifically, supply (or cost) curves are identical for the two, as are demand curves. Thus S_H is the home supply curve and D_H is the home demand curve for either A or B. (For simplicity, the figure represents these curves as straight lines.) P^* is the foreign price for the two activities. Initially, a tariff at the level of t_a is imposed on imports of A, and a lower tariff t_b applies to imports of B. The two domestic prices are thus $P^* + t^a$ for A and $P^* + t^b$ for B. Assume, now, an equal reduction of both tariffs, so that the domestic prices become, respectively, $P^* + t'_a$ and $P^* + t'_b$. Domestic production of A will decline by LM, and production of B will decline by NR, which is equal to LM. Similarly, domestic consumption levels will increase by the same amount in both goods – KH in A and GF in B. Such transitory short-term *costs* as may arise would originate from the

---

3 Consult also Bruno (1972), Corden (1974), and Harberger (forthcoming).

4 A "uniform" scheme of tariff changes is defined here as one in which no activities are referred to by name or by any attributes other than the initial levels of their tariffs.

5 Needless to say, once the tariff level of a good reaches that (zero or positive) floor, no further tariff reduction of this activity will be undertaken. But in our discussion we assume, for simplicity, that this stage is not yet reached.

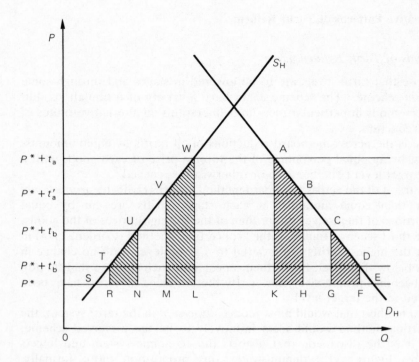

Figure A1.2 Analysis of "concertina" scheme for tariff reduction.

production side, that is, from the lower level of domestic activity. Since the reductions of levels of production will be equal in the two activities (given the assumption of similarity of activities, which amounts to the absence of any specific knowledge of differences between the two), the short-term losses should be identical.

Not so, however, the (permanent) gains from the tariff reduction. In activity A, the production loss from trade restriction will decline from WLS to VMS; the gain from the tariff reduction will hence be the shaded area WLMV. Similarly, the gain from the tariff reduction of B will be the shaded area UNRT. The production gain is thus clearly *smaller* in activity B than it is in A. Similarly, the *consumption* gain from the tariff reduction in A (shaded area ABHK) is necessarily larger than the consumption gain for B (shaded area CDFG). Both the production and the consumption gains, from an equal size of tariff reduction, are thus necessarily larger in the activity in which the initial tariff level is higher.

Discuss, now, an alternative in which the tariff for B is kept at its original level (t_b remains its tariff and $P^* + t_b$ its domestic price). Instead, an equal amount is added to the tariff reduction in A; that is, this tariff will now be reduced not by the difference between t_a and t_a' but by twice that much. The aggregate changes in consumption and in production, and the aggregate (presumed) short-term transitory costs, will be the same as before. But the (permanent) gains from tariff reductions will *not* be the same. The new areas of gains and losses will not be shown in the diagram, to avoid overcrowding. But it should be easy to see that, in this alternative, both production gain and consumption from the tariff reduction must be *higher* than under the former alternative.

The first method illustrated in figure A1.2 represents our first-mentioned scheme, of equal reductions of all tariffs; the second represents the concertina method. It is thus clearly established that the concertina method is superior.

Suppose, now, that the *proportional* scheme of across-the-board tariff reductions is adopted. Assuming the same "average" reduction of tariffs, this would mean that the tariff in A will be reduced to a lower level than t'_a. Again, this would clearly be preferable to the equal-size tariff reductions, since any "transfer" of tariff reduction from B to A would be beneficial. The proportional scheme would be inferior, though, to the concertina method, where the *whole* tariff reduction is "transferred," in a manner of speech, from B to A.

The order of preference for the alternative schemes is thus first the concertina method, next the proportional method, and last equally large reductions of all tariffs.

It is further evident from the analysis that an *increase* of the lowest tariffs – as, once more, a "transfer" of a tariff to the items that carry low tariffs – would be beneficial. This "extended concertina" should constrain tariff increases by the target uniform tariff level: when the latter is zero, no tariff should be raised. Since the planned uniform tariff is normally *not* zero (no actual case has in fact been observed), the zero tariffs at least should be increased.

Normally, duty-free goods are numerous: often they are intermediate inputs and capital goods. The imposition of tariffs on such goods raises further concerns addressed in the next section.

The Imposition of Tariffs on Inputs

This section is concerned with the imposition of tariff duties on previously duty-free imports of inputs. (Inputs here refer to both intermediate and capital goods.)

To isolate the effects of various measures on the *protection* system, we shall assume – as is usually done – that the *exchange rate* is in equilibrium, both before and after any change is introduced. In other words, an exchange rate adjustment is always carried out following a change in the protection system. But it is the *effective* exchange rate that is in equilibrium; in other words, had the (positive or negative) protective devices been removed, the existing formal exchange rate would *not* be at its equilibrium level.

Designate by R_{vj} the *effective* exchange rate (the rate that includes trade taxes and subsidies, in addition to the formal exchange rate) for value added in the production of a good j; or the effective exchange rate for gross value in consumption. R, which is some weighted average of all R_{vj} in the system, will stand for the equilibrium exchange rate. The *protective rate* in each activity j, designated g_j, would then be[6]

$$g_j = \frac{R_{vj}}{R} - 1$$

Had all R_{vj} been equal (that is, in a system with uniform rates of import tariffs and export subsidies), this level of the R_{vj} would also be the equilibrium level of the exchange rate $\overline{R}$; hence all protective rates in the economy would be zero. In the normal case, the R_{vj} will, of course, be different from each other. Hence, some protective rates will be positive; others negative. Specifically, when some imports are subject to tariffs and no export taxes are found, any activity with a zero tariff level must be subject to a *negative protection*; in comparison with a free-trade (or a "neutral") system, this activity is discouraged.

In a system in which export subsidies exist as well as import duties on final goods, and imported inputs are free of duties, the imposition of (low) tariffs on inputs would unambiguously be beneficial. The activities of production of inputs in this case are clearly subject to the highest (algebraically) negative protection, and diminishing that discouragement must be an advantage. Moreover, imposition of input duties will also lower the effective protection rates in the (positively protected) production of final goods, and lower the dispersion of effective protective rates in the system.[7]

The outcome is not unequivocal when some other part of the economy is subject to negative protection. Specifically, suppose subsidies to exports are very low in comparison with the protection of import substitutes; for simplicity, we shall assume that export subsidies are zero, a situation not too far from the norm.[8] Here, exports clearly suffer from the infliction of negative protection and our inferences would have to be qualified.

First, assume that input duties would not apply for the production of exportables – a principle that operates in most developing countries,

---

6 For a fuller elaboration of this formulation, see Michaely (1977).

7 Since protection is defined here in a way in which it is *zero* on average in the economy, only the measure of its *dispersion* would indicate the degree of economic loss brought by the protection system.

8 This is *not* an "extreme" case, since export *taxes* (or export quotas) are quite common.

although their drawback schemes may often be far from perfect. In this instance, some distortions are diminished by the introduction of tariffs on inputs, but another distortion is introduced. The aforementioned benefits of the imposition of input tariffs would still be found; but, whereas without these tariffs the production of inputs and of exportables is equally (negatively) protected, their introduction leads to the discouragement of exportable activities versus the domestic production of inputs. The question of which impact is more important would depend on the elasticities of substitution among the sectors involved. It may be presumed that the welfare-enhancing substitutions will dominate; but this is an empirical judgment, or guess, rather than a logical necessity.

Let us now assume the opposite: no drawback at all of input tariffs is provided to exporters – whatever duties on inputs exist, they have to be fully paid by exporters as well as others. In this case, the imposition of input tariffs would *lower* the effective protection of exportable activities, and would raise the level of dispersion (from initially zero, under our assumptions) of effective protection rates (all of which are negative) in the exports sector. These changes would tend to lower welfare and to offset, in one degree or another, the welfare-enhancing outcome of the inputs tariffs.

To understand the effect on *resource* movements in the economy, the resulting changes in the *formal* exchange rate must also be investigated. We classify all activities into four sectors: final consumption goods (C); intermediate inputs (I); exports (X); and nontradeables (N). Distinguishing, again, between the two extreme situations concerning the availability of drawbacks on input duties in exports, we observe the following.

With a perfect drawback scheme The impact of the imposition of duties would be to reduce domestic production and increase imports of final consumption goods. Imports of inputs will decline too. Any fall of exports arising from the movement of resources into the inputs sector would be matched by falling imports in the latter. Whether an import or an export surplus is created will depend on whether the rise of imports of final goods is larger or smaller than the fall of imports of inputs. Thus the change in the formal rate of exchange is uncertain. Since the average *effective* exchange rate for all tradeables must stay unchanged (to remain in equilibrium), we know that in the end this rate must fall in the final goods sector and rise in the inputs sector; but the result is uncertain for exports.

With no drawback Here, initially exports must fall, because of the decline of effective protection in this sector. Thus a contribution is made toward creating an import surplus, and a *depreciation* of the formal exchange rate. But this result is still not logically inevitable. Once more we know that, in the end, since the protection of inputs increases in relation to that of final consumption goods and exports, the *effective* exchange rate of either one of these two sectors or both must fall. In at least one of these two, resources will move from the sector to the nontradeable activities. In this instance we do not know whether resources will move from the exports sector to the sector of final consumption goods or the other way around, since protection rates fall in both sectors.

The directions of resource flows, and their welfare implications, are summarized in Table A1.1. Note that no impact on welfare is assigned to movements of resources between nontradeables and either of the three tradeable sectors; these combined movements must be "neutral," since the effective exchange rate in the economy is assumed to be always in equilibrium.

Table A1.1 Movements of resources following the imposition of input tariffs

Perfect drawback			Welfare change	No drawback			Welfare change
Direction of resource flow				Direction of resource flow			
C	→	I	+	C	→	I	+
C	→	X	+	C	?	X	?
I	←	X	−	I	←	X	−
C	→	N		X	→	N	
I	←	N		I	?	N	
X	?	N		X	?	N	

←→, direction of movement; ?, ambiguity; +, enhancement; −, diminution; C, final consumption goods; I, intermediate inputs; X, exports; N, nontradeables.

We thus see, in sum, that in either case the welfare effect of the imposition of duties on inputs is uncertain. The presumption of a welfare increase would be stronger with the existence of a drawback scheme for exports than without it (without a drawback scheme, in addition to the ambiguity about movements between final consumption goods and exports, the welfare-reducing movement of resources from exports to inputs production is stronger). But even here, a welfare improvement is not inevitable. In either case, judgment on which flows of resources among sectors would be likely to be important would have to be based on information about specific activities.

Industrial Structure and the Order of Removal of Trade Barriers

In the reduction of trade barriers, should the industrial structure of a branch of production influence the placing of that branch in the schedule of reductions? Specifically, when a liberalization is carried out in stages, should a distinction be made between a competitive and a monopolistic activity?

In addressing this issue, our analysis for simplicity will assume extreme situations: a competitive industry is one with perfect competition; and a monopolized industry consists of a single firm. The compared activities will be assumed to be identical (in cost and demand conditions) except for the difference in industrial structure.

Removal of Quantitative Restrictions

It is sometimes argued that *ceteris paribus*, removing QRs in a monopolistic industry brings more benefits than when the industry is competitive. If so, QRs should be removed first from monopolized activities. The argument seems to be intuitively persuasive. A monopoly leads to distortion and waste, and removal of the monopoly power, through the introduction (or increase) of trade, should enhance welfare by eliminating that waste.

The *ceteris paribus* assumption is crucial in the analysis. Three possible alternatives will be examined: (a) *import quotas* are the same in the competitive and the monopolized industries; (b) *prices* (before liberalization) are the same in both; and (c) *costs* are equal in both. The analysis under these three alternatives is carried out through figures A1.3–A1.5.

It is found that the answer to the basic question of whether more is gained from removing QRs from one industrial structure than another is inconclusive. The following propositions emerge from the analysis.

1   Starting from complete prohibition of imports (zero quotas), and abstracting from other considerations (or in the absence of other relevant information about activities) monopolized activities should be liberalized first as bringing the greatest welfare gain. But an important observation should be made here. The monopolized industries, *ceteris paribus*, would manifest the highest prices, and hence also the highest *differentials* (between the domestic and the international price). A policy rule that requires industries with the highest price differentials to be liberalized first would thus take care of the discrepancy in welfare gains associated with the trade structure. Moreover, such a rule will not have to be concerned with whether the price differentials originate from differences in industrial structure (in otherwise identical activities) or in other attributes of nonidentical activities – such as demand and cost functions or the size of the import quota.[9] There is *no separate* need to specify the industrial structure.

9 In nonidentical industries, differences in size are obviously relevant for the total gain. Properly formulated, the rule should state that the highest gain *per unit of change of imports* (or of production, or consumption) would be realized where the price differential is highest.

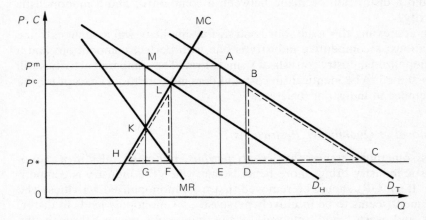

Figure A1.3 Case 1: Import quotas are equal under competition and under monopoly. D_T, compensated demand curve for the good; D_H, demand for domestic production; MR, marginal revenue; MC, marginal cost (= domestic supply, under competition); P^*, international price.

Perfect competition
P^c, consumer price; P^cD (= P^cB), consumption; P^*F (= P^cL), domestic production.

With the removal of quota: gain of consumer surplus = P^cCBP^c; loss of producer surplus = P^*HLP^c; loss of importer rent = FDBL. Therefore, net gain = BDC ("consumption gain") + LFH ("production gain").

Monopoly
P^*G (= P^mM), domestic production; P^m, consumer price; P^*E (= P^mA), consumption.

With the removal of quota: gain of consumer surplus = P^cCAP^m; loss of producer surplus = P^*HKMP^m; loss of importer rent = GEAM. Therefore, net gain = AEC ("consumption gain") + KGH ("production gain").

Comparison
With monopoly, consumption gain is larger by AEDB; production gain is smaller by KGFL. *But*: GF = ED (the difference in consumption between the two cases is equal to the difference in production, since imports are given). Hence, necessarily, KGFL < AEDB. Therefore, the net gain from removal of the quota restriction must be larger under monopoly than under perfect competition. This holds for *any* import quota, including zero, that is, including the case of complete prohibition.

2   When price differentials are equal in otherwise identical activities, the welfare gain would be higher if import restrictions are lifted first from the *competitive* industry. In other words, there is a tradeoff: the welfare gain may be as high in a monopolized industry with a higher price differential as in a competitive industry with a lower differentials. If anything, then, *competitive* industries should be prior candidates for liberalization when the price differential criterion is followed.[10]

10 But this is *not* recommended here as a policy rule. For a variety of other reasons, the gain in adhering to the principle of *uniformity* in the application of a rule (such as that of following price differentials) must far exceed any potential gain from discrimination.

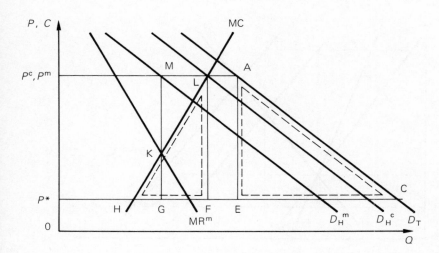

Figure A1.4 Case 2: Consumer prices are equal under competition and under monopoly.
Perfect competition
$D_H{}^cD_T$ (= LA), import quota; P^c, p^m, consumer price; P^*F (= P^cL), domestic production; P^*E (= P^cA), domestic consumption.

With the removal of quota: net gain = AEC ("consumption gain") + LFH ("production gain").

Monopoly
$D_H{}^mD_T$ (= MA), import quota; P^c, P^m, consumer price; P^mM (= P^*G), domestic production; P^mA (= P^*E), domestic consumption.

With the removal of quota: net gain = AEC ("consumption gain") + KGH ("production gain").

Comparison
The consumption gain is identical under competition and monopoly. The production gain must be *smaller* under monopoly. Hence the total gain from the removal of restriction is *smaller under monopoly.*

The rationale is simple. An identical (consumer) price under competition and monopoly may be established only through a *larger* import quota under monopoly. Consumption is the same, but production is smaller (and imports larger) under monopoly. Hence, the gain from removal of the quota restriction is smaller under monopoly.

3   A cost differential criterion would call for the opposite discrimination; but this inference has little practical use. To make any sense, the application of cost differentials as indicators of the expected gains from liberalization would require estimates of *marginal* costs, an effort which is obviously not feasible – even if it were desirable – on the required scale.

Reduction of Tariffs

Whenever imports exist with a given tariff – that is, whenever the tariff is not prohibitive – the industrial structure of the activity is completely irrelevant in the present context: a domestic monopoly has no monopolistic

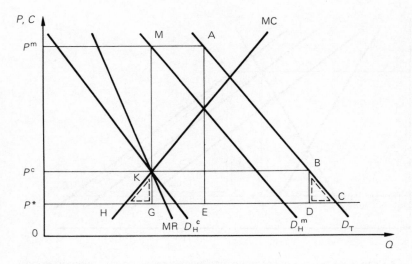

Figure A1.5 Case 3: Costs are equal under competition and under monopoly.

Perfect competition
$D_H^c D_T$ (= KB), import quota; P^c, consumer price; P^*G (= P^cK), domestic production; P^*D, (= P^cB), domestic consumption.

With the removal of quota: net gain = BDC ("consumption gain") + KGH ("production gain").

Monopoly
$D_H^m D_T$ (= MA) = import quota; P^m, consumer price; P^*G (= P^mM), domestic production; P^*E (= P^mA), domestic consumption.

With the removal of quota: net gain = AEC ("consumption gain") + KGH ("production gain").

Comparison
The production gain is identical under competition and under monopoly. The consumption gain must be *larger* under monopoly. Hence the total gain from the removal of restriction is *larger under monopoly*.

This is the reverse of case 2. Identical costs under competition and monopoly must imply a higher consumer price under monopoly. This may be established only by a *smaller import quota*, and hence also smaller consumption. Thus, while production and production loss are equal, consumption (and imports) are smaller under monopoly. Hence the gain from removal of the quota restriction is larger under monopoly.

power as long as imports provide any part of the domestic consumption, so that the otherwise monopolistic firm faces a domestic demand that is infinitely elastic (in a "small country," which is assumed here all along). Industrial structure becomes of consequence only when the tariff is prohibitive.

In figure A1.6 t_c is *the* prohibitive tariff in its strict definition: whatever the industrial structure, it is just at this tariff level that all imports would disappear. An increase of the tariff beyond that level in the competitive

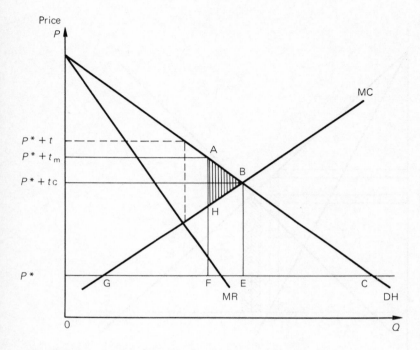

Figure A1.6 Relation of prohibitive tariffs and domestic monopoly.

industry would merely create some tariff redundancy. For the monopolistic industry, however, increasing the tariff level would affect the domestic price, the quantity produced, and the quantity consumed (the last two being necessarily equal to each other).[11] Thus, raising the tariff from t_c to t_m would raise the domestic price from $P^* + t_c$ to $P^* + t_m$ and lower the quantity produced and consumed from P^*E to $P^* + t_m A$. Only beyond the level t would a further raising of the tariff become irrelevant under monopoly. We shall refer to the tariff level t_m as the "actually prohibitive" tariff, whereas t_c will be addressed as the "competitively prohibitive" tariff level.[12] It may readily be seen that the economic loss of the actually prohibitive tariff t_m is *higher* than the loss from a competitively prohibitive

11 We assume, again for simplicity, that no part of the domestic production turns, under monopoly, into *exports*. In view of the existence of transportation costs, and various other costs involved in turning from import substitution to exports, this is in any case not a highly restrictive assumption. As figure A1.6 is drawn, no exports would be forthcoming in the absence of this assumption; but it could be drawn otherwise.

12 Referring to the issue discussed in the first section, another source of a *measured* tariff "redundancy" may be seen here: if the (actually prohibitive) tariff level is compared with the excess of domestic *costs* over the international price, the part AH of the tariff would be found to be "redundant."

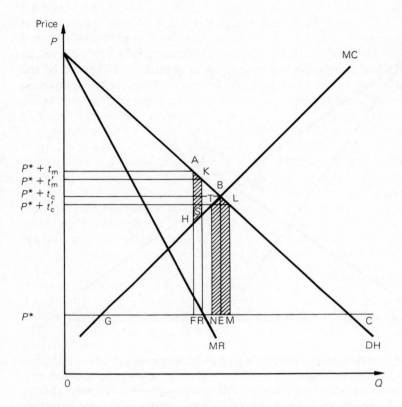

Figure A1.7 Relation between prohibitive tariffs and domestic production.

tariff t_c. The loss from the latter is the combination of the production loss BEG and the consumption loss BCE (that is, the area BCG). The loss of the former, on the other hand, is yielded by the (smaller than competitive) production loss HFG; and the (larger than competitive) consumption loss ACF. It thus *exceeds* the competitive tariff loss by the shaded area ABH. Hence, the *complete* removal of an actually prohibitive tariff, under monopoly, must yield a higher welfare gain than the removal of a prohibitive tariff under competition. The former may always be viewed as being undertaken in two stages: first, a reduction of the actually prohibitive tariff to the level at which it is competitively prohibitive, which would eliminate the excess loss ABH; and then a removal of the remaining part of the tariff, which would have the same effect under monopoly as under competition.

It is thus established – not surprisingly – that if an order of complete removal of tariffs has to be introduced, the prohibitive tariffs should first be eliminated in monopolistic industries. But the same end would be achieved if the elimination of the *higher* tariffs first were to serve as a guiding policy rule. Moreoever, it does *not* follow, from this analysis, that partial reduction, rather than complete elimination, of a tariff should be preferred when a monopolistic industry is in question. This would be the preferred course only if, given the *same level* of tariffs in the two industries, some tariff redundancy exists in the competitive industry, whereas in the monopolistic industry the tariff is only what we have termed "actually prohibitive" (and does not exceed the level t in figure A1.6). The opposite, of course, is not possible. In this case, the partial reduction of the tariff would be welfare enhancing in the monopolistic industry but irrelevant in the competitive industry (as long as the tariff is not reduced below its competitively prohibitive level).

When, on the other hand, no competitive redundancy is involved, the outcome is ambiguous (figure A1.7). Once more, the initial tariff levels are the competitively prohibitive tariff t_c in the competitive industry and the actually prohibitive tariff t_m in the monopolistic industry. Assume, now, an equal reduction of the tariff levels in both industries: from t_c to t'_c in the competitive activity, and from t_m to t'_m in the monopolistic activity. In the competitive industry, consumption will now increase to P^*M; and domestic production will fall to P^*N. The consumption and production welfare losses (in comparison with free trade) will now be LCM and TNG respectively. That is, in comparison with the *initial* tariff, the aggregate welfare gain will be the shaded area BLMNT. In the monopolistic industry, consumption will increase from P^*F to P^*R, and production too will now *increase*, from P^*F to P^*R (imports will still be actually prohibited). The new consumption loss (in comparison with free trade) will become KCR, and the new production loss will be SRG – a higher production loss than before due to the expansion of production. In comparison with the initial tariff, the aggregate welfare gain will be the shaded area AKSH. Now in general it is impossible to tell whether the latter is bigger or smaller than the aggregate gain under competition (BLMNT): the larger consumption gain under monopoly may be either more or less than sufficient to compensate for the fact that the production loss increases, under monopoly, while under competition it must fall. Thus, no general *a priori* presumption is estabished whether, under a scheme of equal reductions of tariffs, a larger or smaller gain will be realized in a competitive or a monopolistic activity.[13]

13 Referring to our discussion earlier, it will be clear that, in a *proportional* scheme of tariff reductions, a higher likelihood is established that the welfare from the tariff reductions will be higher in the monopolistic industry. But that will be due simply to the fact that this industry is subject to a higher level of an initial tariff than is the competitive industry; and hence, also, to a larger (absolute) tariff cut.

Appendix A2

Formal Testing of Hypotheses

Ioannis N. Kessides

Department of Economics
University of Maryland
College Park, MD, USA

In this study we seek to identify cross-country relationships among the attributes of trade liberalization policies, their sustainability, and economic growth. The empirical analysis is based on a cross-sectional sample of several liberalization episodes that were investigated for the research project on "The Timing and Sequencing of a Trade Liberalization Policy." Because the sample included only countries that attempted trade liberalization, all the inferences drawn from the empirical estimates must be *conditional* on such liberalization actually taking place.

All the variables used in this analysis are derived from data provided in the individual country reports except for the territorial size and population of each country (taken from *World Tables*, published by the World Bank) and the rates of growth of exports and imports (based on three-month moving averages derived from *International Finance Statistics*, published by the International Monetary Fund). The variables related to real gross domestic product (GDP) growth performance are from chapter 7. All the qualitative variables defining the attributes of liberalization and the characteristics of the trade regime before liberalization are derived from chapter 3. Finally, the qualitative variables indicating export promotion policies and changes in the real exchange rate in the year of trade liberalization are derived from chapter 12.

The full sample consists of 36 liberalization episodes that have been identified in the 19 country studies in the project. Because of the lack of observations for certain key variables, between five and seven episodes were eliminated. Thus, the final sample consists of at least 29 liberalization episodes to at most 31 such episodes depending on the variable. For example, sectoral growth data are available for 29 episodes, while real annual export and GDP growth rates are available for 31 trade liberalization episodes.

Empirical analysis indicates that the data presented in the country studies provide support for the following empirical propositions.

Proposition 1 The imposition of severe trade restrictions significantly retards growth of GDP. Countries with severely restrictive trade regimes have realized lower pre-liberalization rates of GDP growth than those of countries with less restriction.

Proposition 2 The correlation between growth rates before and after liberalization is lower in countries with severe trade restrictions than in countries with moderate restrictions. Thus, liberalization appears to (partially) remove the constraint on growth imposed by trade restrictions.

Proposition 3 Trade restrictions retard GDP growth in both the traded and nontraded sectors of the economy.

Proposition 4 The correlation between growth rates before and after trade liberalization is higher in the nontraded sector than in the traded sector. Thus the effect of liberalization is more pronounced in the traded sector.

Proposition 5 The strength of the liberalization episodes and the rates of GDP growth before liberalization are negatively correlated. Strong liberalization attempts are more likely in low growth countries, which have more to gain by the process than countries already exhibiting good growth performance.

Proposition 6 Strong liberalization episodes are associated with higher increases in the rate of GDP growth than weak episodes.

Proposition 7 Strong liberalization episodes contribute significantly to GDP growth in the traded sector but not in the nontraded sector.

Proposition 8 Strong liberalization attempts have a much greater impact on growth in countries that have had severely restrictive trade regimes than in countries that have had moderate regimes; that is, countries with severely restrictive trade regimes respond more effectively to strong trade liberalization measures than countries with moderate restrictions.

Proposition 9 Countries with sustained liberalization episodes experienced higher post-liberalization rates of GDP growth than countries where the liberalization attempt collapsed.

Proposition 10 Countries with sustained liberalization episodes experienced larger increases in their rates of GDP growth (as measured from the three-year period preceding each episode through the first four years of the episode) than countries with failed episodes.

Proposition 11 The increases in GDP growth associated with sustained liberalization episodes are larger than those with failed episodes, under both severely and moderately restrictive prior regimes. The effect of sustainability on growth, however, is stronger in countries that had severe trade restrictions before liberalization.

Proposition 12   Countries where liberalization consisted mainly in reducing QRs experienced larger increases in their rates of GDP growth.

Proposition 13   The relaxation of QRs is effective in promoting economic growth in both the traded and nontraded sectors of the economy.

Proposition 14   The relaxation of QRs is highly effective in promoting growth in the manufacturing sector but not in agriculture.

Proposition 15   Sustainable liberalization episodes have a substantial impact on agricultural growth in countries that have had severely restrictive trade regimes.

Proposition 16   Large countries (in terms of territory) are less likely to pursue a long-term (sustained) policy of trade liberalization.

Proposition 17   Liberalization attempts that focus on the reduction of QRs rather than on devaluation or the reduction of tariffs are more likely to be sustained.

Proposition 18   Sustainability is correlated with political stability.

Proposition 19   Sustainability is more strongly correlated with the change in the rates of GDP growth induced by the liberalization attempt than with either the pre-liberalization rate of growth or the rate during the first four years of the liberalization episode.

Proposition 20   Sustainable liberalization episodes are associated with improved trade balances.

Proposition 21   Export promotion policies have been instituted in countries with low rates of export growth before liberalization.

Proposition 22   Liberalization has led, on average, to a significant improvement in export performance.

Proposition 23   Export promotion has significantly affected GDP growth in the traded sector but not in the nontraded sector.

Proposition 24   Export promotion has been especially effective in inducing growth in the manufacturing sector.

Proposition 25   The depreciation of the real exchange rate has been effective in promoting export growth.

Proposition 26   Export performance is correlated with the speed of liberalization – fast episodes are associated with larger increases in the rate of export growth.

Proposition 27 Import performance is correlated with the speed of liberalization – fast episodes are associated with larger increases in the rate of growth of imports.

Proposition 28 The strength of liberalization is correlated with the performance of the trade balance – strong episodes lead to an improvement in the balance of trade.

Impact of Trade Restrictions

A comparison of the rates of growth of GDP before liberalization in countries with severe and moderate trade restrictions leads to the following least squares estimates:[1]

$$\text{Ptl} = 5.398 - 2.013^b \text{SR} \qquad R^2 = 0.147 \qquad \bar{R}^2 = 0.112$$
$$\quad (0.752) \quad (0.989) \qquad N = 25$$

where

$$\text{SR} = \begin{cases} 1 \text{ if the initial trade regime is severely restrictive} \\ 0 \text{ otherwise} \end{cases}$$

Thus, the dummy variable for severe restrictions, SR, is both statistically significant and quantitatively important in the equation explaining cross-country differences in Ptl, the average rate of GDP growth during the three years preceding each country's liberalization episode. These findings support the conjecture that freer trade is superior to more restricted trade and are consistent with the conventional wisdom that there is a crucial link between the extent of a country's foreign trade and the rate of its general economic development.

Proposition 1 The imposition of severe trade restrictions significantly retards growth of GDP. Countries with severely restrictive trade regimes have realized lower pre-liberalization rates of GDP growth than those of countries with less restriction.

The correlation between Avg (the average rate of GDP growth during the first four years of each episode) and Ptl is much higher in the group of countries with moderate trade restrictions than in the group with severe restrictions:

---

1 Here and in subsequent equations, standard errors appear in parentheses. Superscript [a] indicates significance at the 0.01 level; superscript [b] indicates significance at the 0.05 level; superscript [c] indicates significance at the 0.10 level. N indicates the number of observations; R^2 is the coefficient of determination; and $\bar{R}^2$ is the coefficient of determination adjusted for degrees of freedom.

Countries with severe restrictions

$$\text{Avg} = \underset{(0.679)}{3.481} + \underset{(0.159)}{0.250} \text{Ptl} \qquad \begin{aligned} R^2 &= 0.160 \\ N &= 14 \end{aligned} \qquad \bar{R}^2 = 0.095$$

Countries with moderate restrictions

$$\text{Avg} = \underset{(1.441)}{2.634} + \underset{(0.249)}{0.812^a} \text{Ptl} \qquad \begin{aligned} \bar{R}^2 &= 0.542 \\ N &= 10 \end{aligned} \qquad \bar{R}^2 = 0.491$$

The persistence of GDP growth in the group with moderate restrictions is intuitively appealing in that with freer trade the distortions are lower, and hence the corrective and beneficial impact of liberalization will be smaller. In contrast, when growth is constrained by severe restrictions and a policy of liberalization is implemented, then knowing a country's rate of GDP growth before liberalization tells very little about its likely rate of growth after the policy change; hence, the correlation between Avg and Ptl in the severe restrictions group is lower. Thus, although liberalization may not fully neutralize the retarding effect of restrictions, the above provides support for the following.

Proposition 2　The correlation between growth rates before and after liberalization is lower in countries with severe trade restrictions than in countries with moderate restrictions. Thus, liberalization appears to (partially) remove the constraint on growth imposed by trade restrictions.

The analysis of sectoral GDP growth indicates that trade restrictions inhibit growth in both the traded and nontraded sectors of the economy. The SR variable is statistically significant and quantitatively important in the equations explaining TRADEP and NONTRP, the average rates of GDP growth during the three years preceding liberalization in the traded and nontraded sectors respectively:

$$\text{TRADEP} = \underset{(0.937)}{5.312} - \underset{(1.274)}{2.446^c} \text{SR} \qquad \begin{aligned} R^2 &= 0.144 \\ N &= 23 \end{aligned} \qquad \bar{R}^2 = 0.105$$

$$\text{NONTRP} = \underset{(0.685)}{5.759} - \underset{(0.930)}{2.459^a} \text{SR} \qquad \begin{aligned} R^2 &= 0.241 \\ N &= 23 \end{aligned} \qquad \bar{R}^2 = 0.207$$

Proposition 3　Trade restrictions retard GDP growth in both the traded and nontraded sectors of the economy.

We also find that GDP growth after liberalization is more strongly correlated with growth before liberalization in the nontraded sector than in the traded sector:

$$\text{TRADEA} = \underset{(0.620)}{3.505} + \underset{(0.121)}{0.251^b} \text{TRADEP} \qquad \begin{aligned} R^2 &= 0.164 \\ N &= 23 \end{aligned} \qquad \bar{R}^2 = 0.126$$

$$\text{NONTRA} = \underset{(0.927)}{2.466} + \underset{(0.081)}{0.776^{a}\text{NONTRP}} \quad \underset{N = 23}{R^2 = 0.52} \quad \bar{R}^2 = 0.427$$

where TRADEA and NONTRA are the average rates of GDP growth in the traded and nontraded sectors respectively. Thus it appears that in the traded sector liberalization more fully neutralizes the constraint imposed by the restriction of trade. This finding is intuitively appealing, in that one would expect the performance of the traded sector to respond more quickly to the change in trade policy. Alternatively, these results imply that, when a policy of liberalization is effected, knowing a country's rate of GDP growth in the traded sector before liberalization tells very little about the likely rate of growth of the same sector after initiation of the liberalization episode. In the nontraded sector, on the other hand, cross-country differences persist even after a change of trade policy is implemented. Thus liberalization has a greater impact on the traded sector.

Proposition 4   The correlation between growth rates before and after trade liberalization is higher in the nontraded sector than in the traded sector. Thus the effect of liberalization is more pronounced in the traded sector.

Attributes of Liberalization and Gross Domesic Product Growth Performance

There is negative correlation between the intensity of the liberalization episode and the country's rate of GDP growth before liberalization. Indeed, logit analysis leads to the following equation:

$$\text{DST} = \underset{(0.896)}{1.622} - \underset{(0.173)}{0.280^{c}\text{Ptl}} \quad \underset{N = 27}{R^2 = 0.175}$$

where

$$\text{DST} = \begin{cases} 1 \text{ if strong episode} \\ 0 \text{ otherwise} \end{cases}$$

Thus it is more likely that strong liberalization attempts will be observed in countries experiencing low GDP growth rates before liberalization.

Proposition 5   The strength of the liberalization episodes and the rates of GDP growth before liberalization are negatively correlated. Strong liberalization attempts are more likely in low growth countries, which have more to gain by the process than countries already exhibiting good growth performance.

The first four years of each episode do not seem to constitute a sufficiently long time interval to capture the basic corrective features of liberalization fully. Thus, countries with strong liberalization attempts continue to exhibit lower rates of GDP growth – Avg is negatively correlated with DST:

$$\text{Avg} = \begin{array}{ccc} 5.769 & - & 1.752^b\text{DST} \\ (0.537) & & (0.731) \end{array} \qquad \begin{array}{l} R^2 = 0.193 \\ N = 25 \end{array} \qquad \bar{R}^2 = 0.159$$

However, it is implicitly assumed that each country is on a path toward a higher growth equilibrium effected by a freer trade regime. A more appropriate measure of performance, then, might be the change in the rate of GDP growth from the average of the three years before liberalization to the average of the first four years of each liberalization episode, that is, the difference between Avg and Ptl. The results indicate that countries with strong episodes experienced larger increases in their rates of growth:

$$\text{Dif} = \begin{array}{ccc} 0.711 & + & 1.251^c\text{DST} \\ (0.540) & & (0.701) \end{array} \qquad \begin{array}{l} R^2 = 0.113 \\ N = 26 \end{array} \qquad \bar{R}^2 = 0.078$$

where Dif = Avg − Ptl.

Proposition 6 Strong liberalization episodes are associated with higher increases in the rate of GDP growth than weak episodes.

The analysis of sectoral GDP growth indicates that the strength of the liberalization episode can spur growth primarily in the traded sector. The DST variable is statistically significant and quantitatively important in the equation explaining changes in the rate of GDP growth (from the three years preceding each liberalization episode through the first four years of the episode) in the traded sector but not in the nontraded sector:

$$\text{TrdDif} = \begin{array}{ccc} -0.706 & + & 2.093^c\text{DST} \\ (0.951) & & (1.212) \end{array} \qquad \begin{array}{l} R^2 = 0.111 \\ \end{array} \qquad \bar{R}^2 = 0.074$$

$$\text{NtrDif} = \begin{array}{ccc} 0.833 & + & 0.772\text{DST} \\ (0.811) & & (1.034) \end{array} \qquad \begin{array}{l} R^2 = 0.023 \\ N = 25 \end{array} \qquad \bar{R}^2 = -0.018$$

where TrdDif = TRADEA − TRADEP and NtrDif = NONTRA − NONTRP.

Proposition 7 Strong liberalization episodes contribute significantly to GDP growth in the traded sector but not in the nontraded sector.

Strong liberalization attempts have a greater growth-enhancing influence in countries that have had severely restrictive regimes before the onset of each liberalization episode. Analysis of GDP growth rates grouped according to the severity of the pre-liberalization trade regime indicates that the DST variable is statistically significant in an equation explaining cross-country differences in Dif for the group with severe restrictions but not for the group with only moderate restrictions:

Countries with severe trade restrictions

$$\text{Dif} = 0.080 + 2.167^b\text{DST} \qquad R^2 = 0.304 \qquad \bar{R}^2 = 0.241$$
$$\quad\;\;(0.822)\quad(0.988) \qquad\qquad N = 12$$

Countries with moderate trade restrictions

$$\text{Dif} = 1.071 + 0.994\text{DST} \qquad R^2 = 0.022 \qquad \bar{R}^2 = -0.004$$
$$\quad\;\;(0.692)\quad(1.019) \qquad\qquad N = 12$$

Proposition 8 Strong liberalization attempts have a much greater impact on growth in countries that have had severely restrictive trade regimes than in countries that have had moderate regimes; that is, countries with severely restrictive trade regimes respond more effectively to strong trade liberalization measures than countries with moderate restrictions.

Another important characteristic of the liberalization process in its effect on GDP growth is its sustainability. Liberalization episodes were grouped into those that were fully sustained, those that were partially sustained, and those that failed. Ordinary least-squares estimates provide strong evidence that countries with sustained (fully and partially) episodes experienced higher rates of growth than countries where the liberalization episodes collapsed:

$$\text{Avg} = 1.465 + 0.713^a\text{Ptl} + 2.369^a\text{SUSTA}$$
$$\quad\;\;(0.693)\quad(0.121)\qquad(0.668)$$
$$R^2 = 0.652 \quad \bar{R}^2 = 0.624$$

$$\text{Avg} = 1.179 + 0.678^a\text{Ptl} + 2.267^a\text{SUSTB}$$
$$\quad\;\;(0.774)\quad(0.126)\qquad(0.717)$$
$$R^2 = 0.626 \quad \bar{R}^2 = 0.596$$
$$N = 27$$

where

$$\text{SUSTA} = \begin{cases} 1 \text{ if the episode was fully sustained} \\ 0 \text{ otherwise} \end{cases}$$

and

$$\text{SUSTB} = \begin{cases} 1 \text{ if the episode was fully or partially sustained} \\ 0 \text{ otherwise} \end{cases}$$

These results provide strong support for the following.

Proposition 9 Countries with sustained liberalization episodes experienced higher post-liberalization rates of GDP growth than countries where the liberalization attempt collapsed.

Analysis also shows that countries with sustained episodes experienced larger increases (changes) in their rates of growth (again, as measured by the difference Dif = Avg − Ptl):

$$\text{Dif} = \quad 0.191 + 2.389^a \text{SUSTA} \qquad R^2 = 0.295 \qquad \bar{R}^2 = 0.267$$
$$\qquad\quad (0.475) \quad (0.725)$$
$$\text{Dif} = -0.154 + 2.129^a \text{SUSTB} \qquad R^2 = 0.219 \qquad \bar{R}^2 = 0.189$$
$$\qquad\quad (0.632) \quad (0.788) \qquad\qquad N = 27$$

Proposition 10 Countries with sustained liberalization episodes experienced larger increases in their rates of GDP growth (as measured from the three-year period preceding each episode through the first four years of the episode) than countries with failed episodes.

Countries with sustained liberalization episodes experienced larger increases in their growth rates than countries with failed attempts, regardless of whether the prior regime was severely or moderately restrictive. It appears, however, that the effect of sustainability on GDP growth is more pronounced in countries that had severe restrictions before liberalization:

Countries with severe restrictions

$$\text{Dif} = -0.173 + 2.787^b \text{SUSTA} \qquad R^2 = 0.309 \qquad \bar{R}^2 = 0.256$$
$$\qquad\quad (0.731) \quad (1.155) \qquad\qquad N = 14$$

Countries with moderate restrictions

$$\text{Dif} = \quad 0.659 + 1.888^b \text{SUSTA} \qquad R^2 = 0.287 \qquad \bar{R}^2 = 0.222$$
$$\qquad\quad (0.609) \quad (0.897) \qquad\qquad N = 12$$

The conjecture that sustained episodes in countries with severely restrictive prior regimes are associated with larger increases in growth is also supported by the following estimates:

$$\text{Dif} = \quad 0.550 + 2.063^a \text{SRS} + 1.470^c \text{MRS}$$
$$\qquad\quad (0.397) \quad (0.743) \qquad (0.794)$$
$$\qquad\qquad\qquad\qquad\qquad\qquad R^2 = 0.282 \qquad \bar{R}^2 = 0.219$$
$$\text{Dif} = \quad 0.918 + 1.696^b \text{SRS}$$
$$\qquad\quad (0.361) \quad (0.752) \qquad R^2 = 0.175 \qquad \bar{R}^2 = 0.141$$
$$\qquad\qquad\qquad\qquad\qquad\qquad N = 25$$

where

$$\text{SRS} = \begin{cases} 1 \text{ if the initial trade regime was severely restrictive and the} \\ \quad \text{episode was sustained} \\ 0 \text{ otherwise} \end{cases}$$

and

$$\text{MRS} = \begin{cases} 1 \text{ if the initial trade regime was moderately restrictive and the} \\ \quad \text{episode was sustained} \\ 0 \text{ otherwise} \end{cases}$$

Proposition 11 The increases in GDP growth associated with sustained liberalization episodes are larger than those with failed episodes, under both severely and moderately restrictive prior regimes. The effect of sustainability on growth, however, is stronger in countries that had severe trade restrictions before liberalization.

Analysis of the direct elements of liberalization reveals that episodes in which a relaxation of QRs was the only ingredient of the policy package were more effective in promoting GDP growth than liberalization packages that also included tariff reduction and devaluation:

$$\text{Dif} = \begin{array}{c} 0.712 \\ (0.361) \end{array} + \begin{array}{c} 1.566^b\text{RQR} \\ (0.722) \end{array} \qquad \begin{array}{l} R^2 = 0.176 \qquad \bar{R}^2 = 0.139 \\ N = 23 \end{array}$$

where

$$\text{RQR} = \left\{ \begin{array}{l} 1 \text{ if the policy package consisted mainly of QR reductions} \\ 0 \text{ otherwise} \end{array} \right.$$

Proposition 12 Countries where liberalization consisted mainly in reducing QRs experienced larger increases in their rate of GDP growth.

The analysis of sectoral GDP growth indicates that liberalization episodes that consisted exclusively of QR reductions were effective in promoting higher rates of growth in both the traded and the nontraded sectors of the economy:

$$\text{TRADEA} = \begin{array}{c} 0.277 \\ (0.715) \end{array} + \begin{array}{c} 0.858^a\text{TRADEP} \\ (0.123) \end{array} + \begin{array}{c} 2.964^a\text{RQR} \\ (1.019) \end{array}$$
$$R^2 = 0.773 \quad \bar{R}^2 = 0.749$$

$$\text{TrdDif} = \begin{array}{c} -0.383 \\ (0.433) \end{array} + \begin{array}{c} 2.793^a\text{RQR} \\ (1.017) \end{array} \qquad \begin{array}{l} R^2 = 0.274 \quad \bar{R}^2 = 0.237 \\ N = 21 \end{array}$$

$$\text{NONTRA} = \begin{array}{c} 0.867 \\ (0.673) \end{array} + \begin{array}{c} 0.985^a\text{NONTRP} \\ (0.124) \end{array} + \begin{array}{c} 2.924^a\text{RQR} \\ (0.819) \end{array}$$
$$R^2 = 0.798 \quad \bar{R}^2 = 0.778$$

$$\text{NtrDif} = \begin{array}{c} 0.796 \\ (0.333) \end{array} + \begin{array}{c} 2.919^a\text{RQR} \\ (0.798) \end{array}$$
$$R^2 = 0.389 \quad \bar{R}^2 = 0.360$$
$$N = 22$$

Proposition 13 The relaxation of QRs is effective in promoting economic growth in both the traded and nontraded sectors of the economy.

Further sectoral analysis, however, shows that the relaxation of QRs is highly effective in promoting growth in the manufacturing sector but not in agriculture. The variable RQR is highly significant and quantitatively important in an equation explaining changes in the rate of GDP growth (from the three years preceding each episode through the first four years of liberalization) in the manufacturing sector but not in agriculture:

$$\text{MfgAvg} = \underset{(1.068)}{0.927} + \underset{(0.129)}{0.695^a\text{MfgPtl}} + \underset{(1.577)}{7.604^a\text{RQR}}$$
$$R^2 = 0.733 \qquad \bar{R}^2 = 0.709$$

$$\text{MfgDif} = \underset{(0.685)}{-1.125} + \underset{(1.713)}{7.102^a\text{RQR}}$$
$$R^2 = 0.428 \qquad \bar{R}^2 = 0.403$$
$$N = 24$$

$$\text{AgAvg} = \underset{(0.747)}{2.098} + \underset{(0.198)}{0.065\text{AgPtl}} + \underset{(1.023)}{1.100\text{RQR}}$$
$$R^2 = 0.064 \qquad \bar{R}^2 = -0.030$$

$$\text{AgDif} = \underset{(0.601)}{-0.802} + \underset{(1.411)}{0.547\text{RQR}}$$
$$R^2 = 0.007 \qquad \bar{R}^2 = -0.041$$
$$N = 22$$

where MfgDif = MfgPtl and AgDif = AgAvg − AgPtl, the difference between the average growth rates during the first four years of each episode and the three years preceding it, in the manufacturing and agricultural sectors respectively.

Proposition 14   The relaxation of QRs is highly effective in promoting growth in the manufacturing sector but not in agriculture.

In agriculture, in contrast, there is a critical interaction between sustainability and the extent to which trade was restricted before liberalization. Sustainable liberalization episodes have been especially effective in promoting growth in agriculture in countries where the prior trade regime was severely restricted.

$$\text{AgAvg} = \underset{(0.481)}{2.337} + \underset{(0.222)}{0.378^c\text{AgPtl}} + \underset{(1.696)}{4.818^a\text{SRSUSTA}} - \underset{(0.016)}{0.040^b\text{POP}}$$
$$R^2 = 0.375 \quad \bar{R}^2 = 0.271$$

$$\text{AgDif} = \underset{(0.691)}{0.636} + \underset{(1.361)}{8.269^a\text{SRSUSTA}} - \underset{(0.018)}{0.056^b\text{POP}}$$
$$R^2 = 0.686 \quad \bar{R}^2 = 0.652$$
$$N = 21$$

where SRSUSTA = SR × SUSTA and POP is the country's population. The critical interaction between sustainability and the severity of trade restrictions is also evidenced by separate analyses of the growth in agriculture in countries with severe and moderate prior restrictions:

Countries with severe restrictions

$$\text{AgDif} = \underset{(1.625)}{0.981} + \underset{(2.009)}{9.392^a\text{SUSTA}} - \underset{(0.032)}{0.082^b\text{POP}}$$

$$R^2 = 0.749 \qquad \bar{R}^2 = 0.694$$
$$N = 11$$

Countries with moderate restrictions

$$\text{AgDif} = \underset{(1.379)}{1.430} - \underset{(1.376)}{3.949^b\text{SUSTA}} - \underset{(0.027)}{0.020\text{POP}}$$

$$R^2 = 0.484 \qquad \bar{R}^2 = 0.381$$
$$N = 12$$

Thus, we observe substantial growth of the agricultural sector in countries with sustainable liberalization attempts and severely restrictive prior trade regimes but not in countries with only moderate restrictions. In countries with only moderate restrictions, sustainability had a negative impact on agricultural growth.

Proposition 15 Sustainable liberalization episodes have a substantial impact on agricultural growth in countries that have had severely restrictive trade regimes.

Sustainability and its Correlates

The analysis in this section seeks to identify the main components of sustained liberalization episodes and to evaluate the factors contributing to the sustainability of the liberalization efforts. Among the possible explanatory variables, country-specific attributes, including the specific types of policy changes implemented, and the characteristics of economic performance before and during the episodes are emphasized.

Logit estimation indicates that the territorial size of the country, represented by the variable AREA, is significantly negative in an equation explaining cross-country differences in sustainability. One potential explanation for this negative relationship is that the territorial size of a country may be an indicator of the country's natural resource endowment:

$$\text{SUSTA} = \underset{(0.596)}{0.841} - \underset{(0.089)}{0.169^b\text{AREA}} \qquad \begin{array}{l} R = 0.366 \\ N = 29 \end{array}$$

Proposition 16 Large countries (in terms of territory) are less likely to pursue a long-term (sustained) policy of trade liberalization.

There is no evidence, however, that population, another measure of a country's size, captures in any way the country's potential gain from international trade and specialization. The population variable is statistically insignificant in the equation explaining sustainability.

Liberalization attempts in which the relaxation of QRs is the only ingredient of the policy package are more likely to survive than attempts that focus on tariff reductions:

$$\text{SUSTA} = -0.955 + 1.649^c\text{RQR} \qquad R = 0.163$$
$$\qquad\qquad (0.526) \quad (1.013) \qquad\qquad N = 24$$

Proposition 17   Liberalization attempts that focus on the reduction of QRs rather than on devaluation or the reduction of tariffs are more likely to be sustained.

Sustainability seems also to be correlated with political stability:

$$\text{SUSTA} = -1.946 + 2.051^c\text{STAB} \qquad R = 0.245$$
$$\qquad\qquad (1.069) \quad (1.164) \qquad\qquad N = 27$$

where

$$\text{STAB} = \begin{cases} 1 \text{ if there is no change in political regime} \\ 0 \text{ otherwise} \end{cases}$$

Proposition 18   Sustainability is correlated with political stability.

Sustainability is more strongly correlated with Dif, the change in the rate of GDP growth from the three years preceding the liberalization episode through the first four years of the episode, than with either Ptl or Avg, the average rates of growth during the three years before and the first four years of each episode respectively:

$$\text{SUSTA} = -0.412 + 0.008\text{Ptl} \qquad R = 0.0$$
$$\qquad\qquad (0.745) \quad (0.142)$$
$$\text{SUSTA} = -2.863 + 0.429^b\text{Avg} \qquad R = 0.357$$
$$\qquad\qquad (1.226) \quad (0.199)$$
$$\text{SUSTA} = -1.886 + 0.945^a\text{Dif} \qquad R = 0.535$$
$$\qquad\qquad (0.804) \quad (0.357) \qquad\qquad N = 27$$

Proposition 19   Sustainability is more strongly correlated with the change in the rates of GDP growth induced by the liberalization attempt than with either the pre-liberalization rate of growth or the rate during the first four years of the liberalization episode.

Liberalization attempts are more likely to survive in countries experiencing an improvement in their trade balance:

$$\text{SUSTA} = \quad 0.054 + 33.733^c\text{BP}_{1\rightarrow3} \qquad R = 0.217$$
$$\qquad\qquad (0.459) \quad (19.638) \qquad\qquad N = 25$$
$$\text{SUSTA} = -0.578 + 55.855^c\text{BP}_{2\rightarrow3} \qquad R = 0.250$$
$$\qquad\qquad (0.508) \quad (31.866) \qquad\qquad N = 23$$

where $BP_{1 \to 3} = (Xeop - Meop) - (Xptl - Mptl)$, $BP_{2 \to 3} = (Xeop - Meop) - (Xavg - Mavg)$, and where Xptl, Mptl are the average rates of growth of exports and imports during the three years preceding each liberalization episode; Xavg, Mavg are the average rates of growth of exports and imports during the first four years of each episode; and Xeop, Meop are the same growth rates during the two years following the end of each episode.

Proposition 20 Sustainable episodes are associated with improved trade balances.

Performance of the Trade Balance

In this subsection we seek to identify the conditions under which export promotion policies have been implemented and to assess the impact of such policies on the performance of the trade balance.

Logit estimation indicates a negative correlation between the rate of growth of exports before liberalization and the adoption of export promotion measures during the liberalization process:

$$EXPD = 0.625 - 80.675^b Xptl \qquad R = 0.329$$
$$\quad\;\;(0.562)\quad(39.434) \qquad\qquad N = 26$$

where

$$EXPD = \begin{cases} 1 \text{ if export promotion measures were implemented} \\ 0 \text{ otherwise} \end{cases}$$

Proposition 21 Export promotion policies have been instituted in countries with low rates of export growth before liberalization.

A comparison of the rates of export growth before and after liberalization reveals a significant improvement in export performance following liberalization for most of the countries in the sample. Indeed, the null hypothesis that the mean rates of export growth (before and after liberalization) are equal is rejected at below the 0.01 percent level.

Proposition 22 Liberalization has led, on average, to a significant improvement in export performance.

Sectoral analysis reveals that export promotion policies have affected growth performance in the traded sector but not in the nontraded sector:

$$TrdDif = -0.963 + 1.984^b EXPD \qquad R^2 = 0.220 \quad \bar{R}^2 = 0.179$$
$$\qquad\quad(0.649)\quad(0.858) \qquad\qquad N = 20$$
$$NtrDif = 0.844 + 0.454 EXPD \qquad R^2 = 0.023 \quad \bar{R}^2 = -0.026$$
$$\qquad\quad(0.492)\quad(0.666) \qquad\qquad N = 21$$

Proposition 23 Export promotion has significantly affected GDP growth in the traded sector but not in the nontraded sector.

The influence of export promotion has been especially significant (and quantitatively important) in the manufacturing sector:

$$\text{MfgDif} = -2.394 + 3.532^b \text{EXPD} \qquad R^2 = 0.213 \qquad \bar{R}^2 = 0.179$$
$$\phantom{\text{MfgDif} = } (0.981) \quad (1.416) \qquad\qquad N = 24$$

Proposition 24 Export promotion has been especially effective in inducing growth in the manufacturing sector.

Further analysis of the relationship between the attributes of liberalization and performance of the trade balance reveals that the depreciation of the real exchange rate has been effective in promoting export growth. Countries in which the devaluation of the real exchange rate was the most important element of the liberalization package have realized higher rates of export growth following liberalization:

$$\text{Xavg} = 6.622 + 5.544^b \text{DRER} \qquad R^2 = 0.091 \qquad \bar{R}^2 = 0.065$$
$$\phantom{\text{Xavg} = } (2.122) \quad (3.001) \qquad\qquad N = 35$$

where

$$\text{DRER} = \begin{cases} 1 \text{ if the devaluation of the real exchange rate was the most} \\ \text{important element of the policy package} \\ 0 \text{ otherwise} \end{cases}$$

Proposition 25 The depreciation of the real exchange rate has been effective in promoting export growth.

Both the strength and the speed of liberalization are important. Countries in which liberalization policies have been implemented rapidly have experienced larger increases in the rates of export growth:

$$X_{1 \to 2} = -0.004 + 0.012^c \text{DF} \qquad R^2 = 0.132 \qquad \bar{R}^2 = 0.094$$
$$\phantom{X_{1 \to 2} = } (0.005) \quad (0.007) \qquad\qquad N = 24$$
$$X_{1 \to 3} = -0.001 + 0.013^a \text{DF} \qquad R^2 = 0.223 \qquad \bar{R}^2 = 0.188$$
$$\phantom{X_{1 \to 3} = } (0.004) \quad (0.005) \qquad\qquad N = 23$$

where

$$\text{DF} = \begin{cases} 1 \text{ if the liberalization is fast} \\ 0 \text{ otherwise} \end{cases}$$

and where $X_{1 \to 2} = \text{Xavg} - \text{Xptl}$ and $X_{1 \to 3} = \text{Xeop} - \text{Xptl}$.

Proposition 26 Export performance is correlated with the speed of liberalization – fast episodes are associated with larger increases in the rate of export growth.

In addition, estimates also indicate that fast liberalization attempts have led to larger increases in the growth of imports:

$$M_{2\to3} = -0.005 + 0.012^c\text{DF} \qquad R^2 = 0.125 \qquad \bar{R}^2 = 0.087$$
$$\phantom{M_{2\to3} = }(0.005) \quad (0.007) \qquad N = 24$$

where $M_{2\to3}$ = Meop − Mavg.

Proposition 27 Import performance is correlated with the speed of liberalization – fast episodes are associated with larger increases in the rate of growth of imports.

The strength of the liberalization episode seems to be important in determining the performance of the trade balance:

$$\text{BP}_2 = -0.009 + 0.008^c\text{DST} \qquad R^2 = 0.140 \qquad \bar{R}^2 = 0.099$$
$$\phantom{\text{BP}_2 = }(0.003) \quad (0.004)$$
$$\text{BP}_{1\to2} = -0.027 + 0.025^a\text{DST} \qquad R^2 = 0.334 \qquad \bar{R}^2 = 0.302$$
$$\phantom{\text{BP}_{1\to2} = }(0.006) \quad (0.008) \qquad N = 22$$

where $\text{BP}_2 = \text{Xavg} - \text{Mavg}$, and $\text{BP}_{1\to2} = (\text{Xavg} - \text{Mavg}) - (\text{Xptl} - \text{Mptl})$.

Proposition 28 The strength of liberalization is correlated with the performance of the trade balance – strong episodes lead to an improvement in the balance of trade.

Appendix A3

Summaries of Country Experiences

Argentina
Domingo Cavallo and Joaquín Cottani

Argentina's economic performance from 1860 to 1929, when it followed an export-led growth strategy, was impressive. By contrast, stagnation and high inflation became endemic under the import substitution model followed after the Great Depression. In the latter 1970s, Argentina made a move to liberalize trade and financial policies following a preliminary move in this direction in the 1960s. Unfortunately, mismanagement of the transition from a highly interventionist to a market-oriented economy led to a balance-of-payments crisis. Within five years, a reversal of liberalization policies had begun.

The inept use of policy instruments is evidenced by the excessive overvaluation of the peso that prevailed during those years, a phenomenon that cannot be blamed on trade liberalization but must be ascribed to inconsistent accompanying policies.

Rationalizing the Tariff System: the Krieger-Vasena Episode

In June 1966 a coup d'etat put an end to the government of Arturo Illia, who had been elected president in 1963. His administration had failed to gain the support of the military and the trade unions. The military government that took power after the coup was committed to establishing the right conditions for sustained development, but it was not until March 1967, shortly after Adalbert Krieger-Vasena was named Minister of Economics, that the government announced an economic plan to achieve this objective.

This new economic team pursued monetary and price stability as a precondition for sustained growth. Immediate measures were taken to reduce inflation and achieve fiscal discipline. An opportunity to initiate tariff reform came with a sharp devaluation of the peso in March 1967, as tariff simplification and reductions were used to compensate in part for the effect of devaluation on the domestic prices of imported inputs. These liberalization steps were mainly conceived of as part of the stabilization package, although some structural effects were expected as well. From an institutional point of view, tariff reform was necessary to facilitate trade negotiations both globally (General Agreement on Tariffs and Trade (GATT)) and regionally (Latin American Free Trade Area (LAFTA)), which were steps toward greater integration with world markets.

Under the previous import regime there had been 60 different tariff rates, which started at zero and reached a maximum of 605 percent. The new system reduced the number of rates to 16 and the maximum tariff to 140 percent. The larger cuts were at the highest levels; duties below 100 percent were reduced less.

Most important prohibitions, prior deposit requirements on intermediate and capital goods, and subsidies to nontraditional exports were eliminated. Export taxes on traditional goods rose at the time of the devaluation but were gradually reduced.

Although tariff reform undoubtedly brought about a more rational tariff structure, in many cases (notably with respect to consumer goods) it did little more than eliminate water in the tariff. Tariffs were lower for intermediate and capital goods than for consumption goods, and tariffs on noncompeting imports were lower than if domestic production had existed. Additional steps would have been required to secure long-term effects on resource allocation and industrial efficiency, but they were not taken.

The overturn of liberal trade policies after 1970 seems to have been linked to popular opposition to the military government. A thorough analysis of this period in Argentina's history remains to be written. Political scientists and sociologists are still puzzled as to the leading causes of social distress during these years, which witnessed a wave of radicalism marked by frequent street riots, student revolts, and emerging terrorism. The unrest cannot be solely accounted for by the economic situation which, if anything, had improved.

Successful wage demands, arising from mounting labor conflicts, rose to a point where the government lost control of inflation. The reversal of trade liberalization policies between 1971 and 1973 was linked to the increase in inflation, since failure to devalue forced the authorities to restrict imports in order to avoid external imbalances. Moreover, a surge in nationalistic sentiments sustained the reversal and paved the way for the return of Juan and Isabel Perón, under whose government (1973–6) economic policies became firmly biased against free trade.

Another Move toward Liberalization

In March 1976 another military government took power in Argentina and the appointed economic team, led by José Martínez de Hoz, started the most ambitious attempt at trade liberalization in Argentina's history.

By that time, Argentina had a repressed economy, both commercially and financially. Domestic terms of trade had been systematically lower than external terms of trade, which was the outcome of implicit and explicit taxes on trade arising from import and export restrictions. Financial policy was similarly repressive. Interest rates were subject to low ceilings, and the government intervened directly in credit allocation. High inflation made for negative real interest rates, with a consequent decline in real money demand. Inflation was high because of large fiscal deficits financed by the Central Bank.

Martínez de Hoz was firmly committed to economic liberalization. In April 1976, immediately following the military coup, controls on domestic prices were eliminated. Exchange rate unification was achieved by the end of 1976, and the black market disappeared. Ceilings on domestic interest rates were lifted in June 1977. Taxes on traditional exports were practically eliminated during 1977, and the capital account of the balance of payments was opened at the end of 1978.

Import liberalization was much more gradual and discriminatory, but the trade account reached record levels of openness in 1979 and 1980. Most QRs were eliminated, and, in most sectors, nominal tariffs were at their lowest historical level. Tariff reduction was intended to continue up to 1984, after which some proportional escalation in the nominal structure would be introduced.

This trade liberalization did not impose the expected adjustment costs. Instead of increasing, the unemployment rate fell to an unprecedented level. Real wages fell in 1976, mainly as a result of wage controls designed to cope with high inflation, but increased again in 1979 and thereafter as wage policy became more flexible. Initially, the increase in imports did not create balance-of-payments problems. Foreign reserves increased steadily up to 1980, and the trade and current accounts improved substantially.

The benefits of trade liberalization became apparent almost immediately. Increases in productivity were observed in agriculture and manufacturing, and the prices of tradeable products fell. Investment rates were relatively high during the period, and gross domestic product (GDP) growth reached acceptable levels, especially in 1977 and 1979. Endemic inflation, uncontrollable under the Peronist government, stabilized at a lower rate for some years and then began to fall in 1980.

Despite these successes, trade liberalization was abandoned in 1981–2 in the midst of a severe balance-of-payments crisis. By the end of 1983, when a new civilian government took power, Argentina had an external debt of US$45 billion, a sixfold increase since 1975–6. Despite drastic adjustment policies, such as import restrictions and currency devaluations, the surplus in the trade account was significantly less than the amount needed to service the debt. Inflation was high again, and the fiscal deficit was clearly out of control.

What went wrong? This question has been posed by many economists. The most persuasive explanations point to accompanying macroeconomic policies leading to excessive real appreciation of the peso. Domestic macroeconomic policies were geared to reducing inflation rather than to the needs of the trade liberalization program. Real appreciation was the direct consequence of a lack of coordination among the fiscal, monetary, and exchange rate policies used to disinflate. The timing and sequencing of liberalization reforms may also have been a source of undesired fluctuations in the real exchange rate.

Two periods of exchange rate policies can be distinguished. From the last quarter of 1976 to the end of 1978 the government followed a crawling peg rule. Changes in the level of reserves and expected inflation influenced the rate of the crawl. In January 1979, government officials introduced an active-downward crawling peg based on pre-announcement of future rates of depreciation. To induce a fall in inflationary expectations, the crawl decreased gradually. Forthcoming changes in exchange rates, called "tablita," were announced daily. The government pegged the nominal exchange rate at different points in time while committing itself to the pre-announced values. But exchange rate policies are not sufficient to explain why the domestic currency appreciated so much from 1977 to 1981. Three additional factors must be taken into account.

Failure to Link Export with Import Liberalization
The elimination of export taxes was an important element in the initial appreciation of the peso between 1977 and 1978. Export liberalization induced a significant output response in the agricultural sector. The trade balance improved substantially and, since import liberalization was slow, export surpluses were monetized. Eventually, real appreciation reduced the competitiveness of nontraditional exports, inducing fresh distortions as export subsidies were used to keep effective exchange rates high. At the same time, the low real exchange rate created a disincentive for foreign investment because foreign investors received fewer pesos per dollar in real terms. The real appreciation also favored activities such as tourism outside the country and contraband imports, further complicating the process of opening the economy and stabilizing the balance of payments.

These problems could have been avoided if imports had been liberalized simultaneously with exports.

An Undisciplined Fiscal Policy

According to official publications, the deficit of the public sector fell from 14 percent of GDP in 1975 to 9.8 percent in 1976 and 3.2 percent in 1977. This decline was achieved mainly through increased tax collection. On the expenditures side, current spending fell but this was matched by a rise in public investment. Current spending increased again between 1977 and 1981 and, despite a fall in public investment and a further increase in tax revenues, the deficit doubled as a proportion of GDP.

This measure of the deficit does not include interest payments on domestic and foreign public debt, including interest paid on bank reserves held at the Central Bank. When these nominal payments are added, the monetary expansion implied by the fiscal deficit increases significantly.

Excessive Capital Inflows

Like other South American countries, Argentina received an influx of foreign capital during the late 1970s, fostered by domestic policies and international financial conditions. And in Argentina, domestic policies helped to transform an otherwise healthy borrowing opportunity into a debt crisis.

The government was unable to control the money supply and the exchange rate at the same time. Restrictions on capital mobility were eliminated in 1979. Once the government started to prefix nominal exchange rates with free capital mobility, the money supply became endogenous, the stock of reserves being the adjusting variable. The Central Bank set a target for domestic credit expansion in 1979 (70 percent) that was more or less consistent with the pre-announced rate of devaluation (65 percent). But the actual growth of domestic credit was 130 percent, mainly because of a significant reduction in the minimum reserves ratio required on all kinds of deposits from an initial level of 45 percent in December 1977. Reserves fell most steeply during the last quarter of 1978. In December of that year, the ratio was 16.5 percent. Lack of monetary discipline remained a keynote of policy in 1980, when domestic credit grew by 90 percent while the exchange rate was devalued only 25 percent. This time the source of monetary expansion was the large fiscal deficit.

Conclusion

The main lesson to be extracted from the Argentinian experience is that trade liberalization policies must be internally consistent and accompanied by supportive macroeconomic policies. A more open imports policy would have allowed a greater increase in imports in 1977–8. This would have reduced surpluses in the current account resulting from the liberalization of exports. To achieve this, the tariff program should have been implemented earlier and more rapidly. The expansion of domestic credit should have been in accordance with the rate of pre-announced devaluation in 1979 and 1980. This would have required a reduction in the fiscal and quasi-fiscal deficits. Finally, the opening of the capital account should have taken place only after fiscal equilibrium was reached and inflation was brought under control.

Brazil
Donald V. Coes

During the 1970s Brazil was widely regarded as one of the successes of the developing world, having experienced average annual increases in GDP of over 10 percent between 1968 and 1974, before the first oil shock began to slow growth. The late 1960s and early 1970s also witnessed greater openness in Brazilian foreign trade than at any other time in the post World War II period.

High rates of income growth and relatively greater trade openness were not coincidental. Both were features of an economic experience that began with a radical political change in 1964, when a democratic but disorganized populist government was overthrown by the Brazilian military. Beginning in 1964, a series of reforms in trade and capital account policies resulted in a modest opening to imports and much more openness to both exports and international capital inflows. Brazil's political system, in contrast, was probably more closed and authoritarian than at any time in its modern history.

The Brazilian experience does not fit a neat conventional model of trade liberalization in which local prices are brought into closer alignment with world-market prices through a large-scale reduction in tariffs and other trade barriers, with current account balance maintained through a real depreciation. In Brazil, liberalization on the import side was modest and even timid compared with export promotion and capital account openings; the real exchange rate was a key variable in both the initiation and demise of the liberalizing policies.

The style of Brazilian policymaking in the post-1964 period was also instrumental in the initial success and eventual failure of the experiment. The bureaucracy never relinquished control of trade flows to markets; as a result it naturally turned to administrative measures, rather than to prices, as the means to restore balance-of-payments equilibrium after the first oil shock.

The massive and historically unprecedented foreign capital inflows into Brazil after 1968 were a third critical feature of the Brazilian experience. A result both of Brazilian capital account policies after 1964 and changes in international capital markets, the inflows profoundly affected the balance of payments, the real exchange rate, and the eventual outcome of Brazil's attempts at greater trade openness.

In retrospect, while the Brazilian experience cannot be judged a complete success, the retreat from the more open trade policies cannot be blamed on the policies themselves.

The Reforms

Trade reform was not at the top of the agenda for the government that assumed power in April 1964. Real income growth, high in the late 1950s and early 1960s, had come to a halt, with per capita product falling in 1963. Inflation was at unprecedented levels – over 100 percent in the first part of 1964. Capital inflows had ceased, and in 1963 were negative. The priorities of policymakers were thus macroeconomic stabilization and the restoration of Brazilian access to international capital markets, rather than any potential long-run efficiency gains from trade liberalization.

Initial trade reforms focused on exports, which had stagnated since the early 1950s as a result of both exchange rate overvaluation and import-substitution-based development policies. The structure of the Brazilian protection system in 1964 reflected the policies of the preceding decades, which had almost completely eliminated imports of consumer goods and had decreased import coefficients in most sectors of Brazilian industry. The protection system tended to favor capital intensive industrial activities, concentrated in Brazil's southeast, particularly in the state of São Paulo, at the expense of agriculture and other activities that used unskilled labor more intensively.

The first important trade reforms attempted to eliminate some of the anti-export bias inherent in a system in which manufactures were sold primarily in a protected domestic market. Among the reforms was a "drawback" or exemption from duties on imported inputs into manufactured exports, implemented in mid-1964. This was followed in 1965 by an exemption from value-added taxes paid on manufactured exports.

On the import side the first significant reform did not occur until the reduction of *ad valorem* tariffs on most imports in March 1967. Both the level and the dispersion of tariffs were reduced, with effective rates in most manufacturing sectors falling to less than half their levels before the reform. Although some of the reductions were cosmetic, since many tariffs had included a high level of redundancy, there is little doubt that Brazil did become more open to imports. Between 1966 and 1970 imports grew more rapidly than production in most industrial sectors, despite the unprecedented growth of production after 1968. Although timid by comparison with some other developing countries that have liberalized their trade, the Brazilian reforms of 1967 do appear to have been genuine.

The move toward greater openness was interrupted in late 1968, when tariff rates on many items were raised, although not to pre-1967 levels. In the early 1970s the trend toward less import restriction was resumed, primarily through specific exemptions and tariff concessions, which often depended on administrative approval of the particular transaction. Between 1970 and 1974 Brazilian trade policy was thus increasingly open, in the sense of facilitating a rapid growth in imports, but was considerably less liberal in the sense that trade remained subject to a high degree of government discretion.

Coordination with Exchange Rate and Capital Account Policy

Conventional accounts of trade liberalization tend to identify a greater openness to trade with a relaxation of import restrictions. The resulting increase in imports is assumed in the conventional model to force a depreciation of the real exchange rate to maintain current account balance, thus opening the economy on the export side as well.

This model is inappropriate for Brazil's post-1964 experience. The early and sustained emphasis on export promotion, which began more than two years before the 1967 import liberalization and continued after the oil shock, avoided some of the current account deficit that would have resulted from an import liberalization alone. Even more important was the massive increase in external capital inflows that began in the late 1960s. These inflows were more than enough to finance any current account deficit that might have arisen from import liberalization, as the immense increase in Brazil's foreign exchange reserves in the period indicates.

The effect of both the export promotion program and the capital inflows was to permit a real appreciation of the cruzeiro well above the level required to maintain current account balance if imports alone had been liberalized. In August 1968 exchange rate policy was significantly changed by the introduction of a crawling peg. The new policy did not in principle require that the real exchange rate be fixed; it in fact ended the earlier problem of the wide variations in the real rate which had discouraged exports before 1968.

Real exchange rate stability, however, is not always appropriate, particularly if there are real external shocks, as there certainly were in Brazil in 1973–4. The response of policymakers to this sharp deterioration in Brazil's terms of trade and the resulting current account deficit was not to adjust the real exchange rate but to turn to the capital account and to commercial policies to maintain balance-of-payments equilibrium.

In retrospect, policymakers' preference for commercial policy and external borrowing in response to an adverse real shock may explain why Brazil's attempt at greater economic openness eventually failed. Reluctant to permit a real depreciation of the cruzeiro and encouraged by Brazil's relatively favorable position in international capital markets, the government nearly doubled external borrowing between 1973 and 1974. At the time there was little hint of any future limitation on Brazil's capacity to tap external sources of savings.

The adjustment of the current account that did occur was brought about primarily through tighter administrative controls on imports and extension of the export promotion program. The program, which could be characterized as "liberalizing" in the early stages when the policies functioned primarily by removing the anti-export bias, became much less so after 1973, when incentives to export increasingly relied on credit policies rather than fiscal incentives. The export promotion program in its later stages thus moved prices faced by Brazilian exportables producers away from world market prices rather than closer to them.

Brazil's move toward greater trade openness in the 1967–74 period was thus undermined in several ways. The bureaucratic preference for administrative control on imports and incentives for specific exports made it easy to reverse the trend toward greater import openness after the first oil shock in 1973, while making export expansion increasingly dependent on policymakers' decisions rather than the real exchange rate. Even more damaging may have been the concurrent liberalization of capital flows, since it effectively eliminated any possibility of improved real exchange rate competitiveness arising from the liberalization of imports.

The Costs and Benefits of Greater Trade Openness

Even if one accepts the argument that greater openness to world prices will in the long run improve efficiency and increase welfare, there may be short-run costs. Since such costs, real or imaginary, influence policymakers, who must function in the short run, they cannot be dismissed.

The most obvious costs – temporary unemployment of labor and other factors – might be measured in a variety of ways, including unemployment or labor force trends by sector, idle capacity, or bankruptcies or other forms of business failure.

Brazil's trade reforms did not discernibly bring such effects. Data on industrial employment for 15 sectors, classified at the two-digit level, were examined as a potential indicator of disruption due to greater import penetration. Between 1967, when tariffs were cut, and 1973, when the oil shock led policymakers to reverse the liberalizing trend, employment rose each year in eight of the 15 sectors. In four more the upward trend faltered in only one or two years. Even in the remaining three sectors (chemicals, textiles, and tobacco products), there is little indication that slower employment growth had any relation to imports.

This conclusion is reinforced by the data on business failures, available for the city of São Paulo, the center of Brazilian industry, at an aggregate level from 1962 and at a sectoral level from 1969. Failures did not increase after the 1967 import liberalization; rises in the failure rate between 1964 and 1966 (and again in the 1980s) were clearly associated with credit restriction during the stabilization program. Between 1969 and 1973, the period of greatest openness to imports, failure rates were generally flat or falling. As growth slowed after 1974, failure rates in most sectors increased, particularly after 1977. Since the Brazilian economy became substantially more closed to imports after 1974, the evidence lends little support to a hypothesis that greater openness to imports led to more business failures in Brazil.

Conclusion

Brazil's move toward greater trade openness in the post-1964 period cannot be called a trade liberalization in the conventional sense. Although the export promotion program was extensive and lasting, it combined both liberalizing and protective elements, particularly in its later stages when it relied in part on activity-specific credit incentives.

Import liberalization, to the extent that it occurred, was timid and partially reversed in 1969, before being resumed over the 1970–3 period. One important feature of Brazilian trade policy, on both the import and the export side, was that the government held onto its potential administrative control over trade flows. This facilitated the reversal of the liberalizing trend after 1974 and permitted policymakers to use commercial policies rather than the real exchange rate for current account adjustment.

The other important feature of the Brazilian experience was the capital account. The unprecedented rise in foreign capital inflows to Brazil after 1968, far in excess of that required to finance the current account deficit, permitted the real exchange rate to remain overvalued in relation to its level of the mid-1960s. The introduction of the crawling peg in 1968 had a positive effect on trade through reducing exchange rate uncertainty, but did not end overvaluation. The resistance of policymakers to a real depreciation in 1974 in effect spelled the end of Brazil's experiment with greater openness, for the current account deficit then had to be both financed by continued capital inflows and reduced by the adoption of protective commercial policies and by a slowing of income growth.

Chile
Sergio de la Cuadra and Dominique Hachette

Like many developing countries, Chile has had a long tradition of protectionism in favor of manufacturing, a protectionism which intensified after the Great Depression of the 1930s. Economic growth, based on an import substitution strategy and the sheltering of industry behind high trade barriers, became dependent on the roller coaster of copper prices and soon lost momentum as a consequence of the limited domestic market and increasingly inefficient industries. Aware of some of the basic shortcomings of protectionist policy, three governments made modest attempts to liberalize in the 1940s and 1960s; all failed. But unlike many countries in similar circumstances, Chile then went on to mount a major and ambitious trade liberalization between 1974 and 1979.

The country study of Chile focuses on two episodes of trade liberalization since 1950. The first was unsuccessful; the second is alive and well 11 years after it was fully implemented.

The First Episode: 1956–1961

At the inception of the first episode, the economy was in shambles. On the domestic front, inflation was high and growing, output growth was low, income per capita was falling, industrial production was at a standstill, and investment barely reached half the average rate for Latin America. Ever-increasing fiscal deficits produced by a rapidly growing and inefficient public sector and large increase in social security benefits to public employees were financed by Central Bank credit. The domestic prices of tradeables were completely divorced from international prices leading to further misallocation of resources.

On the external front, bonanzas from copper exports had come to a halt after the end of the Korean conflict, with exports falling both in volume and prices. The policy response was to increase import controls in number, depth, and intricacy: exchange rates, quotas, and import prohibitions multiplied. This reaction was consistent with prevailing doubts about, if not contempt for, the market system, whose efficacy in resource allocation, it was felt, had shown serious limitations.

But government intervention on a case-by-case basis in Chile had generated a highly distorted system of incentives. The economy was more or less closed and found itself moving from one foreign exchange crisis to another. Gross inefficiencies in trade management had generated serious import shortages, hindering production in some sectors while severely limiting expansion and diversification of exports. Massive devaluations led to speculation and capital flight, and inappropriate demand management prevented the devaluations from achieving necessary changes in the domestic terms of trade.

The 1956–61 episode was characterized by a shift from a discretionary to a more neutral system in which the price mechanism played a more important role in determining imports. QRs were replaced by a list of goods which could be freely imported, subject to prior deposit. The number of items on the list was steadily increased, while prior deposit charges, initially raised, were being reduced. The reduction in prior deposit amounts was compensated for by a cost-equivalent tax on imports – an additional duty. These duties fluctuated from zero to 200 percent of the cost, insurance, and freight (c.i.f.) value of imported goods. As a consequence, both tariff dispersion and the average tariff were lower. The nonweighted average tariff was reduced from 151 percent in 1959 to 102 percent in 1960, and then increased to 135 percent in 1961. These changes affected only the manufacturing sector.

During this episode, the trend was to simplify the exchange rate system and to increase the stability of nominal and real exchange rates, but at the cost of significant and erratic changes in trade restrictions. The nominal exchange rate was fixed, ensuring full convertibility for foreign capital. Exchange rate stability was considered critical to domestic price stability. So were monetary and fiscal policies. Money supply growth was reduced, credit was redirected from the public to the private sector, quantitative controls were eliminated, and the source of the Central Bank's high-powered money became foreign rather than domestic assets. Fiscal policies also began to be tailored to stabilization goals. Public expenditures were initially financed with foreign loans to avoid inflationary pressures and to increase the availability of imports.

As a consequence, imports grew rapidly while export performance was modest. The trade balance, badly disturbed by these developments, worsened in 1961 when the credibility of exchange rate policy was shaken. The ensuing capital flight brought foreign reserves to an unsustainable low level, given Chile's limited access to the foreign capital market.

To avoid inflationary pressures and disruption of the stabilization program, the authorities shortened the list of permitted imports and established a prior deposit of 10,000 percent on all imports. These measures – a significant setback to liberalization – were maintained indefinitely. Furthermore, the government suspended foreign exchange operations for three weeks before reactivating them early in 1962 after establishing the following: a dual exchange market; a fixed exchange rate for most trade operations but a freely fluctuating rate for tourism and capital transactions; an administrative delay of 90 days for exchange remittances; elimination of automatic access to foreign exchange; creation of a future market for a few essential commodities, and later for exports; a reduction in the list of permitted imports; and an increase in the prior deposit rate. Although the peso was devalued twice during 1962 and the authorities let the exchange rate fluctuate freely thereafter, QRs and prior deposits were maintained. Unfortunately, a disastrous earthquake in the mid-1960s siphoned off a great many resources. New taxes were introduced, but delays in obtaining additional tax revenues and foreign aid brought pressure on the authorities to resort to Central Bank financing.

The Second Episode: 1974–1979

In the early 1970s the socialist government of Allende made a major effort to redistribute income, control the means of production, and enlarge state ownership. Expansionary fiscal and monetary policies were the basic tools. At first, progress was spectacular, but serious problems soon arose as aggregate supply became strained to its limit, with subsidies increasingly distorting the price structure. Meanwhile, the distribution system began to crumble. Labor–management conflicts multiplied, foreign reserves were exhausted, and the demarcation lines between private property and so-called social ownership grew dimmer, to the point where the basic rights of production and consumption of specific goods were put in question. Aggregate production declined precipitously, decapitalization accelerated in numerous sectors, inflation jumped high above any previous levels, and shortages developed in retail markets. The fiscal deficit in 1973 surpassed 20 percent of GDP, the real income gains achieved in 1971 were reversed, and labor conflicts escalated.

Allende's loss of control over the coalition that had brought him to power, together with the chaotic economic situation, led to a military coup in September 1973. The new government's principal long-run objectives were to correct the fundamental disequilibria that had long characterized the Chilean economy and to reorganize the economic system. The keystones of policy were (a) the restoration of market prices as the principal determinant in economic decision making, (b) reinstatement of the private sector as the main agent of development, (c) nondiscriminatory treatment of all productive sectors in order to improve resource allocation, and (d) a greater opening to foreign markets to exploit comparative advantage, reduce the pervasive distortions brought by trade controls, and stimulate exports.

With the exception of six minor items, all QRs were eliminated between 1974 and 1976. The 10,000 percent prior deposit, though not officially eliminated until August 1976, had become defunct before then. Official approval for importation was discarded in 1974. In the meantime, tariffs were reduced in three stages. During the first stage – 1974–5 – the maximum tariff was reduced from 750 percent to 120 percent, the simple average dropped from 105 percent to 57 percent, and the modal tariff declined from 90 percent to 55 percent. Some tariffs, however, were raised in an effort to reduce disparities. In August 1975 the president of the Central Bank announced the second stage of tariff reform. The goal was a tariff structure of 10–35 percent, to be reached in five equal semi-annual reductions by the first half of 1978. All tariffs were to be reduced by the same proportion. After the third reduction in January 1977 the dates of the remaining two reductions were advanced, and the entire adjustment was completed by August 1977. In December 1977 the Minister of Finance announced the third stage – a uniform 10 percent tariff. This was attained in 18 months, by June 1979. The only exception to uniform treatment was the tariff on automobiles and other vehicles. Furthermore, a value-added tax applied to both domestically produced and imported goods replaced all existing indirect taxes. Import duty exemptions were eliminated except for those required by international agreements and a few minor products. Import duties on capital goods could be spread out over a long period in semi-annual installments.

This trade liberalization was carried out in the midst of substantial efforts to reduce inflation and reorganize the economy along market economy lines. A major recession in 1975 made it necessary to adopt restrictive fiscal and monetary policies to stabilize the economy, and fiscal deficits were fully eliminated by 1979. Similarly, after a major devaluation in 1975, the exchange rate was used from 1976 to 1982 to slow down inflation, while wage adjustments were geared toward the same goal, at least until 1979. After 1978, wage and exchange rate policies were no longer compatible. This development, on top of large increases in private expenditures stimulated by over-optimistic expectations and financed by large inflows of foreign credit, kept pressure on prices, causing the real exchange rate to appreciate and delaying the desired outcome. Nevertheless, the annual inflation rate decreased from about 750 percent at the end of 1973 to about 10 percent in 1982.

Along with stabilization policies, massive institutional changes were carried out. Price controls, multiple exchange rates, and interest rate ceilings were eliminated to improve resource allocation. The financial market was liberalized, and controls on inflows of foreign capital were gradually lifted. A more flexible foreign investment code was introduced. Public sector employment was reduced, partly through the privatization of about 500 public enterprises. Surviving public enterprises were required to become self-financing and were given pricing freedom. Last but not least, the labor market was significantly liberalized in 1978.

The principal hindrances to the success of liberalization have been the 1982–3 recession (the worst since the Great Depression), the dumping practices and protectionist policies adopted by trading partners, a domestic financial crisis, the growing burden of foreign debt, and domestic protectionist lobbies. Despite these considerable pressures, Chile's trade policy today differs in only two respects from that of 1979. The application of countervailing duties is limited by GATT rules, and the uniform tariff is 15 percent instead of 10 percent.

Colombia
Jorge García García

This is an analytical history of the factors that contributed to the creation of a more or less open trade regime in Colombia between 1967 and 1982 and the reversal of trade liberalization in 1983–4. Trade liberalization understood as the dismantling of tariff and nontariff barriers to trade did not stand high among the objectives of policymakers in Colombia, nor did trade liberalization designed to reduce the premium associated with quota restrictions. But other policy goals such as export promotion and the avoidance of recurrent crises in the balance of payments led to the adoption of policies that resulted in trade liberalization in both the first and second senses mentioned above.

Although there were four episodes of trade liberalization (1951–2, 1954–5, 1965–6, and 1967–82), only the last was long enough to permit a detailed analysis of the impact of liberalization on industrial employment, where most of the negative short-term effects of liberalization are normally felt. During this period the speed at which tariffs and nontariff barriers to imports were reduced varied, in part because the commitment to reduce them was not strong enough and in part because the foreign exchange problems that might have given Colombia a greater incentive to encourage exports and provide protection to import-competing activities via a high real exchange rate rather than tariffs and QRs did not persist. In addition, misconceptions about the impact of import liberalization, as well as faulty economic reasoning, inadequate macroeconomic management, and the opposition of vested interests all helped to reverse much of the liberalization achieved by 1981.

Reduction of tariffs and QRs did not encounter much political opposition between 1967 and 1974, chiefly because a high rate of general economic growth (6.4 percent per year) and a much higher rate of growth in the industrial sector (8.9 percent per year) minimized the negative impacts of such reduction. Another important reason was that an increasing real exchange rate offset, in part, the reduction in protection produced by the lowering of trade barriers.

From 1975 on, however, reduction of these barriers aroused substantial opposition. There seemed to be a real possibility that enlarged inflows of imports would become permanent, since a foreign exchange shortage did not appear likely to occur any time soon. Furthermore, the high rates of economic growth enjoyed prior to 1975 had disappeared. Thus, reductions of import barriers slowed down between 1975 and 1978. This trend accelerated in 1979 as part of a general policy of macroeconomic stabilization. But the poor economic performance of the country during this period – and, in particular, the poor performance of the industrial sector – brought an end to import liberalization in 1983–4. However, the large foreign exchange inflows enjoyed by the country since the mid-1970s reduced the premium associated with the QR component of Colombia's protective structure. The reduction of the premium eased the overall management of QRs, but protection for some pockets of the industrial sector was still well entrenched. Thus, although an official reduction in QRs is not observed, a more relaxed management of QRs did in fact take place in the mid-1970s.

Although the premium on QRs probably fell considerably between 1967 and 1982, by not reducing tariffs and QRs sufficiently the country missed the opportunity to liberalize as much as it could have. Therefore the story of trade liberalization in Colombia understood as the reduction of tariffs and dismantling of QRs is one of lost opportunities. Policy-induced distortions in the domestic capital market and the use of inadequate instruments of monetary management prevented proper management of foreign exchange inflows. The situation was than exacerbated by inflationary financing of the government's budget deficits.

Of course, the worldwide recession of 1980–2 did not help matters. Colombia's annual rate of economic growth, which had been declining since 1979, fell to 0.95 percent in 1982, its lowest level since 1950. Industrial production in 1982 decreased by 2.1 percent, the largest decrease since 1950. Given these circumstances, import liberalization became an easy target. It was frequently criticized on grounds that it was primarily responsible for the country's poor economic performance.

Attributing the recession in the industrial sector to liberalization was mistaken, however. Liberalization reduced industrial value added by an average of less than 2 percent in 1980–2.

The development of a large current account deficit in 1982 (7 percent of GDP) and projections that the deficit would be just as large in 1983 were a bonanza for industrialists and the better-off industrial workers, who successfully pressed the government to terminate liberalization. Otherwise, they argued, Colombia would suffer a balance-of-payments crisis. Both vested interests and economic ideology played important roles in the policy shift that led to a massive increase in import restrictions in 1983 and 1984.

Import liberalization was never seen as a primary policy objective in Colombia. Nor was it seen as a way to accelerate the nation's rate of growth or to improve the allocation of economic resources. As a result, its direction and speed were determined mainly by internal macroeconomic policies and international economic conditions.

Greece
George C. Kottis

In the early 1950s Greece was a poor and basically agricultural country struggling to recover from World War II and two civil wars. Strong trade and other economic controls imposed by the government during the 1930s and 1940s were still in place.

Greece's first steps toward trade liberalization were taken in 1953, but trade balance problems brought a slowdown in the shift toward freer trade in 1955. A second liberalization period began in 1962 when Greece became an associate member of the European Economic Community (EEC).

The Post-war Period

Until 1951, foreign aid made up for virtually all of Greece's considerable annual budget deficit and most of its trade deficit. But the United States reduced its aid to Greece that year and notified the Greek government that US aid would end within the next few years. Greece then took measures to reduce its dependence on external aid. The government cut its administrative budget, suspended hiring, and abolished certain subsidies. Special levies (ranging from 25 to 200 percent) were imposed on many imported goods, and direct subsidies (ranging from 15 to 50 percent) were created for a smaller number of export goods.

Imports then decreased, while exports increased. The balance on current account showed improvement, and foreign exchange reserves grew. The budget deficit dropped sharply as a percentage of gross national product (GNP), and monetary policy became tighter. Inflation decreased drastically. Although economic growth slipped, not all the deterioration can be attributed to the austerity measures. A drop in agricultural production caused by crop cycles and bad weather had a ripple effect on nonagricultural sectors.

The First Episode: 1953–1955

In April 1953 a new and stable government announced the immediate (overnight) implementation of several significant trade liberalization measures, including devaluation of the currency from 15 to 30 drachmas to the US dollar, the abolition of all special levies on imports, and the elimination of import licensing and QRs. Moreover, export subsidies were ended.

These trade reforms were accompanied by measures to attract foreign capital and to promote Greek ownership of ships under foreign flags by tax revisions and changes in monetary and credit policies. The rate of inflation increased soon after the trade reforms were put into place, but in 1954 it began to decrease. An initial setback to imports caused by devaluation eventually disappeared. To prevent trade balance problems in the presence of fixed exchange rates, the government gradually, and to a limited extent, increased protection for certain domestic industries and subsidized exports. These measures did not appreciably hamper the liberalization process.

The value of both imports and exports then increased considerably, but imports continued to exceed exports. There was no external payments problem, though, since increases in receipts of invisibles and net capital inflows financed the trade deficits.

Nor did liberalization cause budgetary problems. The substantial increase in imports meant rising revenues from regular tariffs and other indirect import taxes which exceeded the revenues lost through the abolition of the special import levies.

The economy's growth after the first liberalization episode fluctuated, but on a rising trend. The manufacturing sector grew substantially, but growth in the agricultural sector was not as vigorous. While there are no data on employment as such, other indicators pertaining to employment showed positive trends. The number of hours worked per week increased, as did wages. Meanwhile, the unemployment rate went down. There was, it is true, substantial emigration, but mostly from rural areas that would not in any case have been seriously affected by the liberalization measures.

The Second Episode: 1962–1981

In 1961 the Greek government signed an association agreement with the EEC which became effective in 1962. The agreement provided for the establishment of a customs' union between Greece and the EEC, and EEC tariffs on certain key Greek agricultural export products (such as tobacco and raisins) were reduced immediately. EEC tariff residuals on such agricultural imports, and tariffs on manufactured imports from Greece, were to be phased out within five years.

Greece was required to abolish tariffs on manufactured imports from the EEC by 1974 if the goods were not being produced in Greece in 1961, and by 1984 if the goods were produced in Greece before 1961. Greece was also required to abolish QRs on imports from third countries and phase out bilateral trade. The Community's Common Agricultural Policy was still being formulated, but Greece agreed to abolish tariffs on a number of agricultural products imported from the EEC within 12 years and on others within 22 years.

There was a provision for the abolition of restrictions on the movement of labor between Greece and the EEC within 12 years, but none for liberalizing the movement of capital. The agreement included a protocol stating the provisions under which Greece would receive financial assistance from the Community and other protocols setting special terms of treatment by EEC countries for Greece's main export products. Service sectors like tourism and shipping were not covered.

The Greek economy performed well following its association with the EEC. Remarkable price and exchange rate stability, high rates of economic growth, expansion of manufacturing production and trade, rapid increases in foreign exchange earnings from exports of goods and invisibles, and surpluses in the government budget and the balance of payments characterized the economy during this period. Labor scarcities occurred in the early 1970s, owing to fast economic growth and substantial emigration. Heavy inflow of foreign private capital was also characteristic of the period.

The oil price shock in 1973 and the Cyprus troubles of 1974 brought a sudden increase in prices, a drastic drop in production and investment, and an increase in outlays for oil imports and for military assistance to Cyprus. Economic performance improved somewhat in 1975, but the improvement was followed by deterioration that increased sharply after the 1978–9 increase in oil prices and after 1981 when a socialist government initiated new economic policies. The GNP growth rate decreased, and has fluctuated around zero since 1981. Inflation has remained high, and private investment low. The public sector expanded enormously in the 1980s, as did the government's budget deficit. Internal and external public debt showed a similar pattern. Net immigration and economic slowdown made employment in the nonagricultural sector an important issue despite large-scale hiring by the public sector.

Conclusions

Trade liberalization was not associated with serious unemployment, production, or balance-of-payments problems in either the first or the second episode. Generally good macroeconomic performance until 1981 helped absorb whatever shocks were caused by opening up the economy. The economic problems that occurred after 1973 were due to external events over which the country had no control (the increases in world oil prices and the conflict over Cyprus).

Indonesia
Mark M. Pitt

Dutch colonial trade policy in Indonesia established a pervasive system of import and production quotas whose level and distribution were controlled or influenced by associations of affected trading firms and manufacturing enterprises. Price control was widespread. The discontent of the export regions of the islands outside Java was manifested in widespread illegal trade. This was countered with various "inducements" that took the form of negotiable certificates linking export and import rights. The same measures characterized the pattern of policy during the first two decades of Indonesia's independence.

Nationalism, not unnaturally, was a dominant influence on policy in the years immediately following independence. This potent force was increasingly associated with interventionism and anti-liberalism in the economic arena, because the economic system created by the Round Table Agreement (under which the Netherlands recognized Indonesia's independence in 1949) in practice left the private sector of the economy under foreign control. As a result, the cabinets of 1949–58 faced the problem of devising economic policy which, if liberal, would be attacked by a nationalist electorate as benefiting the structures of the colonialists and neo-imperialists.

The chauvinism that guided trade policy included Indo-Chinese enterprise in the category of "alien capital." During the 1950s, strong anti-Dutch and anti-Chinese feelings led to the process of *Indonesianisasi* (Indonesia-nization), which entailed official racial discrimination in allocating import rights and eventually led to a prohibition of all Chinese trading outside urban areas. A privileged group of indigenous Indonesian importers and traders emerged, who earned substantial rents and became a powerful lobby for QRs in trade as they disproportionately enjoyed the resulting import premiums. In time, these *Benteng* importers became attached to Sukarno's Partai National Indonesia (PNI), which fostered their interests while they, in return, became a major source of income to its ministers. Corruption, always a problem in the administration of the Indonesian economy, increased markedly.

Attempts to Liberalize: 1950–1952; 1955; 1957–1958

The post-colonial years consequently saw Indonesia moving steadily toward increasing state control of trade, prices, and production. The three episodes of liberalization can be seen as fairly superficial interruptions to the progress toward a controlled economy. The first attempt, initiated by a minority of "economically minded" politicians in the first cabinet after Independence, was briefly acceptable because it replaced most of the quotas imposed by the Dutch with a free-list importing system, and as such was seen as a means of reducing Dutch power. However, liberal policies had little hope of survival in a political climate where economic liberalism was equated with support for alien vested interest; the liberalization collapsed with the end of the coalition government in 1952, and progress toward restriction resumed with increased momentum.

The second attempt, introduced by a caretaker government in 1955, suffered a similar fate. Its reforms, put together in three weeks and introduced in a single day, were sweeping: the entire quota system that had been reintroduced, together with monopoly importing, was abolished. The reason for haste was the coalition's desire to impress its economic philosophy on the electorate before the national elections scheduled to take place in three weeks' time. The electorate was unimpressed; the elections were lost and the restrictive regime returned with renewed vigor.

Like the first two episodes, the third episode was both initiated and ultimately reversed for predominantly noneconomic reasons, though this liberalization had a firmer base of popular support in the interests of the traditional export regions outside Java, particularly Sulawesi (Celebes) and Sumatra. The import-biased trade regime, and the *Benteng* system in whose benefits they did not share, led these export regions to boycott the foreign exchange surrender regulations in 1957 and to threaten secession. The liberalization episode of 1957–8, launched to placate the regions and forestall secession, failed to prevent civil war and ultimately foundered in the suppression of the regions' attempt to secede in 1958.

Guided Democracy: 1958–1965

The government's victory over regional secession led to the centralization of power in the hands of President Sukarno and the end of constitutional democracy. On a popular platform of destroying the last remnants of capitalism and leading the economy toward the social goals of the Indonesian Revolution, Sukarno propounded the notion of "Guided Economy" to justify direct state control of production and trade. Dutch enterprises were nationalized in response to the conflict over the status of New Guinea (Irian), and state enterprises became predominant.

The rents once sought by indigenous importers were now sought by the new state trading firms, but the beneficiaries of the import premiums came from the same political circles as before: rent seeking and quota seeking were now a part of the official state apparatus.

In the ensuing years corruption and black-marketeering became rampant and mismanagement staggering; the economy disintegrated. Foreign exchange reserves were negative, price inflation exceeded 1,000 percent in the months before liberalization, and service on the debt exceeded foreign exchange revenues. The fiscal deficit, 163 percent of fiscal revenue in 1965, reached seven times such revenue in the first half of 1966; the terms of trade were at an all time low. Much of the debt was incurred for costly military adventures and prestige projects. Per capita GDP in 1965 was 9 percent lower than in 1958. Capacity utilization in manufacturing was 20 percent or even lower, and there were significant food shortages in many parts of the islands.

By 1965, "Socialism à la Indonesia" had been completely discredited, and the adherents of the system were swept away in the violent political and economic turmoil of 1965–6. The "New Order" that eventually emerged from the chaos was virtually untrammelled by any effective opposition. Its first actions, impelled by the urgent need to seek aid from the West, were to move quickly toward liberalization.

The Liberalization of 1966

The period 1966–71 saw sweeping changes in the regulation and organization of the foreign trade sector. The liberalization, like many of the earlier attempts, began with the introduction of a certificate linking exports with imports. Government policy shifted dramatically from the direct control of almost all aspects of the modern economy toward heavy reliance on market signals and price incentives. This period saw the end of most direct allocations of foreign exchange, the elimination of most price controls, an opening to foreign investment, and the acceptance of the private sector as the primary source of economic growth.

The important distinction between this liberalization attempt and its numerous predecessors is that it encompassed not merely liberalizing acts but also the destruction of important antiliberal forces – replacing a strongly antiliberal state ideology with one that was nominally liberal, virtually eliminating powerful antiliberal political parties, and dismantling some important institutions of state control.

Imports could not be liberalized until after the "export drive" initiative (of which certificates linking imports with exports and legalized export underinvoicing were the central elements) began to yield results and until Indonesia could reschedule its enormous debt and obtain fresh credits abroad.

Readmission to the International Monetary Fund (IMF), the World Bank, and the United Nations brought visiting missions from the IMF and the World Bank to assist in formulating economy policy, to help arrange a moratorium on Indonesia's debt commitments, and to provide assurances of new grants and credits.

Indonesia was now (1966) in a position to initiate its first direct import liberalization measures while intensifying liberalization of the export system. Import license restrictions were almost entirely swept away. Direct foreign exchange allocations to manufacturing firms were ended. Importers were free to buy almost any good they wished. Reinvigorated legal export flows, a large infusion of foreign grants and loans, and the guarantees of support (and perhaps the insistence) of the donor countries brought an end to QRs, notwithstanding the virtual absence of foreign exchange reserves.

The political situation explains why the economic changes of 1966 were both so radical and so rapid. The regulatory and trade apparatus were managed by Sukarno's cronies who could not be trusted to carry out a staged liberalization and were actively opposing the emerging New Order government. Ending their control over international trade was an effective method of reducing their power, and that of the rentier class.

The speed of the liberalization may also have been impelled by the need to impress creditors with the genuineness of reform. In early 1966 imports had almost come to a complete halt, foreign reserves were negative, Japan had cut off most of its exports to Indonesia, and borrowing from the Soviet Union and China was no longer possible. Indonesia desperately needed foreign credits from those nations and institutions it had spurned as "neo-colonialist and imperialist" just months earlier, many of whom had had their assets nationalized without compensation. Thus, its desperate economic straits, the end of aid from the Communist bloc, and its reputation as mercurial and untrustworthy in international affairs may have required Indonesia to put its liberalization program in effect *before* qualifying for aid and rapprochement with the West.

The Indonesian government suffered from a lack of credibility, as much with its own people as with other nations. This was a nation familiar with the announcement and abandonment of grandiose schemes; earlier liberalization attempts had been scuttled soon after their initiation. To establish credibility, the government could only hope to alter behavior of economic agents through immediate and profound implementation of policy rather than announcement of change.

The performance of the Indonesian economy improved enormously in the years after 1966. Recorded exports, actually declining before 1966, grew rapidly after 1969, despite historically low levels of export prices. Imports grew rapidly as well. GDP, almost flat in the years before liberalization, increased steeply after 1967. Manufacturing value added, which had actually been falling, increased faster than GDP, as did gross domestic capital formation. The stabilization attempts of the government were seemingly effective. The rate of price inflation was reduced from 635 percent in 1966 to single-digit levels in just a few years.

In the months before the liberalization the instruments of economic control were widely evaded by black markets. As a result, much of the response to liberalization (as typically measured) represents the redirection of illegal market activities into legal market activities. Producers of exports benefited from the existence of illegal trade even if they merely resold their produce to middlemen. The domestic price of some exportables was double or possibly triple the return from their legal export – and yet legal export took place. This phenomenon, known as price disparity, was the result of the competition among those engaged in misinvoicing exports to purchase goods in the domestic market for export. The smuggled portion of exports was then resold at the higher black-market exchange rate. It was found for example that the real return to the leading export, rubber, *inclusive* of illegal receipts, was no greater after the liberalization than before. Furthermore, econometric evidence suggests that most of the post-liberalization increase in smallholder rubber export reflected the redirection of smuggling into legal channels. Thus, while the pre-liberalization trade regime was in principle extraordinarily restrictive, the pervasiveness of illegal transactions meant that in practice resource misallocation – though still large – was probably less than it might have been. Nonetheless, this was unquestionably a liberalization.

While every liberalization episode and every country has unique aspects, the Indonesian experience of 1966 differs considerably from many of the liberalization episodes of the project. Issues of the speed and staging of liberalization and the uniform or discriminatory treatment of sectors are important when there are influential economic and political groups whose fortunes are closely tied to the liberalization process and who, by virtue of their political power, can reverse the process if it harms them enough. Manufacturing in Indonesia was probably less important, economic straits were probably more desperate, and standard avenues of political expression less open than for any other liberalization episode of this research project. The Indonesian liberalization, although dramatic by most standards, was dwarfed by the revolution of which it was a part. The experience strongly suggests that the ensuing improved economic performance was a result of the liberalized trade regime; but the liberalization itself occurred at a time of such chaos that general inferences on sequencing and desirable discrimination are nearly impossible to draw.

Israel
Nadav Halevi and Joseph Baruh

The economy of Israel developed rapidly during the 30 years before Independence in 1948, mostly because of massive inflows of Jewish immigrants and capital. Thereafter Labor Zionist socialism and the heavy burdens of mass immigration led to substantial government intervention in the economy – manifested in a large government sector, in price controls (in the early years), exchange controls, and virtual government domination of investment activity. Over the years, the role of government gradually declined. This is not apparent in the relative size of the budget, dominated as it is by defense expenditures, but the role of government in investment decisions has diminished, and even where intervention has been retained it has switched from direct administrative intervention to use of the price mechanism.

This gradual, increasing, reliance on market prices as the major allocative mechanism is also strongly evident in trade policy. The three episodes of trade liberalization discussed in the country study marked periods when basic changes were made, but Israel's trade liberalization experience has actually been continuous, if uneven.

The First Episode: 1952–1955

During the first three years after Independence, the Jewish population doubled, foreign exchange controls were strict, and price controls and rationing of basic commodities were imposed to maintain a fairly egalitarian level of basic consumption while devoting a substantial portion of resources, first to the war effort, and later to investment.

In late 1951 it was clear that the austerity program had outlived its usefulness: inflationary pressure was no longer under control, black markets were the norm, the highly overvalued exchange rate was creating evident distortions, and foreign exchange reserves were exhausted. Contractionary monetary and fiscal policies were adopted in late 1951, and in February 1952 a New Economic Policy was adopted whose traded and exchange components constituted the first liberalization.

The major policy change was the replacement of a single official exchange rate of IL0.37 to US$1 by three *formal* rates: the previous rate, *plus* two additional rates of IL0.74 to US$1 and IL1.00 to US$1. Different types of transactions were conducted at each one of these rates with the effect of raising the price level drastically. By these means the real value of accumulated cash balances held by the public was reduced, absorbing much of the accumulated, previously repressed, inflationary pressure.

Was this really a liberalization policy? The new policy made no promise to reduce domestic protection or to dismantle the existing licensing system and replace QRs by tariffs. Imports were decreased, not increased. The liberalizing aspect of the policy was the greater reliance on the price mechanism to determine the level of noncompeting imports. Gradually, as most transactions were transferred to the highest rate, much of the QR system became redundant, and the rate dispersion among imports and between imports and exports narrowed considerably.

The combination of the exchange rate reforms with a more restrictive monetary–fiscal policy, whose main contribution was to abandon the practice of financing government deficits by printing money, did achieve the principal objectives: the balance-of-payments deficit was curtailed and the inflationary pressure was sharply reduced. Following a brief but severe recession in 1959, the economy entered a period of sustained rapid growth. The episode itself was over by late 1955; restrictions on various aspects of economic activity continued to be removed gradually over the following six years, until the next more dramatic step in 1962.

The Second Episode: 1962–1968

From 1955 to 1962 there was no further change in the official rate of exchange, which had been unified in 1955 at IL1.80 to US$1. The erosion in the real exchange rate resulting from domestic inflation, though in this period at a relatively low annual rate, was counterbalanced by use of "informal" components of the exchange rate: tariffs on imports, and a complicated system of export subsidies. However, by 1962 these informal components amounted to about 30 percent of the effective exchange rate, and the rate dispersion was substantial.

In February, a second New Economic Policy was announced, in response to dissatisfaction with the multiple effective exchange rate system (and IMF pressure to change it), the need to transform the economy to deal with the long-term balance-of-payments problem, and the need to make Israel's industry more competitive if it was to be integrated in the European economy. The two main liberalizing components of the policy were a substantial formal devaluation and concomitant reductions in import duties and export subsidies, which changed both the level and dispersion of effective exchange rates; and a program of gradual reduction of the protection of domestic industry.

The government originally intended to reduce protection fairly rapidly but the opposition of vested industrial interests, and of the Ministry of Industry, made this impossible. As a result a very slow process of changing the form of protection from QRs to tariffs was implemented. Committees examined goods individually and replaced QRs by tariffs designed to keep effective protection at more or less the same level. As late as 1968, the average level of effective protection in industry was no lower – in fact somewhat higher – than in 1965. There was a decrease in the dispersion of effective protection. Though competitive imports increased somewhat, the total effect was negligible: in 1968 the import penetration ratio (that is, the ratio of competitive imports to the total domestic market) was only 18 percent, compared with 16 percent in 1965.

Attempts to keep rising domestic prices down to preserve the real effects of the 1962 devaluation were only temporarily successful: they were not an adequate substitute for contractionary fiscal and monetary policy. The ratio of prices of tradeables to nontradeables, which had risen by 20 percent in 1962, declined thereafter, and by 1966 had almost returned to the 1962 level despite renewed use of informal exchange rate components. Moreover, the 1962 devaluation raised the effective rate for imports more than that for exports, again increasing the dispersion between rates for imports and exports.

The protracted switch of protection from QRs to tariffs and the postponed lowering of protection levels prevented this aspect of liberalization from having significant effects on the economy. But the failure of the devaluation – or more exactly of the accompanying macroeconomic and wage policies – seriously affected the balance of payments. To counteract the deterioration, the government adopted a recessionary policy in late 1965 and in 1966, initiated by curtailment of housing construction. The recession became much more severe than expected. Had the government adopted a policy of real devaluation, the recession could have been at least partly averted and a more fundamental export-oriented restructuring of production could have taken place. The country resumed rapid growth following the 1967 war.

The Third Episode: 1969–1977

By 1968 the form of protection had been switched, and the government turned its attention to reducing levels of protection. This was not an even process owing to external events with serious impacts on the economy – among them the Yom Kippur War of 1973, the oil crisis, and the ensuing world recession. However, the trend was clear. In 1977 the average level of protection of domestic industry was 25 percent (compared with 96 percent in 1968 and 62 percent in 1972). Furthermore, the dispersion of rates of protection between industries had been markedly reduced. This gradual reduction in protection was incorporated in a policy designed to prepare Israel for closer integration with Europe; negotiations with the EEC leading to a free trade area in industrial goods was part of the process.

No less significant was the reduction in anti-export bias. Whereas the dispersion of the average effective exchange rate had been reduced much earlier, the disparity in effective protection rates for exports and import substitutes was sharply reduced in the 1972–7 period.

The decline in the rates of protection of import substitutes is reflected in the increase in the import penetration ratios, from 18 percent in 1968 to 26 percent in 1972, and 29 percent in 1977. Though regression analysis did not show a significant relationship between changes in the effective protection rates and increases in import penetration, significant relationships were found between changes in the nominal protection rates and imports.

Strong results were obtained in cross-section regression examining the relationship between percentage changes in the ratio of effective protection rates of import substitutes to those of exports and changes in the export-to-product ratio: clearly, the decrease in the anti-export bias, mainly due to the lowering of protection levels for import substitutes, did push (or pull) many industrial branches into export markets.

The two arms of the 1969–77 liberalization – reduced protection levels for import substitutes and reduced anti-export bias – work in opposite directions on employment. Employment increased when the positive (increased exports) effect outweighed the negative (increased imports) effect. The net effect was positive, and was positively correlated with the reduction in anti-export bias.

The liberalization was protracted; consequently general growth effects over an extended period more than masked the direct effects of the liberalization itself. A rough estimate of the effect on expected industrial employment from changes in protection rates had there been no other changes in the 1968–77 period shows that there could have been a decline of no more than 9 percent. This would have been considered large in Israel, where increases in unemployment are a very sensitive political issue. The protraction of the liberalization process, in preventing this from happening, certainly contributed to the sustainability of the process.

There were fluctuations in economic activity and policy during the period: after 1972 the economy never resumed earlier rates of rapid growth and balance-of-payments deficits and inflation attained new levels, combated sporadically by recessionary policy initiated by contractionary fiscal and monetary policy. Occasionally, adjustments in the exchange rate were made, and in mid-1975 a crawling peg was adopted. But these policies did not result from nor substantially affect the liberalization policy of gradually reducing protection of domestic industry.

Conclusion

Trade liberalization in Israel during the 1952–77 period has been an extended fairly continuous process during which the trade regime has been transformed from extreme controls to a quite liberal, though as yet far from completely open, economy. The process was marked by three stages, forming the basis of identification of episodes: switching from administrative controls to greater reliance on the price mechanism for determining the level of noncompetitive imports; switching from administrative to price protection of import substitution industries: and a significant reduction in the level of protection of import substitutes and decreases in anti-export bias. No significant negative effects on the economy resulted and, perhaps as a consequence, liberalization suffered no serious setback or reversal. After 1977 (a period not covered in the country study because the next liberalization episode concentrated on capital transactions), the process continued. In light of the agreement made with the EEC and the United States, the process is expected to continue until the Israel economy eventually becomes more open to international competition.

Korea
Kwang Suk Kim

Partition and the ensuing Korean War (1950–3) brought serious economic disruptions to the newly liberated Republic of Korea. But 1963 began a turnaround in Korea's economic development, and the growth of the country's GNP since then has been consistently high. The sudden increase in output growth is generally ascribed to changes in development strategy during the early 1960s. Undoubtedly, other influences were also at work, but the shift from an inward-looking import substitution strategy to an export-oriented development strategy must be accounted central. Since the shift of development strategy in 1962, the total volume of merchandise exports has expanded by about 25 percent annually, stimulating the growth of the domestic economy.

Despite the rapid growth of exports, the country's current account balance on goods and services was almost always in deficit until 1985 (when it turned to a surplus). The persistent deficit was mainly attributable to the concurrent expansion of imports from a base in the 1960s much larger than that of exports. The rapid growth of output created increasing demand for imports. As a result of this precarious balance-of-payments situation, the Korean government's approach to import liberalization was gradual and cautious even after export trade had been liberalized in accordance with the new export-oriented strategy.

The First Episode: 1965–1967

Efforts to liberalize trade, particularly imports, began in 1965 when Korea had almost completed the system of incentives needed for export-oriented industrialization and had gained some confidence in export expansion. The first episode of trade liberalization was characterized by the loosening of QRs on imports. Export trade was also somewhat liberalized beginning in 1965, but with negligible impact on the index of trade liberalization as a whole. A tariff reform, following a relaxation of QRs, reduced the simple average rate of legal tariffs, but resulted in a minor increase in the rate, weighted by domestic production. However, the trade liberalization for this period could properly be regarded as a change from QRs to tariffs because the loosening of QRs was substantial and the increase in tariffs minor.

QRs on imports began to be relaxed in 1965, after the exchange rate reform of 1964–5 had brought in a significant devaluation and a unified exchange rate. Since QRs had been tightened severely during the previous two years of foreign exchange crisis, the initial loosening in 1965 was no more than a return to the pre-1963 level of import control. The government did not have a consistent long-term program of import liberalization in 1965; it simply gradually increased the number of automatic approval (AA) items in its semi-annual trade program as the country's foreign exchange situation improved after the exchange rate reform. This kind of gradual import liberalization continued until 1967.

In mid-1967 an important step was taken toward import liberalization. For the second half of 1967 the government reformulated the semi-annual trade program from a positive to a negative list system. Under the old system the program specified items that could be imported (whether freely or with government approval) implying that the importation of all the rest was prohibited. The new trade program listed only commodities whose import was prohibited or restricted, implying that all items not listed were AA items.

The number of AA items increased substantially as a result, and the overall index of trade liberalization increased correspondingly. But the real effect of the program on domestic industries was considered rather small because the program did not liberalize imports that were expected to increase rapidly under the existing structure of tariffs.

Although the government promised continued import liberalization, after the first half of 1968 it was not able to increase liberalization as measured by the ratio of AA items to total tradeable commodities. In response to a deteriorating balance of payments, arising from accelerating domestic inflation, and increased foreign debt service burdens beginning in that year, the government tightened import controls. Trade liberalization remained at a standstill for a decade, while the government faced continuing balance-of-payments difficulties.

The Second Episode: 1978–1979

In early 1978 the government resumed its efforts to promote trade liberalization, concentrating on reducing tariffs as well as loosening QRs. Unlike its predecessor of 1965–7, this episode heralded sustained progress in trade liberalization thereafter (with the exception of the recession year of 1980).

Because of a favorable external environment, Korea's exports expanded rapidly and its balance of payments improved substantially in 1976–7. Expanding construction services to Middle Eastern oil-exporting countries helped improve the country's balance of payments. But by 1977 the rapid improvement in the external balance caused excessive monetary expansion and problems in domestic demand management. An initial proposal for import liberalization in early 1978 was a response to the monetary expansion.

The Import Liberalization Committee worked out a new program of import liberalization in February 1978. The committee recommended that (a) QRs on imports be liberalized, with priority for items whose domestic prices exceeded import prices; (b) tariffs should initially replace QRs in protecting domestic industry, and then be reduced in the long run; (c) an "advance notice" system should be adopted to prepare domestic industries for import liberalization; and (d) both semi-annual trade programs and trade administration procedures should be simplified. On the basis of these recommendations, the government increased the number of AA items in its semi-annual trade program in three steps: in May 1978, September 1978, and January 1979. As a result, the ratio of AA items to total tradeable items increased from 53.8 percent in early 1978 (before the first step) to 68.6 percent by early 1979.

The government introduced two devices, not used in the first episode, to alleviate the impact of import liberalization on domestic industry. "Advance notices" listed commodity items targeted for future liberalization, while the system of "observation items" allowed the government to examine specific imports for possible restrictions after liberalization. For instance, when the first step of the program was put into effect in May 1978, the government provided a list of items to be liberalized in 1979–82 and specified 28 of the 75 commodity items to be liberalized as "observation items."

Relaxation of QRs was discontinued in 1980 owing to the balance-of-payments difficulties and the severe domestic recession arising from the second oil shock. The program resumed in 1981, increasing the ratio of AA items to total tradeable items from 68.6 percent in mid-1980 to 84.8 percent in mid-1984 and to 95.2 percent by 1988.

Meanwhile, the customs law was revised, effective from January 1979, in order to reduce tariff barriers on imports. As a result the average rate of legal tariffs (weighted by domestic production) declined from 41.3 percent to 34.4 percent. The tariff reform was not, however, planned as part of a comprehensive package of import liberalization, although the reform significantly reduced the average rate of legal tariffs. The government introduced another tariff reform, effective from early 1984. This reform not only reduced the average rate of legal tariffs, but also specified gradual reduction in many tariff rates over the 1984–8 period. In effect, the 1984 reform introduced a system of "advance notice" for the gradual reduction of tariff protection, on the pattern of the system used in the liberalization of QRs.

Conclusions

The significant progress in trade liberalization discernible in the two episodes was the outcome of deliberate government policy. The 1965–7 program was avowedly short term in its aim: the program took the form primarily of revision of an existing semi-annual trade program. Specific plans were for six months at a time, so that there was no delay between announcement and implementation. The 1978–9 episode involved longer-term planning only in that it instituted an "advance notice" for import liberalization. In all other senses, announced programs and their implementation were simultaneous. Even the advance notice system presupposed implementation, as evidenced in the gradual progress in liberalization after 1979.

Against the background of the stated but generalized intention to liberalize trade, the actions taken during the two episodes were piecemeal and *ad hoc* rather than stages in a detailed long-term strategy. All announced schemes were implemented; none was reversed or aborted. This being so, what differences made trade liberalization sustainable after the second episode whereas it faltered after the first? One may be the advance notice system. Another is that the second episode was followed by a more successful stabilization policy than the first episode. And a third difference is that Korea's industrialization was more advanced in the late 1970s than a decade earlier, so that domestic industries could successfully accommodate themselves to trade liberalization.

New Zealand
Anthony C. Rayner and Ralph Lattimore

In many ways, New Zealand's experience of trade liberalization might appear to differ from that of the other countries in this study. New Zealand started the period, in 1950, from a position of considerable wealth. The level of real income per person was surpassed by only two or three other countries in the world.

Despite this initial advantage, the economy displayed many of the characteristics of a developing country, being largely agriculture based, with a small and highly protected manufacturing sector. This protection was part of a long tradition of intervention in the economy, which had the particular aim of ensuring full employment. (The success of the policy can be seen from the fact that the country had only around 50 people unemployed in 1950.) Attempts at trade liberalization in New Zealand started from as restricted a base as any in the project.

The dominating policy of protecting the economy from the world was undoubtedly an expensive failure, whose legacy was an import-competing industry flawed by gross inefficiencies. In tracing New Zealand's attempts at trade liberalization since World War II, it is interesting to observe how the political will hardened and the acceptance of adjustment costs increased as the costs of protection began to make themselves felt.

The First Episode: 1951–1956

The relative wealth of New Zealand in the 1950s probably impeded the first attempts to liberalize trade: the high standard of living masked the losses that the economy was suffering as a result of high protection. The early movements toward liberalization failed to include the essential ingredient of a true liberalization – improving efficiency of resource use by allowing domestic industries to compete against cheap imports.

In 1950, imports were subject to tight quantitative controls through import licensing. In addition, there were high tariff levels and very restrictive exchange controls. From this illiberal base the country had its first flirtation with trade liberalization. The fortunate coincidence of a recently devalued currency together with a world commodity price boom, in part engendered by the Korean War, led to a balance-of-payments surplus. The government reacted to this by removing import licensing. This liberalization appears to have been merely a method of permitting increased import consumption, much as the removal of wartime rationing allowed general increases in consumption. Safeguards were built into the relaxation of import licensing to allow its reimposition if domestic industry demonstrated damage resulting from the imports.

During the early 1950s the causes of the trade surplus disappeared and the newly freed imports increased the movement into deficit. Import licensing was reintroduced as a rationing device, since its reduction had no deeper economic justification. The percentage of imports requiring licenses, falling from 100 percent in 1948 to 40 percent in 1957, returned to 100 percent in 1958. The first episode of apparent trade liberalization had concluded.

The Second Episode: 1962 Onwards

The second episode was much more complex than the first, and at the same time contained a greater degree of economic rationalization for the policies involved. For ease of exposition the episode has been divided into three phases, although the divisions chosen do not mark changes in the full spectrum of trade policies. Rather, they represent significant new initiatives in some aspects of the policy mix.

The first phase (1962–78) can be characterized as an attempt to move closer to neutrality in trade intervention by providing compensation to exporters for the effects of import protection. The forms of compensation varied widely, from direct export subsidies to input subsidies and a number of tax concessions. The policy began slowly, with the interventions few in number and small in size. As the years passed, it built up an accelerating momentum aided by a chronically overvalued exchange rate.

The oil shocks of the middle and late 1970s increased the country's trade problems and reinforced the perceived need to boost exports artificially. From this period until 1983–4, export promotion policies rapidly grew to levels that became unsustainable. Overseas reaction to the export subsidies began to build up, and the fiscal cost of the policy increased until it was having a major impact on the economy.

The roots of the *second phase* (1979–84) were set in the middle to late 1970s, when the policymakers were becoming aware of the real costs of protecting the import-competing industries. As a result, two new initiatives were introduced. The first identified the industries least able to face international competition. Each industry was investigated and a unique "Industry Plan" was developed, the explicit intention of which was to improve international competitiveness. The initial steps in designing the first phase of these plans began at the end of the 1970s and the full set was completed by 1985.

The second trade policy initiative was perhaps even more significant. Again, it stemmed from a recognition of the costs of protection. It phased out import licensing for industries not under the Industry Plan. Continued protection, if it was necessary, would be through tariffs alone. The method of removing licensing was through tendering ever increasing amounts until the license premium fell close enough to zero that the system could be abolished. Tendering began in 1981.

Both these trade policy initiatives were designed to force domestic industry to face greater international competition, with the expectation that some rationalization would result. For the first time, a liberalization policy was put in place to obtain some of the real gains of adjustment.

Continued growth in export subsidization and major public investment in import-competing industries coincided with this reduction of protection. As is suggested above, this aspect of policy became unsustainable. The costs of the "Think Big" investment projects and the relatively large-scale subsidies for agriculture helped create an economic crisis. Tight central controls on prices were unable to remove the root cause of the crisis: the high internal deficit.

Relative economic stagnation has led to a fall in New Zealand's world ranking of per capita income, from third in 1950 to around twenty-fifth by the early 1980s. Inflation and balance-of-trade deficits continued to worsen. Although still not high by world standards, unemployment had grown to levels unprecedented in post-war New Zealand. The main justification for government intervention was thus untenable.

The crisis led to a collapse of confidence in the government and the election of the Labour Party in July 1984. This was followed by a dramatic shift toward economic liberalism, which was to be the hallmark of *phase three* (1984 onwards). The government stance altered from strongly interventionist to reliance on the market system.

The impact was less dramatic on trade than on domestic economic policies. While the main thrust of policy was to lessen government intervention in the economy and rely more on market forces, the reduction of protection proceeded along the lines already determined in the early 1980s. The phasing out of licensing and the implementation of the Industry Plans may have gone faster, but the acceleration was not dramatic. Even the announced moves toward tariff reduction had been planned before the 1984 election.

The third phase, then, saw continued and perhaps accelerated reduction of protection. More substantial changes were made in the other aspects of policy that influence trade. An initial devaluation of 20 percent was followed by a floating of the New Zealand dollar six months later. Exchange controls were removed over a short period of time. Interest rate controls were removed and the ensuing rise in rates strongly influenced the exchange rate. Almost all export promotion and subsidization were discontinued. The cumulative effect of these changes on the export industries was considerable, particularly since the exchange rate did not move to levels that even approximately balanced trade through export stimulation.

The root of the problem was that the government was unable to reduce the internal deficit sufficiently. While the removal of the costly tariff compensation policy brought a significant fall in the deficit in the year after the election, the government was unable to sustain this reduction in expenditures. The effect of the internal deficit on interest rates and the real exchange rate raised the costs of adjustment to trade liberalization.

While it is too early to see the concrete results of the policy changes in terms of a major restructuring of the economy, an accleration of change is clearly taking place. As the need for structural change becomes more widely accepted a return to the old aim of preserving the status quo becomes less and less acceptable.

The structure of the economy has yet to change radically enough to break out of the stagnation of the past; but it is much more likely to do so than at any other time in the last 40 years.

Pakistan
Stephen Guisinger and Gerald Scully

Pakistan began a process of liberalization in 1959 that, for all intents and purposes, has continued throughout the ensuing decades. Certainly, setbacks have occurred. But viewed broadly, and especially when contrasted with the sharp twists and turns in liberalization efforts in Latin American countries, Pakistan appears to have plodded steadily toward a more open trading regime. This is not to say that Pakistan has entered the ranks of the outward-oriented developing countries. But in view of the extreme poverty of the country and a devastating reconfiguration of its national boundaries twice within 25 years, Pakistan deserves special credit for its efforts to liberalize.

Pakistan began its life with a per capita income of US$100, little industry, abundant agricultural land, a strong civil service tradition inherited from the British Raj, and a tiny entrepreneurial class. Through import substitution policies, industry grew rapidly in the 1950s, but toward the end of that decade the government saw that easy import substitution possibilities were shrinking fast. A chronic shortage of foreign exchange earnings coupled with the normal vicissitudes associated with agricultural exports drove planners to think of ways to broaden the source and expand the level of foreign exchange earnings.

Twice in the 1960–80 period the pace of trade reform rose to the level that could be called a liberalization episode.

Episode One: 1959–1965

The first step toward liberalization during the initial episode was, paradox-ically, to increase the level of distortions, specifically creating an export bonus scheme that rewarded exporters of manufactured products with import privileges that effectively devalued the rupee for a portion of manufactured exports. The scheme worked and was followed by other measures, such as the Open General License and the Free List. These were designed, as their names imply, to automate a cumbersome process of import licensing that had hopelessly outlived the days when it was used to curtail import consumption after the bottom dropped out of Pakistan's export markets following the end of the Korean War boom. The newly installed Ayub regime listened carefully to the market-oriented advice of foreign economic advisers, and aid donors responded with increased loans and grants.

Pakistan's exports of manufactured goods improved markedly and the supply of imports earned from the bonus vouchers fueled an expansion of manufactured goods consumed domestically. The early 1960s saw substan-tial economic growth arising from increased foreign aid and liberalization in trade and other areas. These halcyon days were brought to an abrupt halt by the Indo-Pakistan war. Aid donors cut off aid in protest, and emergency measures reinstated many of the controls that the 1959–65 liberalization measures had succeeded in lopping off.

Episode Two: 1972–1978

The second episode began with a bang. The transformation of the eastern wing of Pakistan into the new country of Bangladesh ushered in a new regime led by Zulfikar Ali Bhutto. In the space of a few months Bhutto introduced sweeping reforms – some quite remarkably liberalizing, such as devaluation of the rupee from Rs4.76 to Rs11 to the US dollar, accom-panied by the elimination of most import licensing and the export bonus scheme. Other reforms, such as the nationalization of much of basic industry, were antiliberal.

Bhutto's reforms were undertaken at a time of domestic political and economic stress – floods and droughts plagued Pakistan between 1972 and 1974. If that were not enough to undermine the reforms, the price of oil shot up in 1973. A heavy importer of oil, Pakistan had to tighten its belt to accommodate the increase in the real price of oil. The ensuing world recession yielded no favors for oil importing countries, and Pakistan suffered erratic and generally slow growth. The 1972 trade liberalizations were overcome by outside forces.

Conclusions

What broad patterns emerge from these two episodes of liberalization? Pakistan's careful pay-as-you-go attitude may be of some use to developing countries saddled with entrenched protectionist interest groups. However, trying to sort out cause from effect in Pakistan's liberalization story is a frustrating task because external events and flukes of nature affected the indicators of success, such as exports, output levels, and employment.

First, in neither episode was there a grand design, a comprehensive plan for substantial reform of the trade policy system. In both episodes, newly installed governments adopted liberalization measures to combat a perceived crisis or near-crisis situation: a shortage of foreign exchange in Ayub's case; a political upheaval in Bhutto's. Governments in Pakistan have not undertaken liberalization as part of a stabilization program.

Second, the Bhutto shock treatment excepted, liberalization was always administered in small doses and the "patient" was studied carefully for signs of adverse reaction. Even the Bhutto reforms, on close inspection, turn out to be much smaller in effective magnitude than appears at first sight. The preference for small continuous liberalizations over discrete jumps suggests to us a kind of formula that might have been implicit in determining the amount and timing of liberalizations. The difference between projected levels of foreign exchange holdings and a minimum safety level was regarded as a fund that could be "spent" on liberalization. Even though liberalizations often turned out to be net foreign exchange earners, the ever cautious civil servants followed a piecemeal pay-as-you-go strategy that minimized their risk.

On the assumption that trade liberalization produced no improvements in efficiency, we calculated the additional amount of foreign aid that would have been necessary to finance the ensuing imports, given the elasticities of import and export demand observed over the 1960–80 period. For only a 33 percent increase in the flow of foreign aid, Pakistan could have substantially liberalized in 1960 and maintained the liberalization throughout the period. With a threefold increase in foreign aid, Pakistan could have achieved near-free trade.

Perú
Julio J. Nogués

Peru's economic policies were unique among Latin American countries in the immediate post-World War II period. Unlike its neighbors, Peru liberalized its trade and payments regime and maintained a liberal policy environment until the latter part of the 1950s. It then began to intervene in trade and continued to do so during the 1960s. Protectionist policies reached a peak between 1968 and 1975 under the socialist government of General Velasco Alvarado.

Our statistical analysis suggests that these anticompetitive policies severely hampered economic performance and long-term prospects for trade and growth, even though many of the policies began to be dismantled after 1975. Moreover, some of the policies had a long-term negative impact on the sustainability of Peru's trade liberalization effort.

Ideologically, the military regime that replaced Velasco Alvarado in 1975 was not as interventionist as its predecessor. In fact, some members of the cabinet held distinctly liberal views. But the new military government concentrated its energies on reducing macroeconomic imbalances. By 1979 the fiscal deficit had been reduced to 1 percent of GDP from a 1975 level of 8 percent, and a significant real devaluation of 60 percent had helped bring the current account deficit – 11 percent of GDP in 1975 – to equilibrium.

The Introduction of Trade Liberalization

In 1979 a major dismantling of tariff barriers left only nine out of 5,012 imported goods on the prohibited list, while the proportion of goods on the free-import list increased to 75 percent. Moreover, maximum tariff rates were reduced.

Significant barriers to trade remained in place at the end of 1978, however. Only 38 percent of all imported goods were on the free-import list, with the rest either under import licensing (22 percent) or on the prohibited list. Maximum tariff rates, and the number of goods affected by tariffs, remained very high.

Further trade liberalization measures introduced in mid-1980 after the democratic government of Belaúnde Terry came to power increased the proportion of goods on the free-import list to 98 percent and reduced the maximum tariff rate to 60 percent. This reformed structure remained relatively unchanged during 1981, but a reversal began in 1982. By 1984 much of the tariff structure had been restored, and by 1985 tariffs had once more been imposed on all imports.

The Reversal of Liberalization

What explains the reversal? For Peru, 1980–5 was a period of expansionary fiscal policies and significant public sector deficits. Domestic currency was used as an anti-inflationary tool and therefore appreciated significantly. During 1982, for example, the real exchange rate was only 90 percent of what it had been in 1979. Worse, the terms of trade declined by 30 percent during the period, and the current account deficit by 1985 was US$1.6 billion, equivalent to 8 percent of GDP and 49 percent of exports. As a consequence, trade liberalization policies were not accompanied by greater exports.

Peru was also unlucky. In 1983 its GDP declined by 11 percent, a heavy blow mainly attributable to the effects of "El Niño," a periodic shift of ocean currents and atmospheric conditions that led to serious droughts in some parts of the country and floods in others.

As current account deficits developed and Peru's arrears mounted, the supply of financial capital dried up. By 1985, when Alan García, a young and charismatic leader, was elected president, the foreign external debt of Peru had reached US$13 billion, or 70 percent of GDP.

Also working against the liberalization attempt were labor market regulations that were a legacy of the socialist period. Our statistical analysis indicates that the labor laws made it difficult if not impossible for firms facing increasing competition from imports to adjust their workforces. Consequently, profit rates in what used to be the protected manufacturing sector declined significantly. Furthermore, the labor laws were used by the protected group as an argument against trade liberalization.

There are also political economy explanations for the reversal. Peru's socialist era left a lasting mark on Peru's economic institutions and strongly influenced public perceptions of the benefits and costs of alternative policies. For a liberalization to be successful and durable, institutional foundations as well as economic policies must be remade. Liberalization will only work if the commitment of the nation's leaders to such policies is clear and forceful. The leaders must demonstrate to the public that there are more gains than costs in liberalizing an economy. The evidence – obtained chiefly from studying the news media – suggests that commitment and leadership were absent in Peru during its liberalization attempt.

Why, then, given the bias of Peru's institutions in favor of government intervention, were trade liberalization policies introduced at all? The answer to this question is in our view surprisingly simple. In Peru, different policy instruments are managed by different government offices. Policymaking is thus characterized by fragmentation, considerable discretion, and independence of action. It just so happened that the policymakers who led the Ministry of Economy in 1980 believed that an appropriate course of action for Peru was to liberalize trade. But since these ideas did not spread to the rest of the government or to society at large, the commitment to liberalization remained weak.

The Philippines
Geoffrey Shepherd and Florian Alburo

In the study we concentrate on three episodes of trade reform, each terminated by a partial reversal of the reform measures: the foreign exchange decontrol of 1960–5; the promotion of nontraditional exports in 1970–3; and the "Tariff Reform Program," designed in 1980 for the phased reduction of tariff protection and elimination of quantitative import restrictions. This last program began to be reversed in 1982 and was derailed after a massive balance-of-payments crisis in 1983.[1] The program was resumed in 1986 under very different political circumstances, but the period of the present study ends around 1984.

The First Episode: Foreign Exchange Decontrol, 1960–1965

The Philippine peso became progressively overvalued in the 1950s: in the first instance because, after its independence from the United States in 1946, the country did not gain full sovereignty over its exchange rate until 1954; in the second instance because foreign exchange controls came to suit the import-substituting industrial sector that they had spawned. Under pressure to restore incentives to the export sector and to eliminate the corruption associated with import licensing, the government was finally in 1960 induced to promise a gradual decontrol. This was to be achieved by 1964, through a multiple exchange rate system.

This gradual process went wrong for several reasons. In 1960 the government deliberately pursued an expansionary macroeconomic policy to ease the pains of decontrol, a policy which became excessive in 1961, a presidential election year. In addition, export prices and receipts fell steeply in 1961, adding to the pressure on the balance of payments and fueling speculation on the eventual value that a devalued peso would assume. A new administration in 1962 interrupted the gradual decontrol process with a float of the peso and the lifting of all foreign exchange

---

1 The 1980–3 episode is not covered in the synthesis study because its brevity makes it difficult to isolate effects.

controls except for a tax on exports that was not removed till 1965. Macroeconomic policies also became less expansionary. At the same time, import duties were substantially raised in 1962 and subsequent years, in an effort to maintain levels of protection.

Several notable features in economic performance followed the decontrol effected by 1962:

1 The balance of trade improved considerably by the mid-1960s (at a time when the international terms of trade were deteriorating), thanks largely to the performance of export agriculture and to improvement in the services account.
2 Decontrol reduced the level of protection to industry (in spite of policymakers' intentions), so that industrial performance stagnated – with the apparent loss of some jobs in manufacturing – in the early to mid-1960s. Industry, if leaner, was not noticeably fitter, except that decontrol initiated, from small beginnings, a process of growth of nontraditional manufactured exports.
3 The direct impact of decontrol on import prices was mild because the inflationary effect of nominal devaluation was countered by the deflationary effect of eliminating the import premium associated with controls. Indirectly, decontrol, by stimulating land use for export agriculture, contributed to rising prices for food produced for the domestic market.

The 1960–5 decontrol was the most important of the three episodes. Its achievement was to restore external equilibrium rather than set the economy on a higher growth path. But this achievement, though not entirely reversed until 1983, was not fully sustained. The immediate reason was that, after 1963, inflation and the deteriorating terms of trade were not offset by exchange rate adjustments (except for the 1965 improvement in the export exchange rate). From 1966 the new Marcos administration fueled the inflation with expansionary policies. It reacted to reemerging balance-of-payments problems with a stepwise reintroduction of nontariff import controls between 1967 and 1969. Decontrol came to be perceived by many as something of a failure, particularly in view of the stagnation of manufacturing industry: the experiment in free markets had gone too far.

The Second Episode: Promoting Nontraditional Exports, 1970–1973

In early 1970 the peso was substantially devalued, though many of the controls reintroduced in 1969 were kept in place. In the same year duties on traditional exports were introduced. On the other hand, several incentives to nontraditional exports were legislated from 1967 to 1973. In all, the early 1970s was not a period of unambiguous trade liberalization.

The 1970–4 period saw a stabilization of the external sector, with an improved situation for balance of payments, reserves and foreign debt. Macroeconomic restraint helped make devaluation effective until 1973. The gradual loss of effectiveness from then on can be ascribed to more expansionary macroeconomic policy, but above all to the terms of trade shock after 1974 which was insufficiently offset by exchange rate adjustment.

Nontraditional manufactured exports (NTMEs) – dominated by the labor intensive assembly of imported inputs, particularly in clothing and electronics – accounted for only a modest share of export growth in the early 1970s. But between 1974 and 1983 they grew from 10 percent of total exports to 51 percent, a remarkable change in the structure of exports. There are several reasons for this.

1 The real effective exchange rate (REER) for manufactures had been rising since 1960. The rise was rapid during the 1960–2 decontrol and smaller, but substantial, following the 1970 devaluation. Thus both episodes laid the basis for NTME growth.
2 From 1969 to 1974 real manufacturing wage costs fell dramatically: the real unskilled wage appears to have been halved. The real wage recovered slightly by 1980 but remained well below its pre-1970 level.
3 While the subsidy element of the incentives to NTMEs introduced in the early 1970s was actually quite modest, these incentives were important in allowing exporters to acquire imported inputs at world prices.
4 There was a surge of foreign investment receiving fiscal incentives in 1973 and 1974, the early years of martial law (proclaimed in 1972).

The long-term fall in the real wage in the Philippines has emerged as a crucial factor to the changing structure of exports in the 1970s, not only supporting the growth of NTMEs but also turning the Philippines into an important direct exporter of labor (mainly to the Middle East). But a real wage fall of the magnitude apparent in the period 1969–74 is difficult to explain. Consistent with the Stolper–Samuelson theorem that protection raises the relative price of the scarce factor, and consistent with the historical scarcity of land relative to labor in the Philippines, the devaluations of 1960–2 and the early 1970s reduced the protection to labor and hence its price.

The Third Episode: The Tariff Reform Program, 1980–1983

From around 1974–5 there were signs of a revival of protection, much of it aimed at giving economic privileges to political allies of the government.

A major staged program of tariff reform and liberalization of residual import controls was designed in 1980, and implementation began in 1981. While the tariff adjustments continued to their planned conclusion in 1985, the removal of import controls started to be partially reversed from 1982. In the economic crisis that developed in the early 1980s and came to a head in 1983, the allocation of foreign exchange came to be fully controlled by the government. With direct import controls reintroduced, many tariffs no longer had a protective effect and the whole import liberalization program was stalled.

The trade liberalization movement of the early 1980s was politically fragile, but it was undoubtedly broad circumstances, both external and internal to the economy, that aborted the liberalization. Externally, the period 1974–81 marked the sharpest decline that the Philippines had experienced in its post-war terms of trade, while recession and high interest rates in the Organization for Economic Cooperation and Development (OECD) countries after 1979 exacerbated Philippine debt problems. The magnitude of these external shocks presaged a very sizable adjustment in exchange rates and government expenditure, but this simply did not occur until the partial collapse of the economy from 1983.

From 1975 onwards the Philippines sustained a current account deficit – equivalent to around 5 percent of GDP – that was extremely high by historical standards. This deficit was partly related to the enormous increase in investments in the mid-1970s, much of it financed by foreign loans. The investment was often of dubious quality, and by the early 1980s the government, responsible for more and more failing firms, resorted to increasing public deficits and foreign borrowing. From 1981 macro-economic policy became very expansionary. There was insufficient adjust-ment of the exchange rate to accommodate growing balance-of-payments difficulties. By the first half of the 1980s the current account deficit had reached unmanageable proportions and it only remained for a political event, the assassination of Benigno Aquino in August 1983, fully to trigger the economic crisis.

A Lack of Commitment to Trade Policy Reform

It is difficult to perceive any long-term commitment to trade liberalization in the Philippines. The 1960–5 decontrol was partly triggered by political reactions against corruption, certainly not by a government turning against the principle of protected imported substitution. The export promotion measures of the early 1970s arose from the compromise reached in the late 1960s between stronger forces wanting to increase intervention, planning, and protection and weaker forces wanting a more open economy. Undoubt-edly the hand of the pro-intervention lobby was strengthened by generally negative perceptions of the effects of decontrol. As for the third episode, the Tariff Reform Program, it is difficult to see any build-up of support to a point where the majority of the government favored such a potentially thorough-going reform. Indeed, the reform decision may more appropriately be seen as a kind of "palace coup" brought about by a "technocratic" minority in government.

One plausible reason for the lack of long-term Philippine commitment to trade reform can be suggested. The country's rich resource base – the backbone of its development since the middle of the nineteenth century – provided the surplus on which a high cost import-substituting manufacturing sector could be built from the 1950s onwards. By the same token the primary-product-exporting sector was sufficiently resilient (until the later 1970s at least) to respond rapidly to balance-of-payments crises (in the early 1960s and early 1970s). There was never any pressure on manufacturing to become more efficient. Resource-poor countries in contrast, have little choice but to overcome crises through creating an efficient industrial sector that can export.

Since the beginning of the 1970s the Philippine economy *has* responded to its progressive loss of comparative advantage in primary product exports by exporting manufactures; but these exporters have largely developed in the enclaves of bonded warehouses and export-processing zones without much undermining the inherited strength of the protectionist lobby. Nonetheless, the logic of the Philippines' changing comparative advantage is that primary exports can no longer solve external crises, that manufactured exports must increasingly do so, and that trade policies must change accordingly.

Two further explanations of the lack of commitment to more liberal policies may reflect factors specific to Philippine history. First, public hostility toward traditional agricultural exporters, a consequence of the politics of the 1950s, meant hostility toward the more liberal trade policies these exporters espoused. Second, the country's "love–hate" relationship with its ex-colonial power, the United States, has helped breed an autarkic brand of nationalism that continues to fuel protectionist sentiment.

Portugal
Jorge B. de Macedo, Cristina Corado, and Manuel L. Porto

Portugal is a relatively small country with a population of roughly 10 million (in the mid-1980s). Despite a respectable rate of growth in the post World War II period, it has remained one of Europe's poorest nations, with an annual per capita income (in the mid-1980s) of about US$2,000. Its industrial structure reflects this position. Agriculture, despite a dramatic decline throughout the last generation, still accounts for about one quarter of the country's GDP, and employs 44 percent of the economy's labor force.

A very high degree of labor mobility and labor migration has always characterized Portugal. This is reflected both in the sizable portion of Portugal's labor force that migrated abroad, temporarily or permanently, first to the colonies and then to European countries, and in rapid shifts of population among the country's regions – with the two major urban centers of Lisbon and Porto absorbing large immigrations from other parts of the country.

The year 1974 represents a watershed line in the country's post-war history. First, following a period of colonial wars, Portugal concluded by that year a process in which it divested itself of its colonies – a fact of major significance for the country's conduct of international trade and for its international orientation. Second, a revolution in 1974 toppled a long-established dictatorial government and introduced a democratic regime – with a strong bent (at least in the beginning) toward socialism and state management. As a result, various sectors of the economy (including the financial sector) were nationalized, and a large sector of public enterprises was established.

Except for the interruption of the trade liberalization episodes that will be surveyed shortly, Portugal's trade regime has been highly restrictive throughout. Exports, originating primarily from small-scale labor intensive "traditional" industries, have been discriminated against, whereas import-substituting activities – with a heavy representation of capital intensive large-scale firms – have been highly protected, through both high tariffs and, often, import prohibition or import quotas.

The first – and still the most significant – trade liberalization occurred between 1970 and 1974, the last five years of the authoritarian government. The introduction of this episode was due to the convergence of several factors. One was the transfer of the dictatorial powers, upon the death of Salazar in 1968, to Marcelo Caetano, who was more disposed to opening the economy and integrating Portugal with Europe. Another factor was the culmination, around 1970, of several gradual tariff reduction processes agreed upon in earlier years with the EEC and GATT. Still another facilitating factor was a rapid accumulation of foreign exchange reserves, due to an impressive growth of exports, a large inflow of remittances from Portuguese workers abroad, and, to a lesser extent, an inflow of external private investment capital.

Liberalization consisted, first and foremost, in an overwhelming reduction in tariff levels; less important was a partial relaxation of QRs. Export subsidization was not materially affected. On the domestic front, some restrictions on prices and investment were removed or relaxed, but other interventions, such as financial or fiscal subsidies to selected activities, were maintained and even expanded. The foreign exchange rate, supported by a persistent favorable balance due to export expansion and the inflow of remittances, was kept constant throughout. Monetary policy, determined to a large extent by the fate of foreign exchange reserves, was expansionary. Domestic prices responded, and the inflation rate was substantially higher than before the start of liberalization. The real exchange rate thus *appreciated*. Domestic unemployment remained on a low level throughout the episode, apparently unaffected by the opening of the economy to imports. Imports in particular, but also, until a short time before the end of this episode, exports, grew at a rapid pace, and the economy's openness in terms of the ratio of trade flows to income increased substantially.

In 1974, the policy of trade liberalization was completely reversed. This was due to several factors, economic as well as political, with the latter most probably related to the former. The continuous real exchange rate appreciation essentially led to the interruption of export growth, while imports kept rising. This coincided with the increased bill for oil imports, after the first oil crisis at the end of 1973, to put pressure on the country's foreign exchange reserves. Trade liberalization, reducing the wage bill, came to be perceived as being "unfair" to labor and, at the same time, resented by many business leaders. The coup of April 1974, which ended the authoritarian regime, also brought an immediate reversal of liberalization by the new regime. Whether liberalization would have survived had the political regime not been changed remains an open question.

The second trade liberalization episode started in early 1977 and lasted through 1980. It was launched with the government's announcement of its application for full membership in the EEC. Indeed, the latter provided the major rationale for the liberalization policy, with expectations of the effect of membership on social and political stability and moderation (as well as development aid from the organization) apparently outweighing any direct economic benefits expected from trade liberalization.

In contrast with the first episode, balance-of-payments circumstances were definitely unfavorable when trade liberalization was introduced. Exports had been relatively stagnant for several years, and foreign exchange reserves had been gradually depleting. In addition, external debt had been growing, following continuous borrowing from abroad. The balance of payments reflected, in turn, an expansionary macroeconomic policy – in particular, persistent deficits of the central government and state-owned enterprises.

It is thus not surprising that in this episode strict trade policy measures were secondary to changes in macroeconomic policies. Some tariff reductions were started in the trade area, as well as a minor relaxation of QRs. Import surcharges were lowered, and compulsory import deposits were abolished. To the extent that QRs became less restrictive, however, this was primarily due to a significant devaluation, which for some time (close to two years) reversed an earlier trend of a real currency appreciation. Beside this devaluation, the major macroeconomic steps of stabilization were a fiscal contraction and a tightening of credit to both the private and the public sector – reflecting the use for the first time of an active monetary policy.

This change in macroeconomic policy, however, was reversed within a short time – and with it trade liberalization. By 1979, fiscal policy turned again in an expansionary direction. Monetary policy, too, changed course by the spring of 1979: the trend of the increasing discount rate and market interest rates stopped, and credit ceilings were relaxed. Consequently, the real exchange rate started appreciating after 1979.

Trade flows responded to changes in the real exchange rate. Trends of a slow increase in imports and a fast rise in exports, following the introduction of the stabilization *cum* liberalization package, were reversed in 1980, and the import surplus again began to expand. A reversal of trade liberalization followed in 1980, although it was only partial: no further tariff reductions were undertaken, and QRs became somewhat more restrictive. Just as trade liberalization itself was moderate in the second episode compared with the first, the reversal of the policy was much less dramatic and abrupt.

Singapore
Bee-Yan Aw

Traditionally an export-oriented economy with a historical heritage as an entrepôt port, Singapore adopted an import substitution strategy in the early 1960s in anticipation of political and economic union with neighboring Malaysia. But Singapore's putative merger with Malaysia was doomed by political and racial differences, and ended in 1965. Once Malaysia's large domestic market for industrial goods was no longer available without restrictions, Singapore gradually switched to a policy of once again promoting exports. Although the main liberalization effort was made between 1968 and 1973, certain steps toward freer trade were taken both before and after that period.

It should be noted that even after Singapore opted for an import substitution strategy in 1963, its tariffs and import quotas provided only a modest degree of protection for domestic industries. Moreover, there was an understanding among protected industries that tariffs and quotas were temporary and subject to frequent government review.

The policy of using tariffs and quotas as protective devices underwent a major change after 1965: quotas were replaced with low tariffs for existing industries deemed likely to serve export markets as well as the domestic market efficiently. Higher tariffs were created for infant industries. From 1966 to 1969, about a third of all new duties announced each year were used to replace import quotas, and by the end of 1973 all import quotas had been abolished.

No strong link has been established between the shifts in protection provided by tariffs or quotas and corresponding movements in industry performance. However, a simple model relating the performance variables of Singapore's industrial sector to the liberalization efforts between 1967 and 1973 provided evidence suggesting that the gradual replacement of quotas with tariffs did affect those variables. Quotas were shown generally to have encouraged inefficient production and therefore resulted in reduced output.

Central to Singapore's adoption of trade liberalization was a shift from trade to fiscal incentives to foster investment. Under the Economic Expansion Incentive Act of 1967, 90 percent of the profits of exporters were exempted from taxes, with the period of relief ranging from three years for nonpioneer companies to five years for pioneer companies. The government increasingly encouraged foreign investment and entrepreneurship. Subsidies in the form of low interest loans and cheap access to the infrastructure were provided more readily to some industries than to others, especially after 1968 when the government formally adopted a policy of picking winners. The most important incentives took the form of government directives as to which industries should expand rapidly. These directives reassured entrepreneurs that the risks of moving in these industries were lower than for other industries.

Singapore's economy grew strongly during the liberalization episode. The balance of payments was in surplus every year, the average annual GDP growth rate exceeded 13 percent, and export growth exceeded 18 percent a year. Growth rates of gross domestic fixed capital formation were also remarkable, averaging over 20 percent a year.

Conclusion

Trade liberalization in Singapore during the 1968–73 period was a gradual process. Nonetheless, domestic policies on such matters as real wages and private savings often had to be modified to bring them in line with the economy's gradual opening to international conditions.

Two factors were broadly responsible for the success of the policy. The first was that the modest level of protection and the short duration of the import substitution period (1963–5) meant that the adjustment costs associated with liberalization were negligible.

The second was the government's commitment to the principle that Singapore's surviving industries would be those that were able to compete in international markets. The role of such government intervention is, of course, controversial. But given that intervention existed, government subsidies to export industries are more self-limiting than import restrictions. To put it another way, the visible costs of subsidies cannot continue indefinitely without drawing criticism. Moreover, Singapore's subsidies to individual industries were modest. The government's not unreasonable intervention in various sectors was counteracted by its strong commitment in general to free trade.

Spain
Guillermo de la Dehesa, José Juan Ruiz, and Angel Torres

Trade liberalization in Spain can be characterized as a generally liberalizing trend beginning in the late 1950s and marked by major upswings in 1960–6, 1970–4, and 1977–80. The chief characteristics of the three episodes were tariff cuts, reductions in QRs, and improvement of export promotion schemes. Multilateral trade agreements reinforced the trend toward greater liberalization.

Before liberalization began, Spain's trade was controlled through extensive restrictions on imports, heavy reliance on bilateral clearing agreements, and a complex exchange rate structure. This system brought Spain to an economic dead-end: a highly overvalued exchange rate, a permanent balance-of-payments deficit, extremely low reserves of foreign currency, a rising rate of inflation, and a small and inefficient industrial sector.

The First Episode, 1960–1966

As domestic economic circumstances deteriorated in the late 1950s, Franco's advisors persuaded him to alter Spain's economic policies. A stabilization program ushered in the first episode of trade liberalization in 1959. During the episode, import restrictions were relaxed in several stages. A uniform exchange rate replaced multiple exchange rates, implying a substantial devaluation of the peseta, while government intervention in trade shifted from QRs to tariffs and other import duties. A list of unrestricted imports was created in 1959 and enlarged several times. Nondiscriminatory quotas were established for imports previously controlled by bilateral licensing. In addition, the government reduced tariffs and initiated export incentives to reinforce the integration of the Spanish economy with international markets.

This stabilization and liberalization program produced the most sustained wave of economic prosperity in the modern history of Spain. During the 1960s, annual per capita income grew by 6.4 percent, substantially above the 2.8 percent attained in the 1939–59 period and the 0.9 percent registered in 1906–30.

The gradual opening of the economy after 1959 allowed Spain to share in the European economic boom of the 1960s. Europe's prosperity boosted foreign direct investment and tourism in Spain while stimulating a large emigration of labor that reduced unemployment. Remittance of funds from Spanish workers in other parts of Europe increased.

Changes in relative prices brought about by trade reform improved Spain's comparative advantage, including large gains in productivity. This, in turn, led to considerable internal labor migration and, in combination with worker emigration to other parts of the continent, appreciably raised labor income.

But a more thorough transformation of the economy was prevented by failure to reform the inequitable tax system and to revamp the antiquated financial system. Those "sins of omission" arose from the inherent conflict between trade liberalization and the authoritarian nature of the political regime.

Spain's economic expansion began to lose momentum in 1966. The inflation rate rose, and Spain's balance of payments began to erode despite a growing surplus in net services. In late 1967, Spain's economic authorities approved a program that included a devaluation of the peseta, tighter financial policies, and a freeze on prices, wages, and other income. The inflation rate then plummeted, and the external account improved. These changes were compatible with a high rate of GDP growth, and by 1970 Spain seemed to have recovered macroeconomic stability.

The Second Episode, 1970–1974

The second episode began when Spain signed a preferential agreement with the EEC in 1970 and adopted a unilateral policy of tariff cuts and reductions in QRs. The unilateral measures were ended in 1975 as economic conditions, including the balance of payments, deteriorated. As a result, trade in mid-1975 was no freer than it had been in 1966 except for Spain's obligations under the EEC preferential agreement.

The Turmoil of the Late 1970s

The closing years of the Franco era were marked by political turmoil and economic disequilibria which reached a climax in 1977, the year of the first general election in Spain in four decades. A newly elected government had to tackle a raging inflation rate, large deficits in the balance of payments and the government budget, and rising unemployment.

To deal with these problems, the major political forces negotiated an agreement whose principal goals were to reduce domestic expenditures and to end the growing disequilibrium in Spain's external accounts. The peseta was devalued, ceilings were placed on wage increases and public sector expenditures, and tighter monetary targets were adopted. This program brought about a small surplus in Spain's current account and a reduction in inflation in 1978. But success was bought at a high social cost: domestic demand and GDP stagnated, and unemployment rose. Meanwhile, a deliberate expansion of social benefits caused the public sector deficit, as a percentage of GDP, to triple.

The Third Episode, 1977–1980

The third liberalization episode involved "voluntary" steps to prepare Spain for joining the EEC. As in the second episode, the main measures adopted were across-the-board and selective tariff cuts, further easing of the QR system, and tinkering with Spain's export promotion scheme, chiefly through a large injection of funds to support export credits and export tax rebates. No specific trade goals were established, possibly because the government thought that Spain would soon become a full member of the EEC.

Although Spain did not, in fact, become a member of the EEC until 1985, trade liberalization was encouraged by two events during the 1977–80 period. In June 1979 Spain signed an agreement with the members of the European Free Trade Agreement (EFTA) gradually to eliminate all barriers to trade between Spain and EFTA and to extend to the EFTA countries the same benefits accorded to EEC members under the 1970 preferential trade agreement. Then, in mid-1980, reductions in tariffs negotiated during the Tokyo Round of the GATT were approved by the Spanish government.

After the second oil price shock in 1979, Spain's economic situation worsened and the political climate deteriorated. As a result, further liberalization was delayed until Spain finally joined the EEC.

Conclusions

Continued price distortions impeded the functioning of factor markets during the period covered by this study. Labor mobility was limited by regulations that made it difficult and costly to fire redundant workers. Furthermore, the wage boom that preceded the transition from dictatorship to democracy in 1977 paved the way for formal income policies that had a substantial impact on the wage structure and contributed to a higher level of unemployment.

Spain's capital market also suffered from government intervention. Credit rationing was the norm in the 1960s and early 1970s because of ceilings placed on domestic interest rates to keep real interest rates negative, and strong barriers impeded entry by domestic competitors. Foreign banks were barred from the market until the late 1970s. Moreover, exchange controls on capital outflows isolated the Spanish capital market from the world market.

The level of foreign currency reserves had a decisive influence on economic reform. Only when the level of reserves was high enough and the balance of payments was in surplus or equilibrium was it possible to implement trade liberalization. All three liberalization episodes were preceded by worsening economic conditions corrected by tighter financial policies combined with devaluations in the nominal exchange rate. During each episode, the loosening of other macroeconomic policies gave rise to new disequilibria (higher inflation, appreciation of the real exchange rate, and so on) that weakened Spanish competitiveness in the trade sector, and hence the country's balance of payments.

The Spanish experience suggests the superiority of a gradual and multistage liberalization over a one-stage process. The international agreements that Spain signed, especially those with the EEC, influenced this gradual approach. But the absence of significant adjustment costs indicates that liberalization could have proceeded slightly faster with minimal additional cost.

Trade liberalization did not greatly affect employment, which grew slowly from 1960 to 1974. In 1977, when the third episode began, Spain was suffering a general and sharp decline in employment, but neither trade liberalization nor trade flows were the forces underlying this decline. Rigidity in the market, typified by slow and costly adjustments in the work forces of individual companies and by excessive growth in real wages, was the main cause.

Exports grew substantially during the three liberalization episodes, offsetting losses in employment. Export promotion schemes were steadily intensified and were augmented by elements that helped to reduce sectoral anti-export biases. In the long term, however, export promotion schemes did not contribute to efficient allocation of resources.

Although Spain's trade balance is normally negative, tourist receipts and remittances from migrant workers have usually financed the trade balance deficit. In the 25 years after the first liberalization episode, tourist receipts covered, on average, 77 percent of the trade balance deficit, and remittances covered an average of 28 percent. Invisibles, in short, have often allowed Spain to achieve surpluses in the current account which have served as buffers against external shocks. While not vital to the survival of liberalization, the income from services and invisibles probably allowed Spain to pay less attention to labor intensive exports than would otherwise have been necessary.

Sri Lanka
Andrew G. Cuthbertson and Premachandra Athukorala

In nearly 40 years of modern independent rule Sri Lanka has seen two identifiable trade liberalization episodes. These episodes took place in an environment of economic management featuring regular swaps of government from center-right to center-left. A constant challenge for governments of either persuasion was to manage the fluctuations in commodity prices from the tea, rubber, and coconut sectors of the economy. So important were these sectors to economic well-being that times of low commodity prices severely affected the Sri Lankan economy. From time to time, these downturns triggered import barriers which, once established, became hard to remove. The episodes described in this study reflect two concentrated efforts to dislodge these barriers.

Sri Lanka became independent of colonial British rule in 1948. At that time, by conventional economic indicators, it was well placed for continuing economic achievement. Its national income was higher than that of many Asian countries, and its balance of payments was healthy and backed by large foreign exchange reserves. The budgetary position was sound, the population healthy, well educated, and well fed, and the public administration competent. It was regarded by some as "the best bet in Asia." Its economic achievements are generally considered to have fallen short of this original promise.

The origins of protection for weak manufacturing sectors may be traced to the industries sponsored by the government during wartime emergency, which could not cope with competition following the end of the war. This early protection of government-owned industries saw the first diversification of the economy away from the traditional export sectors – tea, rubber, and coconut – and services.

Ebbs and Flows in Trade Policy

The story of the swings in Sri Lanka's commercial policy since Independence begins with a relatively open economy which persisted for some ten years. An initial closing up in the late 1950s was associated with dwindling foreign reserves, falling output of the main crops, and an ambitious food subsidy program with a large import content. Punitive taxes on the main export commodities and impediments to management of their efficient production gave rise to a long series of low export years, which in turn saw a steady tightening of import controls. While there were some reversals during good years, by and large the moves to bar imports dominated those aimed at easing import controls – at least until 1977, when a quite significant assault on import barriers occurred. This was the second liberalization episode for Sri Lanka. The first took place in 1968; it had petered out by 1970.

The 1968–1970 Episode

The gradual tightening up after 1948 led, by 1965, to an economy that was practically closed to imports and operating with a highly overvalued rupee. The main instrument of the 1968 episode was a form of multiple exchange rate and partial import liberalization package. Under the Foreign Exchange Entitlement Certificate (FEEC) scheme, external transactions were divided into two categories. On the export side, one category included earnings from the traditional export crops. On the import side, in that same category were essential food imports along with other government imports. These transactions took place at the official rate of exchange; those in a second category took place at a premium rate. Exporters of goods receiving premiums did so in the form of certificates which were negotiable and could be used to buy foreign exchange to pay for imports.

These changes in incentives, while not far reaching, were reversed by 1970. At first, economic performance had been quite good and growth and employment had seemed to respond favorably to the liberalization. But by 1970 export revenues had fallen again and the government had tightened up on imports once more. The study found that the prime reason why this episode ran out of steam so early was that the government was not really committed to it, and moreover not very well entrenched – compared with the complete domination of the Jayawardene Government in 1977. This lack of resolve, furthermore, was clearly evident, and because the intent was therefore not credible it was easily reversed by pressure groups opposed to liberalization.

The 1977–1979 Episode

The 1977–9 episode was a liberalization of substance and durability. The instruments included a pronounced shift from quotas to tariffs, a devaluation and managed float, and the introduction of moderate export assistance measures. The government also foreshadowed general moves to free up the economy in the areas of labor and capital markets. The thrust of the program for liberalization was left open; policymakers apparently felt that they had gone far enough in the first round. Indeed, a number of actions in the late 1970s involved holding the line rather than carrying it further.

In this regard a tariff review body was established to hear appeals from manufacturers about the new regime. The appeals body through the next few years increasingly assessed these appeals in an economy-wide context and against the backdrop of measures of assistance, such as effective rates of protection. In consequence, subsequent tariff reforms in Sri Lanka became a "long hard slog" approach compared with the relatively spectacular progress of 1977.

What Else Happened?

The main accompanying policy to the 1977 trade liberalization was a massive program of public investment. There were three so-called lead projects: the acclerated Mahaweli program, a public housing program, and an urban development program. These were all largely financed by foreign aid. These ambitious projects made it difficult for the government to maintain fiscal balance. Some local resources had to be devoted to the projects and this, combined with political reluctance to cut their scale back, fueled continued budget deficits.

Export Development

Within a couple of years of the initial liberalization the government had set about actively promoting exports. A new institution was established and various promotional measures were set in place – improved duty drawbacks schemes, for instance. But, there was one big blemish on this export development activity, which largely removed its prospects for contributing to neutrality. The blemish arose from the manner of financing export assistance – primarily by a cess or surcharge on dutiable imports. Thus exports – the disadvantaged sector – were to be helped by raising the protection given to the already advantaged import-substituting sector.

Apart from this fundamental failing, the export drive in Sri Lanka would not have had much impact even if it had been funded in a less distorting way. Most of the measures were selective, with selection driven by administrative opinion rather than market performance. Often so-called local value added was encouraged by measures which effectively taxed exports of products in their traditional and probably most competitive form. Thus the main contribution to neutrality in Sri Lanka happened by substitution of a quota control regime by tariffs.

Employment

The short-run disruption that is often regarded as an inevitable consequence of a trade liberalization episode, especially one as vigorous as Sri Lanka's was in 1977, did not seem to occur in Sri Lanka. While this conclusion is qualified in a number of ways, the detailed quest aimed at identifying unemployment by sector and region could not uncover any significant signs. This applies not just to this particular study but also to specific inquiries and surveys undertaken by the government in the early 1980s.

Now to the qualifications: the first of these relates to data. The organized sector data do show a steady growth in almost all sectors – even though data sources are scattered and the levels differ, the story over time for organized sector data is consistent. The data for the unorganized sector are much less satisfactory and we cannot rule out the possibility that the unorganized sector before the brunt of the unemployment that occurred.

But there are other explanations also. One of these is that the huge inflows of foreign aid and investment simply took up any available surplus labor, and that without this investment program there would have been quite significant unemployment. Another somewhat begrudging explanation is that Sri Lanka was simply lucky to have a demand from quota-protected markets for supplies of garments and textiles. However, we observe that being lucky required some liberalization in the first place – that without the trade liberalization that did occur Sir Lanka would not have been able to take up this good market, be it fortuitously available or otherwise.

Prognosis

From about 1982 Sri Lanka has been beset by domestic conflicts which have significantly impaired economic performance and management. Nonetheless the liberalization stance seems to have remained in place. Indeed, the ideas and understanding of the benefits of liberalization are now bipartisan policy. To that extent the bold policy begun in 1977 seems to have had a long-lasting impact.

Turkey
Tercan Baysan and Charles Blitzer

From the founding of the Turkish Republic in the aftermath of World War I until very recently, economic policy was characterized by strong nationalistic overtones. The most important economic manifestations of this ideological outlook (sometimes referred to as "etatism") included (a) primary emphasis on rapid broad-based industrialization, (b) a leading role for the central government in planning and determining the allocation of investment, (c) a dominant role for state-owned firms in the banking and large-scale industrial sectors, (d) discouragement of foreign ownership, management, and investment, and (e) import substitution to minimize dependence on foreign trade. Although the emphasis and form have changed from time to time, this basic approach was never seriously challenged: economic nationalism survived wars, elections, and military governments for more than 50 years, until the beginning of the 1980s.

During this long period, trade policy was restrictive, using quotas and a positive licensing system for all imports (and some exports); extensive tariffs and taxes on imports; tight foreign exchange and capital controls; and government control of investment to support growth of import-competing industries. Generally, while not actively discouraged, exports were suppressed indirectly by an overvalued exchange rate and meager allocation of investment.

But the degree of the trade distortion was never constant. Periodically, steps were taken – typically, a large nominal devaluation accompanied by some reduction in the tax rates on imports – to reduce distortions and encourage additional exports. Sometimes this was done by a government with a more liberal outlook toward trade, but more often it was in response to a severe imbalance in the external accounts. At least four such liberalization episodes occurred in the 30 years following World War II. In each case, however, the government was conducting a "mid-course correction" or "fine-tuning" to ease balance-of-payments problems or improve economic efficiency at the margin; none could be regarded as an attempt to change the fundamental inward-looking direction of Turkish economic development.

In addition to reviewing the broad outlines of Turkish economic history and trade policy beginning in 1950, in the Turkey country study we analyzed the motivation, policy changes, and results associated with the last of these "corrective" liberalization attempts, which began in August 1970. This episode is interesting as an example of the short-run impact on trade flows of a rapid change in exchange rates.

The second episode examined in the study began in 1980 and is still in progress. The economic policy reforms are aimed at a radical reorientation and restructuring of the economy through liberalizing imports, promoting export-led growth, reducing the role of the public sector, expanding the private sector, and increasing foreign investment. As such, this represents the first effort at long-run trade liberalization.

Episode One: 1970–1973

The 1970 episode had its roots in the severe balance-of-payments difficulties of the late 1960s. The government was attempting to maintain a 7 percent growth target coupled with an import-substituting industrialization strategy. This led to rapid increases in demand for raw material and capital goods imports. To reduce the pressure on the balance of payments, the government, rather than adjusting the exchange rate, chose in the late 1960s to adopt a more restrictive regime through increases in the tax rates paid on imports. It also tried to encourage foreign exchange earnings. The exchange rates for tourists and for workers' remittances were raised twice in the late 1960s. Tax rebates for nontraditional exports were also increased.

Nevertheless, the balance-of-payments situation continued to deteriorate. As the foreign exchange shortage became increasingly acute, the premium on import licenses increased, exceeding 100 percent of the official exchange rate by early 1970. Foreign exchange shortages forced the government to delay issuing letters of credit even when all other licensing procedures had been satisfied. The black-market exchange rate was increasing rapidly.

The pre-devaluation period was dominated by social unrest and political instability. Clashes between right-wing and left-wing extremists, the closing of universities, and street demonstrations were widespread. Political violence continued through 1970 and into early 1971. Severe social unrest, allegations of corruption, continuing violence, and internal opposition within the ruling party all began to weaken the government. The proposed 1970 budget was defeated in the National Assembly early in 1970.

In August 1970, the government devalued the lira by two thirds. A uniform exchange rate system replaced the existing multiple exchange rates. In addition, some minor modifications were made in accompanying trade policies, designed to minimize the inflationary impact of the devaluation and to reinforce the incentives for exports. These included lowering the stamp duty on imports and reducing import guarantee deposit rates. No major changes in tariff and quota structures were made. The export regime remained the same except for some simplification of the export tax rebate system.

These reforms were a once-and-for-all attempt to remove the overvaluation of the lira and thereby to tackle the balance-of-payments problem. There is no indication that the government intended to liberalize foreign trade activities permanently or to establish a more neutral trade regime. Indeed, the pattern of investment allocation after 1970 showed no shift away from its prior emphasis on import substitution industries.

The package was successful in achieving its main objective of improving the balance-of-payments situation. Exports and workers' remittances quickly increased in response to the more favorable exchange rate. This allowed for a large expansion in imports as well as a dramatic short-run improvement in the balance of payments. The current account showed a surplus and reserves increased in the year following the devaluation.

But the early momentum was short lived. Export growth slowed, partly because of the onset of deterioration of the real effective exchange rate. Meanwhile, expansionary macroeconomic policies accelerated import growth. These developments soon brought back balance-of-payments difficulties, which were then exacerbated by the first oil shock.

The main inference to be drawn from this episode is that, even in a very inward-looking economy, exports can be quite responsive to the real effective exchange rate. A sharp devaluation led to substantial export growth. Then, slow deterioration in the real effective exchange rate was associated with export stagnation.

Turkey entered the late 1970s facing dire economic circumstances. Severe balance-of-payments problems necessitated long and detailed negotiations with its creditors and with its NATO allies to come up with large amounts of increased aid. Inflation was accelerating, unemployment was rising, shortages were common, and labor unrest had reached crisis proportions. Even worse, political violence was rampant and spreading.

Episode Two: 1980 to Present

In the face of these problems, the government announced a broad series of policy reforms in January 1980. These included a near 50 percent devaluation of the lira, increases in direct export incentives, and limitations on public spending and credit – much like the actions taken in similar economic circumstances, such as in 1970. This time the government went much further, however, declaring its intention to gradually, but fundamentally, change the way the economy was managed. Longer-run trade objectives included dismantling the QR system, opening up the foreign capital account, and allocating resources to export sectors through market mechanisms.

No specific plans, timetables, or sequential orders of change were announced. It is unlikely that a comprehensive program was formulated.

Nonetheless, subsequent actions revealed the basic elements of a reasonably coherent plan. The immediate problem in 1980 was foreign exchange. Consequently, the first steps were aimed at increasing foreign exchange earnings. The initial devaluation was followed by regular smaller devaluations which soon occurred daily. These attempted to establish and maintain an exchange rate consistent with rapid export growth and external balance, including stimulating remittances and limiting excess demand for imports.

In the first stage, direct export incentives were the principal instrument for increasing exports. The rise in exports coincided with real devaluation, increased rebates, interest subsidies for exporters, and other benefits. Although a great deal of noise was made about import reform, in part to satisfy the World Bank and other sources of nonproject credit, not much was actually done. Some commodities were shifted from the more restrictive to the less restrictive list. In 1981 some licensed imports were liberalized and the explicit import quota system was abolished. There were few other shifts until 1984. The system remained dominated by licensing QRs, protection for domestic industry, and so forth.

The second stage began at the end of 1983. About 60 percent of previously licensed imports were liberalized. Even more important in the long run were structural changes in the administrative system for importing. Instead of banning all goods that had not been explicitly included on a list (the old system), now any goods not explicitly prohibited could be imported. The number of prohibited items is small. In addition, there is a list of imports subject to licensing (mostly domestically produced goods) and a list of goods subject to a special levy (mainly luxury items). Almost 75 percent of current imports can enter Turkey without a license. A number of tariff changes were also made at that time. These affected about 20 percent of imports and, on average, lowered nominal protection on these by about 16 percent. Effective rates of protection, due to the escalation of tariffs, might be higher for some domestically produced import substitutes. It appears that a wider range of goods (particularly consumer goods) is being imported.

In terms of success and failure, the record is mixed. The government has succeeded in maintaining a flexible and realistic exchange rate. The devaluation of 1980 has not been eroded. Exports shot up beginning in late 1980 and, after a pause in 1983, resumed their rise, although not at the 25 percent annual rate of the early 1980s. Progress has been made on imports as well. The import system became more liberal than at any previous time. The balance of payments now is much stronger than at the beginning of 1980. The trade deficit is lower, whether measured in nominal dollars, real 1980 dollars, or relative to national income. Although the currency is more convertible than before, there are few signs of capital flight. Of course, the process of macroeconomic and balance-of-payments adjustment was significantly eased by the extensive credits supplied to Turkey directly and indirectly by OECD countries since 1979. Turkey's reform program, in turn, has reinforced her creditworthiness with both official and commercial lenders.

On the negative side, the most obvious failures (which generally are not directly related to trade policy) have been in reducing inflation, promoting real economic growth, and maintaining real wages and employment. After falling during most of the first stage, inflation accelerated in late 1983 and 1984 and remains in the 40–50 percent range. Public investment has been directly squeezed by austerity measures and by the desire to reduce the role of the government. Private investment has declined even more sharply, and so far shows no signs of recovering.

Because the episode is still in progress, any general inferences must be tentative. Nonetheless, the following conclusions seem warranted. First, the implementation of liberalization has been too slow. There is no evidence that the liberalized trade regime has contributed to Turkey's continuing macroeconomic difficulties. On the contrary, expanded exports permitted firms to maintain higher output levels, contributed to the restoration of creditworthiness, and supported modest real growth since 1980. Import liberalization was probably delayed for too long; little or nothing would have been lost in terms of employment if it had begun in 1980 or 1981.

Second, in the Turkish case it was probably necessary for export promotion to be the most important initial focus. Exports are an important means of compensating for weak domestic demand and maintaining employment, while promoting creditworthiness. Moreover, to promote investment in export industries when that had been discouraged for more than a generation, appropriate signals need to be given early, firmly, and credibly. That seems to have been done. However, the attempt to offer different subsidy rates to different categories of exports seems not to have been an important explanatory variable of export performance.

Third, the major threat to sustained trade liberalization at present comes from the macroeconomic side. While in many ways the trade policy reforms have been successful, they have occurred in the context of declining real wages and per capita real consumption. Trade liberalization is highly visible and widely publicized. In a country with a strong nationalistic tradition, it may prove difficult to persuade the electorate that it will produce long-term benefits unless real growth and real per capita disposable income begin to increase measurably. Indeed, it may prove all too easy for the political opposition to use trade policy as the vehicle for mounting a major attack on the new directions that the Turkish economy has taken since 1980.

Uruguay
Edgardo Favaro and Pablo T. Spiller

The post-World War II history of Uruguay took Uruguayans and foreign observers alike by surprise. This small country, with a well-educated and stable population of just above 2 million in the 1940s, enjoying a relatively high standard of living, was deemed likely to become the Switzerland of South America. Instead, Uruguay's experience during the second half of the century has been one of stagnation, inflation, and instability, not too different in a sense from that of the other Latin American countries.

The Uruguayan political system responded to the major events of the first half of the century by increasing the extent of government intervention in the economy. By 1950, Uruguay's public sector comprised all major public utilities (electricity, water, telecommunications, and railroads), and there were state monopolies for the provision of insurance, alcohol, and petroleum refining. The economic impact of the public sector, however, extended even further. By 1950, Uruguay had a welfare system which provided benefits unparalleled elsewhere in the region. Moreover, public sector employment was the major driving force behind employment growth in the post-war period. Finally, and perhaps most importantly, Uruguay pursued a policy of import substitution, with foreign trade restrictions reaching their highest level in the early 1970s.

By then, however, the dream of becoming a Switzerland was replaced by the reality of stagnation. By the late 1960s, economic stagnation and the rise of an urban guerrilla movement paralyzed the political system as well. A military coup followed in 1973.

Uruguay reached the early 1970s, then, with an overly taxed agricultural sector, an export sector almost totally based on agricultural products, a labor market characterized by emigration and public employment, a depreciated industrial capital stock, and a strongly regulated financial sector with recurrent capital flights and currency crises.

The ability of the economy to respond to the oil price shock of 1973 by maintaining its foreign trade structure intact was very limited. Further import substitution was impossible, and an export drive was required. In July 1974 the military appointed a new economic team which responded to the balance-of-payments crisis generated by the oil shock by introducing major foreign exchange, trade liberalization, and tax reforms.

The economy reacted to the new reforms with a flexibility unseen during the post-war era. From 1974 to 1981 the annual rate of growth reached record levels, with an average of 4 percent for the period; the investment-to-GDP ratio also reached a record level of 20 percent; and the emigration process that started during the 1960s was reversed by 1981. Foreign trade increased substantially, as did capital inflows. Furthermore, the structure of imports and exports changed. Before reform, traditional exports accounted for more than 75 percent of total exports; afterwards, they accounted for only 40 percent. Similarly, the share of intermediate goods in total imports almost halved following the trade reforms.

In 1982, in the midst of a deep recession, the trade liberalization program was partially reversed and then halted. By then, however, the success of the reforms in reallocating resources away from the import-competing sectors was significant.

The failure of trade liberalization to produce further structural changes in the economy did not necessarily derive from the trade liberalization program itself. Accompanying policies may have impacted more strongly on the economy than the trade reforms themselves.

The experiment, however, was successful in other dimensions. First, it provided the Uruguayan economy with new export industries and markets; second, it increased the efficiency of its industries; third, the structure of the export sector was permanently changed; and fourth, and perhaps most importantly, it proved, for the first time in almost 40 years, that when given the proper domestic incentives the Uruguayan economy could be a very dynamic one, even in the face of adverse international conditions. The new democratic system that started in 1984 cannot help but take the lessons of the 1974–82 reforms into account when developing new economic policies.

Our main results are, first, that the reforms were introduced in timely fashion, but their sequencing and coordination with other policies could have been improved upon. Second, the relationship between macro-economic policies and commercial reforms appears crucial in determining the path of the economy following liberalization. Third, the speed of implementation could have been increased and the discriminatory nature of the early stages could have been reduced without serious adverse employment effects. These changes would have generated more lasting effects and might therefore have produced greater political support for liberalization.

Yugoslavia
Oli Havrylyshyn

Policy analysts, watching Yugoslavia's economic experimentation, have paid primary attention to the unique middle-of-the-road approach of workers' management, intended to combine the efficiency of "capitalist" profit incentives with the equity of "socialist" ownership. But another important economic experiment took place in Yugoslavia in the mid-1960s: an attempt to liberalize trade relations. The objectives were increased international competitiveness, balance-of-payments stability, and full convertibility of the dinar. At that time, Yugoslavia had a considerable and typical array of trade intervention policies; hence its experiment with trade liberalization can provide some lessons for developing countries today.

After World War II, the Yugoslav economy was modeled on Soviet central planning, which included a state-trading monopoly. With its break from the Soviet camp in 1948 and the consequent "turning to the West," trade policy became increasingly liberal. But it was not until the 1960s that a major reform of the trade regime took place. A unification of the exchange rate and the establishment of a tariff regime in 1961-2 gave Yugoslavia associate member status in the GATT and set the stage for the true liberalization steps taken in 1965-7. These steps consisted of reductions in tariffs, quotas, and other import restrictions; realignment of domestically controlled prices; removal of export subsidies; and concomitant devaluation of the dinar.

Opening the economy was part of a general reform aimed at greater liberalization of economic decision making and increased influence of market forces. The reform was to achieve greater productive efficiency and full implementation of workers' self-management principles. Neither the reform nor the trade liberalization were a success. The changes in trade policy to be implemented over five to ten years soon began to be modified, reversed, or postponed. The trade regime of the 1970s, while more open than that of the 1950s or early 1960s, saw a series of reversals and limited revivals of liberalization. Perhaps most indicative that the experiment was largely a failure was the introduction of another broadly similar reform in 1983, known as the Economic Stabilization Program. The focus of the country study is on the major episode of trade liberalization in 1965-7 and its first reversals in 1967-70.

Economic Circumstances at the Time of Liberalization

Yugoslavia in the 1950s had a record of strong growth, including a rapid structural shift toward industrial activity; a negative but manageable balance of payments, with export growth exceeding import growth; a debt-to-GNP ratio in 1960 of about 17 percent; a debt service ratio of about 15 percent, counting only convertible currency exports; and low inflation rates.

For a year or two before the 1961 liberalization the trade and current accounts were deteriorating and inflation was rising. The balance of payments improved again by 1962, only to resume its decline the next year. Thus both the 1961 and 1965 policies came on the heels of a balance-of-payments crisis, and both entailed devaluations that apparently helped to correct the crisis.

Export performance for the period 1960–4 remained as strong as it had been earlier, with only brief setbacks in the years 1961 and 1964. External price movements were on the whole favorable. Yugoslavia's major trading partners were experiencing high rates of growth in the first half of the 1960s, but 1965–7, when trade liberalization was implemented, was a period of slowing trade activity and, more important, of increasing barriers to Yugoslav exports to the EEC, especially for agricultural goods.

Availability of long-term capital inflows and their terms were largely unchanged in this period. Development assistance was increasingly available at below market terms, and Yugoslavia had no difficulty in obtaining short- or long-term credit. During the 1961 and 1965 liberalizations the IMF extended credits of US$75 million and US$110 million respectively. No major economic or political shocks occurred at the time of liberalization, with the exception of a very poor harvest in 1960–1 and a very good harvest in 1966.

The 1965 Reforms

Despite the move away from state-trading monopoly in 1952, Yugoslavia did not attempt significant liberalization until 1965. In some respects the 1965–7 policies repeated those of 1961. The dinar was devalued again, IMF credits were obtained to help the adjustment, tariffs were reduced sharply to 10.5 percent, and coverage of liberalized imports was increased from 25 percent of value in 1965 to 41 percent in 1966 and to 36 percent in 1967. But the 1965 liberalization went much further than the liberalization of 1961, and differed on the export side in abolishing virtually all subsidies. Retention quotas of 7 percent, however, were maintained, as apparently were other export supports including selective fiscal and credit benefits.

The economic context also differed. While the 1961 program was mostly a trade policy reform, trade policy was only one aspect of the 1965 program, whose primary thrust was the development of the workers' management system. The basic mechanism of the system had been established by 1952, but the central power was still dominant. The reforms of 1965 were intended to decentralize power: to shift resource allocation decisions increasingly to workers in factories and to decontrol domestic prices, making price-setting more subject to market influence. Trade liberalization, while clearly consonant with the philosophy of the reforms, was only one element.

The substantial momentum of reform in the years 1965–7 was slowed by reversals beginning in 1968–9. Attempts to reinvigorate the liberalizing process in the early 1970s were abandoned in 1974, when a major decentralization of power shifted control of foreign exchange allocation, price-setting, export credit and subsidies, and even import restrictions away from central government to self-management enterprises and local governments. Though this exercise in federalism by no means emasculated central power, it undermined it considerably. For trade policy, the decentralization resulted in a balkanization of the regime with local interests dominating national objectives. But decentralization was not the only or even the principal reason for the failure of the liberalization, which had, after all, a decade to operate and become ingrained.

The Reversal of Liberalization

The immediate reasons for reversal and failure were inappropriate macro and exchange rate policies accompanying the liberalization. The underlying long-term failures included persistence of distorted prices and incentives that were never eliminated in the short-lived liberalization, substitution of *ad hoc* and compensatory export support programs for true import liberalization, and deterioration of financial discipline as firms and local governments were given freedom to make decisions but were not held responsible for failures.

The main reason for the economic slowdown in the early years of the liberalization was that the complementary macro policies were too restrictive given the noninflationary conditions of the economy. Inflation pressures, though high by Yugoslav historical standards (over 10 percent), were by no means critical. Monetary authorities also reacted strongly to the one-time "inflation" adjustment of decontrolled prices in 1965 (prices of some goods were adjusted by as much as 25 percent) and imposed severe monetary restraint. The growth of money supply fell from about 10 percent in 1964 to 4–5 percent in the next two years, and to −5 percent in 1967. This economic downturn frightened authorities into an overreaction in the other direction, with growth in the next four years averaging nearly 20 percent, fueling the very inflation they had earlier tried to contain.

Another problem was inadequate devaluation. While the 1965 devaluation spurred export growth, the nominal exchange rate was unchanged until 1971 despite an annual inflation rate of 15–20 percent. Hence the real exchange rate depreciation was not sustained, undermining export performance and encouraging imports that (at least until 1969–70) were less restricted than they had been before 1965. The combination of the worsening trade balance with the slower growth of output and especially industrial employment engendered political pressure to reverse liberalization, which was blamed for job losses. This perception was not consistent with the fact that in the first three years of the liberalization (1965–7) export growth exceeded import growth (9.6 percent compared with 7.4 percent) owing to the sharp one-time devaluation of 1965. Indeed, as the liberalization measures were gradually reversed after 1968, import growth outpaced export growth, despite the tightening of imports and foreign exchange allocation, because the real exchange rate was allowed to appreciate.

The first fundamental problem of the liberalization itself was that it was too brief and too small in scope to generate any benefits. While tariffs were lowered considerably and remained low, other restrictions were only partially reduced before they began to be reintroduced in 1968. The share of liberalized imports went up, the use of foreign exchange allocation as the binding restriction reappeared, and export subsidies were reinstated. The correction of the price distortions, which were severe before 1965, was far from complete by the time the reversals began three years later. The export gains that did occur were probably due more to the devaluation than to reallocation in response to correction of price distortions.

A second difficulty manifested itself more slowly: such correction of the anti-export bias as was achieved was effected not through gradual reductions in import restrictions but through compensatory export support policies to offset the import-cost effects of protection. While this may have helped to reduce the bias in the short run, such policies were not successful in promoting exports in the long run since the underlying protection costs remained, and the export interests themselves became as dependent on government assistance as import-competing industries. The allocative inefficiency of this compensation system was aggravated by its selectivity: shipbuilding, machinery, electrical equipment, and others were favored over other industries in the allocation of export-related credits for investment, foreign exchange allocation, and so on.

The third problem was that the policy of workers' management, far from promoting mobility of factors, may have impeded it. The system of workers' management itself is thought to reduce factor mobility because of the nontransferable asset participation of workers. It is unclear whether this did indeed play a role. What is clear is that a "soft-budget" climate for losing enterprises was created. The reforms of 1965 decentralized power to the worker-managed enterprises, but the responsibility for errors and consequent losses was never effectively decentralized. Loss-making enterprises were rarely forced to close or go bankrupt, but were instead propped up. The decentralization of fiscal and banking activities from the central government to regional and even local governments may have increased the political importance of saving jobs; it certainly meant that local authorities had the power to support weak enterprises. This environment – called the monopoly of the backward in Yugoslavia – gave little incentive for enterprises to be efficient or to move into new product areas of import substitution or exports in response to any trade liberalization signals. Whatever the impact of the system on factor mobility, the "soft-budget" climate reduced that mobility even further.

References

Balassa, Bela and Associates (1982) *Developing Strategies in Semi-Industrial Economies.* Baltimore, MD: Johns Hopkins Press for the World Bank.

Bhagwati, Jagdish N. (1965) "On the equivalence of tariffs and quotas." In R. E. Baldwin et al., eds, *Trade, Growth and the Balance of Payments: Essays in Honor of Goldfried.* Chicago, IL: University of Chicago Press.

Bhagwati, Jagdish N. (1978) *Anatomy and Consequences of Exchange Control Regimes.* Cambridge, MA: Ballinger for the National Bureau of Economic Research.

Bruno, Michael (1972) "Market distortions and gradual reforms." *Review of Economic Studies*, 39, 373–83.

Calvo, Guillermo (1988) "Notes in credibility and economic policy." Mimeograph.

Cavallo, Domingo, Joaquín Cottani, and M. Shahbaz Kahn (forthcoming) "Real exchange rate behavior and economic performance in developing countries." *Economic Development and Cultural Change.*

Corden, W. M. (1971) *The Theory of Production.* Oxford: Clarendon Press.

Corden, W. M. (1974) *Trade Policy and Economic Welfare.* Oxford: Clarendon Press.

Cottani, Joaquín and Raul E. García (1989) "The determinants of the real exchange rate in Argentina, 1976–85." Washington, DC: World Bank and IEERAL-Fundación Mediterranea, March.

Dornbusch, Rudiger (1983) "Panel discussion on Southern Cone." *IMF Staff Papers*, 30, 173–6.

Edwards, Sebastián (1984) *The Order of Liberalization of the External Sector in Developing Countries.* Princeton, NJ: Essays in Liberalization Finance No. 156.

Favaro, Edgardo and Pablo T. Spiller (1989) "The determinants of the real exchange rate in post-war Uruguay." Washington DC: World Bank, May.

Frenkel, Jacob (1983) "Panel discussion on Southern Cone," *IMF Staff Papers*, 30, 164–73.

Hachette, Dominique (1989) "The opening of the capital account: the case of Chile: 1974–82." Washington, DC: World Bank.

Halevi, Nadav (1987) "Capital movements and liberalization in Israel." Washington, DC: World Bank.

Harberger, Arnold C. (1986) "Welfare consequences of capital inflows." In Armeane M. Choksi and Demetris Papageorgiou, eds, *Economic Liberalization in Developing Countries.* Oxford: Basil Blackwell, ch 6.

Harberger, Arnold C. (forthcoming). *Trade Policy and the Real Exchange Rate.* Washington, DC: World Bank Economic Development Institute.

Krueger, Anne O. (1974) "The political economy of the rent-seeking society." *American Economic Review*, 64, 291–303.

Krueger, Anne O. (1978) *Liberalization Attempts and Consequences.* Cambridge, MA: Ballinger for the National Bureau of Economic Research.

Krueger, Anne O. (1986) "General issues in economic liberalization." In Armeane M. Choksi and Demetris Papageorgiou, eds, *Economic Liberalization in Developing Countries*. Oxford: Basil Blackwell, ch 2.

Lal, Deepak (1987) "The political economy of economic liberalization." *World Bank Economic Review*, 1, 273–99.

McCulloch, Rachel (1973) "When are a tariff and a quota equivalent?" *Canadian Journal of Economics*, 6, 503–11.

McKinnon, Ronald (1982) "The order of economic liberalization: lessons from Chile and Argentina." In K. Brunner and A. Meltzer, eds, *Economic Policy in a World of Change*. Amsterdam: North-Holland, pp. 159–86.

Michaely, Michael (1977) *Theory of Commercial Policy*. Oxford: Philip Allan, and Chicago, IL: University of Chicago Press.

Michaely, Michael (1983) "The floating exchange rate in Israel: 1977–1980." In D. Bigman and T. Taya, eds, *Exchange Rate and Trade Instability: Causes, Consequences, and Remedies*. Cambridge, MA: Ballinger, ch. 12.

Michaely, Michael (1986) "The timing and sequencing of a trade liberalization policy." In Armeane M. Choksi and Demetris Papageorgiou, eds, *Economic Liberalization in Developing Countries*. Oxford: Basil Blackwell, ch. 3.

NBER (National Bureau of Economic Research) (1974–8) *Foreign Trade Regimes and Economic Development*, 11 volumes: I, Turkey, by Anne O. Krueger (1974); II, Ghana, by J. Clark Leith (1974); III, Israel, by Michael Michaely (1975); IV, Egypt, by Bent Hansen and Karim Nashashibi (1975); V, The Philippines, by Robert Baldwin (1975); VI, India, by Jagdish N. Bhagwati and T. N. Srinivasan (1975); VII, South Korea, by C. R. Frank, Kwang Suk Kim, and L. E. Westphal (1975); VIII, Chile, by Jere R. Behrman (1976); IX, Colombia, by Carlos F. Díaz-Alejandro (1976); X, Liberalization Attempts and Consequences, by Anne O. Krueger (1978); XI, Anatomy and Consequences of Exchange Control Regimes, by Jagdish N. Bhagwati (1978). New York: Columbia University Press (vols I–XI) for NBER; Cambridge, MA: Ballinger (vols X–XI) for NBER.

NBER (1981–3) *Trade and Employment in Developing Countries*, 3 volumes: I, Individual Studies (1981); II, Factor Supply and Substitution, ed. Anne O. Krueger (1982); III, Synthesis and Conclusions, by Anne O. Krueger (1983). Chicago, IL: University of Chicago Press for NBER.

OECD (1970) *Industry and Trade in Some Developing Countries*, 6 volumes: I, Brazil, by Joel Bergsman; II, India, by Jagdish N. Bhagwati and Padma Desai; III, The Philippines and Taiwan, by Hsing Mo-Huan, John H. Power, and Geraldo P. Sicat; IV, Mexico, by Timothy King; V, Pakistan, by S. R. Lewis; VI, A Comparative Study, by Ian Little, Tibor Scitovsky, and Maurice Scott. London: Oxford University Press for OECD.

Rodrik, Dani (1987) "Trade and capital-account liberalization in a Keynesian economy." *Journal of International Economics*, 23, 113–29.

World Bank (1987) *World Development Report*. Washington, DC: World Bank.

Index to Volume 7

Cumulative Index to Volumes 1–7